The Act of Being

Translated by Jeff Fort

The Act of Being

The Philosophy of Revelation in Mullā Sadrā

Christian Jambet

ZONE BOOKS · NEW YORK

2006

The publisher would like to thank the French Ministry of Culture for its assistance with this translation.

ZONE BOOKS
1226 Prospect Ave.
Brooklyn, NY 11218

Printed in the United States of America.

Distributed by The MIT Press,
Cambridge, Massachusetts, and London, England

Originally published in French as *L'Acte d'être* ©2002 Librairie Arthème Fayard.

Library of Congress Cataloging-in-Publication Data

Jambet, Christian.
[Acte d'être. English]
The act of being : the philosophy of revelation in Mollâ Sadrâ / Christian Jambet ; translated by Jeff Fort
p. cm.
Includes bibliographical references and index.
ISBN 1-890951-69-2 (hardcover) –
ISBN 1-890951-70-6 (pbk.)
1. Sadr al-Din Shirazi, Muhammad ibn Ibrahim, d. 1641.
2. Ontology. 3. Philosophy, Islamic – Greek influences.
4. Sufism. I. Title.
B178.V413 2005
180-dc22

2006046144

Contents

To my daughter Pauline

Preface to the English-Language Edition

When a philosophical work written by a Westerner attempts to articulate the essential elements of a philosophical system constructed by an Iranian Shīʿite of the seventeenth century, the potential reader has the right to ask: For what reasons has the author of this book spent so many years reading the works of this man who will always remain a foreigner, whose very face he will never know, and whose beliefs belong to the intellectual universe that came to an end, in the West, with the mathematization of physical space, with the end of political theology, and with the great revolutions that radically modified the image of reason?

Rarely does such a question fail to become an objection. After reading *The Act of Being*, an erudite and attentive friend, who had long before included my first work on Islamic philosophy in the series he was then editing,[1] wrote to me in all honesty that for us today there is not much to learn from my dear Mullā Sadrā. Working before the age of modern science, deeply rooted in the soil of metaphysics, subject to the demands of religious revelation, Sadrā, like all the thinkers of Islam, is merely an object of learned study and of the history of philosophy, a kind of scholarly curiosity or even an antiquated exhibit fit for a museum.

This objection is not entirely without merit. I would even like to add a few arguments to it, in order to see whether it is possible to refute it in a serious manner.

The first argument against such an undertaking is of a historical nature. The interest that Western culture has shown for Islam, for its thinkers, poets, and mystics, has its own history. Roughly speaking, this history has had three major phases since the eighteenth century: first there was the "Oriental Renaissance," as Raymond Schwab has called it.[2] Then, in response to the positivism of Ernest Renan, there was the discovery of the great spiritual figures of Islam, as part of a quest aimed at starting a dialogue between the mystics of the three religions of the Book – Judaism, Christianity, and Islam. Finally, today, the intent is no longer to gain self-knowledge in proximity with Islam, but rather to come to know Islam in its foreignness, or even its fundamental hostility toward ourselves. A concern no longer for the *same*, for similitude, but for the other, for *difference*, for the absence of any common space. This more recent perspective, which is eager to take up the vocabulary of war ("clash of civilizations," and so on) is the unreflective response to the political emergence of Islam at the present moment of world history.

The first phase can be associated with the names of Goethe and Hegel, the second with those of Louis Massignon, Henry Corbin, Richard Walzer, and Seyyed Nasr. The third phase, our own, is seen as the time of the sociologists and the political scientists. The history of this research would thus show that the period when Orientalism was closely linked with the colonial era, and with that of the emancipation of colonized peoples, has ended. The present is seen as a time involving the reciprocal criminalization of the West and the Islamic East, the hegemony of "revolutionary" doctrines in Islam, and the ruin of all "dialogue" between the peoples of the Book. The major conflicts centered in the Middle East are said to overwhelm a more *spiritual* Islam, drowning it in blood – a spiritual Islam whose death knell was rung during the Islamic revolution in Iran.

The second argument is closely related to the first. Islam, it is said, is above all a political religion and gives rise essentially to political theologies, such that the only reason to study its ideologues would be to illuminate this politics, identified entirely with the "struggle on the path of faith." The philosophers, mystics, and poets should be placed on the shelf of curiosities because they lack any concrete effectivity and reflect a scholarly culture cut off from the popular masses who make history. This observation is not false. The works of a thinker such as Sadrā, like those of Avicenna, al-Fārābī, and Ibn Hanbal, remain unknown to the people and are of interest only to scholars. The separation between philosophy, spirituality or Qur'ānic studies, and popular culture obviously promotes a religion for simple, ordinary people characterized by a naive adherence to the letter of the Qur'ān, to traditional customs, and to the teachings of local preachers, who may be more or less well informed. The simplicity of Wahhabism no doubt partially explains its success, and it promotes the expansion of the Islamist political ideologues. These considerations certainly do little to weaken such an argument.

Let us remark, however, that the culture of religious scholars is more consequential than is often acknowledged. In Iran, and more broadly in the Shī'ite world, the actors on the political stage use the discourse of classical philosophers or theologians, citing it and adapting it for their own purposes. It suffices to recall the example of the Ayatollah Khomeini, or one of his successors. If Khomeini turned his back, in a way, on Mullā Sadrā's thought, he nevertheless knew it very well, and his political gesture cannot be explained without taking into account his internal dialogue and his critical relation with the great Iranian mystic and philosopher. You turn your back only on someone who rules over you — and who for that reason influences you in the very gesture of separation.[3] In the Sunnī world, the rupture between mystical religion and political religion is in itself a major historical fact that only the study of the spiritual philosophy of Islam allows us to illuminate in a satisfactory way.

It therefore seems to me that the doubts and confusions can be dispelled if we examine their presuppositions.

The first objection to there being any present interest in studying the philosophies of Islam emphasizes the irreducible fracture that separates the Western system of thought based on the discourses of Descartes, Locke, and Kant from the system of thought that finds its completion and fulfillment in seventeenth-century Iran. Islamic metaphysics is said to have only a single virtue, namely that it transmitted Aristotle to the Latin Middle Ages, despite which it subsequently lost itself in the sands of perpetual commentary and sterile repetition. To the extent that Western metaphysics arrives at an end with German Idealism in the nineteenth century, it would be doubly useless to search for any living truth in the books of the Muslim philosophers. If there is any truth, it can only be modern, stripped of metaphysical illusions or else located in the deconstruction of the truths of metaphysics. Only those amateurs of mystical sentiments, who have no ambitions to attain the concept, could find any interest in these "Oriental" thinkers.

An attentive examination quickly undermines such certainties. It is now well established that the flourishing of philosophical thought in Islam did not come to a halt in the thirteenth century. The image, presented by Ernest Renan in his well-known work on Averroës, of a Muslim philosophy disappearing after the immense work of the Andalusian commentator, no longer exerts as unchallenged a seduction today as it used to.[4] On the contrary, reasonable scholars will admit that one cannot treat Islamic thinkers after the thirteenth century as if they were simply "mystics" or "spiritual masters" devoted entirely to an inner salvation devoid of any conceptual intelligence. One goal of the present work, among the other purposes it attempts to serve, is to show how a number of discourses, including metaphysics, the exegesis of the Qur'ān, the sciences inherited from the Greeks, Sūfism, and morality, were progressively constituted into coherent *systems*. The internal movement of the spirit toward its perfection, in the form of the spiritual worship offered to God, and the work of the concept in no way exclude one another but rather express one another — to the point that this form of knowledge was able to actualize the ontological wealth of the Islamic religion, and that it did so in the work of Mullā Sadrā, which I attempt to study here.

The interest one may bring to these thinkers is therefore not simply an antiquarian passion. It is a matter of discovering not an old and worn-out artifact but rather what Islam says about *being as being*. It is also a matter of knowing what Islam says about *its* own being, its own decision concerning being, in the way it conceives the physical universe, man, destiny, moral obligations, and the relation between concrete existents or intellectual realities and their ultimate foundation. It is a matter of understanding the ontology of Islam in both senses of the expression: the doctrine of being that Islam slowly brought to completion, and that which constitutes the being of Islam itself, its ontological foundation.

The faithful Muslim has little concern for this last question, since he is persuaded, in his faith, that the existence of Islam is the norm, is self-evident, is inscribed in the nature of things willed by God. But the philosopher's mission is to interrogate this *ontology of Islam*, less to "deconstruct" it than to understand it. This means understanding the ontology of Islam in the thought of the authors of Islam, *in their texts*, somewhat in the sense in which Michel Foucault considered the work of genealogy or archaeology and in which he spoke of an "ontology of the self."

If we admit this much, then the "political" argument loses its force – and with it the epistemological argument. Studies in political science are too often susceptible to the illusion that it is possible to sever political discourses from the classical metaphysical ones, and then to study them separately, connecting them only to the modern political or religious practices that correspond to them. But this view of things, insufficient in the study of the concepts of Western knowledge, becomes downright absurd when it comes to Islam. In Islam, as in ancient Greece, politics is the discourse on legitimate authority. What kind of authority deserves to be respected? What kind of authority deserves to be the foundation of power? In Islam, the only legitimate authority is that of God, as he is revealed in his books (announced by the prophets), in his "messengers," and in the acknowledged successors of these "messengers" (for example, in Shīʿite Islam, the imams). How could one understand political practices, however shocking or contestable in our eyes, without illuminating them through the exegesis practiced by Muslim authors on the religious revelation of these practices and, consequently, without paying precise attention to the ontology of Islam that is unveiled by the philosophers and theologians, or even by the mystics? It is not in the surface discourse perpetually rehashed by the Muslim jurists that the truth of the political order is best revealed in Islam, but in the works of the philosophers, whether they turn away from politics or attempt to found it. Most often, philosophical and theological syntheses are conscious testimonies to the profound tension that animates Islam, a tension between a temporal vocation and a spiritual vocation that are simultaneously united and opposed.

The choice of an author like Mullā Sadrā thus becomes very clear. In order to understand this choice, we must not forget the importance of messianism for the ontology of Islam. Related to the "Servant" whose coming was announced by the prophets of Israel, to the "Suffering Servant" in the Old Testament, and to Jesus, and not without influence from the figure of Mani, who invented the notion of the "seal of prophecy," Muslim spirituality is an intense meditation on the essence, the prerogatives, and the demands of the complete Servant in proximity to his Lord. He is the Perfect Man, and the thinkers of Islam, inspired by the work of Ibn al-'Arabī, focused their thought on the definition of this Perfect Man, on his future coming, and on his silent and active presence in this world and in the other metaphysical worlds. Already, Shī'ite thought, particularly Ismā'īlism, had thus proposed a scheme of sacred history, unfolding from its origin in the creation of Adam until the coming of the awaited Resurrector.

The study of such an *ontology of history*, one of the richest versions of which we are presenting here, is extremely important if we want to move forward in the comparative study of the three messianisms – Jewish, Christian, and Muslim. Such a study reveals a conception of human becoming that includes the exigency of man's divinization, or rather of his fulfilled resemblance to God, who made man in his own image and established him as "caliph of God on earth." The concept of the *essential motion* of all existents toward that point where the Perfect Man becomes the mirror of the divine names, a concept that we find in Mullā Sadrā, remarkably illuminates the dynamic orientation of Islam. Part of what is at stake in such a study is a philosophy of history that renounces the assertion of a supposed "disenchantment of the world," and that renounces any abdication before a supposed "secularization" of historical time, seeing the every day as only a surface phenomenon, beneath which the conflict internal to biblical and Qur'ānic messianism carries on its work. Toward what end? Toward what reconciliation? Toward what irreducible alterity? These are the very questions we face today.

The epistemological argument that maintains that these systems of thought are rendered obsolete by modern science or by the ascendancy of modern political thought disregards something that is nonetheless glaringly obvious. It is pointless to say to an entire culture that it is "behind," or that it has not completed the necessary journey to the age of scientific truth. It would be more useful to ask: Why, today, has such a culture, combined in a very complex way with multiple contributions from the West — in technology, economy, and ideology — begun to move, on the historical stage, so decidedly against the grain, and in such a flagrant way? Why is the present historical moment characterized by such a historical *initiative*?

To answer this by attempting to justify the "modernity" of Islamic science is pointless. To answer by deploring the "perverse" effects of a dead thought or a culture blocked in its development is to proffer a contradiction in terms. How, indeed, could a dead thought have any living effect (contestable or not, that is not the question here) if it is truly dead? What it would be necessary to understand, rather, is the following.

On the one hand, we would need to understand how the philosophy of Islam has a certain living power, from the very fact that it is not foreign to world history, because it is connected to and even interlinked with our own metaphysical destiny, both Greek and biblical. In the past, it already gave life to some of the most enduring categories of our vision of the world. A central example is provided here, when I examine the question of the existence of essence, in an attempt to give what I call the *Avicennian moment* its full importance.

On the other hand, we would have to ask how, against the background of a common metaphysics, Islam has maintained convictions foreign to those that made possible the development of modern philosophy in the West, as well as the worldviews that derive from these convictions. That is, we would have to ask how it is not a thing of the past but rather lives according to its own rhythm, in a mode of historical life with its own logic, its own time, and its own autonomous finalities.

Such work goes far beyond the ambition of the present study. But it is at least within this perspective that I have written it. I would like to specify my method. My goal here was not primarily that of a historian of Islamic philosophy, although I do believe that I have been faithful to history and its demands. It is as a philosopher that I have attempted to read the philosophers, whether Western or Eastern, who are interrogated here. My only ambition has been to receive as faithfully as possible what Sadrā and those associated with him were trying to say, and to render manifest, in the language of a Western philosopher living today, the mode of appearance of being evident for these spirits in their immediate and direct vision. My method strives to be the phenomenology of a becoming, of a metamorphosis of thought, from its Hellenic bases to the Islamic figure of an *absolute* that is different from the absolute unveiled in Western Christian thought. That is my obvious debt to Hegel, whose teaching still seems indispensable to me, whatever the contestations with which practically all contemporary discourses have assailed it.

Finally, I would like to express my gratitude and admiration for the scrupulous and rigorous work done by Jeff Fort in translating this work into English — for he has done more than translate it; he has given it another life in a fitting and adequate philosophical language (and that is his specific contribution to this text), in all faithfulness to the original French. His work provided the occasion for a number of corrections and specifications, and in that sense, too, it cannot be seen as the passive reconstruction of a book in another language. Any errors or omissions in this book fall to me; the improvements and elucidations, however, owe a great deal to him. And for this I offer him my warmest thanks.

Christian Jambet
Paris, August 2004

Introduction

It is presumptuous to explain the truth of a religion. Only someone who practices it knows anything about it, in his or her experience of God or of the word that reveals the absolute. Religion, like most forms of human knowledge, is made up of beliefs. But the content of religious faith is *the true*, not this or that truth: the foundation of the truth in a word, a teaching, a revelation. Hegel is right when he says that "it lies essentially in the concept of true religion – the religion whose content is absolute spirit – that it be *revealed*, and, in truth, revealed *by God*."[1] What is "true religion"? How and why did Hegel claim that Christianity was the true religion? These questions involve a particular judgment concerning the process internal to monotheism. What matters to us here is the conviction that initially compels them: if the question of which religion is the "true religion" has been posed, it is because prophetism and monotheism have spoken the true and have an originary relation to the essence of truth.

For each of its followers, Islam manifests its truth in prophetic revelation, and the ultimate content of their faith is not what Hegel means here by the concept of "absolute spirit," but rather the identity of God and "One": "Say: He, God, One."[2] The aim of this book is to provide an introduction to one of the greatest philosophers of Islam; it is an attempt to guide the reader toward the generative center of his philosophy, by presenting the concepts through which this philosophy remains faithful to the revelation of the identity of the real and the One. How did Mullā Sadrā conceive of the meaning of this revelation, and how did he meditate on the foundation of all reality, in a real that would be "one"?

In the Muslim world, philosophy aspired from the beginning to be a meditation on the meaning of revelation, a meditation that maintained the identity of the reality of being and the unique reality of God. Without this close connection between metaphysical speculation, spiritual experience, the elaboration of morality and politics, and eschatology and scriptural revelation, this philosophy would have had only a historical role: the transmission of the Greeks to the medieval and the modern world. We will be concerned here not with such a history but with the relation between Islamic philosophy and the prophetic revelation of the truth of the real.

Indeed, for our purposes, Hegel's statement communicates the following prescription: to recognize that revealed religions are not mere "cultural phenomena," that they are even less discourses of illusion or error or metaphors for rational truths that remain foreign to them. They are a moment of the revelation of the true, they have a truth because they have intrinsically to do with truth. In saying this, I am not judging the "truth" of what is stated in a particular dogma accepted by a particular "sect" of Islam. I am not interrogating the validity of any such contents of faith, as if faith could be judged according to the norms of a knowledge external to it—as if, for example, molecular biology could confirm or disprove a prophecy! Nor am I asking what the truth is for a particular adherent who receives the normative discourse of the Qur'ān as truth, or how such a person's desire is constituted. On the contrary, I will begin from this very simple fact, which Hegel calls to our attention: God is a subject. God is a subject of enunciation, and He is also often a subject of statements. The sacred books of Islam (the Leaves of Abraham, the Torah, the Psalms, the Gospels, the Qur'ān) say the true because they inscribe into the letter the act of the subject that is God, an act of enunciation and creation, since the letter of the book will create its own reader.

The truth of the book is the creation of man as prophet: not only the individual who is a prophet but also the prophetic essence of man, whose essence as a speaking being is defined by the fact of speaking the particular language of the book.[3] Truth is thus not the adequation of the representation to the thing but the inadequation of man as prophet to the language of the divine speaker, the absolute subject supposed to speak—an inadequation experienced in anguish (Muhammad seized with terror after the visitation of the angel), an inadequation struggled against but never vanquished, in the infinite exegesis of the letter. What is said, in this inadequation of the prophet to his language, is a certain mode of the truth of being. In this sense, Islam is the bearer of an immanent ontology.

Islamic philosophy can no more be considered an epiphenomenon of Islam than Islam itself can be considered a cultural epiphenomenon. This philosophy is the ontology of Islam; it is the discourse that says, at each of its stages and according to prophetic revelation, what being is. As a discourse on being, it is also a discourse on revelation. As an exegesis of revelation, it accedes to being as being. It thus states the relation of Islam to the truth of being, that is, a constitutive moment of our own relation to being, of our own practice of truth.

The Qur'ānic equation between God and the name of the One is equivalent for Sadrā to the equation between the first foundation and being. That God is being, that he is being itself, is a decision that can in no way be taken for granted, since Ismāʿīlī Shīʿite theology, for example, maintained the power of another conviction, which claimed that the principle was beyond being and beyond the negation of being. In Sadrā, ontology, or the discourse on being, becomes capable of saying the truth of the revelation of divine unity, and the word "being" (*al-wujūd* in Arabic) means not only existence but, more radically, the real in all the senses of the Arabic term *al-haqq*: that which has a right to impose itself as true, authentic, that which is verified beyond all representation and all manifestation, but which also gives to all revelation its power as truth.

The focal point of the meditation on being is this: that there is *the* real, that this real is one, and that this real is revealed in all sensible and supersensible reality. Reciprocally, according to Sadrā's conception, one can approach the *real* only through a particular grasping of being. This is why we will show by what means – and by what paths – Mullā Sadrā organizes his search for a real that is "being," and for a being that is worthy of designating the real. The identity of the real, the One, and being finds its philosophical fulfillment in Sadrā and thus allows us to investigate the meaning of the ontology of Islam, in which Islam interprets itself in the completed ontology offered to it by philosophy as its mode of exegesis.

I do not claim to provide an exhaustive presentation of the arguments or a full account of a philosophical system that is among the richest and most prolific in all of Islamic philosophy. That would require thousands of pages and a synthesizing knowledge able to encompass the multiple derivations of an almost infinite flow of concepts. Mullā Sadrā never ceased reworking his demonstrations and his speculative "illuminations" or intuitions and giving them multiple forms. The summa of his investigations has become the basis on which what is called traditional philosophy has been practiced in Iran up to the present day. It is titled "The Supereminent Wisdom in the Four Journeys of the Intelligence," and this somewhat heavy-handed title is most often given, by Sadrā himself, a rather evocative abbreviation: the *Four Spiritual Journeys*, or simply the *Journeys* (*al-Asfār*).[4] It contains an ontology, a metaphysics of motion and of time, a doctrine of the intelligence and of knowledge, a physics, a theology, a psychology, and an eschatology. Sadrā first prepared for it, then distilled it, in various works, in letters, in his commentaries on the Qur'ān and on the traditions of the imams, and even in his didactic poetry.[5] Recent commentaries in Iran are already innumerable, and an international congress held in Tehran in 1999 consecrated Mullā Sadrā as what could be called the conclusive point of Islamic philosophy.[6]

These are the symptoms of a philosophical situation that justifies the work I am presenting here. Sadrā became aware that he was creating a revolution in the field of philosophical thought with his intuition that the entirety of the tradition he was inheriting, particularly from Avicenna, Nasīr al-Dīn al-Tūsī, and Suhrawardī, had to be completely rethought, in terms of what is called the "preeminence of the act of being." He recapitulated all the teachings of the Neoplatonist philosophy that had preceded him, as well as the illuminative philosophy of the Ishrāqīyah (the school of Suhrawardī), by synthesizing their schemes with the theosophy of Ibn al-'Arabī and his disciples and with many of the theses accepted among the masters of Sunnī theology, which he argues against or adopts, without contradicting his profound fidelity to the sayings of the imams collected by Kulaynī in the volumes of the *Book of the Principles of the Kāfī*.

Sadrā often says of himself that he is the first, the one who inaugurates the true philosophy of Islam. This claim, quite common among our philosophers, rings true for Sadrā in a way that will be of much concern to us. But this inauguration also seems to me to be an end and a last word. Of course, during Sadrā's lifetime, and after him, there were many thinkers who did not think as he did and who developed very original propositions. We might think of Qāzī Sa'īd Qummī, for example, or the group of teachers belonging to what has come to be known as the Shaykhi sect. But it is Mullā Sadrā who completes the constitutive ontology of Islam; it is he who thinks it in its systematic purity, in such a way that he determines the problems and refutations that will provide the substance of his successors' concerns.

But this metaphysical gesture, as an illustration of the "renaissance" of philosophy in the Safavid period, is no less a moment of conclusion. It would be absurd to predict that there could be no new type of philosophy in the Muslim world, just as it would be absurd to claim that metaphysics has been "completed," so that it is no longer valid as a practice. Does not the completion of metaphysics, for those who announce it, signify in fact its full transhistorical retrieval and repetition? The empirical end points to the task of a permanent return, a thinking of what has been thought. I therefore do not claim that Sadrā henceforth forbids a new flourishing of philosophy in the Muslim world – which, I repeat, would simply be foolish.

One can say, however, that he gives to the philosophical exegesis of Qur'ānic revelation – in the equation of the real, being, and the One – its maximum power, a power that enables it to take its place in the completed system of thought on the absolute, at the level of a radical philosophy of *identity*. The real conceived of as an energy infinite in itself, unity conceived of as the origin and end of reality, being conceived of as the effectivity of the being.[7] This is the full deployment of the ontology of *light*, whose principal moments were Avicenna's systematic construction of metaphysics, Suhrawardī's interpretation of being in the ontology of lights, and finally the Sadrian synthesis.

The philosophical situation in Islam would no doubt have been completely different if two events of great importance had not taken place: the marginalization of the admirable Ismā'īlī Shī'ite theology after the tragedy of Alamūt, and the massive integration of Ibn al-'Arabī's thought into Twelver Shī'ite philosophy. The situation would have presented a very different face if Iranian history had not favored this recapitulation and this diffusion of traditional knowledge in the seventeenth century, a recapitulation and diffusion that Mullā Sadrā's work attests to in the highest degree. Finally, it would not have been what it was without the generative power of Avicenna's work, that is, without what I call the Avicennian moment.

We cannot separate the flourishing of Islamic metaphysics, understood as a system of knowledge that says the real of all reality, from another important event, namely the adoption of Neoplatonic schemes by Ismā'īlī Shī'ite thinkers in the tenth century. This Ismā'īlī decision is contemporaneous with the construction of the systems of al-Fārābī and Avicenna. It engendered a number of theses on the nature of the first principle and on the instantiation and emanation of existents. These theses culminate in a radical apophatism, opening a disjunction between a real that is not "being," that is not even "principle," that is not "one" – except in a paradoxical sense — and what is called "the principle" but has no foundation in this first real, from which, however, it is enigmatically instantiated, and which is thought under the concept of a "prime instantiated," or "Prime Intelligence."[8] This approach to the real, comparable in its force to the procedure of Proclus or especially Damascius, receives a lengthy and polemical treatment in the works of the Qarmatian and Fatimid theoreticians, from Nasafī to Hamīd al-Dīn Kirmānī (d. 408/1017). The inflections introduced by later Ismā'īlī systems of thought, particularly in the highly eventful period beginning with the proclamation of the "great resurrection" in 559/1164, also belong, quite rightly, to the history of Islamic metaphysics and cannot be reduced to a nonphilosophical "gnosis."

It is very clear that the historical failure of Ismā'īlī political theology — which does not mean that it lost all value for a deep understanding of the question of questions in the Muslim world, namely, the question of authority and its foundation — nevertheless translated into a marginalization of these ways of thinking. The apophatic scheme shifted into the background. Avicennism, on the contrary, became dominant as it was protected and revitalized by both Sunnī thinkers (such as Suhrawardī) and the Twelver Shī'ites. It allowed the adequation of the *real* and *being* to become, in a way, obvious — an uncontested point of departure admitted by all. The "principle" is not secondary in relation to an unsayable real; rather, it is primary, it is necessary being, it is the real. The fact that Ibn al-'Arabī (d. 1240) had such great influence on Iranian philosophers suffices in itself to explain the force acquired by what was "obvious." Mullā Sadrā, following others before him, elaborated his own system on the basis of his constant reading of two texts, which he attempted to harmonize: the *Theology of Aristotle* and Ibn al-'Arabī's *Fusūs al-hikām*.

We must not neglect, in this coming together of doctrines, the importance of Suhrawardī, the Shaykh al-Ishrāq (d. 1191). The abundant glosses written by Mullā Sadrā on Suhrawardī's *Philosophy of Illumination*, and the repeated confrontations with other works by the shaykh, who was put to death on the orders of

Saladin, remind us that Sadrā saw himself intellectually constrained within Suhrawardian metaphysics, even as he contested virtually all of Suhrawardī's theses or rethought them within his own metaphysics of the act of being. Suhrawardī's point of departure, at least in his final work, is the equation of the real with the light of lights, itself identified with the being that is necessary by itself. Real, absolute being, the originary light, and the unity of being (*wahdat al-wujūd*): these became the major concepts whose problematic fecundity had to be accepted by metaphysics. The problem of the real had indeed become the problem of being.

That the question of the real would be thought within the horizon of necessary being seems to imply a definitive victory for Aristotelian ontology. Mullā Sadrā is not a Peripatetic in the strict sense, but he brings to completion two Aristotelian assertions: God is pure act and *energeia* is the truth of being. But in order to carry the energetics of being to its furthest consequences, he willingly inscribes it within a theoretical framework that hierarchizes the existent according to Platonic models. The metaphysics of Ismā'īlism, briefly mentioned above, is characterized, for its part, by an inverse scheme. Radical apophatism situates "Him," the unknowable ipseity or rather the real, beyond the act of being. But at the same time, the conception of emanated existents is much more Aristotelianizing than it would appear to be. The Sadrian scheme is the completed ontology of Islam, made possible by the decision to inscribe this ontology onto the Avicennian moment, in order to think the real within the split and reconciliation of essence.

All too often, we still have the impression that Avicenna's work derives whatever value it has from its role within an "Aristotelian tradition." In this view it modifies or transmits a certain heritage – that of the Greek commentators – and plays its principal, if not its only role in the elaboration of questions that will reach maturity only after being transmitted to Latin Scholasticism, in the medieval debate with Averroism, and in the Western doctors' use of the Latin version of the *Book of Healing*. This prejudice is handed down to us by Ernest Renan. But the power of Avicennism became manifest in the future that it came to have in Islamic philosophy. The future of a thought speaks the *truth* of this thought, whereas the history of its sources fixes its exactitude. The metamorphoses of a philosophy are the effective act of being of this philosophy because philosophy has no history but rather, in the time of systems, expresses schemes whose fecundity or capacity to be transformed through a confrontation with the present, is expressed by its future power. Its "history" is the record of the positions it has taken within the real, which it embodies and engenders.

Even if philosophy has no history, philosophers do. The life of Muhammad ibn Ibrāhīm Sadr al-Dīn Shīrāzī, referred to familiarly as Mullā Sadrā, unfolded in perfect conformity with the singular figure of the *'ārif*, the man of spiritual knowledge and science (*'irfān*) as it emerged in the new space of Safavid Iran. Sadrā was born in Shiraz, in 979 or 980 of the Hijri calendar, 1571 or 1572 of our era, during the last years of the reign of Shāh Tahmāsp I. He lived most of his life under the reign of Shāh 'Abbās I, having been born into a family with close ties to the court (his father, Ibrāhīm ibn Yahyā, is said to have been the vizier of Sultan Hamza Mīrzā's mother and of the future Shāh 'Abbās I).[9] After his early studies in Shiraz, he left for Esfahan, which would become the capital of the new state in 1598. Esfahan was the seat of both royal and religious power, and the capital was consciously thought of as a center for the diffusion of learning Shī'ism needed to flourish as a "state religion."

It is useful to recall the main features of this "Safavid renaissance." In 1501, Shāh Ismā'īl, the leader of the religious and military order of the Safavids, proclaimed Twelver Shī'ism the religion of the state he was founding in Iran. This master, like his predecessors, did not hesitate to present himself as the manifestation of the awaited imam, the twelfth, hidden imam, or, even more radically, as the messianic manifestation of God. Consider these verses, which have come down to us from him: "I am Very God, Very God, Very God! / Come now, O blind man who has lost his path, behold the Truth! / I am that *Agens Absolutus* of whom they speak."[10]

Grounded in such a messianic perspective, the Savafid state would necessarily encounter a difficulty confronting other Muslim states that were also founded on a messianic type of insurrection (the Qaramatian state of Bahrain, the Fatimid state, the Ismā'īli Shī'ite state centered in Alamūt, and even the 'Abbāsid state, and so on). It is remarkable that a very large number of figures of state authority in Islam owe their emergence to this type of proclamation. The problem is not foreign to the messianic question itself: how is it possible to claim to be the immediate coincidence of God and the face of man live in the time of duration, in the necessary transaction with the necessities of this world? The compromise solution involved the creation of a special body of religious teachers, a sort of clergy of religious experts and scholars, charged with transmitting the king's authority by upholding his absolute power and by emphasizing the teaching of integral prophecy, as conceived by Twelver Shī'ism, beginning with the letter of the Qur'ān and including the collections of the sayings of the successive imams.

The scholars who taught in this context did not engage in a disinterested practice of philosophy, for not only was philosophy integrated into a traditional curriculum that was deeply militant, but its ultimate goals involved nothing less than reinforcing the specifically Shī'ite teaching on the contents of revelation. Hence the following question was continually posed: what should this teaching be? Should it tend toward a spiritual exegesis of the legacy of prophecy and the imamate, or should its main focus be the rational elaboration (*ijtihād*) of the doctrines of law, suitable as a whole — though not without conflict — for strengthening royal power and the power of the Shī'ite clergy? This question carries with it a much broader problem: what is the meaning of an engagement in the cause of the imamate? The Safavid dynasty was able to take power in Iran through a confrontation with the Ottomans thanks to the affirmation of its eschatological and messianic mission. How could the mass of believers be converted to the Shī'ite cause, which was merging into the "national" Iranian cause? How to provide a solid basis for a power that would be supported by two pillars: royalty (whose claims went back to the ancient Persian royalty) and religion? The institutional response was the creation of a clergy made up of scholars — scholars, that is, in the service of power. The figure of the Shī'ite *mujtahid*, already present, was then solidified, and it acceded to its modern dignity.

This religious scholar was, and still is, confronted with his own position regarding the figure of the master par excellence, the twelfth imam, who brings together in his person the complete fullness of revelation and the light of the imamate. The greater occultation of the latter in 330 / 942, like the wait for his Parousia at the end of time, governs Twelver Shī'ite consciousness.

Twelver or Imāmī Shī'ism is characterized by the following profession of faith: "There is no divinity but God and Muhammad is the prophet of God and 'Ālī is the friend of God." This *shahāda* thus includes three affirmations: the existence and the unicity of God, the prophetic mission of Muhammad, and the mission of 'Ālī ibn 'Abī Tālib — son-in-law and cousin of the Prophet — which consists in being God's "friend," his *walī*, and thus in carrying out the complex function of the *walāyah*, which is to maintain the power of revelation after the closure of prophecy, in its exoteric and esoteric aspects.

The Twelvers are so named because they recognize twelve imams, beginning with the founder of their line, 'Ālī, up to Muhammad al-Mahdī al-Hujjah, son of Hasan al-'Askarī, the eleventh imam, who died in 260 / 873. We know that the twelfth imam mysteriously disappeared at the age of about five, when his father died. We know that this disappearance caused great turmoil within the community of faithful Imāmī, since it seemed to invalidate a dogma according to which the presence of the twelfth imam was necessary to the life of Islam and the very permanence of the universe. The response to this disappearance was the elaboration of a doctrine of "lesser occultation," which lasted until 329/940–41. During this period, the imam continued to correspond with his community through the intermediary of four principal representatives, although others among the faithful also had some contact with him.[11] The lesser occultation was followed by an indefinite period of occultation referred to as "greater," which will come to an end only with the awaited return of the imam.

The religious scholars persisted in their investigations concerning the proper conduct to adopt in relation to this occultation of the imam. Was it necessary to suspend all representation of the imam, or was it permissible for the clergy – composed of the scholars themselves – to make itself the collective representative of the imam? From the moment that royal power was upheld by the exercise of the Shīʿite faith, was it not legitimate to complete the work that had been begun long before: the usurpation (according to some) or legitimate leadership (according to others) of the temporal prerogatives of the imam, of powers that are ideological (leading Friday prayers), economic (managing ritual alms and the *khums*, the "one-fifth" tax – one-fifth of all income paid as a tax), and political (the struggle for the faith)? Bound up in these questions was the problem of the destination of knowledge, and thus of the place – central or peripheral – of philosophy.

Mullā Sadrā's teacher, Shaykh Bahā' al-Dīn al-ʿĀmilī (953/1546–1030/1621), distinguished himself by taking positions favorable to the sovereign and to the expansion of the clergy's power within the state.[12] Another of the philosopher's teachers, Mīr Dāmād, was noted for his political and religious practice as someone close to the king, but also for being one of the most profound philosophers and gnostics of Shīʿism.[13] Mīr Dāmād, known as "the third teacher" (along with Aristotle, the first teacher, and al-Fārābī, the second), agreed to a theologico-political decision of the greatest importance for the future. Shāh Ismāʿīl became aware of how few teachers he had attracted to spread his conception of the Shīʿite faith in Iran. He fostered the establishment in Iran of a large number of learned men from the traditional lands of Shīʿite Islam – for example, Lebanon, Arabia, and present-day Iraq. This explains, among other things, how Arabic became the language of the clergy in Iran at the time, in competition with Persian, which was the language of culture and of the poets, the language of the people and of literature.

Among these learned scholars, there was a wise and sensible man, Shaykh ʿĀlī al-Karakī (d. 940/1534), who was from Syria. On a number of occasions, he counseled Shāh Ismāʿīl, but he saw the full success of his undertaking under the latter's successor, Shāh Tahmāsp, under whom he was designated the representative (*nā'ib*) of the hidden imam.[14] This was the culmination of a long history during which the Shīʿite clerics persistently stood in for the hidden imam by elaborating this notion of the imam's representative. This, however, had become a thing of the past after the passing of the four particular "representatives" during the greater occultation. One consequence of this transgression was that it endowed the imam's collective representative – that is, the clergy, made up of religious scholars and experts – with the iman's spiritual prerogatives, before the particular representative seized his temporal prerogatives: this would be the issue at stake in the Islamic revolution in Iran in 1979. The political silence of Twelver Shīʿism was followed by constant intervention in the affairs of the state, which seemed to many scholars to be a disturbing reorientation of the original intentions of the Shīʿite faith. Mullā Sadrā thus had his path laid out for him: to become a traditional man of knowledge, engaged in developing religious sciences, with the double aim of reinforcing not only royal power but especially the power of the class destined for domination, the Shīʿite mujtahids.

But that is not at all what happened. Unlike his teachers, Sadrā took no part in the affairs of the court. He clearly perceived the growing conflict between a juridico-political Shīʿism and the Shīʿite gnosis which, for him, was alone faithful to the teaching of the imams and to eschatological waiting. As with Mīr Dāmād, it would be overly schematic and false to decide who among these great scholars was primarily committed to one path or the other. Rather, it was often a matter of placing gnosis itself in the service of constructing the new juridical order, not of destroying or weakening it. But in the end, Sadrā took a decisive position, maintaining that Shīʿite gnosis had to be central to the exercise of true spiritual power, not at the periphery of a temporal power. Sadrā's treatise *The Three Principles*, written in Persian, attests to the vigor with which he courageously opposed the legalitarian mutation, in all its forms, of the Shīʿite vocation.[15] Whatever the importance of the conflict between the religious scholars who considered the practice of *ijtihād* – the personal effort to elaborate new consequences for the discourse of the imams – legitimate and those who refused it, the issue at stake was, among other things, the very destination of Shīʿism. Sadrā's life unfolded entirely during the time of such a conflict, which, during a brief period under Shāh ʿAbbās II, turned to the advantage of the "gnostic and mystic scholars" (*ʿirfānīyūn*).

The introduction to the *Journeys* (*al-Asfār*), often cited in research on Sadrā, gives a few signs of the moral crisis that he had to overcome. Here the philosopher expresses a belief that gives his entire life meaning. According to him, nothing surpasses the perfection proper to the human species, a perfection in which the very substance of the essence of man can be realized. "It is the conjunction with the intelligibles and the proximity of the Creator, the separation from sensible realities."[16] At stake here is the creation of one's own life, a preference given to the search for authentic beatitude once the sensible pleasures have demonstrated their vanity. According to Sadrā, salvation through contemplation is effected by God in the intelligence of the contemplator, in the conjunction at the terminal point of the soul's ascension after it has been torn away from sensible realities. It is a matter of leading not simply the life of a man of knowledge, but the highest life, the life which transfigures the very substance of man as he realizes his most intimate desire, a desire veiled by the seductions of this world. At the dawn of the long ordeal that would lead Sadrā to solitude and a preoccupation with intelligence alone, there is this certainty – fully experienced – that nothing is valid except the truth of desire. For Sadrā, the truth of man's desire is this conjunction with the divine world. That is why he tells us that entering on the path of philosophy was for him a conversion, a reorientation of the gaze toward the intelligible face of God. It was a conversion that signified for him the gradual perfection of the self and that implied a rupture with all compromised transactions: "It is necessary for him who devotes himself to the intelligible (*al-'āqil*) that he be converted to the most important occupation of all, and that he not abandon his desire to dedicate his entire life to the most complete perfection of the self, after acquiring the other forms of science and knowledge."[17]

Sadrā is distinctly melancholic when he speaks of the age in which he lives; he describes it as a time of darkness when the enemies of truth are triumphant. This feeling contrasts with the familiar image of the Safavid renaissance and the unquestionable brilliance it shed on Muslim civilization. In the conclusion to his *Treatise on Resurrection*, Sadrā addresses his readers with these words: "You must hide this epistle and conceal it from the eyes of the inexperienced. Beware of offering it to men of blindness, who are the most numerous sons of this time, but give it to the few whom none but God knows, because they are hidden under the domes of mercy, away from the eyes of all creatures, be they men or jinn."[18]

In the introduction to the *Journeys* (*al-Asfār*), Sadrā alludes to the persecutions he suffered after beginning his studies of the Greek philosophers and the philosophers of Islam.[19] This climate of incomprehension forced him into a solitary life, a life rewarded by the birth of illumination in the philosopher's heart:

> I was led initially to act according to the words of my lord, my master, and my support, the first imam, the first heir of the Prophet (*wasī*), the father of the martyred imams, friends of God, he who divided heaven and hell, practicing dissimulation (*taqīyah*) before the evildoers, . . . and I did not allow myself to be swayed by any concern for people or for their company; I withdrew far from their society and their gregarious conviviality, escaping the stubbornness shown by the sons of this age. I freed myself from their disagreements as well as their agreements, taking their esteem and their insults as equal, and I turned my face toward the cause of causes; I humbled myself, imploring him who makes difficult things easy. As

> I remained in this state of withdrawal, incognito, and solitude for quite a long time, a very long period, my prolonged inner struggles caused my soul to become enflamed with a luminous fire, and because of many spiritual exercises my heart burned with an intense fire, and the lights of the Malakūt flowed over it. My heart received the secrets of the Jabarūt.[20]

Sadrā found this ascetic and studious solitude in the village of Kahak, near Qom. Writing the lines just quoted, the philosopher characterizes his entire work in terms of an imitation of the first imam, 'Ālī ibn 'Abī Tālib. But he takes as his model neither the imam's political authority nor his notorious practices as a warrior but rather the spiritual authority conferred on him by his seat in the pleroma of the immaculate, among the imams considered the original witnesses, the martyrs par excellence. Dissimulation is the practice he adopts in conformity with the life of the imam. We know that this dissimulation consists in the faithful Shī'ite keeping his beliefs a secret, in order not to attract the ill regard or condemnation of those who disapprove of them. More generally, dissimulation is permitted to the Muslim when he lives in a country ruled by infidels. But here this practice takes on a precise meaning. It is a matter of imitating the imam in the secret that protects the secret, in the silence imposed on the esoteric teaching of Islam, in order to avoid scandal among the supporters of the legalitarian religion reduced to what is "obvious" in this world. As a consequence, the practice of philosophy aspires to the continuation and imitation of the esoteric revelation possessed by the imam and taught by him to a select few among the faithful.

But who could oppose such a revelation, such an example, in Safavid Iran, where Shī'ism had become the state religion? It is clear that the "sons of this age," the "ignorant" persecutors, cannot be equated primarily with the adherents of Sunnī Islam. The division Sadrā has in mind does not seem to be that between Shī'ites and Sunnites; rather, it opposes the sage and those who restrict themselves to an external religion focused on legal obligations and reduced to these obligations—in short, those who are loath to practice the exegesis of what is given in the *sharīʿah*. In sum, Sadrā says that—unlike the Shīʿites who persecute him—he remains faithful to the imam by choosing the path of intelligence and wisdom as he wishes to express them in his great work.

It is remarkable that he gains access to this wisdom precisely through the conclusions he draws from his persecution: conversion to God, ascetic practices, solitary life, and spiritual exercises, without which there would be no illumination. Finally, the awakening of the flame in the heart. This blazing of the heart is the authentic destination of man, his intelligible perfection, for it brings to fulfillment the natural love that man (like all existents) has for the cause of causes, that is, for the final cause of all existence and all desire. Sadrā says:

> It is established that natural realities have final ends, and that no deficient existent lacks the natural power which God gives it and by which it moves, or the natural desire by which it journeys in search of the perfection that conjoins it to its finality and completeness. That is why metaphysical philosophers speak of the flowing of the light of love and of the desire oriented toward God within the whole of existents. There is no existent that does not love God, that is not ardently passionate for him, whether at rest by his side or journeying toward him, and whereas God remains, all things must perish.[21]

The *Journeys* (*al-Asfār*) expresses in philosophical terms the experience of the amorous and spiritual journey and the illumination of the heart, which can be awakened only in withdrawal.

Sadrā's hopes were probably disappointed by those who did not make philosophy the royal road to God. But our interpretation may be unilateral. Sadrā does not like the "philosophers" any more than he does the jurists and the theologians, and he often stigmatizes those who "philosophaster." He reproaches them with being unfaithful to the ancient exemplars—the "first teacher," Aristotle, as well as Socrates and Plato. It may be that the "deniers," from whom Sadrā wanted to protect himself through dissimulation and withdrawal, are the philosophers who deny the truth of the Qur'ānic promise, the reality of a paradise and a hell effectively lived by the chosen and the damned. For these philosophers, the practice of dialectics allows one to regard the future retribution of human actions with skepticism. They believe that representations of paradise and hell are imaginary, and they ask where they are located. They have only contempt for the imagination of ordinary people who hope for sensible pleasures or fear physical pain in the other world.

This is how Sadrā speaks of them:

> The extraordinary thing is that most of those whom we just evoked are plunged into the intelligibles, but they do not know the sensibles. They speak of divine things but know nothing of natural realities; they provide demonstrations and analogies but do not in fact practice logic and syllogistic reasoning. When it comes to the religious sciences, they are familiar with only the most controversial questions, and they do not strive to know the medical art that treats the soul and the purification of the inner man, the cleansing from the heart of impurities left by attributes and habits. No, instead they seek the power that comes from being a leader and subjecting men to their own fatwas and their own judgments.[22]

The "deniers" deny future retribution, opposing it to a beatitude that consists of intellective cognitions. Sadrā, too, thinks that salvation lies in a conjunction with the intelligible. But he refuses to treat Qur'ānic promises as mere metaphors addressed to the humble and the ignorant. He has no contempt for "sensible things," even if he turns his gaze to the pole opposite the sensible. If salvation were simply the eternal possession of the "first intelligibles," what happiness would there be in possessing them? He questions Alexander of Aphrodisias, as well as Avicenna's apparent agreement with him. He questions Themistius, who thought that imperfect souls had nothing better to hope for than some weak, imaginary happiness culminating in an understanding of such elementary truths as "the whole is greater than the part."[23]

Here, it seems to me, Sadrā is denouncing an extreme form of contempt for the people.

Sadrā responds to the argument that paradise and hell cannot be located in this world with an admirable analysis of the very notion of "world." The idea of "world" is the idea of an absolute totality, such that there is nothing external to it. Consequently, a "world" has no place. Understood correctly, the "world" is perfect and complete in itself and, consequently, has neither a "where" nor a "place." On this point, he says, Aristotle is right. From this it follows that it is absurd to ask where hell is or where paradise is. They form a world in and of themselves and are not "parts" of this world; they constitute "the land of the other-world." This land is the land of the soul; and it is in the world of the soul that the torments of hell and the joys of paradise take place – physical torments and sensible joys that occur through the intermediary of the senses of the soul, that is, through the sensibility internal to the soul. These sensations are infinitely more intense than what we feel with our physical bodies, and that is the truth of the Qur'ānic promises and the divine warnings. At stake in moral life is something that ordinary people understand very well and that philosophy must take into account: the soul's eternal suffering or permanent enjoyment [*jouissance*], in the singular mode of its "resurrection."[24]

The persecutors whom Sadrā had to confront may well have included some who denied a fully lived eschatology. This hypothesis is all the more plausible in that Sadrā considered his philosophy of the soul, which posits the successive "births" of the soul and the substantial motion of metamorphosis, the major consequence of his ontology. Indeed, it is possible that Sadrā faced opposition on two fronts: on the one hand, from the jurists, skilled in fashioning their own interpretations of the revealed texts, enamored of themselves and their authority; and, on the other hand, from the Peripatetic philosophers, distant readers of Avicenna, reticent about the legacy of the imams and the *sharī'ah* (understood in the sense that Sadrā gives it in his meditations). Indeed, it should be clear that Sadrā has no desire to disavow this *sharīʿah*, for he uses the term to designate the complete teachings of prophecy, not the juridical doctrines that claim to be a substitute for inwardly lived religion and indispensable moral ascesis.[25] All his efforts are aimed, on the contrary, at finding a way out of the never-ending debate between jurists and philosophers, between those who reduce the gnosis of the imams to a matter of social jurisprudence and those who reduce Aristotle to a blinkered exercise in understanding. He was persecuted, no doubt, because he believed in the possibility of a return to the rational truth of revelation – according to his understanding of reason as the faculty of the highest problems of the spirit. Reason is that power man has to intuit the very act of existing and to think its consequences for the sum total of created existents. In this sense, Sadrā bore witness to Islam and to the universal destination of philosophy.

Later, thanks to the governor of Shiraz, Allāhwirdī Khān, Sadrā was able to teach in a *madrasah* that was built for him. Mullā Sadrā was thus not, strictly speaking, part of the school of Esfahan. Although he studied in the capital, he exiled himself and only found a public audience in Shiraz, in the Fars region. We must not allow the solitude of Kahak to disguise the influence and celebrity that he gained at the time. He did have disciples. For example: ʿAbd al-Razzāq Lāhījī (d. 1072/1661–62) and Muhammad Muhsin Fayd al-Kāshānī (d. 1091/1680), who were his sons-in-law, and Husayn Tunkābunī (d. 1101/1690 or 1105/1694). He also had enemies, and it could be argued that Islamic philosophy from the seventeenth to the nineteenth century in Iran can be partially explained in terms of the conflicts that arose among the schools of Mīr Dāmād, Mullā Sadrā, Rajab ʿĀlī Tabrīzī (d. 1080 / 1669–70), and Qāzī Saʿīd Qummī (d. 1103/1691).[26] Sadrā undertook the pilgrimage to Mecca seven times; he died on his return from the seventh pilgrimage, at Basra, where he was buried in 1050/1640. The life of Mullā Sadrā – a philosopher's life lived in the cultural milieu common to the Shīʿite scholars – has few notable rough patches. This life disappears beneath the weight of an imposing body of work that bears the mark of those teachers unconstrained by any obligation to be concise – an infinite commentary, that provokes its own glosses and commentaries in turn.

The major work, the summa of Sadrā's philosophy, is the *Four Journeys*. The principal works that also discuss many of the subjects addressed there are *al-Shawāhid al-rubūbīyah* (Divine Witnesses), *al-Mabda' wa-al-ma'ād* (The Beginning and the End), *Mafātīh al-ghayb* (The Keys to the Invisible World), *Kitāb al-Mashā'ir* (The Book of Metaphysical Prehensions), *Risalāt al-hashr* (Treatise on Resurrection), *Risālah fī al-hudūth* (Treatise on the Eduction[27] of the World), *al-Hikmah al-'arshīyah* (The Wisdom of the Throne), *Tafsīr al-Qur'ān al-karīm* (Commentary on the Qur'ān), *Sharh usūl al-kāfī* (Exegesis of Kulayni's *Book of Principles of the Kāfī*), *Ta'līqāt 'al Hikmat al-ishrāq* (Glosses on Suhrawardī's *Philosophy of Illumination*), and *Ta'līqāt 'al-Ilāhīyyāt* (Glosses on the *Metaphysics* of Avicenna's *Shīfā'*).

The conflict between philosophy's gnostic destination and its placement in the service of juridical and political discourse had a familiar result: the institutional triumph of the clergy's effort to reinforce its temporal power through the exercise of spiritual power. In a way, this signaled that philosophy was obliged to think of itself as a threatened, fundamentally interior practice geared toward personal salvation. Mullā Sadrā could not have known what a strange destiny would befall his work once it was taught in modern Iranian religious universities: how can one ever forget that this work lies at the heart of internal debates among clergy, at the heart of what still today remains essential to the framework of the Islamic republic?

It is strange that the founder of this republic had taught Sadrā's work for a long time, that he had adapted a few of its major concepts (that of existential revolution, for example) to a task that was the exact opposite of Sadrā's intentions, through a "conversion" to the old clerical project of the collective representation of the hidden imam. This "conversion" – of gnosis to law and Islamic politics – also justifies the study of Mullā Sadrā, because his work offers the remedy for what could well be the extinction of Islam in Iran, after having been its provisional temporal triumph.

It offers the completed ontology of the Islam that was, as a whole, the philosophy of the doctors and the gnostics, and is today a major reference for gnostics when they face their opponents, especially because Islam brings to completion within this set of conflicts its own philosophical self-knowledge.

I would like to say a few words about the conditions affecting the Western philosopher today when he reads the works of the philosophers of Islam. Thanks to the editorial work of the past twenty years, particularly in Iran, such a reader has access to a larger number of printed texts than ever before. The work of Muhammad Khvājavī is much appreciated; it has greatly facilitated the reading of a number of Sadrā's works. The pioneering work undertaken before him by Jalāl al-Dīn 'Āshtiyānī also deserves appreciation. However, at times it is necessary to consult old lithographs or to observe that some manuscripts still await editors. The printed texts are not critical editions in the usual sense of the term. To take only one example, the nine-volume Qum edition of the Arabic text of Mullā Sadrā's *Four Journeys (al-Asfār)* provides a very rich philosophical commentary but includes no references. Sadrā refers to authors both in a familiar and an allusive way; he cites texts from memory; he dictates or writes while briefly consulting manuscripts that serve as an aide-mémoire — manuscripts whose exact title or reference, of course, he does not supply. While the more recent editors indicate verses cited from the Qur'ān, they do not clarify Sadrā's references to the collections of prophetic traditions or to the sayings of the imams, and they give no references to modern editions of texts that are cited or mentioned. The reader must find the Arabic text and identify its author or, depending on the case, must identify the corresponding Greek text.

There is a reason for this, which has nothing to do with negligence or contempt for erudition but with a traditional practice of knowledge. The reader of these books is a teacher or a teacher's disciple. Beginning at a very young age, he learns the texts by heart and can identify a passage from memory, without even the aid of a note. The art of memory, so greatly lacking in Westerners, is the technique of the Eastern reader; the child learns it upon first discovering the Qur'ān, and it is strengthened by traditional studies in the exegetic and philosophical sciences.

In the pages that follow, I am therefore responsible for the bibliographic work that is indispensable for discussions and elucidations. The reader must make do with the almost complete absence of translations into Western languages, since the overwhelming volume of Mullā Sadrā's work seems largely to have discouraged translators.[28] Following the 1999 "World Congress of Mullā Sadrā," a vast movement of editing and publishing began to develop in Iran. This is most welcomed. As for the quotations from philosophical texts written in Arabic or Persian, all translations are my own unless otherwise noted.[29]

I would have lacked the necessary endurance to complete this project if I had not been encouraged and supported, as well as enlightened on many points, by the attentive considerations of Olivier Bétourné, to whom I offer my gratitude.

Souâd Ayada knows how much this book owes to her.

Christian Jambet
Paris, February 2002

Part One

The Metaphysical Revolution

Chapter One

The Witness of the Real

"Is it not enough that your Lord is a witness present in all things?" Sadrā quotes this verse in the prologue to *The Book of Metaphysical Prehensions*, and this quote clarifies his conception of his undertaking as a whole.[1] God testifies to himself in all his manifestations, which are all existents proceeding from his light and his infinite act of being. In return, the philosopher is the witness of the real, restoring to God the testimony whose source can only be in God and thus practicing the most authentic *shahādah*.

Sadrā's conception of wisdom (*hikmah*) encompasses his definition of metaphysics. This conception presupposes the hermeneutics of the Qur'ān and the traditions of the imams, because it aspires, above all, to be faithful to the internal meaning of the Holy Book:

> We know that an understanding of the symbols of the Qur'ān, of its depths and its secrets, cannot be realized through sharpness of thought or by much examination and research, if there is no pilgrimage of the pure along the road of purification through the esoteric and education through mystery, and, by the return to the people of the house of divine friendship,[2] the acquisition of the lights of wisdom in the tabernacle of prophecy and in the source of what by the perfect prophets and the immaculate imams bring about, the illumination produced by their lights, heeding their secrets, faith in their

> guidance, and fidelity to their lights, so that the pilgrim may attain some part of the lights of the Book and of the tradition, and so that he may be freed from innovating arguments.[3]

Ultimately, the knowledge of the act of being is the understanding of the revelation granted to the prophets and its concentrated interpretation in the spiritual teachings of the imams.[4] Conversely, metaphysics makes an essential contribution to the exegesis that leads to the hidden meaning of the letter of the Qur'ān. To the extent that he is a Shī'ite philosopher, Mullā Sadrā aspires above all to be a "gnostic," an *'ārif*, a practitioner of the gnosis (*'irfān*) that is transmitted in the light of the imamate. He locates his search at the heart of the literal or apparent meaning (*zāhir*) of the book, in order to raise it to the hidden meaning (*bātin*), such that metaphysics would have little relevance without this hermeneutical horizon. But it is no less important to observe that, for the very same reason, the methods of metaphysics have the power to lead to the effective reality (*haqīqa*) of being, to sustain the effort of spiritual intuition that grasps the concrete truth of existing, in which the very essence of God is concentrated.

Philosophy is not a discipline separate from exegesis; rather, it is a style of exegesis, although it uses its own means: judgment and demonstration. Metaphysics remains closely connected to other hermeneutic procedures, since its object—being—can be conceived only as the *real* and as coinciding with the nature of God, and since God gives himself over to being known in scriptural revelation.[5] Thus we can speak of an *exegetic philosophy*, a philosophical exegesis of God, an exegesis of the book and its interpreters, an exegesis of the self.[6]

Wisdom and Existence

Metaphysics is indeed the "divine science," or the "divine wisdom" (*al-hikmah al-ilāhīyah*). The science or knowledge we can have of being as being is, to be sure, unworthy of the science God has of himself and all possible existents. But the difference is not one of essence; our science is the reflection of divine science in the mirror of our intelligence, which is infinitely far from perfect but is an expression of the intellection of the subject par excellence, the divine subject. Sadrā's definition of metaphysics conforms with the teachings of Aristotle and Avicenna: metaphysics is the science of the existent as existent. It culminates in the recognition of the highest existent, the existent that is necessary by itself:

> Since we have established and verified that the first wisdom and the highest science is the search for the states of the existent and the first divisions of the absolute existent — which, however, is not a particular species — within the register of mathematics or physics, then its subject is the nature of the absolute existent, or the concept of the existent as existent. It is therefore necessary that its subject have a self-evident reality that does not derive from a representative definition or a prior demonstration.[7]

From the concept of the existent we pass to its presence, to the immediacy of its reality. We return to what is most immediate, the obvious, which cannot be founded by any representation or demonstration. Metaphysics will thus have to consider the pure intensity of existing, of the *act* of being. There is nothing, then, that formally distinguishes Sadrā's definition from that put forth by Avicenna, except a decisive insistence on showing that, as the cognition of the very act that determines existence, metaphysics differs from derivative sciences whose objects are the respective quiddities of existents. These sciences all say what existents are, whereas metaphysics attests, above all, to that in which the existent exists, to what constitutes its act of being, and to the nature of the activity (*fi'līyah*) through which it is effectively established. If God is existence, the object of our highest knowledge will be the nature of the act of existing rather than the quiddity of things .[8]

The act of being (*wujūd*) is the object of "divine science," for what occurs in the first instance always arises from a certain position within existence. Metaphysics, unlike other sciences, is not primarily concerned with the formal definition or subject matter of a particular theoretical teaching. It does not present the essence of a being according to just any form of *mathesis*; rather, it bears on the *reality* of being. The act of being does not belong to the being as a being, as one of its properties would belong to it; a being is what always expresses a certain degree of existence. It is through its act of being that a being affirms its effective reality, from which it follows that the being will be this or that, and thereby possess a certain quiddity. The division between act of being and quiddity determines Sadrā's entire undertaking, and his interpretation summarizes the entire enterprise of metaphysics. According to this initial division, divine science is distinguished from particular sciences devoted to knowledge of the nature of these or those types of beings.[9]

These sciences are always regional and assume that their objects undergo a certain transformation, a mutation dependent on the point of view from which they are envisioned. They must be turned from existents, in the absolute sense, into particular beings "among movements and things moved, or among continuous and discrete quantities." The characterization of metaphysics as ontology, the science of being, implies this transcendental condition, the separation of the act of being from the quiddity of the being, since the sciences of particular beings are distinct from metaphysics to the extent that, unlike the latter, they are disciplines and forms of knowledge whose objects are limited exclusively to the quidditative attributes of beings.

How did Sadrā parse the series of manifestations of the act of being, and how did he experience the metaphysical quest? He considered it self-evident, first of all, that the science of the act of being does not need to have been preceded by another science. The act of being asserts itself in the immediacy of its presence. Furthermore, ontology is not, in itself, theology, although God is the act of being par excellence. God is not the first object to be examined in the order of discovery. For the act of being to unveil its reality, it is appropriate to begin — as Avicenna teaches, drawing directly from Aristotle — with the existent in general. This order of investigation is a reversal of the hierarchy of the acts of being, and it must lead us to reestablish the effective order, such that God will be not only the first of all existents but also the constitutive reality of every act of being.

Henceforth, ontology will be irresistibly converted into theology. When Sadrā formulates the program ontology will pursue, he testifies to this conversion: he will establish the whole of effective realities – whose reality is that of an act of being *(al-haqā'iq al-wujūdat) – on the basis of* the Creator. From this follows the program of theology properly speaking: the unicity (*wahdānīyah*) of the Creator, knowledge of his names and attributes, knowledge of the angels, exegesis of the holy books and of the message of the prophets, and establishment of the otherworldly region (*al-Dār al-Ākhīra*). Eschatology brings ontology to its end; it is the *raison d'être* of metaphysics. For anyone who reads Sadrā, it is as clear as day that the most refined exercises of speculation would be no more than a futile game for him if it were not necessary to justify, for our intelligence, the prophecies concerning the future retribution of the good and the wicked as a whole and in detail. Ontology is completed in a spiritual morality which itself presupposes the hierarchical structure of the universes and the philosophy of resurrection. As an exegetic philosophy, the system reaches its fulfillment in the form of an eschatological metaphysics.

This doctrine of the destination of all created existents, deduced from the act of being in its essential truth, would found a mystical psychology which, in turn, would verify the "births" or successive growths of the soul, and would proceed to think the formation of the spiritual body and the intellectual union with the divine proximity. If the intelligence is our true reality, if intelligible man is at the center of an anthropology – inherited from Plotinus – that makes him the origin and the end of both psychic man and natural, sensuous man, the intelligence is therefore the metaphysical power par excellence. But the intelligence and the heart are one, such that "love follows from the perception of being, since the latter is pure good."[10] Intuition of the presence of being leads to the practices of contemplation, which Mullā Sadrā is not afraid to name using the following three modulations of love: passionate love (*al-hayamān*), spiritual love (*al-'ishq al-rūhānī*), and divine love (*al-mahabbah al-ilāhīyah*).[11] Metaphysics teaches the practice of a certain freedom, in imitation of divine freedom; this freedom is inscribed in the very nature of the intelligence, which is linked directly to God and eminently expresses the creative spontaneity of the divine imperative: to intelligize is to liberate one's own self from all mortal attachments, from the oppression of matter and the passions. Conversely, the practice of the self requires intellection, in the sense of grasping being in its immediate givenness, in its originary surging forth. That is why the intelligence must not be confused with a ratiocinative understanding. Here is one definition among others that Sadrā gives:

> The intelligence mentioned in the book of the *Ilāhīyāt*, and in the gnosis of lordly things, is the existent delivered from every attachment, whatever it may be, except for the attachment to its own principle, which is God, the Provident (*al-Qayyūm*);[12] it is the existent that has no attachment to a substrate (as an accident would have), or to matter (as a form would have), or to the body (as the soul would have). It has no perfection in potency; there is in its essence no modality of nonbeing and potentiality, or of ontological deficiency, except for what follows from its being subjugated to the omnipotent necessity of the act of being of the divine real, because of which we name its "world" the world of the Jabarūt.[13]

This intelligence is the Intelligence thought according to the Neoplatonic scheme, to which the intelligence of man is linked by virtue of the trace of this free totality of being and thought that man bears within himself. Metaphysics is, *de jure*, the free deployment and exercise of a thought that thinks itself and thinks with itself and in itself all the hierarchies of existence, all the lights of being.

Metaphysics is the science of origin and return. It is sustained by cognition of the act of being that depends on the concept of substantial motion and unveils the free movement of the real, whose impetus resides in the hierarchized whole of its manifestations. It comprehends all cognitions of the various degrees of divine worlds, particularly the lower and upper Malakūt; it comes to completion in the science "descended from the divine throne," a gnostic and illuminative science, homologous to the spiritual teachings of the imams. Sadrā thus aligns his definition of metaphysics with spiritual unveiling (*kashf*) and the *ta'wīl* or hermeneutic of higher worlds (the imaginal world, or the world of images, and the intelligible world), in which the destination of all possible existents — all the way up to man in his becoming angelic — is realized.[14] This cosmology requires the fixed determination of the ten predicaments of being, through which Sadrā rejoins the Peripatetic program. But it also requires the elucidation of the "universal realities" that characterize every existent: one and multiple, potency and act, universal and particular, cause and effect, the anterior and the posterior, the four causes — agent, end, matter, and form. Ontology attempts a synthesis, necessarily problematic, between the Aristotelian definition of the being as a being and pure intuition of the act of being.[15]

Life Made Divine

In the prologue to *The Beginning and the End*, Mullā Sadrā expresses the sense and the final goal of what he means by "wisdom," *hikmah*, and thus also the nature of a metaphysics that has reached completion. Wisdom consists both in the integral, ordered knowledge of existents that proceeds from cognition of their principle, and in the attainment of real happiness, of life made divine. Within this wisdom, the science of the true is also — and immediately — practice, a lived experience of divine goodness. Wisdom is revelation, in that it unveils the realities of things, from immaterial Intelligences down to substances condemned to generation and corruption. It is also revelation in the sense that God himself, in his being, which is identified with his science, manifests himself in human wisdom, through which the epiphanies of his most beautiful names are experienced. And it is revelation in the sense that it opens up to men the path to self-knowledge, where they awaken from oblivion, learn their destiny, and come to satisfy moral demands – where their practical intelligence illuminates the decisions of their will and turns their freedom into a liturgy and a perpetual glorification. Gnosis is a transfiguration of the subject through the actualization of its highest potentialities. These potentialities are never completed through the promises of this world (natural perfection) but carry supernatural perfections within themselves: the constitution of the body resurrected in the otherworld and the ascent toward the intelligible angelic realities.[16] Wisdom is a becoming angelic of man.

The point of departure for metaphysics is "the existent as existent"; its final goal is integral wisdom, which reveals God in all things and restores to men the truth of their own act of being. That is why it is so difficult to distinguish the definition of metaphysics from that of wisdom. It is as if wisdom, as absolute knowledge, enveloped metaphysics, overflowing it on all sides, the way a circle expresses its own generative center. God is the origin of two congruent types of cognition: intellectual demonstrations, on the one hand, and opinions transmitted by the religious tradition, on the other.[17] The common source of practical philosophy and religious knowledge is the agent intelligence, identified with the archangel Gabriel. Thus the "tabernacle of lights" of the prophecy is the providence of the contemplative. The unity of the truth of faith and the truth of the intelligence is the unity of divine revelation, which takes place equally along these two paths.

Integral wisdom, both theoretical and practical, includes both religious tradition, founded in the Holy Book and in the exegeses of the imams, and philosophical wisdom, culminating in spiritual intuition and the transformation of the self. Wisdom is the exegesis of faith, whereas the hidden content of the sayings of the imams, like the prophetic revelations, is made explicit in the discourse of metaphysics and is extinguished in the extinction of the self in proximity with God, the conjunction with the "world of the *mysterium*." Intelligence is knowledge [*savoir*], presence, and intuition of being, greatly exceeding the formal representations of understanding and discursive thought, while the religious tradition offers to the initiated faithful the manifestations of this same absolute being, in the word of the Qur'ān and in the hermeneutics inspired by the divine throne itself. Henceforth, "canons of wisdom" and religious principles conform to each other.

The goal of wisdom is happiness. Here we encounter the Greek ideal again, the finality that Aristotle clearly assigns to human existence. The quest for happiness lies in man's very nature; it illuminates his form and his end. It is the reward for contemplative activity. Sadrā does not think that man is a "political animal" but that, by his fundamental nature, he is not an animal at all. Nevertheless, the human soul begins its development in the lowest stages of matter and then passes through all the degrees of the structure of worlds, from elementary existence to pure immateriality. In his essence, man is made for contemplation. His practical life is illuminated by his contemplative life, and the latter is the completion and perfection of the former.

The notion that perfect happiness is perfect knowledge is no doubt the most widespread commonplace of ancient wisdom. But if we look carefully, we can see that it is quite a bit more than a commonplace. It is the spirit of the Western world, the result of an unstated decision. This decision made it possible for the sciences to flourish, just as it authorized the search for a holy life in the renunciation of the world. It encompassses both knowledge of the world and a possible exit from the world. Mastery and ascesis are two poles of existence that are hardly strangers to each other. Sadrā justifies this model of life:

> Certainly, the treasures and the beatitudes, as well as the best means for attaining the highest degrees and the most eminent good, consist in a perfection of the contemplative power through the actualization of the sciences bearing on essential realities, and of the most certain gnoses, which are precisely what human souls seek. This is the noblest of those means by which material intellects are perfected, since, through these sciences and gnoses, man becomes a pilgrim on the road of cognition and gnosis (*'irfān*), leading to his conversion

> toward the *Ka'ba* of science and faith; he is purified of impurities and depravity, and he directs himself toward beatitude and the merciful proximity, passing beyond similitudes and the things one associates with God, as the divine books show, and as announced in the prophetic symbols and in the evident truth of the theses of philosophical wisdom.[18]

The contemplative power is the theoretical intelligence. It must pass from the stage of material intellect to that of actual intellect, by receiving the agent intellect's illuminations. Thus the natural sciences, the mathematical disciplines, and – at the highest degree – metaphysics are born and progress toward their completion as total knowledge. These sciences unveil the forms of existents and lead to the experience of certainty, or a cognition of the very presence of existing. All knowledges are gnoses, and fully so, for they are the direct experience of the profound unity of the knowing subject and the object known, of the one who is a witness of being and the being he contemplates. Certainty in and through God is a pilgrimage; it engenders the concrete existence of man and gives him a sublime meaning far beyond the contingencies of his sensible life.

Metaphysics is a conversion, a turning of the soul, an ethical purification, which has its pole in the temple, not simply the material temple toward which the believer makes his way, but also the spiritual temple where the secret of prophetic revelation is revealed to be the secret of science. We cannot overestimate the importance of this transfiguration of the temple. It is no longer the site of a blind obedience but the terminal point of a lived, transformative experience, an illumination through higher forms of cognition.[19] To become like the "intimate angels," to receive all the influxes of divine mercy, and to recognize in each thing the expression of this mercy, is to be turned toward the good, that is, to be turned toward being.

Science and gnosis are, in principle, a totality, but the human soul is incapable of actualizing all their "branches," all their various forms, because it is itself rooted in this corporeal "birth." That is why the metaphysical quest and the scientific search illuminated by it are infinite tasks for us, a pilgrimage that we must constantly begin anew. In this life, we are not detached from corporeal matter, the very principle of all darkness and error. The destiny of metaphysics cannot be separated from knowledge of the human soul.

To be sure, the science of the soul is a natural science, the highest there is, and not a part of metaphysics. But the famous *hadīth* that states that "he who knows himself knows his Lord" justifies the notion that knowledge of self reflects a knowledge of being. For Avicenna, the unveiling of the self was the very experience of existence.[20] According to Sadrā, this knowledge is an exegesis of the self that leads to proximity with God, in his hierarchized universes, through the discovery of one's own spiritual nature, which, for its part, is a "luminous word" (*kalimah nūrīyah*), a "spiritual essence" (*dhāt rūhānīyah*), a "flame of the Malakūt" (*shu'lah malakūtīyah*).[21] Since the soul is "word," it belongs in principle to the reign of intelligible existents, in which the divine Word is expressed. As a spiritual essence, it has an angelic nature. As a flame of the Malakūt, it is a spark of the intelligible world. In it the two worlds that are superior to the sensible world – the psychic world and the angelic world – reflect each other, giving rise to the higher births of the soul as it ascends the spiritual hierarchy. The human soul is not material, at least not in its higher faculties, which are the imagination (homologous to the Malakūt) and the intelligence (homologous to the Jabarūt). That is why the goal of metaphysics is to illuminate the soul's becoming, to draw out all the consequences "from the fact that the soul does not die with the death of the body." It prepares the progressive perfection through which the soul reconciles with its true nature and ends by "resembling the angelic substances."

Perfection of the Self

The natural science of the soul is thus converted into a supernatural science directly preparing the way for metaphysical contemplation, while the latter, in return, confirms and grounds the former. The posthumous becoming of the soul is the object of a knowledge of the otherworld and of ultimate ends; it is the object of a philosophy of bodily and spiritual resurrection. The soul accedes to knowledge: it becomes "intellective" and imprints itself into angelic substances. The classical doctrine of the actual intellect, of the union with the agent intellect, maintains that the intelligibles become "actual" after having been "potential." In Sadrā, this doctrine is extended to constitute the entire landscape of the existent: the material intellect is "the flowing together of two seas," as it is said in Qur'ān 25:53: "It is he who has made the two seas flow together: one fresh and sweet, and the other bitter and briny; and has placed a barrier (*barzakh*) between them, a partition that it is forbidden to pass." The material intellect is the limit between the "briny" sea, which is material nature, and the pure water, which is the otherworld. Man is the microcosm that recapitulates the macrocosm – the totality of universes, from nature to Intelligence – and the *barzakh* is his material intellective faculty, which requires the theurgic operation of the angel of knowledge.

The knowledge of the soul allows one to cross this barrier; it accedes to pure existence. That is why it is the "mother of wisdom" (*umm al-hikmah*), the foundation of happiness, such that it unveils the goal of metaphysics: to grasp the separation of man from matter, his superexistence (*baqā'*), which is indistinguishable from certitude (*al-yaqīn*). Metaphysics is thus transmuted into wisdom, into a concrete experience of this permanent abiding in proximity to God. The doctrine of spiritual salvation is the living heart of metaphysics, its effectively lived ethics.

The human soul is thus concerned, in its very destiny, with the knowledge of metaphysics, while the definition of first philosophy reciprocally envelops that of the human soul. In the introduction to his exposition of the cognitions needed by man in the sciences as a whole found, in the general prologue to the *Four Spiritual Journeys*, Sadrā proposes a synthetic definition of philosophy (*falsafah*): "Philosophy is the perfecting of the human soul through a cognition of the effective realities of existents as such, and of the status of their act of being, by a determination of truth (*tahqīq*) according to demonstrations and not according to any received opinion or blind acceptance (*taqlīd*), and this in proportion to man's capacity."[22] It is a question here of first philosophy, and the word *falsafah* is synonymous with *hikmah*. Among the thinkers of the school of Esfahan, the two terms are generally used interchangeably. Philosophy is wisdom, and wisdom is philosophy. The two constitute an encyclopedia of philosophical knowledge, and a *progressive perfection*, a cognition that is a practice and intensification of the self.[23] The path leading to the full actualization of the intelligible is salvation, not a theoretical prerequisite to salvation.

The object that concerns this philosophy, and allows us to distinguish it from the physical sciences, is indeed the existent as existent; in this respect, Sadrā is faithful to Aristotle and Avicenna. Knowledge of the existent as such is a cognition of its reality (*haqīqah*), of its act of being (*wujūd*). The term *al-haqīqah* designates the *reality* of the existent in question through which the existent occurs in the real, constituting it as real. It is therefore, in a way, synonymous with the essence of the thing. But let us be clear about the word essence; it must be understood that the essential reality of the thing derives from the divine essence, which is the real par excellence, the constituting and constitutive ipseity of every existent. Cognizing essence means going back to its foundation in God, understanding how it expresses the divine real, how it finds in this real its origin but also its return, how it proceeds from it and is converted back to it.

Essence is therefore in no way reducible to the quiddity of the existent, to the content of its formal definition, which answers the question "What is it?" (*mā huwah?*). Quiddity (*māhīyah*) expresses the degree of actualization of a certain essence but does not exhaust the essence. According to Sadrā, it is the shadow of the act of existing, the consequence of its determination. Cognizing the effective essence, the reality of the existent, means above all cognizing the act of existing that is primary with respect to a certain necessary quiddity. For without existence, quiddity would be nothing. Metaphysical research bears on the "status of the act of being" that determines essence. The act of being — existence — is precisely what is affirmed according to the degrees of intensity or weakness, perfection or imperfection. It is the foundation, in the existent, of essence, in that it is an expression — a "trace" or an "effect" — of the absolute act of being (*al-wujūd al-mutlaq*) which is the essence of God. Consequently, first philosophy is the knowledge of the act of being, and of the ways these acts are produced — according to the hierarchized ranks passing from the immaterial essences (the Intelligences) down to primary matter, in which existence fades and passes away — by the various degrees of celestial souls, human souls, lower souls, then celestial bodies, sublunar bodies, and the elements.

This knowledge repudiates opinion (*zann*) and blind assent. Opinion, belief, and blind assent are different sides of the same ignorance. The word *taqlīd* designates an intellectual attitude of obedience devoid of true knowledge. Should we see this as a discreet critique of the jurists? Probably, if the jurists repudiate the philosophical sciences in the name of a blind acceptance of canonical principles, from which they deduce their prescriptions using the methods of the *ijtihād*, the effort based on a literal reading of scripture. Sheer adherence is contrary to philosophy, since it proceeds without spiritual exegesis, demonstrations, or proofs. But there are two orders of proof: the metaphysician can give demonstrations that follow the paths of the intellect, or he can prove by means of illumination (*ishrāq*) received from the lights of the divine throne.

Syllogistic activity, whether it is fully apodictic or dialectic, is subject to illumination; it is combined with the lessons of this illumination and finds there its highest confirmation. In Sadrā, the doctrine of illumination is directly inherited from Suhrawardī's "Oriental" wisdom. Illumination is not "irrational," a simple mystical influx without intellective content; rather, it is the synthesis of mystical aptitude and intelligible knowledge. It translates the point of unification with the angel, the agent intelligence.[24] The definition of metaphysics involves a redefinition of the intellect itself. This faculty is not the finite ratiocinative understanding, nor is it the power of proof by means of natural light alone. The intellect receives a supernatural, angelic light, which is authentic reason, equivalent to the *nous* of the Neoplatonists. Proofs are hierarchized according to the degrees of logical reasoning and the "illuminative" unveiling that confirms it. The highest intellective knowledge leads to a "presential" grasping, indistinguishable from illumination, and in which the presence (*hudūr*) of being is unveiled.[25]

Without "presential knowledge" (*'ilm hudūrī*), metaphysics would simply be impossible, since this knowledge alone is capable of uniting a grasp of the act of being with a gnosis of the hierarchical universes. According to Sadrā, knowledge (*'ilm*) actualizes in intelligence the very ipseity of the thing. There are three ways of gaining knowledge of a thing. First, the thing can reveal itself by itself, in a giving that, through the act of knowing, renders it present in its concrete ipseity, in its independent act of being, so that the actualization is then effectively real. In this case, the thing is there, in itself, by itself. Second, the thing can be known through a knowledge of its separate essence, in an actualization that is a judgment, still in its ipseity itself, in what it really is. Third, the thing becomes known by its form, not by what it is itself, in its independent act of being. It is not then present to the knowing subject, but is cognized through an abstract form that is its own form reproduced in the intelligence. The first two modes of knowledge are called "presential knowledge" (*'ilm hudūrī*), because the reality of the object known in itself and through itself is one with its existence in the intelligence, or its act of being for the intelligizing subject.

In other words, the thing no longer exists according to two types of existence – existence in itself and existence for the subject – rather, it is one, and our knowledge of it consists in the unity of the act of being of the subject and that of the object. This is the sense in which we will speak of the *presence* of a thing. Formal knowledge differs from the experience of *presence* in that what is actualized in the intellect is only the form of the concrete existent thus known — in other words, a representation. What, then, is the essence of knowledge? It is actualization (*husūl*) itself; it is real being in absolute terms. There is no act of knowing unless there is an act of being, and everything that exists is known through that which is existent for it. That is why independent existence, free from any attachment to a substrate — as is the case with the intelligence — is a knowledge of self, whereas what subsists through something other than itself is not known by itself. Presential knowledge is specific to immaterial substances, for which being is knowledge and knowledge is existence. This presence to itself of the intelligence expresses "concrete existential attachment," or better, the unification (*ittihād*) of the subject and the object that characterizes the essence of the act of knowing: "Every existent that is free in its act of existing, subsisting by itself, knows itself, through the unification of self with self." In knowledge through forms, it is the forms that the subject knows, and not the real presence of the thing, its effectivity. This formal knowledge takes place by accident; it is a "metaphorical" (*bi-l-mijāz*) knowing.[26]

Freedom, existence, and knowledge of self by self, unification of self with self: all these themes have a distinctly Stoic flavor. They define the field of an illumination in which the subject knows itself in its presence to itself, in which the soul is at once subject and object of its act of cognitive presence, which is its act of being itself. How can we doubt that this is what makes metaphysics possible, if metaphysics is supposed to be the grasping of the act of being in the unity of the act of knowing? "He who knows himself knows his Lord": the act by which the soul knows itself is its act of existing itself, and it is also the act by which this soul, independent of all material attachment, returns to its higher principle, to God.

Order and Resemblance

Metaphysics is the discovery of an order — the order of creation — emanating from the world of order. This intelligible order is actualized in the human mind, which can be perfected to the point of resembling the Creator. This is how these two central themes of metaphysics are emphasized: metaphysics is the discourse of order, and it is the royal road to the imitation (*tashabbuh*) of God. Nothing escapes from order (*nizām*). Philosophy combines the war waged by the intelligence against the enemies of God – against animal and satanic desires – with the supreme peace of enlightened obedience.

We must insist on the polemical function of illuminative wisdom, on the gnostic intention of this philosophy. We must recall that it saw itself as an escape from the "Occident," a redemption from exile, and a striving for the Orient of lights. Thus it was possible to carry out a synthesis between philosophy and the teachings of Shī'ism, which professes such an escape. But the rebellion against the shadows of this world harbors a deep desire to reestablish the most perfect order. This is the central motif of political philosophy in Islam, from al-Fārābī to Nasīr al-Dīn al-Tūsī.[27] The gnostic and the metaphysician are deeply distressed by the disorder and injustice inherent in "corrupted cities," and by the irruption of evil at the lowest degrees of the existent. They do not offer a necessarily "political" remedy for these maladies, rather they search for a personal salvation that would be the ferment of a collective metamorphosis.

Existential revolution, as Sadrā will call it, is the rational hope of humanity; it lies at the heart of his eschatological metaphysics. But it is difficult – for the great mass of men are forgetful and negligent. Gnostic philosophy is resonant with the most somber tonalities of prophecy. Muhammad, like the prophets of Israel before him, never ceases to deplore men's resistance to conversion. The imams of Shī'ism will see the confirmation of this resistance to truth in the persecutions of the just. Philosophy will see these persecutions as the effect of corporeal matter, the passions attached to it, the blindness of the greatest number. That is the reason why gnostics and philosophers always distinguish the elite (*al-khāss*) from the common (*al-'āmm*). We should understand this in terms of the conviction, originating with the Greeks, that places the philosopher and his disciples at the highest rank, distinguishing them from common men by virtue of their moral concerns and spiritual practices. This belief has been a commonplace ever since Plato.

But we should also understand it in the very sense that Plato gives it, in terms of this other belief: the real order, the order of the real and of truth, is refused precisely by those who are sick from being deprived of it. The ideal city cannot be realized in history,[28] and the Idea remains cut off from its sensible imitations, distorted and confused. The refusal of the disorder of the world is carried out only in the secret recesses of men's hearts, through the assumption of true order, which science unveils when it comes into contact with the intelligible. Whether it is a matter of gnosis and Ismāʿīlī Shīʿite philosophy, or of the philosophies elaborated by the Twelver Shīʿite thinkers of Esfahan, it is always a discourse of perfect order, for in its essence the intelligence can unveil being only in the register of order.

That is why there is no politics other than imamology and eschatology. Among the fruits of metaphysics we do not find any specific discourse on the political.[29] Politics is replaced by gnosis itself, such that metaphysics, the discourse of the order of worlds, becomes the authentic political theology. The divine *nomos* is unveiled in the other world, in the imaginal world — where each soul receives its retribution — and in the world of the Intelligence. The city does not lie at the heart of the investigation. It can only be changed and perfected by the imam himself, upon his return. We must also understand that the imam's gathering of men and all living creatures will be an eschatological gathering. Politics, as understood by al-Fārābī or Fatimid Ismāʿīlism, is absent here.[30]

Because it unveils the order of the world, philosophy is an imitation of the Creator, the production of a work that "resembles" his very act of creation, his Imperative. We find the source of such a destination in al-Kindī: "Philosophy is resemblance to the actions of God, insofar as this is possible for man."[31] In Sadrā, *homoiōsis* — conformity to God in a resemblance — is the passage from the sensible "birth" to the supersensible "birth." This passage is in the nature of man: it is a sort of drug, a very strange *ma'jūn.*[32] This "drug" has two components: a spiritual form belonging to the world of the imperative and a sensible matter subject to the world of Creation. The form-matter composite must be dissociated, not for death but for the body's resurrection after death, when form returns to its spiritual world, in which matter is left behind in its creaturely unreality. Wisdom is the contemplative path, that of detachment from matter; it points to and prepares for the eventual separation. The final goal of metaphysics is the salvation of the imperative form, its return to its source in the divine Word.

Wisdom is both contemplative and practical.[33] A dialectic, or at least a kind of movement, is established between the exercises by which one purifies one's soul and the knowledge by which one knows oneself and accedes to the various degrees of immaterial realities: each prepares for the other and leads the way to it. The notion that joins them is strict obedience to God. Sadrā comments on the following saying of the imam: "O Hishām, the true is manifest through obedience (*al-tā'a*) to God and there is no salvation except through obedience, and obedience comes through knowledge and knowledge comes through teaching and through intelligence. There is no knowledge that does not originate from the divine world, and the gnosis of knowledge takes place through the intelligence."[34] It is a question of passing from the stage of the first growth, in which man is a shadowy substance created "from worldly matter and from shadows," made of "filth" (*wasakh*), to a second growth, in which he becomes an inhabitant of the higher world.

Shadow and light: this fundamental opposition organizes a series of practices that constitutes wisdom: purification (*tasfīyah*), education (also in the sense of moral purification, *tahdhib*), conversion (radical change of self, inner revolution, *tabdīl*), discipline (*ibta'dīb*, the acquisition of a true cultivation of the self). This revolution of growth, its reversal of orientation, changes natural sensible growth into immaterial intelligible growth. Only this conversion will make it possible to enter paradise. Salvation consists in "going from the world of shadows to the world of lights"; it is not the simple increase of its original growth, its first condition (*fitrah*), but rather the birth of another condition, the foundation of a new origin. The gradual perfection of man is thus fundamentally revolutionary, and intensification through wisdom substitutes a new nature for the old one.

This revolution of the self is a purification of the self, a practice of purity (*tahārah*), but also a stripping away or despoliation, a leaving behind of what makes one blameworthy, something like a negative ascent that imitates the stripping away carried out on the representations of God in order to reach his transcendent unity (*tanzīh*). This is possible only through the renunciation of all revolt against God. The self's work on the self is centered in this other-than-self, which is nonetheless at the center of itself—that is, in God, in whom one recognizes the omnipotence of the real subject by intensifying in oneself the state of the servant (*'ibādah*). But this conversion is one with knowledge. It requires a master, who is either God himself, the sage, or the complete philosopher, designated here by the expression "the lordly man of knowledge" (*al-'ālim al-rabbanī*)—the one who possesses the gnosis of the worlds of divine lordship.

This knowledge includes within it the entire program of metaphysics; it also contains prophetology, angelology, and imamology. The only giver of knowledge is God. Man understood in the sense in which he is only a man has nothing to give in this respect. To know authentically is to draw one's knowledge from God, directly, as the prophets and the imams do, or to derive it from these privileged men, from their guidance in spiritual pilgrimage and practical acquisition. Instructed by prophecy and by the imamate, the other possible master is the divine philosopher (*al-hakīm al-ilāhi*), who is under the influence of divine attraction. Thus "every lordly man of knowledge is lordly only because he is pure and luminous intelligence." Contemplation and practice are intimately linked. They fashion the new birth of man. They are governed by divine attraction and are expressed in a total obedience to God. Such is the spirit of wisdom according to Sadrā.

Ontology and Theology

Sadrā rarely gives any clear, explicit definition of the final aim of metaphysics, or any systematic investigation of its object. The pages I have just discussed leave us with several difficult questions: What relation must one establish between wisdom or philosophy – in a general sense – and metaphysics or first philosophy? Does Sadrā make God the privileged object of this metaphysics, or does he remain faithful to the object proposed by Avicenna, that is, the existent as existent? If he remains Avicennian, how are ontology and theology bound together in his system?

What is "first philosophy"? Sadrā appropriates the definitions we find clearly presented in Suhrawardī, clarifying the relation between wisdom (*hikmah*) and philosophy (*falsafah*): these two terms, we have said, are synonymous. It would be preferable to say that most often one can be taken for the other in their respective usage, with the understanding that wisdom and *first* philosophy are not strictly synonymous. Suhrawardī writes: "The realities are such that some among them are not connected to our actions, like the sky and the earth, while some among them are connected to our actions. The science relating to the former is called theoretical wisdom, and that which relates to the latter is called practical wisdom."[35] Practical wisdom is subdivided into the moral, the economic, and the political. Theoretical wisdom has its own divisions: the object of the highest science is "what relates to immaterial realities, absolutely speaking, such as the necessary, the real, the Intelligences and what concerns them, absolute being. Its subject is the most general of realities, and that is absolute being."[36]

Theoretical wisdom has a broader extension than first philosophy, since, beyond the objects of this science, it embraces existents that are separable from matter through thought, such as mathematical objects, and objects that are not separable from matter, such as the physical substances and their properties.[37] Here we are confronted with a division that goes back to Aristotle, and which Sadrā maintains, as we saw above. Theoretical wisdom contains first philosophy but does not come to completion with it. When we use the word "wisdom" as an equivalent of the word "philosophy," what is meant is "the highest wisdom," or the first science. The latter, for Suhrawardī as for Sadrā, reaches full completion in "Oriental wisdom," a union of metaphysics and illuminative gnosis.

From another perspective, and to return to our other question concerning the *object* of metaphysics, we must distinguish the object of the search from the subject of this same search (as Avicenna teaches in a famous text that we will analyze later). This object, according to Suhrawardī, is God, the Intelligences, absolute being. But here we find absolute being again as the *subject* of the very same search. For the sake of clarity, let us adopt the division proposed by Suhrawardī: universal science, *metaphysica generalis*, is concerned with the division of beings while divine science has to do with God. According to sound logic, therefore, we must begin by studying general metaphysics, in order to arrive at the special metaphysics that unveils the nature of the divine real—the being that is necessary through itself. The subject—the point of departure—is thus indeed the existent as existent, understood absolutely. Nevertheless, this priority of general metaphysics over theology remains problematic, especially if it is true for Suhrawardī and Sadrā that there is no metaphysics without God. Must we not then reserve the word metaphysics for divine science itself? We are going around in circles.

In his course on Suhrawardī's *Talwīhāt*, Henry Corbin asks: "Is there a science of the universal distinct from metaphysics or 'divine science,' or is the former merely a chapter of the latter?"[38] It seems that for Sadrā, if the analysis of the existent as existent precedes that of divine nature, first science and divine science merge together. As proof of this, I need only quote a brief remark made in the commentary on an imam's saying: "Philosophers first establish the attributes and the unity of the necessary Being in their science, called universal science, and through first philosophy."[39] The imam's statement is very interesting in itself. It claims that "it is through the lowest kinds of knowledge, or the smallest, that the entry into Islam takes place." Thus metaphysics is located at the heart of the progress of knowledge, which begins at the lowest degree – the literal faith in the unicity of God, the rejection of associationism – and proceeds to the illuminative knowledge of this same unicity, a metaphysical knowledge that, as we have seen, is the highest wisdom. This relative disqualification of literal faith has enormous consequences in other respects, for it refers back to the Shīʿite hierarchy of apparent and hidden, superficial knowledge and the divinely inspired knowledge of the imams.

To clarify the very status of this question, we must take it up again at its origin, in the founding gesture by which Avicenna, at the beginning of his *Metaphysics* – eloquently named the *Divinalia* (*al-Ilāhīyāt*) – elucidates the discourse of Aristotle. To do this, it is necessary also to appreciate the difficulty that Aristotle's metaphysics presented to its Muslim interpreters. The following facts should be kept in mind. First, there was the preestablished unity or harmony between Plato and Aristotle, and Aristotle was read not as we might read him but as if he belonged to a tradition of Greek sages – in which he does not diverge from Plato – and according to an intention that considers Aristotle the thinker of the unique and immaterial divine principle. Next, there is the fact that for Avicenna and his successors, Aristotle was referred to as the author of the famous *Theology*, which is in fact a collection of translated, rewritten, and annotated passages from Plotinus's last three *Enneads*.[40]

Avicenna is searching for the subject (*al-mawḍūʿ*) of first philosophy, thereby determining the essence of this philosophy insofar as it is distinguished from the other sciences. He analyzes the "philosophical sciences," dividing them into theoretical sciences and practical sciences.[41] The definition of the theoretical sciences based on their final goal turns out to be the one we also find in Sadrā: It is "the gradual perfection of the soul's theoretical power through the realization of the actual intelligence, which itself occurs through the realization of the representative knowledge of forms and the knowledge gained by judgment, whose objects are realities which, as such, are not our works or our ways of being."[42] But we must immediately modify our statement: Sadrā will not accept this definition as is. He will say not that knowledge through forms is sufficient, but that the highest theoretical activity is presential knowledge.

However important this mutation — which follows from Sadrā's reading of Suhrawardī's *Philosophy of Illumination* — let us point out that Suhrawardī and Sadrā accept this provisional "definition" of Avicenna's as self-evident. Indeed, Avicenna is drawing the obvious conclusion from his investigations of the human soul, which demonstrate the existence of the intelligence and its intelligible objects, its division into theoretical intellect and practical intellect. Theoretical science is subdivided into physics, mathematics, and finally metaphysics. The latter is "divine science" (*al-ilāhīyah*). Must we think, then, that its subject is God? If it is not, how can we determine the place of theological investigations?[43]

Avicenna examines the traditionally accepted elements of the definition. They are in agreement with Aristotle himself: metaphysics "studies the realities separated from matter in terms of subsistence and by definition. You have certainly heard also that metaphysics is the science in which one studies the first causes of natural being and of mathematical being and what relates to them, and in which one studies the cause of causes and the principle of principles, which is God."[44] There is nothing here that does not agree with Aristotle's *Metaphysics*, if we take Book Twelve (Lambda) at its word. Thus we find God and the Intelligences at the heart of metaphysics. Avicenna does not reject this definition, as one might expect, but he displaces its terms and its validity. He refuses it as a way to render the *subject* of metaphysics but accepts it as a statement of the *aim* of metaphysics, the *object* of its research. And this is the source of all our difficulties: the point of departure of metaphysics, its *subject*, is not God or the Intelligences. Instead the theological *center* — which is in turn precisely God, and, after God, the procession of separate Intelligences — is the *object* of this metaphysics.[45]

Avicenna therefore questions this "definition," which, in his eyes, does not define the subject of metaphysics. He poses the question to which Sadrā will respond in his own way: Is metaphysics necessarily, and by definition, rational theology? Does it by definition posit the first cause, such that the first science would be knowledge of the attributes and operations of God? In other words, is philosophy the same thing as rational theology, as *kalām*? If that were the case, the independence of metaphysical investigations in relation to the rational theology of Islam would no longer be assured, since a science founds its originality through its subject. It becomes necessary to provide, at all costs, a ground for the distinction between philosophy and *kalām*, and to give the former a guarantee of validity in the Muslim world.

Other definitions have been proposed in an attempt to ground "authentic" philosophy – the philosophical knowledge of effective reality, or first philosophy – in its epistemological function: this function could provide a foundation for the truth of the principles of the other sciences, which would thus be true wisdom. Whether it is theology or epistemology, wisdom would have three properties: it would be the noblest science of the noblest known object (God); it would be the truest and most precise knowledge; it would be knowledge of the first causes of the whole. The question whether this set of properties is the one we find in al-Kindī, or whether Avicenna is thinking of someone else, is of no importance here. What is important is the work of analysis he will carry out based on these premises, which he admits as the point of departure for a dialectical argument, the only one that can hope to discover the "point of departure" of a science.

Avicenna's entire undertaking depends, then, on the logical distinction between the subject of a science ("something whose existence is admitted in this science," its *mawḍū'*) and the object sought by this science (its *maṭlūb*). The subject is what is initially [*antérieurement*] posited as primary. It is what is accepted without dispute (*musallam*), whereas the object is what is sought, the final aim of the investigation: it comes later, or even last. But the being of God cannot be incontestably accepted in the first science, as a subject of the first science must be.[46] The being of God is a goal, *one* object of research for metaphysics. Metaphysics seeks the being of God, after physics has led to an awareness of the existence of this first principle, and after our desire has been strengthened to move toward the station (*maqām*) that is "beyond," in order to attain a true knowledge of it.[47] That is how Avicenna displaces the accepted definitions: they may be valid for the object of metaphysics, but they are not for its subject.

Let us return to the word "cause," which is essential to physics, and which led us to the apprehension of a "first cause" or a cause of causes. This moment is essential, for in the long passage that concludes his first chapter, Avicenna shows that we study causes only because they are existent. If that is the case, then the existence of the existent, or more precisely the existent as existent, precedes causes and must be admitted as a subject of metaphysics.

In Chapter Two, Avicenna leads us from the subjects of physics, mathematics, and logic to the existent as existent. Let us, he says, leave logic aside, for it is an instrument of thought, and let us turn toward substances. "The state of substance insofar as it is existent," of the body insofar as it is substance, of measure and number insofar as they are existents — the "how" of their existence, whether it is a question of immaterial formal realities or of forms in composition with a corporeal matter — these presuppose at least a separation, a distinction through study. We observe that all the subjects of the particular sciences subsist independently of the sensible: separation from matter is their very subsistence.[48] The concept of subsistence (*qiwām*) is determinative here. Indeed, later it will lead us to the search for the principle of this subsistence, which will be God. For the moment, let us consider it for itself. The common subject, of which the subjects of the particular sciences must be "states" or modes (*ḥālāt*), can only be the existent (*al-mawjūd*). Consequently, "it is impossible for any signification grounded in the real and the true to be common to both of them, unless it be the effective reality of the signification of being."[49] This is the definition of the subject of metaphysics that Sadrā will take up, but not without radically modifying its intention: the truth of the signification of being is the signification of the truth of being.

The presentation of the existent according to the logical path has a defect, or in any case it falls within an operation that remains quite obscure. We begin with a proposition, "causes are existent," in which "existent" is in the position of predicate. From there we move to a proposition in which "existent," having become "the existent," is in the position of subject: the *existent* is the common signification of the subjects of the particular sciences. To be sure, this operation is legitimated by the exceptional nature of the predicate "existent": the latter cannot belong to the class of predicates expressing the essential properties of substances conceived in each of the particular sciences. For example, "existent" is not comparable to "extended" or "continuous," or to "light." But then is "existent" a predicate? We know that Kant would maintain that it cannot be one. In his own way, and in a context that has nothing to do with critique in the Kantian sense, Sadrā would affirm something similar. But can one say that Avicenna treats the existent as a predicate before making it the subject of metaphysics? He tells us rather that it is a term whose signification (*ma'nah*) is common to the two subjects of the particular sciences. But meaning, intention, is not merely a logical reality. The word *ma'nah* also designates a concrete reality. The existent has a "signification" that, ipso facto, possesses an effective reality (*haqīqah*), and this effective reality becomes the subject of metaphysics. The predicative movement by which we have posited that causes are "existent" is predicative only in appearance, since the originary effective reality is indeed that of the common existent, whereas the causes and the subjects of the particular sciences are particularizations of this existent. The existent has never ceased occupying, however silently, the position of subject.

It remains true nonetheless that the mere possibility of logically situating the existent in the provisional position of predicate opens the way to all the subsequent difficulties: existence, in turn, will be in danger of being placed in the position of predicate. Above all, the existent is presented at the end of a dialectical argument, not in the evidence of an originary given. The existent thus becomes the common existent, whose being is common being. How to avoid confounding it with mere universal significations? How to avoid making it a mere concept? These are the major objections that Sadrā makes against the deduction of the existent. Even as he situates himself within the framework of Avicennism, he contests its fundamental theses. For him, the truth of being (*wujūd*) would be primary, constitutive of the reality of the existent, and the meaning of this truth was necessarily the subject of metaphysical elucidation.

If being, in its truth, is the subject of metaphysics, can one speak of an onto-theology? I believe that this term is quite obscure, and very inappropriate to understanding the link between the search for being and the search for the divine principle. Avicenna is perfectly clear: the existent is the subject of study; God and the Intelligences are some of the objects sought by this science. The point of departure of ontology is the meaning of the existent, and this leads ultimately to God, who is the subject of theology. From another point of view, this articulation is faithful to the respective destinations and roles of the philosopher and the prophet, and Sadrā, like his contemporaries, respects this order. Mīr Findariskī explains it very well: the philosopher moves from the sensible to the intelligible, whereas, for the prophet, the intelligible becomes an object of sensible perception. The prophet's knowledge begins where the philosopher's ends.[50] Prophetic knowledge is therefore the descent of truth from the world of the *mysterium*, whereas ontology is an ascent to that world.

This division is reproduced at the heart of metaphysics itself, in which theology arranges the existent in gradations, beginning with God, whereas ontology moves toward God. There is thus no onto-theology, if by this term one means an ontology that is condemned to be theology, or a theology that is the truth of ontology. But the hyphen that unites – and distinguishes – the terms "ontology" and "theology" has the merit of identifying a problem, which is *the* problem of this metaphysics: how to reconcile the fact that the existent is a subject and God is an object? How does the object clarify the subject? Better, how do the subject and the object end up revealing that they are one? This is the price of the unity of metaphysics and of its authorization in the discourse of prophecy.

In question here, in the unity of metaphysics, is the truth of the fundamental proposition "there is no being but in God."

Mullā Sadrā distinguishes the task of ontology from that of theology. But he was not influenced only by Avicenna. He is also an attentive reader of the Neoplatonic text that is for him the philosophical revelation par excellence and that he constantly quotes to corroborate his own statements: the *Theology of Aristotle*. In this text, philosophy is identified with theology, with the discourse of divine "sovereignty." Here are a few lines from the prologue, which formulate the quest for being as it will appear in Sadrā, providing the elements of its essential structure:

> Our aim in this book is the first discourse on Sovereignty and the explication of it: that it is the first cause, that eternity and time are beneath it, that it is the cause and originator of causes, by a certain path of origination. And that the luminous power effuses from it over the Intelligence and, through the medium of Intelligence, over the universal celestial Soul, and from the Intelligence, through the medium of Soul, over Nature, and from the Soul, through the medium of Nature, over the things that undergo generation and corruption. And that this activity arises from it without motion, and that the motion of all things comes from it and is caused by it, and that things move toward it by a kind of desire and longing.[51]

The emanative activity of divine sovereignty would be being itself, conceived no longer as common being but as the intensity of the real proceeding from its source through the hierarchy of worlds. The movement of the energy of being would make it possible to think the source together with what is derived from it—God together with the existent—to arrive at the concept of substantial motion. How does the essence of the act of being authorize this circle, which consists of an arc leading to God and another leading back to the hierarchy of created existents? This is the question that will be taken up in the following pages.

Chapter Two

The Light of Being

Being Is the Name of the Real

In order to examine systematically Sadrā's doctrine of being, it will be helpful to recall its fundamental theses. One text is particularly useful in this regard: the opening chapter of *Divine Witnesses* which can be seen as an epitome of Sadrā's ontology. This text is divided into nine "illuminations," the first of which is this:

> The act of being is the most real of things with respect to real effectuation, because what is other than it becomes effectively real through it. Consequently, the act of being is that through which all that possesses a real obtains its effective reality. How, then, could it be an abstract reality, as is asserted by those who are separated by a veil from its evident testimony? Thus, indeed, it is essentially instantiated, to the exclusion of what one calls quiddity.[1]

The term *al-wujūd* is often translated as "being" or "existence," and its meaning is well rendered by these words if one excludes the copulative function of the verb "to be" and admits only the existential function.[2] Most often, I prefer to say "the act of being," for when I am talking about *being*, I mean being as an *act*. We will even see that it is an act in the imperative: not the act that actualizes a potentiality, but the actualization of this act, which always bears within it the mark of the divine imperative. The act of being imposes itself on us. Without any possible doubt, it is identical to the reality of what is real: *al-wujūd huwa-l-haqīqah*, the act of being, is effective reality, as Sadrā often says. He thus states that the act of being is the most *real* of things.[3] Everything that lies within the *tahaqquq*, the effectuation of all reality, depends, in the last instance, on the act of being. All that is other than it becomes effectively realized, acquires a *haqīqah*, a reality, through the act of being and through it alone. Reciprocally, ontology is not an "existential" philosophy but a doctrine of the reality of the real.[4]

There are two modalities of the effectuation of the act of being, which Avicenna had already recognized: first, effectivity *in concreto*; second, the affirmation of being in mental existence, in the reality of the objects of thought. The mental existence of representations is no less an act of being than the concrete act of being, although the latter has much greater intensity and dignity. There is no distinction between them in terms of being and non-being; rather, there is a difference of degree. A thought, in order to be thought, must have an act of being in the mind, in a manner analogous to the existence of a sensible object or of a supersensible concrete reality (for example, a body, a soul, an intelligence).

All that is real possesses its effective reality solely through its act of being. Whatever belongs to the domain of quiddity is thus dismissed from the foundation of the existent. To be sure, there is nothing that does not possess a quiddity (except God); there is nothing that does not unfold its act of being in an essence whose formal content is defined by and in quiddity. If anyone professes the inevitable unity of the act of being and quiddity for the existents derived from God, it is Sadrā. If anyone maintains that, in concrete reality or in the reality of thought, the act of being must actualize a quiddity, it is Sadrā. But such a unity is not a union; it does not unite two realities that possessed separate existences. The act of being does not possess an existence, because it *is* existence; it does not receive a second existence, which for it would be like an accident, which in turn would have its own existence, and so on to infinity.[5] The act of existing is the immediate luminous presence of the thing itself, its pure immanence. Quiddity has no other being than that which is conferred by the act of existing. Sadrā thus explains that it is the *shadow* of the act of being. The quiddity of an existent is the share of darkness and shadow that marks the limit of its act of being.

Hence Sadrā's first critique – one that he often repeats – is addressed to Suhrawardī and to all who have professed a philosophy of the primacy of quiddity over the pure act of existing. For them, the act of being becomes an abstract reality, for they forget that it is the very act of constituting reality. They begin with a concrete existent and abstract *being* from this existent in such a way as to make it merely a *point of view* from which to regard the thing. "Abstraction" here translates the Arabic expression *amr i'tibārī*, the "reality of a mere point of view." To take a point of view, to place oneself in a perspective, is to forget the totality of what is in question, in and by itself, and to mistake an aspect of the existent for the existent as a whole. Suhrawardī maintains that the existence of the existent is only a point of view from which to regard the existent in question. Ipso facto, he sees as real an inessential aspect, the formal definition of the existent, its quiddity – the very thing that, since Aristotle, has constituted the *ousia* of the thing in question.

Quiddity is always an abstraction that does not capture the concreteness of the thing, whether it is effectively existent in the gradations of nature, the soul, and the Intelligence or a "mental thing" in the human mind. In Sadrā's language, an "abstraction" is always opposed to a real, effective thing, *amr haqīqī*. The *i'tibār*, the quidditative "point of view" is opposed to *al-haqq*, the real, as the limit is opposed to the unlimited, as finite determinations are opposed to the indeterminacy of the infinite freedom of divine effusion. Sadrā rejects the thesis that the act of being is a common reality, that it is an *ens communis*, identifiable with any common being whatever. If the act of being is ascribed, analogously, to all existents, it is nonetheless not common to them, in the way that one makes it abstract, by force of language, when speaking of being in general. It will never be an attribute common to beings. The act of being is anything but that height of abstraction which could be converted into pure nothingness. Sadrā rejects and tirelessly denounces in the philosophy of quiddities, and particularly in Suhrawardī, an inconsistency: how can we say that being is *light*, effectively living and evident, and still maintain the primacy of quiddity over concrete existence? Not only is essence determined by quiddity, but existence, thought of as an attribute of essence or as a "point of view" from which to regard essence, is no longer anything but itself; it is no longer essence's act of being; it is no longer anything at all.

Is Sadrā's indictment of Suhrawardī correct? The problem is worth examining, particularly since, in his commentary on *The Philosophy of Illumination*, Sadrā interprets Suhrawardī's doctrine according to his own metaphysics of the act of being.[6] In any case, Suhrawardī makes many statements claiming that what exists at the origin are pure lights, that is, pure luminous essences, whose existence, considered separately, is only a "point of view" from which to see what they are. What exists is not the *existence* of the luminous essence but the luminous essence itself. This is the "point of view" that, according to Sadrā, forms the first veil obstructing pure and simple reality. The abstractive operation through which one withdraws beings from the different existents prevents "obvious knowledge." The evidence of being lends itself to testimony. All Sadrā's thought aims at this evidence and seeks to rejoin or preserve it. The act of being precedes all reflection, all predication; it is pure presence, brilliance of light. It illuminates vision and spirit. It illuminates the senses, though more dimly. This evidence allows Sadrā to reconnect with Suhrawardī, although he criticizes him for making existence a mere abstract reality, an *amr i'tibārī*. Indeed, Suhrawardī is a witness to the primordial certainty according to which all knowledge is an illumination (*ishrāq*), a rising of the light of being over the soul. The evidence of being is concentrated especially in the heart.[7] What does witnessing reveal? That the act of being is "instantiated essentially." From the outset, the evidence of being leads us back to God, light of lights, who instantiates the lights' existence by effusing his own constitutive existence.

We should not underestimate Sadrā's use of the vocabulary of "instantiation" in a sense close to that of Ibn al-'Arabī when he conceives the self-revelation of God in the divine names and in the production of eternal essences. The instantiator is pure act of being, of which nothing can be said except that he is an infinity beyond infinity. But this infinity, incommensurate with any measure, does not rule out a fundamental unity between the instantiated and the instantiator. It is simply that the concrete act of being, or the act of being of our thoughts, to the extent that it is secondary to the divine infinity, is always determined; it is rendered passive (instantiated, *maj'ūl*) by this act of instantiation, while also being the mirror of the actuality and the activity expressed in it. That is why it will have the shadow of a quiddity that bears witness to the determination given to the existence instantiated at a certain degree of the modalization of being—whereas the act of being in itself will be the pure mirror of instantiation, of the imperative act through which something real triumphs over nonbeing. The act of being, which bears witness to itself in the grasping of the evident, is not called quiddity, since it is the divine effusion itself and not its finite determination. The unity of the act of being and quiddity is not a dialectic but rather a tension between the light of effectivity and the darkness of its limit.

The Contemplation of the Real

Everything that refers to quiddity in the language of our understanding veils the act of being: either language speaks of the abstraction of a "being" that is the most general property of the existent, or it articulates quiddity. This intimate solidarity between language and quiddity led Aristotle to conceive of quiddity as the rightful object of the investigation into being, because the quest for being could only be in agreement with the essence of language: "There are several senses in which a thing may be said to be.... In one sense, it means what a thing is or a 'this,' and in another sense, it means that a thing is of a certain quality or quantity or has some such predicate asserted of it. While 'being' has all these senses, obviously that which is primary is the 'what,' which indicates the substance of the thing."[8] Sadrā is haunted by the proper name, by the impossible name of the singular act of being, because language always produces common ways of naming.[9] That is why "it is impossible for the effective reality of the act of being to be actualized in a thought."[10] No thought is representative of existence, and existence has no being in thought, no mental existence.

Mental existence is the being of our representations. The human soul has the power to instantiate the forms of things in its own world, a psychic world, which is immaterial and expresses the "root" of the soul, its intelligible nature. To be sure, here below, the soul does not have the power to create effectively real beings through sheer force of thought. But it does have the power to actualize their forms in itself, through its imagination and intelligence. After the death of the body, when the obstacles connected with matter have been lifted, the imagination will be able to give both a mental and a concrete existence to forms of the soul—the infernal or heavenly forms perceived in the "lesser resurrection." From that point on, our representations and, *a fortiori*, our acts of presential knowledge are not mere mirages without substance; they exist, according to the mode of existence of our soul determined by its degree of purity and intensity. They populate our souls and outline the contours of the world of the soul, whose center is our very act of existing.[11] But here we see that the act of being, which is expressed, among other things, in our power of representation, does not itself have a representation. Therefore, it has no mental existence. The soul cannot actualize it in itself as it does the forms; it can only prove it through the intelligible grasp of its own act of being an intelligence, in the presential unity of subject and object.

Sadrā writes in the second "illumination" of his chapter on being:[12]

> The act of being cannot be represented by a definition (*hadd*) or a description (*rasm*), nor by a form (*sūrah*) congruent with it, since the representation of the concrete thing designates the actualization of its signification, and its transference from the limit of concrete reality to the limit of thought. This is the case for what is other than the act of being. As for the act of being, this simply is not possible, except through pure and simple contemplation (*mushāhadah*) and through the vision one has with one's own eyes, to the exclusion of what is indicated by definition and demonstration, and to the exclusion of the understanding as intellectual abstraction and explanation. Since the act of being has no mental existence, it is neither universal nor particular, neither general nor singular. It is not absolute, and it is not determinate (*muqayad*), but these things are implied by it according to the various degrees and to what exists, among the quiddities and their accidents, through the act of being. As for it [the act of being], it is, in itself, a simple reality to which neither genre nor difference occurs, and which has no need, in its effective actualization, for the addition of some determination through difference or through the accident that classifies or particularizes it.[13]

Since quiddity exists only through the act of being, all discourse on quiddities means forgetting the reality that grounds them. On the one hand, quiddities have no reality by themselves, since their beingness is actualized by the beingness of the thing itself — the concrete individual — and through its act of being. When thought conceives quiddities, it conceives only abstractions. On the other hand, Sadrā attributes to quiddities a being which is at the heart of the divine science: "In the tradition of a group among the people of unveiling and certitude, the quiddities refer back to eternal essences, which eternally breathe the fragrance of being."[14] In order to think the status of the quiddities, he adopts the conception of Ibn al-ʿArabī. Existing not through themselves but in God and through God, quiddities are shadows of the existent, because divine existentiation projects them as consequences of positing the created existent. It is in fact necessary that the essences exist only through the act of being, if the latter constitutes the whole reality of the existent. It is, however, also necessary that they have an eternal reality, if we want to understand why each concrete individual never actualizes its act of being without its accompanying shadow, that is, without a certain essence. Only God is pure light without shadow: all other things have shadows, which translate their oblique position in being. God alone is in the noontime of being.

The position Sadrā takes with this thesis is decisive. When we return to the definition of the existent in Aristotle and in Avicenna, the meaning of this existent is principally rendered by its quiddity. Sadrā maintains that this meaning is abstract and illusory. In it we undergo a veiling, rather than an unveiling, of the real. Conversely, the discourse on the existent, in order to remain faithful to the unveiling of the originary act of being, must be fundamentally *negative*. It is a matter of setting into action the power of negation (of which there will be many examples in Sadrian theology) and setting out on an indefinite *via negationis*. This method consists in negating both a term and its contrary, and then negating the negation.

The presential affirmation of being presupposes, in this discourse, the radical negation of all determination, even if this determination is itself the negation of a determination. In fact, we are dismissing every mode of access to the act of being that could be found by way of representation (*tasawwur*). The act of being cannot be represented; there are no grounds for considering it an object of thought, and it has no mental existence. Concrete existents possess another mode of being in the mind, namely, that of their representations. But there is no representation of their act of being. The act of being is the real of all reality, not a reality that could be represented and thought. That one cannot represent being has the most profound consequences: being is indeed grasped in and by the mind, but this grasping is the mind's experience, not the object of its representation. This experience is the intuition of the act of being in the intensive growth of spiritual reality, in the becoming intelligence of the soul. It is the life of the soul leading up to its final term in God, its spiritual resurrection.

At its root, knowledge is existence itself, not the duplication of the external thing in a psychic form.[15] It reveals the central, immaterial light by which the existent exists. It is, therefore, a recognition of the intelligible in the intellect, a certain mode of unification of the intellect and the intelligible. The act of being, which is predisposed to this union of the intellect, the intelligible, and the act of intellection, cannot in turn be the formal object of a representation that ruins illuminative presence. Cognition by way of concepts is fundamentally inadequate to it. We have learned to distinguish two types of knowledge: representative, conceptual knowledge – or knowledge through forms (*'ilm sūrī*) – and presential knowledge (*'ilm hudūrī*), which offers the passionate feeling of being (*al-wijdān*). Presential knowledge is testimony itself. In a way, it remains unnamable, such that the divine science, metaphysics, is only a substitute for a fleeting and superior illumination, which for the perfect man is the very *habitus* of the soul. The prophets, says Sadrā, see things *as they are*, whereas the entire discourse we tirelessly weave around the real only allows it to escape. That is why we can speak of it only negatively, even though it is pure affirmation and immanence: like Rousseau, Sadrā writes in order not to have to write.

If the act of being is not representable, then it has no definition and no quiddity. It is not delineated or configured in any image, even though it engenders a profusion of images: to the iconoclasm necessary for grasping the act of being in and for itself corresponds the extraordinary multiplication of the icon in the vision of being's epiphanies. The aesthetics of sensible and imaginal forms is based on the radical absence of the image in the very principle of the act of being.[16] Sadrā thinks the concept is incapable of allowing the essence to appear. All representation of a form in the mind posits the existence of a concrete thing, and that this thing will have a signification (*ma'nah*, Latin *intentio*). The significative intention duplicates the concrete thing by transposing it into the mind, where it engenders the intellectual form. Using an image, Mullā Sadrā says that one then passes over the "limit" or edge of concrete reality to the limit of thought. This transferal is admirably suited to the quiddities. But it is not suited to the contemplation of what has no form, the act of being.

There is, on one side, abstract reality, according to the point of view of representative intelligence, and on the other side, the concrete reality of the act of being, intuited by the extreme edge of illuminative intelligence. There is, on one side, the actualization of signification (*husūl al-ma'nah*) and, on the other, sheer contemplation (*mushāhadah*). Contemplation is not the perfection of signification but a completely different mode of intellection, one that suspends representative signification. Contemplation grasps not *what* the existent is but its reality, its existence. Contemplation neglects the limit and the figure in the existent, in order to perceive in it the eternal intensity of being; it is always outside time, in the eternity of the instant. To grasp existents *under the aspect of eternity*—is this not to celebrate their astonishing refusal of nothingness? Not their quiddity but the point of *reality* that is expressed in it. In Arabic, contemplation is *al-mushāhadah*; it implies the coincidence of the perceiving being and the perceived act of being. In conceptual knowledge, as we have seen, a space is opened between reality and thought, the space of the transferal of representation, whereas in the contemplation of the act of being, we are beset by the real. Such, then, is the indissoluble unity of the perceiving subject and contemplated reality.

Grasping the act of being is possible for whoever sees with his own eyes, in the solitude and freedom of a witnessing that no one else can experience in his place and that can never take the form of a common assertion communicable through human chatter. The sight of the beautiful, the good, and the true is not the abstract knowledge of innocuous transcendentals but the immediate grasp of the beauty, truth, and goodness of being in the eternal center of every concrete existent, at the point where its victorious reality shines forth in its proper light. Contrary to this, conceptual representation (*tafhīm*) leads inevitably to abstraction and demonstration. Sadrā's metaphysics, although it uses definitions and demonstrations, takes as its subject that which cannot be a substrate of inhesion, namely, the act of existing. Since it is not in principle the subject of a predicative judgment, the act of being refuses every form of logical knowledge, so that there will always be something paradoxical about binding together hundreds of pages of subtle arguments, whereas the real subject of metaphysics is foreign to the syllogistic order.

This is because the act of being cannot be configured in the mind and has no mental existence. All our ideas have mental existence, and we cannot form a single one whose object – the form that we think – does not exist in the soul. Mental existence is not merely the objective reality of the idea but indeed a formal, actual reality, a psychic reality of form accommodated by the world of the soul.[17] But existence does not correspond to any logical representation. The idea of the act of being has no being. This is why, with regard to the act of being, Sadrā rejects determination according to genus and difference, universality and particularity. In itself, effective being is neither common nor particular. It is neither divided into classes (*musannaf*) nor particularized (*mushakhkhas*). It will be necessary to grasp a pure singularity that is not the opposite of the universal and that corresponds to the unique status of the act of being in each effective existent.[18] It is not the singularity that attests to a particular existence of the same order as it (as when we say that a man is an individual, whereas man is universal). This singularity is contrary to abstract being but fundamentally united to it. Instead, this pure singularity is the unspeakable brilliance of the existent as existent. The double negation grasps not a thing but the very substantiality of substance in its inimitable existence.[19]

Faced with the real, we can speak only negatively and in a constantly sustained negation. To be sure, in God the act of being is free and absolute (*mutlaq*), whereas in the derivative existents it is "bound," "linked," determinate (*muqayad*). But God is not the absolute act of being, if he is worthy of being grasped as the act of being itself, in itself and at its highest degree of power. Mullā Sadrā, reading Ibn al-'Arabī, constructs the different levels of the divine essence at the heart of a single unity. And if God is not identified with absolute being, the act of being is beyond the absolute and the determinate. To be sure, on numerous occasions,

Sadrā calls the act of being "absolute being." But, in all rigor, the negative path also excludes the possibility that being could be determined as absolute, since the absolute is also a representation, the opposite of the representation of determinate being.[20] Thus the universal, the particular, the common, the singular, the absolute, and the determinate correspond to degrees of being that proceed from the act of being as such but are negated by its supereminence and priority. Sadrā applies to the act of being the negative approach, adopting the quest for supereminence that Plotinus applies to the principle, to the One.

Flow, Hierarchy, and Difference

The act of being is arranged hierarchically in degrees (*darajāt*). This structure merely expresses the ascent toward being, the consequence of the negative path. Everything we can know about the exemplifications of the act of being presupposes this hierarchical order, the majesty of the ordering of nature, of souls, of Intelligences, the order of the three worlds (sensible, imaginal, intelligible), culminating in the pyramids of angels that border on the divine throne. This hierarchy is an increasing intensification of the act of being, an upward scansion of the movement that traverses and metamorphoses all substances, changing the lower ones into higher ones, all the way up to the final return to divine unity. From God, the free instantiator, to primary matter, we will cognize the processive hierarchy of the degrees of the act of being. How is their differentiation to be thought?

The differentiation of the degrees of the act of being has nothing to do with what Aristotle's logic calls *difference*. The latter effects the production of a species within a genus. The differentiation of the act of being is completely unlike this, since in the act of being there is neither genus nor difference nor species. Although there is an infinity of degrees, the act of being always remains a simple reality (*amr basīt*). Whatever the multiplicity of existents, we will always have to grasp the simplicity of being that manifests the real in them. But this simplicity, in turn, has nothing to do with the common being that abstraction draws from the various existents. The notion of common being is purely imaginary. Common being is not simple – it is nonexistent. Furthermore, unity and multiplicity are not exactly reciprocal in any given existent. The latter will not be considered "one" and "multiple" on the same level or according to the same type of perception.

The following points thus allow us to avoid a possible vicious circle: First, unity belongs to existence, and "for everything that we say to be existent, we also say that it is one." Second, unity is all the more perfect when the act of being is more powerful: an angel is more "one" than an imaginal form, which is more "one" than a sensible form, such that the degrees of the act of being correspond to an increasing intensification of existence and an increasing perfection of unity (*wahdānīyah*), from the sensible forms and corporeal realities up to the intelligibles and the intelligences, in which being is powerfully one, to God, who is at the maximum degree of being and unity. The hierarchy of existents is an increasing gradation of the monads of existence. Third, the multiple is better known by the imagination, because the imagination first receives sensible impressions, which manifest multiplicity and veil unity. Unity is better known by the intelligence. Unity is, fundamentally, an intelligible reality. We know the multiple through unity, in acts of intellectual knowledge, because we consider unity primary in representation. And we know unity through multiplicity in the acts of imaginative knowledge. It is therefore necessary to break the possible circle of the one and the multiple by referring to the hierarchy in which the intelligence is more potent than the imagination. First comes the intellective act of knowing, through which the multiple intention of imaginative signification is grasped in its unity; then comes the presentation of the intelligible unity in the multiplicity registered through the imagination.[21]

The act of being has no genus, at least not insofar as it is a pure real. Therefore, it cannot have a contrary. Two contraries oppose each other if they fall under a single genus. Here Sadrā remains faithful to the Peripatetic teaching that the opposition reigning between two beings or two states of a being must take place in a common matter, or that the specific difference and the absence of this difference are revealed against the ground of a single genus. Still faithful to Avicenna, by liberating the act of being from the contrariness that characterizes predicates under the regime of opposition, Sadrā invites us to think differentiation among the acts of being outside of all opposition or all contradiction.[22] For there to be "the most extreme mutual difference" between two realities — a difference that can only be opposition — these two realities must be opposed to each other. But this opposition supposes the common substrate of a genus. Two acts of being are such that they never possess a single genus, since the act of being has no genus. The difference of acts of being therefore does not fall under opposition and contrariety. The unities of existence are not subject to a differentiation brings with it the least negativity; rather, they are juxtaposed according to the variable intensive positivity of their perfections.

By evacuating opposition from the pluralities in which the flow of acts of being is expressed, Sadrā also dispels all potentiality or privation, and he refuses to submit the unities of the act of being to any dialectic, reserving the unity and opposition of contraries solely for realities that have a genus, which will be thought under the heading of the quiddities: "Yes, the particular realities of the act of being — if one considers their particularization through significations and concepts, which are not the effective reality of the act of being — are such that mutual opposition and mutual similitude occur for them."[23] The realities of existence must be interpreted according to their limits, their conceptual fixity, so they may enter the universe of similars and opposites. This universe is that of language, in which the existents grasped by representative thought are delineated. All opposition is representation; all identification is imaginary. In this travesty of existences, we cannot fail to have a sense of sameness and otherness, and we always assume the community of a specific differentiation. Which means that this world of significations or intentions is the world of reality but not the real of the world, or, rather, it is *the world*, acts of being reduced to the commonness of a single meaning, which in turn allows for oppositions and resemblances.

Acts of being, in their effectivity, do not form a world, since they are not subject to mutual opposition and resemblance. They are instead hierarchized according to a series of worlds, which typify their potency and their relative attachment to matter. This series expresses the nongeneric unity of existence, even while differentiating it and opening it onto the infinite potency of the principle. It is an open-ended series. The real of being is unity, but this unity is not that of a genus; it is difference, but not one of species. Each act of being is singularized outside all dissimilitude; each monad expresses unity in a multiplication that exceeds every multiplicity signified in the registers of the same and the other. This singularity is affirmed by itself, without a dialectic to unite it with other acts of being: "Two opposites and two similars are two contrary existents or two existents in perfect mutual similitude, whereas the beingness of the act of being by itself is nothing more than itself." The real differentiation of effective realities is neither opposition nor similitude but an ontological differentiation that must be given priority, and that is nothing other than the real positing or effectuating opposites or similars. The act of being is never the "opposite" or the "similar" but rather "that which manifests itself in the ipseity of two similars," or "that which is manifested through the form of two opposites." Opposition and resemblance are qualifications that "fade away" in the act of being. By itself, the act of being is when the real self-posits itself in such a way that all the "dimensions" are united—so many attributes of existentiality, which will receive their names from the predicative properties of quiddities. But "whether they are mutually opposites or similars," these attributes "are consumed in the very reality of the act of being (*fi-ʿayn al-wujūd*)."

The intensive differentiation of acts of being, which the quidditative order translates and disfigures, fundamentally returns to the unity of the real, such that the act of being is a disappearance or a fading away of the fabric of the world of the quiddities.[24] The act of being is the *fading* of the relations of similitude and opposition:

"There is no alterity except in the considerations carried out by the intelligence."[25] The unity of being is neither similitude nor dissimilarity but a consumption of meaning in the real of actualization. The subject's becoming thus consists in a re-ascent, a return to this actuality of the real in being, where he will undergo his own consumption, which will be both extinction (*fanā'*) and eternal existence (*baqā'*) in closest proximity to the divine real. If we persist in thinking that something can be opposite or similar to the act of being, then the homonymic predication attributing this act of being to things will turn it into an accident of what was supposed to be opposite or similar to it. Reduced to accidentality, the act of being would no longer be anything.

We might think that the act of being does have an opposite: nonbeing. But nonbeing, understood here as privation or negation, is, as it were, enveloped in being. Take the attributes of negation: expressing nonbeing, they can only "return," in a way, to being. For nonbeing is experienced in the various aspects of the alteration or mutual contradiction of qualifications. But these dimensions and qualifications are annihilated as pure attestations of nothingness, and they "return toward the effective reality of the act of being." We will distinguish the concrete act of being, which is always one of the degrees of the emanation of being, from the act of being as such, the pure generative source and center of this emanation. The first of these designates a "birth," a "growth" proceeding from the generative source. It may be that negations, contradictory qualifications, do not converge in the direction of the unity of being. But in the act of being taken as an absolute real, negativities, alterity, and contradiction are abolished, fading into the effectivity of the generative source.

Vanity of Nothingness

Another way to show that nonbeing is enveloped by being is through an examination of language and rational concepts. The conceptual reality of nonbeing does not contradict being absolutely, since it has a certain signification. It has a certain mental existence, that of a universal signification. Nonbeing is thus completely enveloped by being. That is why we intelligize nonbeing, and the nonbeing of nonbeing. Absolute nonbeing, the impossible reality, has a way of being intelligible. The intelligence can direct its signifying intentions even to nonbeing, to the "absolute unknown," just as it conceives of two contradictory things. To be sure, what it conceives of possesses no reality, if only because everything that occurs in the intelligence and has merely a mental reality does not possess any effective reality. Nonbeing is enveloped in thought's being, but the latter in turn falls under a sort of nonbeing that hinders its own potential.

Intelligence directed at a concept whose object is a nonbeing does not aim at any essence. It does not aim at the essence of the absolute unknown, at the effective reality of contradictories, nor at the concrete individuation of absolute nonbeing. Thus the concept of "he who is on a par with the Creator" is absolutely empty of all reference to an effective real. Here is an example of mental nonbeing: when the intelligence conceives of nonexistents, it conceives of significations in which, to be sure, nonbeing is enveloped in the being of pure thought. But this mental quasi being refers to no essential signification. No eternal nature corresponds to what is then intelligized, whether concretely or even in the intelligence. In the case of every figure, whether nonbeing returns to being—as when it is a matter of a contradiction whose terms "resemble each other" in the generative center of being or a question of a logical impossibility—the only reality of nonbeing is nothingness, without the least positivity. Far from contradicting the act of being, it underscores its identity with all that is real. Being and the real are one.

The intelligence conceives of nonbeing as a simple, uniform reality, possessing a single signification: "not to be" is always equal to "not to be"; the negation does not seem to be able to differ from itself. In fact, "not to be" knows no differentiation or distinction, just as there is no actualization of nonbeing.[26] The realities of nothingness are nonexistent without, however, being different from each other in their "not-beingness" (*ma'dūmīyah*). The act of being always imposes the differential singularity of its manifestation, whereas the negation of the act of being abolishes every difference. An existent can "fall into the site of nonbeing" and be reduced to being indistinct from every other reality of nothingness.

However, the intelligence always represents realities as distinct from each other, since it cannot fail to conceive of essences and accidents. Thus it makes causes and effects, conditions and conditioned, and so on. It establishes relationships of mutual opposition and, if need be, attributes the concept of nonbeing (*mafhūm al-'adam*) to the realities it distinguishes. The intelligence cannot avoid positing negation as a concept that distinguishes positive essences: for example, it distinguishes the nonbeing of the cause from the nonbeing of the effect. That which is "non-cause" thus still possesses something of the causativity of the cause, but in the guise of its nonexistence, its negation. Thought is led to infer from the difference of the being the supposed particularity of the nonbeing that will come to annul it. If it refrained from such a deduction, it would cease to treat nonbeing as if it were *something*; it would cease pluralizing nonbeing and thinking, for example, of the nonbeing of the hand and the nonbeing of the foot as distinct from each other.

If reality behaved the way our thought expected it to, there would be in each negated thing a doubling of negations, an infinite number of nonexistences. This supposed infinite divisibility of nothingnesses only shows, in its way, that in reality nonbeing is always unique (*al-'adam wāhid*); it can be repeated, but it is one. That is why it has no effectivity or actualization (*al-tahassul*). That is the meaning of its designation by simple privation. Nothingness, like being, has no quiddity; in addition, nothingness is never the answer to the question that invites the acknowledgment of a given act of being: "One will not answer that nonbeing is something, if someone asks what it is."[27] If we consider the causativity of nonbeing, we come back to the negation of the causativity of being. More generally, attributing negation to something means negating the attribution of being to that thing. It never means attributing a position or a positivity of nonbeing. There is no individuation that is not the individuation of the acts of being, and there is no being that is not the being of this individuation. Evils are the absence of existential perfection (*kamālīyah wujūdīyah*), and evil has no essence. It is only the limit of the light of being.[28]

Expansive Being

After approaching the act of being on the negative path, Mullā Sadrā attempts to give a positive definition that does not betray this approach. Indeed, we are on the verge of having to affirm that if being is not something representable, the act of being is nothing. We understand why the supporters of the philosophy of quiddities lost interest in existence: it is nothing conceivable, so it seemed to them to be nothing at all. To rescue being and the evidence of the act of being, it is necessary to give at least a name and a property to this being. But it must be a paradoxical property that cannot be a mental qualification. This definition and this property are expressed in a phrase inherited from the vocabulary of Sadr al-Dīn al-Qūnawī, "extended being."[29] The act of being is expansion, extension, and flow. This is stated in the third *ishrāq* of the summary we have been following:

> The act of being does not comprehend things the way the universal includes particular realities, as we have shown; rather, its comprehensiveness is a matter of extension (*inbisāt*) and flow (*sarayān*) over the temples of the quiddities — a flow unknown to representation. Thus, although it is singularized through itself and is a principle of singularization for what exists through it and possesses universal quiddities, the act of being can be said to have essential realities that are differentiated in terms of the quiddities it determines, each of them according to a rank among its ranks, a degree of its degrees — with the exception of the prime existent, in which no quiddity is mixed. Indeed, the prime existent is the pure act of being, and none is more complete than it. The pure act of being is the one that confirms in being with intensity, the one whose potency is infinite, and whose intensity is infinite. Even better, it is above infinity insofar as it is infinite. No limit circumscribes it, no description apprehends

> it, "no knowledge envelops him, and all faces are humbled before the Living, the Provident (*al-Hayy al-Qayyūm*)" (Qur'ān 20:110–11). There is no discrepancy between what we teach, on the one hand—concerning the unicity of the effective reality of the act of being, the mutual differentiation of its degrees according to priority and posteriority, confirmation in being (*ta'akkud*), and ontological deficiency—and, on the other hand, what the Peripatetics taught concerning the difference of their essential realities.[30]

The doctrine of the simplicity of being is a hermeneutics of divine unity. The simplicity of the act of being, in each concrete existent, is one with the ultimate simplicity of God. This simplicity is not only the condition for the extension of being over all things; it is one with this extension. The word "simple," *basīt*, has the same root as *inbisāt*, "extension." The approach to the act of being occurs no longer within the logic of quiddity and existence, but rather in the register of a completely different configuration of thought, that of the great Andalusian mystic Ibn al-'Arabī, for whom, indeed, being can be located only within the infinite extension of the real (*al-haqq*). Sadrā's discussion of the Avicennian theses in this passage of *Divine Witnesses* is meant less to overturn the order of preeminence between existence and quiddity than to substitute a set of problems inspired by Ibn al-'Arabī for the Avicennian problematic as a whole.

That is the meaning of the critique of universal logic: the comprehension of things within the act of being is not the subsumption of the particular under a generic concept, or of particular substances under a second reality leading to a supreme genus. To be sure, the act of being "comprehends" all things, but not by including them in an abstract totality. Avicenna himself never conceived of being as a supreme genus. But here, we have to deal no longer with a universe constituted by essences or substances whose quiddity is the primary ground of being, but rather with a vast envelopment of every singular thing within the expansive motion of the real. That is why Sadrā cannot be situated within the conflict between nominalism and realism. The structural elements of his thought are completely different: they are act-of-being singularities, liberated and determined by the flux proceeding from the act of being of the real, by the originary effusion that posits divine names in being—what Ibn al-ʿArabī calls the "breath of the Merciful." If no formal knowledge is possible for the act of being, if there is no representation of it, then one could not subsume an individual existence under any generic existence whatever.

Mullā Sadrā opposes the nonrepresentational perception of flux (*sarayān*) to the logic of the concept by which being is eventually grasped in the ten categories. Flux is extension. The word *inbisāt*, extension, also means joy, jovial effusion; it is what one says of someone who is cheerful, welcoming, open. It is the generosity of a heart that welcomes the other unconditionally.[31] The Neoplatonic conception of the superabundance of the One and its emanation in all the degrees of beings is thus interpreted through the vocabulary of joy. The act of being "comprehends" all things, not as the universal carries within itself the ground of particulars, but as joy is communicated to the other, enveloping him with its creative potency, and raising him to a greater potency of existing. This thought of extended potency as joy could be compared with the thought that animates Spinoza, to the extent that Spinoza's own point of departure is Avicenna, whose work is the necessary precursor to Spinoza's doctrine of the potency to act.

The flow of being extends over the "temple of the quiddities." Ordinarily, the word "temple," *haykal*, plural *hayākil*, is used for the body. Here, it means quiddity itself, in its finite determinacy. Quiddity receives its reality from the act of being that constitutes it; it is nothing without the influx and the extension of being, which it does not particularize as a particular thing within it as a species or a genus does. Instead, it bends it to a certain degree, giving it a certain inflection or curvature, beyond which being continues its expansion. The temple of quiddity is a construction of the act of being. Like every construction, it delimits being and translates a certain fixity. The tension between this fixity and the mobility of being will be traversed by all the ethical ruptures and all the weight of the existent, as well as by the irresistible ascension that will carry it beyond itself, toward the higher joy of its metamorphosis.

The flow of being is what Sadrā calls *substantial motion* (*al-harakat al-jawharīyah*), which is not a motion affecting substances with extrinsic modifications but a transformative motion that affects their substantiality itself. This motion can no longer be defined or grasped by representation. Representational cognition is incapable of grasping its flow, which is the expression of the pure simplicity of divine unity. It is in the unmatched singularity of the concrete existent that this simplicity can be intuited. Sadrā denies that being is either particular or universal. Rather, he introduces a term that is not caught in the logical network of the universal and the particular: the word *shakhs*. It refers to simple individuation, the unity expressing the divine One in the plurality of its effusions – the individuation of unity through unity itself. This is a unity that is not a fixity but a singularity of flow, not a part of this flow but an inflection, the entire flow as a whole expressed in a monad of existence. The act of being is always *amr shakhsī*, a monadic reality, singular and singularized through itself, *mutashakhkhas bi-dhātih*: such is the self-positing of the act of being in its singularization, which corresponds to all concrete things around us.

We will say (still following Spinoza): he who knows singular things knows God. The quiddities envelop the species, whereas the act of being is always singular. But the existent is fixed in being through quiddity, not by its expansive singularity. The species entails the fixity of particulars, whereas concrete singularity liberates them, by inflecting a movement that traverses them and modifies them in the direction of a greater potency of acting and knowing. That is why we can speak of monads of existence by reading the expression *al-wujūdāt* in this sense. We could translate this term as "the existences," which would be correct. But this translation does not retain the signifying intention that inhabits the original term. The "existences" are always singular inflections of the flow that is itself the singularity of being, the monadizing monad that pours out its flow over all its expressions.

It is obviously rather difficult to conceive of what a "monad of existence" might be, since the monad seems to be defined rather as a singular essence that is determined by its quiddity and whose being owes everything to this quiddity. But, in truth, this is not so. Thinkers on the monad, from Proclus to Leibniz, insisted on Proclus's remarkable statement "All that perpetually comes to be has an infinite potency of coming to being." And the remarks that follow this proposition would fit quite well within the Sadrian doctrine of the act of being: "All true being is infinite in that it has an inextinguishable life, an unfailing substance, and an undiminished activity.... Its infinitude is in respect to potency. Accordingly, what renders it indivisible makes it also infinite, and a being is more infinite in proportion as it is more one and indivisible."[32] This indivisibility — which is infinity itself — is expressed in the monadic singularity of each act of being. The monadic acts of being, these pure singularities, return to the fundamental unity that is the source of their flow — the source, that is, of the expression of the infinity that constitutes them, the expansion of their joy — and they are converted into the primordial instantiator, God. The differentiation of the simple act of being, according to its degrees, is modalization. Here, too, Sadrā seems to be very close to Proclus: "All things are in all, but in each one according to its proper mode."[33] The law of differentiation proceeds according to distinctions of priority (causativity in expression) or posteriority (the fact of being caused), greater or lesser intensity in the act of being, "confirmation in being" or "ontological deficiency."

Mullā Sadrā later provides an exposition of this gradation of the acts of being and the principles of their distinction (*imtiyāz*):

> Every act of being is singularized by priority and posteriority, by perfection and imperfection, by autarchy or need, or indeed by material accidents if it dwells in matter, accidents that are concomitants of the material individual and its characteristics. Consequently, the occurrence (*wuqu'*), for every act of being, in a station among the stations (*maqāmāt*) is constitutive for it. Priority and posteriority are like two constituents for the act-of-being realities that are above

> generation and movement. And every act of being that takes place in one of the degrees preceding occurrence in matters and dispositions is such that the very fact of its having taken place in this degree of being constitutes it. We do not represent it as disappearing from this degree, given that in itself it would persist in existence. As for the realities of being that are material, they like that as well, except that their disappearance from matter is itself possible through themselves, but not in the sense that their own particularities disappear whereas they themselves persist in being.[34]

The dense passage translated here is governed by the following technical term: *al-wuqūʿ*, occurrence. *Waqaʿah* means to occur, to take place, to happen, to emerge into being. Mullā Sadrā is very careful not to use the verb *ʿaradah*, which also means "to occur," because *al-ʿarad* means accident, that which happens to something, that which occurs in a certain substrate. This is not the case for the act of being. The occurrence of the act of being is determined solely by the station that it occupies in the flow of existence emanating from the infinite potency of God. The act of being is not first "some thing" that then finds itself situated by God in a particular station of the gradation of existents. It is singularized by the very position of this station; it is an inflection of this position. The station is its constitutive principle.

The station is characterized by various differentials, which Sadrā lists. He specifies the status of immaterial and material acts of being. The former, which are the presences or occurrences of the Intelligences, differ only according to priority and posteriority. It is not the quiddity of each of the Intelligences that determines its rank and, therefore, its act of being; rather, the rank, the station, and the differential of priority or posteriority determine the singular mode of angelic existence. The Intelligence cannot disappear from its station and continue to be by and through itself: it *is* its very station. In the case of existents composed of matter and form in the sublunary world, the characteristics of matter also determine the rank they occupy. Thus, a dense body will have a more inferior position than a subtle body. As a whole, the differentiation and the singularization of the acts of being are due to the hierarchy governed by the effusion of being, from its highest intensity to its weakest. How, then, can Sadrā refer to the teachings of the Peripatetics concerning the status of the difference between essential realities? Perhaps he means that the difference between essences imagined by Aristotle's disciples, specific difference, is an *effect* of differentiation according to the degrees of intensity of the act of being, its translation into the order of quiddities.

God Is Pure Intensity of Existing

The apprehension of being in the flow of its own expansion modifies the Avicennian tradition of metaphysics. This is made clear by Sadrā's insistence on presenting being as synonymous with intensity. God is the pure act of being. This makes it possible to say, henceforth, that the prime existent is not, strictly speaking, a being, since he is not characterized by a certain degree of intensity; rather, he is the infinity of intensity as such. Sadrā continues to use the traditional expression for God: the prime existent, the supreme existent. But this existent has no other consistency than the intensity of being itself; it has no quiddity. Avicenna has already maintained that God has no quiddity, that his essence is existence itself. In his summary, Sadrā defines God as "the pure act of being, such that there is none more perfect than he." God is thus the *ens perfectissimum.* What does this eminent perfection consist in? It consists in the intense confirmation in being. God confirms, instantiates, and affirms existence. Power and intensity are synonymous. In order to think about them, if not to understand them – which is impossible – it is necessary to know the meaning of the two divine names of God as they are bound together: *al-Hayy al-Qayyūm.*

We must return to the very precise status of these names in Sadrā's exegesis of the divine names. It is useful to recall that life, power, and knowledge form a well-known triad in the Neoplatonic tradition, and it is not by chance that Sadrā uses these two names when he defines – as much as possible – the maximal intensity of the divine essence. Confirmation in being means not that being is prior to God who confirms it. Rather, this confirmation is the very life of the "living" par excellence, the formation of the being, the constitution of the being as a being. The beingness of God, the most perfect existent, is therefore not a being-entity but the formation, the non-ontic constitution of the beingness of the being. Being is here disjoined from all ontic determination from its source to the last of its derivations.

Why does Sadrā preserve for God the status of a maximal being, when he thinks God as the pure intensity constitutive of beings? Why does he not cross the threshold that was crossed by the Ismāʿīlī Shīʿite thinkers who radically separated God from beings? No doubt he wants to deduce the major attributes of God from the only "property" of the source of pure intensity that we can know: an infinity superior to all infinity. But affirmation of any of the major attributes assumes that God is, in his very transcendence, capable of assuming them, and that he is absolved from his solitude and from his separation. That is why God will be called "the most perfect being," although he has no quiddity and no plurality in him, and although he is not a determinate "being."

The name *al-Qayyūm* means that God is "the provident."[35] He is thus the source of the expansion of being, because in his simplicity he has no need of an instantiator and because he is subsistent by himself, as a pure and constitutive intensity. Incorporeal, without state or dimension, he is the unity of knowledge and power that provides subsistence for all that is other than himself. He knows all the acts of existing that proceed from him, universally and particularly. He is not limited to possessing a universal science of existents, but determines them and knows them in their particular mode of existing. Divine subsistence and providence are one. If the world is brought into being in time, if it must disappear at the end of time, all this is an effect of the inferior limitation of the infinite emanating flux; the material world cannot eternally receive the effusion of being. But there is no trace in this of any divine parsimony, or of a divine caprice, of a reluctance to shed his grace over the emanated existents. The incapacity to be eternal comes solely from the precariousness of the material receptacle. As a whole, life and provident subsistence envelop all God's major attributes, which express the generosity of being, the divine gift of existing given to each thing, a gift that is appropriate to the rank of the thing, without a final goal, without compensation, without need for praise, prestige, or glory.[36]

The divine name *al-Qayyūm* allows one to grasp something of the constitutive dimension of being, that by which the act of being makes beings come into being: *al-qayyūmīyah*. It is the power to found in being. This power is the confirmation in being of monadic acts of being, singular acts of being manifest in concrete existents. This power is one with intensity, *al-shiddah*. God is the principle of extension, joy and effusion. Ontology, which according to Avicenna reaches completion in pure existence, deepens into a theology of power and intensity. The prime existent is constitutive insofar as he is the real, for the real can be apprehended only in a power whose infinity cannot be represented by any figure of infinity itself. He is beyond infinity by its infinity. He is that which is excepted from all reality, while constituting this reality in its existence. The name "the provident," *al-Qayyūm*, designates that which instantiates reality, founds it without losing itself in it, while also being the intensity of this reality. The binding together of the real and reality will lead to the questions of the *nomination* of God and the identity between his hidden essence and his revelation in beings. The infinity beyond all infinity is the One, but only on the condition of barring this One from a limitlessness that liberates it from all *constituted* unity.

The act of being, thought in its maximum degree, is what we name the paradoxical One, the One such that it is conceivable never as a finite or infinite totality but only as a superinfinity.[37] It is the being that sustains beings in being and founds the derived monadic acts of being. The act of being, in essence, is the principle of the erection of beings out of nonbeing. That is why, at this point in the exposition of his doctrine of being, Sadrā's approach takes the form of an exegesis of the two divine names, *al-Hayy al-Qayyūm*, the living, the provident. On the basis of these two names, designating the sole and unique founding essence, superinfinity, we can understand the unity of apparent contraries: on the one hand, the unification of the effective reality of the act of being, *ittihād haqīqat al-wujūd*, and on the other, the differentiation of degrees of act of being, *ikhtilāf marātib*. For Sadrā, constructing a metaphysics means reconciling these two poles, which correspond to the superinfinite One and the One unfolded in the multiple. It means binding together the real and reality. We are beginning to sense that the way to this reconciliation, this bond, is not a dialectic between unification and differentiation, between identity and difference. The very terms Sadrā uses indicate, rather, that this reconciliation concerns a logic of extension, intensity, and potency. *Qayyūmīyah*, that is, the power of constitution, binds unicity to differentiation according to a gradation in the power of being.

In a very brief fourth section, Sadrā takes up for his own purposes the Neoplatonic triad referred to above: "In each thing, the act of being is identical to knowledge, power, and the other attributes of the perfection of the existent as existent."[38] The attributes of perfection express the name "the living." This very brief exposition on the superinfinite One clearly maintains that the bond between the divine essence and its attributes is manifest in each thing, and the exegesis of divine unity is the very exegesis of the existent as existent. Theology and metaphysics are reconciled in the exhibition of the knot between the real and reality, at the heart of absolute extended being.

The Status of the Quiddities

What, then, becomes of the quiddities, which in metaphysics were the essential principles of the existent? Here is what Mullā Sadrā writes:

> Between the act of being and the quiddity existing through it, there is a purely intellective correlation and not a chance accompaniment. On the contrary, in the sense well known among the philosophers, it is necessary for one of the two terms connected in an intellective

> correlation to be made effectively real by the other term. Or else it is necessary for the two terms to be effective realities together, made such by a third term that effectuates the link between the two. The second hypothesis is not correct, for one of the two terms, namely quiddity, is not instantiated in being and is not existent in and through itself, as we have demonstrated elsewhere. There remains, then, only the first hypothesis. And then it is not possible that quiddity implies the act of being. Otherwise, quiddity would be existent before the act of being, and that is absurd. The truth is that the act of being is prior to the other, but not in the sense that it has effects in quiddity through being of quiddity itself, which is not instantiated in being, as we saw, but rather in the sense that the act of being is the ground of effective realization and that quiddity follows it, not as existent follows existent, but as the shadow follows the individual and the silhouette follows the concrete form, without effectuation or reception of effectuation. Consequently, the act of being is existent in itself by essence, whereas quiddity exists through the act of being, that is, by accident, and the two are united by this unification.[39]

Quiddity is the form of the existent, its substance determined by certain essential attributes. Thus the quiddity of Zayd is determined by its substantial form, man, which is differentiated from the animal genus by reason. It is quite evident that this substantial form is connected to existence in Zayd according to a certain necessity. It is this necessity that Sadrā investigates here. He excludes the hypothesis that the quiddity of the existent is united to this existent's act of being by a third term. It remains only to ask which term – that is, which reality, that of the act of being or that of quiddity – could be the connecting principle of the whole. But formulated in this way, the question veils the very reality of the terms presented: quiddity in itself has no reality; it "is not instantiated in being." Sadrā denies quiddity the status of common nature, independent from inhesion in a substrate, the concrete existent, or the existent in thought. Avicenna does not say that a purely indeterminate common nature – "man," for example – exists in and through itself, like the Platonic Ideas. He gave them a status only within divine science. But he did not draw the conclusions that, according to Sadrā, are obvious.

If "common nature" becomes existent only as the quiddity of a concrete particular (Zayd's humanity) or as a universal concept in the mind ("man," rational animal), then quiddity, in order to be, needs a concrete act of being or an act of being of pure thought. Quiddity cannot exist before existing, that is, before the connection that is an act of being. The act of being is therefore not one term that unites with another term but the foundation of the existence of quiddity, either in the concrete (the individual) or in the mind (in the form of a universal concept). Sadrā renounces the Avicennian scheme of the priority of quiddity in the real essence of the thing, in order to maintain that this essence is fully constituted by the act of being alone, whose quiddity is a shadow: what a thing is is the shadow cast by the thing, or the silhouette that is formed when the real individual comes to pass. These eloquent comparisons underscore the inanity of quiddity if one detaches it from the act of being that founds it, in the sense that a shadow is nothing without the individual who projects it.

That said, we are brought back to something already concluded from the purely negative approach to the act of being: it is never the object of a concept that gives rise to intellective judgments; with regard to judgment, it is nothing. But quiddity, for its part, does seem to be something; it even seems to be the thing itself, because it presents itself in the category of substance, and because it then supports the other categories, the accidents — quality, quantity, relation, and so on. But the converse is true: these categories of being are nothing by themselves; substance is nothing except through its substantiality, which is conferred upon it by the act of being. Mullā Sadrā writes:

> The act of being, in its essence, is neither substance nor accident, since both of these are the model for a universal quiddity. Now you know that the act of being is singular by itself, actualized by itself and by the principle of its effusion, its instantiator. If the act of being were subsumed under the category of substance, which one would include within it like

> a genus, or under a generic sense found among the accidents, then it would need something that would actualize it as act of being, as difference, and it would need something that would make its flux flow out among the other actual realities by the act of being. And then the act of being would not be the act of being. This is contradictory.[40]

Once again, we begin with the intuition of the immediate: the act of being is there, prior to all determination of the existent by way of a form or an accident. It is there, in its singularity, reducible to neither the particularity nor the universality possessed by quiddity in the concrete existent or in the mental existent (the existence of the concrete thing is singular, but the existence of the concept in the mind is also singular; that is the very root of its unicity). The immediacy of this always singular act of being testifies to the fact that it does not have an instantiating principle different from itself, since, according to this hypothesis, there would be a cause of the act of being, which would therefore be mediated. The cause of the flow of being would then be one of the realities whose existence is effective only through the act of being.

It is necessary, then, to posit the act of being as the cause of its own actuality, since it is the pure actuality of the existent realities and their quiddities. This does not mean that the act of being of a concrete existent, or of a concept in the mind, is without ground or reason: its reason is God, the instantiator of the act of being, not as an antecedent to the thing of which it is a cause, but as the principle of the flow of which the act of being is an inflection. God does not harm the immediacy of being. Rather, he founds it; he is the principle of its appearance, he is the apparent par excellence. That is what makes it possible to deny Aristotle's ten categories the ability to grasp the act of being – categories which are indeed those of quiddity and are placed in the register of the universal. The differentiation that singularizes an act of being is not the difference that determines a substance.

At this point, Sadrā has finished stripping away from the act of being every qualification taken from the Aristotelian vocabulary of the quiddities. In Aristotle's metaphysics, the approach to the existent as existent is resolutely oriented toward substance and its accidents, neglecting the act of being. It is worth asking why Aristotle is not interested in the act of being, as Sadrā intuits it, and why intuition without concepts is of no interest to Aristotle, to the point that the difference between existence and quiddity is not even truly interrogated. In my opinion, this is not a "forgetting" of being but a decision, one that is very fruitful for the science of the existent as existent. But it is precisely this fruitfulness that Sadrā radically calls into question.

He does this by taking to task one of Avicenna's disciples, Bahmanyār, whose accomplishment was to systematize (and to schematize) the Avicennian conception of the link between the act of being and quiddity.[41]

> Since the abode of your heart is illuminated by the dawning of the light of gnosis over the horizon of proof, and since you have acquired the certainty that the act of being is neither substance nor accident, then cast far from you the shadow of your vain thought and do not be concerned with what you find in one of the philosophers [Bahmanyār]: "The act of being is an accident which requires that the caused act of being possess a substrate, and every accident subsist through an existence in its substrate. Such is the state of the act of being. The act of being of 'man' subsists through its relation with 'man' and the act of being of Zayd subsists through its relation with Zayd, but not in the manner of a thing that is in a place to which the relation comes from without."[42]

According to Sadrā, Bahmanyār's error is that he misinterprets the relation of the act of being to quiddity by identifying it with the inhesion of an accident in its substrate. The error comes from then conceiving of the act of being and quiddity as two distinct effective realities, united by a relationship. Indeed, according to Bahmanyār, the accident subsists only through and in its substrate, but it can still be conceived of separately from the substrate. And indeed, the accident's relationship with its substrate is not that of two things external to one another, but the unity of the two is not primary; it follows the inhesion of the one in the other. To conceive of the act of being as an accident of quiddity is necessarily to first think quiddity alone, as an abstraction, and not the fundamental unity of the existent. "But no!" says Sadrā. "Both of these [act of being and quiddity] are one *in concreto*, and they are also one in thoughts [in the mental realities]."

There is no real distinction between existence and essence, since the thing, whether it is concrete or a representation of the mind, is — taken as a complete whole — both act of being and quiddity; or, rather, quiddity attests to a certain type of act of existing. Quiddity is not the receptacle of the act of being, and the act of being is not received by quiddity. The intellectual analysis of the existent breaks it into two distinct realities, and does not preserve this fundamental unity. It separates matter from form. It distinguishes substrate from accident. Thus envisaging the receptivity of the substrate, the intellect gives birth to this abstraction — quiddity — and fixes it, absolving it of its fundamental unity with effective existence, "separating it from the totality of the act-of-being realities." The intellect extracts quiddity even from this separation, ascribing to quiddity an act of being through itself, by which it would become existent in itself.

Sadrā thus proceeds to the phenomenology of the inevitable act of abstraction performed by the intelligence. He faithfully describes it in order to show the origin of the transcendental illusion to which Bahmanyār falls victim. The intelligence is inevitably confused because it irresistibly produces an abstraction. "Henceforth quiddity becomes foreign to the act of being," whereas, in reality, the two are unified. Whoever abstracts quiddity is obliged to confer an existence upon it, since he conceives of quiddity as a "nature" existing by itself, prior to the reception of existence. He thus inadvertently admits that quiddity is only a typification of the act of being, and, despite himself, he confirms the priority of the real. In Avicenna's analysis, the separation of quiddity from the act of being leads the intelligence to make quiddity into something that truly exists, granting it the act of being, and thus confirming what it claims to refute. "See then how much more comprehensive is the extension of the act of being! And how much vaster is the expansion of its luminescence, precisely there where its affirmation follows from its negation."[43]

The act of being is revealed for what it is: the extension, the expansion of effective reality itself, not just any predicate received by an abstract subject, since this subject would presuppose a certain mode affecting the expansive flow of being. The act of being is therefore not a reality for which we could forge a concept; "the act of being of things is their beingness itself," the fact, for them, of being purely and simply existent – the real of reality.

Critique of Transcendental Illusion

It remains for us to understand "the effective reality of the characterization of quiddity through the act of being" and to dissipate the confusion originating from the real distinction between these two terms. Sadrā is perfectly aware that he is overturning the ontological foundations of the moderns, as he calls them – in other words, the philosophers who think along the lines laid out by Avicennism. In wanting to characterize quiddity with the act of being, one inevitably succumbs to the transcendental illusion that creates the following representation: a quiddity existing before its own act of being. The "characterization" made in this way can have several guises:

> Sometimes the Moderns deny the principle of derivation and replace it with the link of concomitance; sometimes they reserve it for what, among the attributes, is beyond the act of being. Sometimes they argue that the place of beingness is the unification of quiddity with the concept of the derived existent, but without granting to the act of being a subsistence or an affirmation by itself and for what is other than itself – and this is the status of every derivative for one who speaks thus. No one speaks the truth about the true nature of the question at stake here.[44]

Whether the act of being is thought of as a derivation or as a concomitant amounts to the same thing: it does not subsist by itself; it is not the subsistence of the effective existent. If we grant that the existent unifies in itself quiddity and existence, we are still wide of the mark, for we do not grasp the root of this unification, realizing this unification only after positing the abstraction of quiddity and the abstraction of existence. The unity is primary, not secondary; it is extended being itself. That is why the true determination of quiddity is the following: "The act of being is the beingness of quiddity, not of something else that belongs to quiddity, like the rest of the accidents."

We must stop to dwell for a moment on this last formulation. Sadrā first said that the act of being was the beingness of the existent. Now he maintains that it is the beingness of quiddity. Does this mean that the existent is quiddity? Certainly not, if the intelligence hastily concludes the opposite and affirms that quiddity is the existent. It does mean this, however, if we maintain that all existents except God are released into being according to a certain quiddity and are indeed "some thing" expressed by this quiddity. This is the source of the confusions I have discussed: we are dealing with very real quiddities, distinct individuals belonging to distinct species, and we perceive or think distinct existents by virtue of the quiddities. But these real quiddities are real only through their act of being, their beingness. What constitutes them as beings is not something other than their effective reality, that is, their act of being. This constituent is therefore not an attribute or an accidental reality but their source and their principle. The distinction between quiddity and act of being is resolved in the distinction between the being and its beingness, a metaphysical distinction that unveils the effective being of things without ruining the fundamental unity of the thing, which is its beingness itself, its *mawjūdīyah*.

Sadrā does not merely reverse the relation between the act of being and quiddity by refusing to make the act of being the concomitant of quiddity; he profoundly rethinks the consequences of the Avicennian intuition of the existent, which led Avicenna to say that existence is always the concomitant of a quiddity, that is, always accompanies it. If it is true that the act of being always accompanies quiddity, this is because quiddity is always existent through its very beingness, which is the act of being. Avicenna's idea, fully matured and thought out, leads to a reversal of the thesis affirming the priority of quiddity in the concrete essence of the thing. Sadrā's reversal brings Avicenna's metaphysics to completion. Sadrā cannot leave behind the vocabulary of the act of being and quiddity; he is entirely reliant upon it. But at the very heart of this configuration, he thinks quiddity in its existence itself, and he thinks the fundamental unity of this existence and of the quidditative degree realized in and through it. He destroys the abstraction of a quiddity that exists before existing, as well as the abstraction of an existence that exists — as an accident — in the substrate of quiddity. In a profound way, he returns to the unity of the existent, as it was presented in Aristotle.

The ontology of the act of being is faithful to Aristotle not because it gives priority to the definition of quiddities but because it grasps the existent in its substantiality, or its accidentality, without dismantling the beingness of the being, except in the metaphysical consideration of the difference between what is and what makes it be. But the ontology of the act of being reverses the Aristotelian perspective, in that it does not exhaust the metaphysical quest by grasping *ousia* as quiddity but realizes it by grasping *ousia* as the effectivity of an *einai*, of a being. *To on*, the being, is brought back to its beingness, that is, to its *einai*; everything *mawjūd*, everything "that is found" in the being, exists through its *wujūd*, its "finding itself," its being-there.[45]

Mullā Sadrā supports his claims with two quotations from Avicenna. It might seem strange that he would illustrate the reversal of the Avicennian conception of essence through two references to Avicenna himself. Nevertheless, this is not an ironic salute to the master but a very elaborate interpretive strategy, which opposes Avicenna to Bahmanyār and the moderns who followed him and attempts to show that, despite his own declarations, Avicenna is inexorably led to the same conclusions as Sadrā. Here is the first quotation from Avicenna: "The act of being that belongs to the body is the beingness of the body. That is not how it is for whiteness in the body." If the act of being were an attribute of the body, it would have in itself a certain signification (as whiteness possesses a signification) and would then exist in its substrate (as whiteness exists in white things), even if its existence were nothing other than its existence in the substrate. The attribution is a judgment that distinguishes three things: the existence of the substrate, the concept of the attribute, and the copula (the verb *to be*). But, says Sadrā, in the judgment "the body is existent," there are only two terms: "the body" and the act of being, which is not identical to the copula in the judgment of attribution. Thus the judgment of existence confirms what Avicenna says here, which brings us back to what Sadrā says: the act of being is not an attribute. Existence is never a predicate.[46]

Here is the second quotation:

> The act of being of accidents in themselves is the act of being belonging to them in their substrates, except for the accident that is existence. The latter differs in effect [from accidents] because these need existence in order to be existent, whereas existence is free of all need with regard to existence in order to be existent. It is therefore not true that its existence in its substrate is its existence in itself, in the sense that existence has an existence as white has an existence. No! We must understand that its existence in its substrate is the very existence of its substrate. That which is other than existence, among the accidents, is such that its existence in its substrate is the existence of this other.[47]

In Avicenna's hypothesis, the act of being is concomitant with quiddity, here thought as an accident different from all other accidents. Whereas accidents such as whiteness need to have existence conferred on them in order to exist, and therefore need inhesion in a certain substrate, existence *in* the substrate is the very existence *of* the substrate. Whiteness exists by its substrate, but it exists as whiteness of the substrate, and that *is* the existence of whiteness in this substrate; existence, however, exists in the substrate not as something that comes to the substrate and is added to it but as the very being of this substrate. One cannot say "existence exists"; it does not need any existence to be added to it.

Avicenna therefore leads to Sadrā:

> To the act of being there belongs a quite real mode of being *in concreto*, but its "being" has not been added to it by anything, as is the case with the accidents. It has no need, on the other hand, for what is called a substrate in order to exist; rather, quiddity exists through it, since for quiddity there is not another act of being by which it [quiddity] would be prior to existence. As for calling quiddity "the substrate" and the act of being "the accident," this arises from a pure and simple abstractive "taking into consideration" by the intellect.[48]

Avicenna's thesis, according to which the act of being has an accidental reality, contradicts itself. It reveals the inevitable abstraction of the intelligence, the point of view taken by the intellect regarding the concrete thing. But Avicenna has the genius to bring out the strangeness of this "accident" – existence – which has none of the properties of the accident, since, at bottom, it is not an accident at all.

The transcendental illusion leads to an antinomy that is unsurpassable for the understanding; this antinomy was perfectly elucidated by Nasīr al-Dīn al-Tūsī in a remarkable passage in his commentary on Avicenna's *Ishārāt*, quoted by Mullā Sadrā: "The act of being is prior to quiddity *in concreto* and posterior to it in the intellect."[49] It is indeed a question of an antinomy, since reason can take two points of view – maintaining both a thesis and its antithesis – with equal demonstrative force and conviction. This is how Sadrā explains it: "The act of being *in concreto* is a foundation (*asl*) that proceeds from the instantiator, and quiddity follows it, whereas in thought it is a property of the intellect to have an abstract perspective regarding quiddity separately from its connection with the act of being. It is then that the intellect attributes the act of being to quiddity." Presential knowledge grasps the absolute priority of the act of being, the fact that it is the foundation of quiddity. But formal abstractive cognition cannot help but posit quiddity and attribute existence to it.

The power of cognition undergoes a division. It is split between two contradictory theses on being. The lowliest sensation shows that a thing must exist in order to possess a quiddity. The intelligence says that the thing possesses a quiddity in order to be able to exist. According to Tūsī, it seems that the point of view of the concrete and the point of view of the intellect are balanced so we can take one or the other. For Sadrā, this is not so. To the extent that there exists a presential knowledge (which Tūsī does not admit), it is clearly superior to abstractive knowledge, and above all it is not on the same level. There are not really two points of view regarding the real but rather an effective *grasp* of the act of being, on the one hand, and, on the other, a *point of view* based on the fact that the intellect abstracts the form from the existent and does not grasp the existent in its effective existence. This antinomy can be resolved if we distinguish the respective perceptions from each other. The transcendental illusion originates in the intellect itself, which is thought according to the features of an abstract understanding, a producer of abstract forms. As soon as it is reduced to that, the understanding opposes sensation, as the form opposes the testimony of existence. But if we grant priority to the presential grasping of the thing itself, our intelligence discovers that it is the highest power of cognition, for cognition is capable of the most luminous grasp of the act of being, whereas sensation obtains only a veiled revelation of it, confused and obscure.[50]

The act of being is what is most apparent. It is "more known than everything we represent to ourselves," and is thus "the beginning of all representation."[51] Ignorance of the act of being entails an ignorance of "all that comes after it." The defect of the intellect in these matters is that it turns toward what is hidden, toward quiddity, and cannot immediately receive the appearance of pure appearing. Only divine science, which is the very existence of God, is a grasping of appearance, because it is knowledge of the divine essence. Sadrā thus maintains that being is what is most withdrawn, because it is what is most apparent: transcendence (or what we awkwardly call transcendence) is in truth the radical immanence of being to the being – pure manifestation. Necessary here are the tireless metaphysical quest and the unveiling of the meaning of the divine names and the divine essence. What is needed is the link between exegesis and ontology. This link assumes the mind's negative approach to the real.

Chapter Three

The Avicennian Moment

Origin of the Problem of Metaphysics

It is often said that by affirming the priority of the act of being Sadrā reverses the "philosophy of essences" as it was founded by the Peripatetic tradition. Thus Henry Corbin writes: "Mullā Sadrā dethrones the venerable metaphysics of essence, whose reign had lasted for centuries, ever since al-Fārābī, Avicenna, and Suhrawardī."[1] This revolution, however, seems to me less radical than it might appear. In order to evaluate it, it is necessary to measure the extent to which Sadrā remains under the influence of the Avicennian world, less with regard to its detailed determinations and more in terms of an overall perception. To be sure, the theoretical modifications and, in the end, interpretive schemes that allow Sadrā to carry out the exegesis of natural and supernatural realities are so numerous that the Avicennian schema will eventually be effaced. In his interpretation of the Qur'ān and of the sayings attributed to the imams, Sadrā proposes his most authentic ontology, for which the immense edifice of *al-Asfār* is something of a prerequisite and a deductive preparation.

He will take a great deal from the school of Ibn al-'Arabī and from the illuminative Suhrawardian tradition, not to mention mystical numerology, spiritual medicine, angelology, pneumatology, spiritual physics, astrology, and the teachings of Sūfism. Here he will carry out a synthesis of the ontology of Islam, which he discovers in the Qur'ānic text and in an open-ended series of various spiritual disciplines. The question of the priority of the act of being—a logical question—is doubtless only a necessary condition for this exegetical adventure; it does not exhaust the true repercussions of the Sadrian doctrine, which aims to think about the bodily and spiritual salvation of man, the real statuses of paradise and hell.

Nevertheless, Sadrā must begin by demonstrating the priority of the act of being, without which the very notion of the real would not be elucidated. How is it possible to know what authentic salvation is if one does not know what it is "to be?" If one does not know how being constitutes the existent, how it can redeem its imperfection and reach its most eminent position—close to God, the source of being? Sadrā agrees with Avicenna on this important point: the real must be known if one wants to grasp the effective order of realities; the authentic truth must be unveiled. He interprets Avicenna's injunction in this sense: "The goal of theoretical philosophy is knowledge of the real *(ma'rifat al-haqq)*."[2]

The Sadrian revolution is inscribed within the Avicennian moment of philosophy even as it works to exceed it and to undermine its foundations, in an attempt to preserve its ultimate intention by transforming it. Sadrā wants to overthrow Avicenna in order to save him, or to preserve him by overturning one thesis on being in favor of another one derived from Avicenna's inaugural concepts and decisions.[3] If Sadrā proposes the completed ontology of Islam, as I believe he does, this ontology is marked by the development of Avicennism and by the mutations provoked by three major events: Suhrawardī's philosophy, the irruption of Ibn al-'Arabī's teaching (especially *Fusūs al-hikām*), and Shī'ite gnosis. All this is built on foundations Avicenna laid, which provide a defining basis for all the thinkers of what has come to be known as the school of Esfahan.

We should not forget that the Avicennian moment does not comprise the entire native philosophy of Islam, if this moment includes within it the full completion of al-Fārābī's project but leaves out Ismā'īlī Shī'ite ontology. Ismā'īlī philosophy configured reality according to other schemata and led to an attempt to think the unhypothesized—the real—not in the guise of being but as that which is situated beyond being and nonbeing, as a One immediately affected by a negation of its unity, and by the negation of this negation.

We have seen that in his highest speculative reflections on the principle, Sadrā reconnects with this fundamentally Neoplatonic type of thought and attempts to think being in terms of a work of negation. But he will always remain under the influence of the Avicennian moment, to the extent that all his thought, and even his boldest speculative risks, will assume that the ultimate term of the quest must be *being*, the superabundance of being, being "above perfection" (*fawq al-kamāl*), according to a decision of Avicenna's.[4] What would the ontology of Islam look like if we took into account this split between the concern for being and the concern for the One beyond being and nonbeing?

We must therefore go back to the schemata of Avicennism as they appear in Mullā Sadrā's meditations. This presents difficulties that may seem insurmountable. Can we conceive of Avicenna's system, the living totality of his philosophy, as Sadrā was able to conceive of it, as a living source of new problems? Who was Avicenna for Mullā Sadrā?

Answering these questions is delicate work, for the following reason, at least: the organic theses of this system are not isolated; they cross through and govern a logic, physics, and metaphysics, without omitting the major domains of the exegesis of the Qur'ān, prophetology, and eschatology. A traditional Shī'ite thinker like Sadrā would never challenge the fundamental theses on existence and essence, the possible existent and the necessary existent, or the refutation of the Platonic Idea, without bearing in mind Avicenna's highest aim, as it is expressed in the last three books of the *Ishārāt*—a text that Sadrā read through the filter of Nasīr al-Dīn al-Tūsī's commentary. For Sadrā, the doctrine of the Intelligences is, immediately, a personally experienced angelology. The difficulties of psychology (Does the soul come into being with the body? Is the imagination an immaterial faculty? and so on) are governed by the exigencies of an ascent toward an ever more intense activity.

God's love for himself, the infinite enjoyment he receives from himself, the celestial soul's endlessly renewed love for his intelligence, the love of each nature, however humble, for the higher order of reality — these are not subordinate allegorical themes, or mere concepts. The first principle of the existent is the beloved par excellence, and this is what truly unveils his nature as a necessary existent. The revelation received by the exceptional souls of the prophets, as well as that which sometimes touches souls in dreams, are not fictions. The former legitimates the political function of the virtuous man and allows Avicenna to conclude his metaphysics of the *Kitāb al-Shifa'* with a political theology of the greatest importance; the latter opens the way to all the speculations on the activity of the imagination.

Sadrā adopts as the horizon of his thought, as the primary evidence of the existent the logic immanent to a perception of worlds rather than a logic stripped of all concrete presence. It is a logic in which beings are hierarchized according to their potentiality or their actuality, their weakness or their power to act and to exist, and in which goods are harmonized with relative evils in a general order animated by desire. It is within the framework of this intuition of a universal desire, tending toward he who has no desire, that the following reading of the "Avicennian moment" and its significance for Sadrā should be understood.

The Ontological Split

The approach to the act of being is supported by a wide-ranging dialectical discussion that contends with the following thesis: Existence is an accident of quiddity. This thesis presupposes that Avicenna distinguished existence from quiddity and from essence. Now what about this distinction? Can one say it is real? Or is it nothing more than a distinction of points of view regarding the effective existent? What comes to be thought in this thought that was, from another perspective, so important for the development of Western metaphysics? Is it a mere assumption concerning essence?

In his interrogation of this distinction, Mullā Sadrā applies to Avicenna what Avicenna himself says of all complex reality: the simple is prior to the composite, the part to the whole. It will therefore be necessary to examine in its own right that part of the doctrine explicitly concerned with the existence of quiddity, conceived as a series of simple elements into which the manifestation of the existent is broken down. But, on the other hand, the perfection of the final whole determines the development of each of its moments. To read Avicenna is to accept this apparent contradiction, which is in fact generative logic itself. It cannot be a matter of privileging one of the approaches to the detriment of the other; rather, their mutual necessity must be grasped.

For Sadrā, the thesis that clarifies the path to be taken is the following: in Avicennism, the split between quiddity and existence is primary, but it is also constitutive of their reconciliation. Inversely, the substantial unity of being is real only on the condition of being animated by this split. It is therefore precisely this split that Sadrā will reexamine, in order to lead it in another direction, toward the unity of being. Rethinking it and attempting to overturn it, he takes it as his "point of departure" and as the condition of his dialectical reflection. He inscribes himself, *nolens volens*, within the logic of such a split.

The distinction between existence and the thing is a distinction between the signification of existence and the signification of the thing: in our souls, when we represent the former, we do not represent the latter at the same time.[5] For Sadrā, the die is cast: existence has become an object of representation, just like "the thing." *Ipso facto*, existence and the thing are distinguished from each other as two intentions of signification, and their logical or at least semantic distinction leads thought down the path of abstraction. The object of our meditations then becomes existence conceived of as "signification," instead of the act of being, which is never a "signification."

The initial split must be effaced if one wants to regain the truth of the act of being. This does not prevent Sadrā, when he names the act of being using the term for existence, *al-wujūd*, from presupposing what he is criticizing — namely, this very split — even as he interprets it in a very singular fashion. He states that *al-ma'nah* means "signification" — that is, mental signification, the concept. If this term indeed designates the intention of signification, it also often has a more concrete sense, and the entire problem is whether or not it has such a concrete sense in this context. Here is what Guy Monnot writes in an analysis of the word *ma'nah* within the lexicon of the Mu'tazilī *qādī* 'Abd al-Jabbār:

> 'Abd al-Jabbār distinguishes *ex professo* three senses of the word: a) signification (*qasd al-qalb bi-l-kalām ilā-l-murād*; II, 4–8); b) the grounds for validity or the cause (*'illa*, II, 9, 11); c) the thing that is affirmed or whose existence is affirmed (*al-shay' al-muthbat*[*]; II, 12–15). In the technical sense in which it is often used in the Mu'tazili *kalām*, the word means (apparently like an *'illah*) something seen as prior to one's cognition of it.[6]

Similarly, Avicenna means something that has a certain effectivity, that not only is signified by the mind but also preexists this analysis and this knowledge. Not merely a "point of view" but an *effective* sense — the sense content of something real that can properly be said to be, in a certain way. The intention of sense is not only true *a parte subjecti* but also the index of a reality *in objecto*. All the more so in that, if one preserves the sense of "cause," the *ma'na* takes on even more consistency. If we draw the conclusions that follow from this approach, it seems indeed that "existence" and "the thing" possess two distinct realities, or "entities" (as Jolivet aptly translates it).[7] We are thus confronted with the theoretical scheme that conditions Sadrā's two critical perspectives: either existence and the thing are mere abstract "significations," and the addition of an abstraction to an abstraction will never achieve concrete being,[8] or they are two "entities," and concrete being is thus lost once again, since between these two "entities," one will have priority over the other — and this will inevitably be "the thing," reduced to the status of a quiddity.

Mullā Sadrā begins with immediate perception and with presence. If I perceive a determinate individual being, an object before me, this object is quite obviously a thing, and the fact of existing is in no way separable from what it is in its concrete presence. It is indissolubly existent *and* the thing that it is. The two senses of the verb *to be* – to exist and to be something – are fused in the object and do not constitute two separate entities. There is thus no need to reconcile two entities that have split. Nevertheless, Avicenna effects such a split, out of fidelity to language and according to prerequisites of the general structure of existents that have yet to be unveiled. On the one hand, the object is, it exists. "Existing" (*mawjūd*) is synonymous with being established in being (*muthbat*) or that which has received being, received the act of existing (*muhassal*).[9] Note the use of passive voice: the object has been instantiated in being. The language here already presumes what will be demonstrated: namely that being, in the cases of the objects that surround us and all other possible existents (not necessary through themselves), means being necessitated by something other than itself. The analysis of being presupposes that being is not lacking grounds or justification. This analysis is irresistibly oriented toward the horizon of a rational causality and a dominant necessity.[10]

The thing (*al-amr*) possesses, on the other hand, an essential reality (*haqīqah*) "through which it is what it is. The triangle possesses an essential reality through which it is a triangle. Whiteness possesses an essential reality through which it is white." Existence is not this essential reality; rather, it assumes effective establishment (*al-wujūd al-ithbātī*). There is thus indeed a split between the reality by which the triangle is a triangle and the establishment by which it exists. Is this to say that the quiddity of the thing (what it is, its reality) is by itself a reality and that existence is another reality? This is the form that Mullā Sadrā gives to his interrogation as he attempts to account for a split effectively introduced into the heart of the real existent, a split that for him has the blandness of a pure and simple abstraction.

But Avicenna's argument is far from authorizing such a

conclusion. First, the distinction between existence and quiddity might well be only conceptual. This is the argument of Toshihiko Izutsu, for example, when he refutes what he sees as Suhrawardī's misunderstandings in his interpretation of the distinction in question. However one may regard the Suhrawardian decision, can we write, as Izutsu does, that "the distinction between 'quiddity' and 'existence' is in Avicenna a conceptual distinction"?[11] It seems to me that the very notion of a "conceptual distinction" remains poorly elucidated. To be sure, the distinction between existence and quiddity results from a representation in the mind. But, according to Avicenna, all cognition of the existent as existent can only be a representation, since it assumes that concrete being is thought and submitted to a process of abstraction. This presents a difficulty since existence, for its part, is fundamentally attested to by sensation.

But the cognition of the distinction between two "entities" that constitute the existent is not sensation; this cognition gives rise, rather, to two intelligible concepts. This does not mean that these concepts have a merely logical validity, in the sense that the object of logic does not involve concrete determinations. Rather, the two entities, quiddity and existence, although neither has any existence in or for itself (as if it were a question of separate existents) do have a certain effectivity. They do not have existence in and by themselves, if by that we mean that quiddity exists by itself in the manner of a Platonic Idea. The aim of Avicenna's radical critique of the Platonic conception of the Idea is precisely to eliminate all confusion in this regard. There is not the slightest shadow of the Idea, in Plato's sense, in the Avicennian system.[12]

And yet the distinction has a real sense, if for Avicenna the logical analysis of being is the very constitution of ontology. The conceptual distinction between quiddity and existence involves the being of the being in a split that is not merely a game played by the mind — although this split does not determine the occurrence of two existents — but the generative center of the concrete hierarchy of existents, from the necessary to the last degrees of the possible. That it is not a matter of two existents is confirmed by the fact that existence cannot, rationally, be an existent. If that were the case, it would be necessary for this existence itself to exist or, in other words, for it to receive existence — in a foundational moment that would recede to infinity.

Furthermore, the split between the reality of quiddity and the reality of existence (leaving aside for the moment the enigma of what these realities might be and whether they are merely conceptual) is immediately abolished in the reality of the effective existent: "The concomitance (*luzūm*) of the signification [or entity] of existence always belongs to essential reality. Better, the signification of the existent is always implicated for essential reality, for this reality is either existent *in concreto* in individuals (*fī-l-a'yān*) or existent in the estimative faculty (*wahm*) and in the intellect (*al-'aql*). If this were not so, it would not be a thing."[13]

For existence, what is a concomitant of quiddity? We must posit the two terms and define the status of quiddity more precisely. Whatever the situation of existence, it can be considered only in relation to this quiddity, which bears responsibility for the essential reality of the thing, since it is in possessing its quiddity that the thing possesses an essential reality proper to it. But quiddity is different from existence, for it has no need for existence in order to be thought. When we conceive of necessary being, we have to ask ourselves whether we are conceiving of a quiddity whose existence is inseparable from it, or whether we are dealing with being that is entirely existence, without quiddity. This is not an idle question, for it may decide the status of the proofs of God's existence.

The Enigma of Quiddity

Let us return to the question of the existent in general. We can comprehend, in an effective intention (itself realized in our mind) that quiddity is existent (*mawjūdah*) in one of three states: "either in individuals, in souls, or absolutely, such that it is common to both together."[14] Does this mean that Avicenna is positing three states of quiddity, namely, nature existing *in concreto*, nature existing mentally in our representation, and nature common to the two existing natures? What does it mean that all three are said to be existents? We understand very well what concrete individual existence and mental existence are, but what is the existence of their common nature? Why three statuses for quiddity? This question points to a true difficulty and impels Sadrā's critique.

Indeed, strictly speaking, only the statuses of concrete quiddity and quiddity in thought – that of the concrete individual or that of the individual that is the representation of the universal form in our minds – are existential. There is no place here for a reality such as the Platonic Idea. Nevertheless, quiddity requires a status that is neither the one it has in the concrete individual nor the one it has in mental existence. This raises the question of the mode of being of its third status, which is at once indispensable and problematic. To answer this question is, inevitably, to think of God and his providence.

Let us note that the *status* of quiddity cannot be thought without existence, although the *nature* of quiddity must be conceived of without it. That is the split: one cannot be thought without the other, although each must be thought separately, and without the other. This knot of contradictory thoughts is called concomitance (*luzūm*). Its logical definition will be examined below.[15] Existence, as a concomitant of quiddity, is separable from quiddity, and at the same time is never separable from it in the effective existent. This is what is expressed by the verb "to assemble" (*jamaʿah*), which can be seen as a symptom of the split: Zayd "is the assemblage (*majmuʿ*) of man or of humanity with concomitant accidents (*aʿrād lāzimah*), as if these were parts of him"; quiddity and existence are split apart and brought back together like the parts of a whole, where the whole is the effectively real thing.[16] Nevertheless, in this bringing together, existence is not constitutive of Zayd's quiddity.

Speaking of the attribute (not the accident), Avicenna writes: "The attribute (*al-mahmūl*) is sometimes constitutive (*muqawwim*) of the quiddity of the subject, and sometimes it is a concomitant reality of the subject, not constitutive of quiddity, like existence."[17] If what is true of the logical attribute is true of the real accident, then existence (thought here as attribute) will be non-constitutive of the quiddity of its subject: "Existence ... is concomitant and does not enter into quiddity."[18] Mullā Sadrā calls precisely this assertion into question, and yet it also results, with blinding clarity, from the rational analysis of quiddity. This analysis leads inevitably to the conclusion just quoted. Why?

Quiddity confers on the thing the assemblage of significations (of entities) through which the thing is what it is. It is responsible for the fact that man, for example, differs from dog, the barking animal, which differs from dog, the celestial constellation. "We say: each thing possesses a quiddity through which it is what it is, and that is its essential reality, or better, that is its essence (*dhāt*)."[19] Essence can be a "single and unified absolute signification" (which cannot be separated into multiple significations). Therefore, says Avicenna, "it is necessary that its existence be acknowledged." The absolutely simple essence, through its very simplicity, tends toward the necessity of existence.

But if essence is gathered together and unifies a multiplicity of significations, it does not imply the necessity of existence. Nor does existence enter into the constitution of essence.

> For example: this man. Indeed, he must be a substance, possess an extension in space according to the dimensions of length, width, and depth; together with this, he must possess a soul, and his soul must be a soul through which he nourishes himself, through which he senses and moves as he wills; together with this, *he is*—to the extent that he learns to think the intelligibles, learns to know the arts, and in fact knows them, if nothing in external reality prevents him from doing so.... Therefore, when the whole is gathered together, a unique essence is actualized from the whole, and this is the essence of man.[20]

The quiddity of man is not the "common essential" belonging to him and to what is other than him; man is not what he is because he is an animal; rather, *all* his essential attributes must be actualized.[21] Let us return to the distinction between simple quiddity and composite quiddity. What has been said of the identity of quiddity (*māhīyah*) and of essence (*dhāt*) is valid, strictly speaking, for what is simple. Indeed, "there is not here something that receives its quiddity (*qābil li-māhīyatih*)."[22] Otherwise there would be a distinction here between the received (the form) and the receptacle. The composite, however, is not defined by form alone. Its definition "includes also matter, regarded from a certain angle, and through this we know the difference (*farq*) between quiddity and form in the composites. Form is always a part of quiddity in the composites, whereas every simple thing is such that its form is also its essence, since there is no compositeness in it. As for composites, their form is not their essence and *their quiddity is not their essence*."[23]

In the definition of man, there is certainly form, but one also considers a certain aspect of matter—that of the spatial extension of corporeality—without considering the materiality of vegetative and animal powers. This new split, between essence and quiddity, doubles that between existence and quiddity, and expresses the status of the possible existent, necessitated in being [*nécessité à être*] but possessing neither the simplicity nor the necessity of existence. Potentiality, multiplicity, and evil enter into the consideration of essence, with their decisive consequences for the thought of creation as a whole.

We see very well that the two splits are at bottom one and the same: concrete man will be necessitated in being—for example, in the individual Zayd, who actualizes his form in a certain matter. The composition of form with a matter in which it is individualized is a type of creation in which existence comes to the existent as a concomitant, "from the outside." The final unity of the existent will then testify both to the dynamic gathering together of its essence and to the effectuation of existence. But this gathering together will be actualization, not immediate actuality, because matter and privation, the seats of evil and nonbeing, are inevitable components of the definition, leaving it with a fundamental lack in being.[24]

Mullā Sadrā situates himself in his own way within the theoretical framework provided by Avicennism when he poses the following question: Between quiddity and the act of existing, which is the reality that founds the existent? He will accept the terms of the problem – even if it means modifying them – by asking what has priority in being, quiddity or the act of being. But is this question of priority an Avicennian question? Is it already present in Avicenna? This is what must be examined.

In *Logic*, Avicenna provides some very clear elements: "You have accepted that things possess quiddities and that these quiddities exist sometimes *in concreto* [in individuals, *fī-l-a'yān*] and sometimes in thoughts. And that quiddities do not require the actualization of one of the two existences, and that each of the two existences is established *after* the establishment of this quiddity [*ba'd thubūt tilkah al-māhīyah*]."[25] Quiddity really exists only insofar as it is the quiddity of a concrete individual, or insofar as it is thought in the estimative faculty or the intellect. It does not seem to possess any status prior to these two types of existence. However, quiddity must be established so that concrete existence or mental existence can be established *afterward*. Avicenna says it very clearly: "But quiddity is firmly established first."[26]

There is some legitimacy to the claim that, at least within his discussion of logic, Avicenna maintains the priority of quiddity when he considers it without any relationship to the idea of quiddity insofar as it is accompanied by the concomitant of existence, in individuals or in thoughts. But Avicenna also stops speaking in terms of establishment and talks instead of "point of view":

> The quiddities of things are sometimes in the concrete realities of things, and are sometimes in the representation. They therefore possess three points of view: first, the point of view of the quiddity insofar as it is this quiddity, without being linked to one of these two acts of being [concrete or in thought] or to what is connected with them, to the extent that quiddity is [merely] so. Second, the point of view of quiddity to the extent that it is *in concreto*; then there are accidents connected with it that particularize its existence. And third, the point of view of quiddity to the extent that it is in representation.[27]

It can be established, then, that there are two existences of quiddity, and three points of view regarding it, even before considering whether quiddity has priority over its particularization through the concomitance of an act of existing. Quiddity in itself is a simple point of view within the system formed by the three logical points of view, as the following quote shows: "And thus the art of logic does not devote its study to the singularities of these things, insofar as they are according to one of the modes of existence, *in concreto* and in thoughts, nor to the quiddities of things insofar as they are quiddities."[28] This last phrase clearly indicates Avicenna's attitude. He wants rigorously to escape the difficulties that arise from the repudiation of Platonic Ideas. The Idea had the advantage of grounding its own participation in and through individuals, while remaining universal. If this participation turns out to be unintelligible, that advantage turns out to be illusory. We must return to the ipseity of quiddity, not as if it were an Idea but in its mere definition.

Let us take the ipseity of humanity (*huwīyat al-insānīyah*) as humanity. "In the definition of this thing there is only humanity."[29] One must refrain from answering the question "Is this humanity one or multiple?" When humanity is in Zayd, in the concrete individual, it is not "from the point of view (*bi-i'tibār*) in which it is 'humanity' only."[30] It is entirely a matter of consideration, but this consideration, this point of view regarding simple quiddity, has the greatest consequences.

How is it possible to take such a point of view on the mere ipseity of quiddity? By considering it alone, without the least external predicate. Thus the animal, as animal, is neither the common (*'āmm*) animal, nor the individual (*shakhsī*) animal, nor the animal from the point of view of its existence *in concreto* or from the point of view of intellection in the soul. In all these cases, it is the animal *and* something. We must take into consideration "the animal by itself" (*al-hayawān bi-dhātih*), not as an Idea subsisting in a separate intelligible place but as a mere abstraction, which, however, must not be seen as entirely vain, since it is the essence by itself, belonging to the animal through itself: "Its essence belongs to it through itself."[31]

Nature is thus stripped of all that will happen to it, and Avicenna maintains that "this point of view is prior in existence (*al-wujūd*) with respect to the animal that is individual through its accidents – or else universal, existential, or intellective – and this priority is that of the simple over the composite and of the part over the whole. And through this *existence*, it is not genus, it is not species, it is not individual, it is not one, it is not multiple; rather, through this *existence*, it is 'animal' only and 'man' only."[32]

The point of view regarding this simple quiddity, the animal as animal, cannot be a mere "logical" abstraction, in the sense of being a mental representation without the least effectivity. Besides, if that were the case, the animal in itself would be confused with the animal as I intelligize it, and would thus receive an accident, mental existence in me. But, on the other hand, this existence cannot be confused, purely and simply, with the existence that is a concomitant for quiddity, in the concrete existent or in the intelligized existent. Better, simple quiddity, reduced to its mere definition, is approached negatively through the stripping away of predicates (unity, multiplicity, and so on).

Must we decide that existence is attributed to quiddity before quiddity has received a concrete existence? Or must we give the word *al-wujūd* a more neutral sense than "existence"? What would such a sense be? We find ourselves at an impasse. Avicenna says that this existence of quiddity pure and simple has priority over the quiddity affected by predicates, like the accidental or the concomitant. This priority must be taken seriously. But the existence of this priority is that of the simple over the composite – a logical priority. How could a logical priority entail an ontological priority, if the existence of simple quiddity cannot be conceived of in the manner of the supposed existence of "the intelligible man" in the Platonic Idea? In short, what is the existence of the animal by itself?

Before responding to this question – as much as possible – by reverting to the concept of divine providence, I would like to point out that the lines I just discussed are indissociable from the movement of thought that comes after them. Avicenna writes:

> But it is incontestable that it must be one or multiple, since nothing existing lacks these two [modes of being], according to what is externally concomitant to it (*min khārij*). And this animal, [insofar as it is viewed] under this condition (*shart*), although it is existent in each individual, is not *through this condition* a certain animal, although it implies becoming a certain animal because, in its essential reality (*haqīqah*) and its quiddity, according to this point of view, it *is* a certain animal.[33]

Thus the first moment, the stripping away of all accident from essential reality, precedes and engages the second moment, effective existence, in which the existent is either concrete or mental. Nothing existing can be without one of these two modes of being. Simple quiddity is therefore not an existent. But its existence precedes concrete determination. Is its previous "existence" a mere logical presupposition, whereas the regime of the effective existent begins with determinations by external concomitants? If so, the concomitants would risk becoming constitutive of the effective existent, which they are not.

We can escape these difficulties only by hierarchizing the levels at which quiddity is considered and by strictly maintaining the distinction between the two moments of this consideration: on the one hand, quiddity without condition, and on the other, conditioned quiddity (and this second level will in turn be divided). There is nothing existing that is not determined, but quiddity, in itself, is not affected by these determinations, because it is defined without them. It is not nothing, however; it is not a mere concept produced by us or the result of a purely analytic distinction. Rather, it has a status in divine science, and this must, inevitably, be the grounds for the movement of thought that Avicenna has just carried out.

Without God and his attributes, the status of pure quiddity is unthinkable, since it involves a certain enigmatic type of existence. Better, since existence is God himself, it is not inconceivable that quiddity derives, in God, from the existence constitutive of God. This is precisely its enigmatic existence prior to the two modes (concrete and in thought) of the effective existent. For Sadrā, the reversal of the priority between essence and existence is the ultimate consequence of the Avicennian approach.

It is difficult to understand what Avicenna means when he defines quiddity pure and simple. It is not clear whether its status is purely logical or whether, as Sadrā believes, it already implies a presumption of existence. Is the distinction between a logical point of view and a thesis that somehow involves effective existence even relevant?

Here is one of the most well-known passages in Avicenna, in which — it should be noted — existence never comes up. It is an analysis of quiddity with respect to particularity and generality:

> No, but the animal, when it is considered as an animal, and from the point of view of its animality, is not particular, and is not nonparticular, that is, general. Rather, both are negated by it, because from the point of view of its animality, it is only animal. But the concrete sense of the animal (*ma'nah al-hayawān*), insofar as it is an animal, is not the sense of the particular and the general. Nor do these enter into its quiddity. If this is so, the animal as animal is neither particular nor general in its animality. No, it is, rather, animal and nothing else, among realities and states. Yet it implies that it is particular or general.[34]

The concrete sense, that is, the reality of the animal, is nothing other than what is required by the consideration of animality, without adding the particular and the general to it as concomitants. This is not to say that this animal in itself exists prior to its particularization or generalization. On the contrary, if it effectively is, it will not fail to imply one of these two concomitants. And this is indeed always the case. The effect of grasping the animal in itself is therefore not the positing of a third status of existence, but simply the affirmation that in itself, in its quiddity, this animal must be stripped of every concomitant that does not bear on its concept.

Avicenna specifies that the animal is indeed lacking particularity and generality as such, in its animality, but not in its existence (*fī-l-wujūd*). It is therefore when the animal effectively exists that it receives concrete existence or a mental existence along with the concomitant that is existence. It seems, therefore, that the animal in itself has no existential status, and that this lack is necessary for making the distinction, in the concrete or in the general concept, between quiddity and existence. The split between these two realities must be grounded in the logical consideration of pure quiddity, of the animal in itself, which is neither particular nor general.

At this point in the argument, Sadrā intervenes, tirelessly repeating that he cannot understand how quiddity can be prior to existence, while also being endowed, somehow, with an existence. Are there grounds for posing such a question? Probably not, if we grant to Avicenna that nothing in pure quiddity indicates any presumption of existence. But there are if we understand what he says later in the text:

> The animal considered with its accidents is a thing of nature (*al-shay' al-tabīʿī*), and [the animal] considered in itself is that nature (*al-tabīʿah*) whose existence (*wujūd*), it is said, is prior to natural existence, in the sense of a priority of the simple over the complex. This is the existence that distinguishes itself insofar as it is divine existence (*al-wujūd al-ilāhī*), because the cause of its existence, insofar as it is animal existence, is the providence of God, may he be praised.[35]

The animal in itself does not exist, if existing must be understood as concrete existence or mental existence, but it exists with the very existence of God, if it is true that it must be eternally conceived of in God and grasped in his providence.

It is inconceivable that pure quiddity in itself would have no reality, but it is no less difficult to think what this reality could be, if we persist in thinking it outside of divine science and the necessary attributes of the divine essence. The difficulties disappear when one ceases to try to grasp something that is situated on the level of the very eternity of God in terms of temporal priority or posteriority. The priority of pure quiddities is not a priority that would fix them in a sort of quasi existence, before their effective existentiation, whether in concrete individuals or in intellects and thoughts.[36] It is nothing other than the envelopment of natures within the divine existence itself, prior, logically speaking, to their deployment according to the order of causes in the universe of possibles necessitated in being.

It is nonetheless true that, considered in itself, quiddity implies no presumption of *separate* existence. If we understand this, then quiddity is not "existent" in the sense that the Platonic Idea exists. Rigorously speaking, God always existentiates effective existents, either *in concreto* or in thoughts. He confers existence on the existent, which then possesses an existent quiddity. Even when pure quiddity is thought in divine science, it has no other existence than this divine existence and no *distinct* existence prior to its effectivity in the emanated existent. Sadrā will be more faithful to Avicenna than it appears at first sight. He will argue as follows: if pure quiddity has no presumption of existence, and if existence signifies something other than quiddity, then quiddity has no existence at all *by itself*. Consequently, the act of being has an absolute priority over quiddity.

The orientation adopted by the exegetes who make pure quiddity "exist" in God is therefore not entirely clear or absolutely convincing. It seems possible to say only that quiddity is enveloped in an exemplary fashion in divine unity, because it effuses from the latter in the very movement in which the possible existent surges forth into being. But this "divine" existence of quiddity is not separable from the existence of God. We find it again in Ibn al-ʿArabī, in the distinction between the establishment of quiddity in God and its effective existentiation. But Ibn al-ʿArabī is a Platonist, which makes it easier for him to affirm the establishment of eternal essences.

The creative flow of divine providence pours forth from the absolute necessity of God to the derivative necessity of effective or thought existents, such that quiddities or natures, existing in an exemplary fashion solely by virtue of the existence of God, will never cease to exist through the individual concrete existence or mental conceptual existence they receive from this divine existence as concomitants. But their existence will not be necessary, insofar as it will not be implied by them as constitutive; it will depend not on the mere consideration of their essence but precisely on this flow, which is what allows being to institute the possible quiddities — which are thought in God — within the graduated order of Intelligences, and within natural forms composed of matter, species, and individuals, in the heavens and in the sublunary world.

That is why it is indispensable to know God in order to understand how existence, in what is not God, is detached from quiddity, while also being reconciled with it and never failing to accompany it. In the order of reasons, everything that allows the nature of God to be elucidated is prior to the logical debate on essence and existence. This is hardly surprising, if we remember that metaphysics, whose first object is not God, is no less theology for all that — it is a deduction of God but also and especially a foundation in God.

This deduction, which allows Avicenna to write that "it has now been established for you that something exists necessarily,"[37] will require the distinction between modalities of existence — between the possible and the necessary. Although in return, in a sort of metaphysical circle, the definition of modalities assumes the absolute priority of necessity and, consequently, a sort of anticipation of the singular status of God. The deduction of God and the foundation of all things in God imply each other and form two arches in one and the same structure.

This will become clearer when we deal more precisely with the question of the modalities of being, which brings with it another difficult question: Does contingency have any particular signification? Nevertheless, within the metaphysical circle, the real point of departure, that is, the effective ground, can only be God. Indeed, what is established by the deduction of the nature of God, inseparable from the deduction of his existence, is this: God alone exists necessarily, and he is thereby the principle of the necessity of existence for all things; he makes all things necessary, either immediately or via a series of causes.

The necessity of the existence of God is not a predicate of his essence. Avicenna demonstrates this on the basis of the absolute simplicity of God, which is his very unicity. "The First has no quiddity other than existence."[38] Avicenna recalls that he has indeed made it known that the significative reality of quiddity is separate from that of existence, and in what sense it is separate. This might lead to misunderstanding the fundamental necessity of God, of his very existence, and to imagining that God possesses a certain quiddity, and that the latter implies, as a constitutive element, the necessity of existence—just as a man possesses a quiddity that receives the possibility of existence as its concomitant. But this is not the case, for such an argument, by applying to God the predicate of necessary existence, would introduce the distinction of subject and predicate into God, and would abolish the fundamental simplicity of his essence.

The necessity of existence is the very being of God, and one could say, using a term that is only slightly forced here, that it is the very subjectivity of God. This means, incidentally, that the Kantian critique of the "ontological argument" would not truly worry Avicenna, although it might appear that by treating the existence of God logically as an accident, and as a concomitant, Avicenna leaves himself open to this critique.[39] God has no quiddity, "except that he is what is necessarily existent. And this existence is real existence."[40] The existents that possess a quiddity distinct from their existence all have the status of something caused; their existence comes to them only "from the outside," that is, from the series of causes that goes back to the cause of all causes, the First. This latter possesses neither genus nor difference. It has no definition, and acts freely, without any "why" for its activity. Its necessity and its fundamental freedom are one, and it does not imply existence "as a secondary thing that it would need, as being colored possesses an existence that comes to it secondarily."[41]

God has no associate in his freedom from all matter; he transcends all inclusion in the categories of the existent; he is such that one must negate from his constituent existence all similarities with the existent conceived of according to the categories, and he is such that one affirms of him the totality of constitutive relations expressing the procession of all things from him. It is in this sense that God is the principle.

Transcending all definition, God is not "perfect"; rather, he is "above perfection" (*fawq al-tammām*).[42] He does not *possess* existence but is superabundant in being, such that all existence effuses out of him, while remaining in him. This (obviously Neoplatonic) concept of effusion (*fayd*) is absolutely central; it clarifies the notion of providence (*'ināyah*) and is inseparable from it. The procession of possible existents is inscribed into the very essence of God, in his power and freedom, for it expresses the superabundance of his existence and is translated into the fundamental goodness of everything that exists, insofar as it exists. That is why "evil has no essence" but is privation of substance or of "ontological health," that is, of the maximum of perfection allotted to a substance. "Existence is goodness, and the perfection of existence is the goodness of existence."[43] Existence, constitutive in and through God, is pure good, and God is indeed the real, since the necessity of his existence founds his reality in him, from which the being-real of all things emanates.

In this unity of the principle, Avicenna thinks the unity of three major attributes: science, will, and life. God is intelligence, but the objects of his intellection are not ordered and differentiated forms, as happens in the human soul.[44] God "intelligizes things all at once," without a multiplication of self and without things' being represented by their forms in the effective reality of his essence. Pure quiddities, prior in existence to the quiddities that receive concrete or mental existence, are therefore not formal abstractions, represented in the divine science in their ideal multiplicity. They become separate quiddities only in the "time" of their effusion: "The forms of things effuse from him as intelligized forms."[45] Forms "effuse from the being-intelligence" of the principle, and it is insofar as God intelligizes that he intelligizes all things through himself.

It is impossible to understand the status of pure quiddities if one abstracts divine science from will and from life. The quiddities are enveloped in the unity of an originary intuition that is fundamentally free of all formal distinction. They exist through the flow of divine life that provokes their actualization, which is to say, their emanation. God knows himself as the Good beyond all perfection; he therefore knows "the modality of the order of the good in existence," and he engenders this order through the sheer potency of his superabundant life, which is one with his will.

The quiddities have no existence in a "time" prior to concrete or mental existence, and the status of simple natures designates these quiddities through the movement of eduction out of the divine simplicity in such a way that the quiddities express, in their multiplicity, the simplicity of existence from which they proceed:

> The First thus intelligizes his own essence and the order of the good existing in the whole, and how the whole is according to this order, because he intelligizes it—and the whole effuses; it becomes and is existent. And all that is known of the existent that proceeds, the aspect in which the existent proceeds—this proceeds from its principle and dwells with its principle. This order is a good that does not exceed but that follows the goodness of the essence of the principle and its perfection, which are loved for themselves.[46]

In accordance with a classic Neoplatonic scheme, the procession of forms and the immanence of forms in the divine unity are one. It follows that the forms and the quiddities never lack in existence but that the distinction between quiddity and existence is valid only in the procession itself—signifying the lack in being necessary through itself, the relative degradation of existence in the motion of life and will—and in the hierarchy of causes. This degradation is not in itself an evil, but it is progressively accompanied by evil – privation of good – in proportion to the growing privation of perfection. The split between essence and existence in the universe of emanated existents expresses the fundamental unity of existence in the principle; it therefore assumes their reconciliation in the return to the principle. This is the general scheme from which the doctrine of love will be developed.

The general theme of love is of the utmost importance in the Avicennian system. Not only because it clarifies moral motifs and prescriptions for salvation but because it transfigures the knowledge we can have of existence, especially the knowledge of the first, necessary, and absolute existence of God. We will return to this question when we discuss spiritual salvation. For now, we can ask what this very general theme of love, of the loved/lover relationship, can tell us of this providential flow, this effusion of existence that unfolds quiddities and projects them into a derived, precarious existence marked by a fundamental potentiality. We can answer this question only if we remember that Avicenna identifies the most perfect, superabundant existence with beauty (*jamāl*) and splendor (*baha'*), which saturate God with being and effectivity without the shadow of a categorial dimension, of a quantity or a quality.

It is this Platonic identification of the beautiful and the real that justifies the ecstasy of the sage in contact with the dazzling and overwhelming light of the principle: "I am beyond the entire world of intelligence. I remain in this noble and divine place. I see here such a light and such beauty that no tongue can praise its order, no ear can grasp it."[47] In this passing flash that reaches beyond the intelligible, the rational approach of metaphysics allows one to imagine, to name, and to recognize the true nature of this pure, absolutely immaterial, foundational, and constitutive existence – the entire reality of God.

This beauty gives the nourishment of divine unity to the desiccated abstract concept. Order and beauty: these are the true faces of existence – distant, yet very close – that we must decipher in physical realities and that lead us to the incomparable splendor of the principle. The necessary being, writes Avicenna, "therefore possesses pure beauty and splendor, and is the principle of the beauty of all things and of the splendor of all things."[48] But what do love and dilection desire? Precisely such a harmony, such a concord, the self-conformity and the absence of dehiscence that one sees in divine beauty. Thus emerges an aesthetics of perception that will be joined with the highest ethical destination: perception passes through different degrees, from the least perfect to the most intense, from sensation to intellection, by way of the imagination and the estimative faculty, such that the greatest perfection, the greatest nobility of the perceived object, corresponds to the intensification of this perception. At the final term of this gradation is also the end of desire, since the intensification of perception goes hand in hand with the intensification of love and with the gradual perfection of the relation between the subject who loves and the loved object.

In God, the separation of this subject from its object disappears; the perception of self by self is absolute, immediate, and total, and full enjoyment is eternally actualized. In a very beautiful phrase, Avicenna says that God is "himself for himself" (*dhātuh li-dhātih*).[49] God is that unique subject who is absolutely for himself and who is therefore the object of desire and distant imitation for all those who seek truth, reality, wisdom, and political order and harmony. He is the model of love, the object of love, and — above all — the real in which the lover and the beloved coincide. Necessary existence is this fundamental unity of the lover and the beloved. God is thus the one who gives pleasure and the one who takes pleasure. Just as perception and desire are intensified according to the gradation that leads from the sensible to the intelligible, existence is perfected, and the highest enjoyment belongs to the most eminent subject, the subject par excellence, the one who is "himself for himself": God is the most perfect giver of pleasure and the most perfect in enjoyment. This enjoyment of God is the reality of his necessary existence, and we have no adequate words to describe it.

The distinction between quiddity and existence applies to the possible existents that proceed from the necessary existent and express their ontological deficiency in this unfulfilled desire which binds and weaves their nature and orders them in relation to God. The distinction has a logical reality, but it functions also to explain this gradation of love, the truth of the universes and their foundation in the beloved, who is "himself for himself." This theme of the union of love recurs in Sadrā. It provides a basis for his doctrines concerning spiritual salvation, the aesthetics of forms, and moral consideration. It is what authorizes the penchant for order. For the soul, the possibility of being, implies this desire and this love, through which the perfection of existence is and must be sought: all possibles tend toward the necessary.

The Ontological Reconciliation

The possible, unlike the necessary, possesses a definite quiddity. It is ontologically precarious because its essential reality is not constituted through concrete existence. Existence is not essentially constitutive (*al-dhātī al-muqawwim*) of possible existents: the possible existent is caused, "and the causes of its existence are different from the causes of its quiddity."[50] Existence cannot be constitutive of the possible existent, since the quiddity of this existent is not "itself for itself"; it is not the principle of its own existence. The force of the argument lies in this: efficient causality is not a mere representation of causality but must be realized in an effective cause, and the quiddity of the possible is not sufficient to provide this effective cause to the possible so that it may exist. That is why, when we form the concept of a thing, we can always doubt whether the thing really exists. We can develop the concept of humanity, the form of humanity can exist in our soul, and yet we doubt that it possesses an existence in some concrete individual we have not seen. Sadrā would respond that humanity exists *in our souls*, and that it is necessary for existence to be primary and indispensable to it. But according to Avicenna, this objection is not valid, since it is enough that the concept does not imply the concrete thing (a particular one) for existence not to be constitutive.

Existence "comes" or "happens" to the possible existent according to its causes. But it is called a "nonconstitutive accidental concomitant." We cannot say that existence is a purely fortuitous accident that could have just as easily not happened to the existent since, indeed, it really does exist. Having effused from divine providence, how could the existent not exist? Its existence could have not occurred to its quiddity – through which it is a *possible* – and will always bear traces of this potentiality in itself. But, if it exists – by virtue of divine science, will, and life (which are all one) – if pure quiddity has effused into its effective concrete quiddity, the possible has been caused in being, it has been existentiated. Existence belongs among the concomitant accidents of effective reality that it is impossible to strip from the existent, although it is not constitutive of this existent.[51] Concomitant existence shares with the constitutive a certain necessity in the thing itself, although the necessity of the constitutive is essential, whereas that of concomitant existence is external to the essence of the thing. It shares with the accidental the fact of coming to the thing "from the outside," that is, from a certain cause, which goes back, ultimately, to the cause of all causes.

Can we speak, henceforth, of "contingency" in reference to existents that are not God? In his classic work, *La pensée religieuse d'Avicenne*, Louis Gardet writes of an "essential contingency" of created realities, concluding that: "The created contingent is not, as created, posterior to a nonbeing that would limit it: but all the being that is in it, including its essence – not as such, but as existent – comes from a *necessary* emanation of the first Being who *necessarily* thinks it as *possible*."[52]

Can we give meaning to, and confer reality on, contingency in a system of thought governed by the split of the existent into quiddity and existence, and by the reconciliation of the one with the other in the order of providential causality? It seems that the existent, proceeding from God through a certain chain of causes that leads to its existence, is never exempt from a certain form of contingency, from the mere fact that nothing in its own essence forbids it not to be. Gardet considers this absence of any necessity-through-itself responsible for what he calls contingency. It is the slender difference between pure quiddity and existentiated quiddity — between equinity or humanity without condition, and the concrete horse or man (or the universal horse or man in thought) — that would be translated here by the term contingency: pure quiddity is possible if its constitutive elements are not contradictory, or rather it becomes possible when God conceives it in his eternal science.

Rigorously speaking, humanity (for example) is not, in itself and without condition, "possible"; it is not affected by any modality of existence. It is enveloped in the simplicity and the unity of the science of God, from which it effuses as possible, and from which it effuses necessarily, as Gardet aptly puts it. But in this motion of effusion, quiddity — here, humanity — gains an inseparable concomitant of its essence, an existence that does not constitute it but that is nonetheless indispensable to it. This existence does not eliminate the fundamental potentiality of the being of the existentiated and caused existent, whether it is individual and concrete or universal and imagined. But this existence is indeed necessitated; it can no longer not be, since God has willed it and decreed it, and since it expresses the emanative power of God. It remains "contingent," however, because, being unable not to be, it still *could have* not been, if we think of it simply in the first and absolute nakedness of pure quiddity, in which existence is in no way constitutive.

Contingency is not a modality that is added to the possibility, necessity, or impossibility of being as a fourth term; rather, it is a type of necessity, different from the absolute and intrinsic necessity of divine existence. It is a necessity that has never been able not to be, since its instantiation makes it such that it can no longer not be: the future anterior of necessity. It translates the difference between the principle and the whole of created existents, all affected with a delay in being necessary, which justifies their desire and their love for the primordial loved one.

Contingency is not a "state" (*ḥāl*) of the existent. Nor is it *the* property of existence, revealed in the experience of a truthful unveiling. There is no question in Avicenna's ontology of a contingency synonymous with an absence of ground, the silence of the principle of sufficient reason that we find in literature – in the well-known passages of Jean-Paul Sartre's *Nausea*, for example.[53] Here, however, existence is saturated with necessity. We have proof of this in Avicenna's definitions of the possible, the impossible, and the necessary, which are for him the only three "states" of the existent as existent. He says that it is difficult to define these three modalities and that the ancients, from whom we inherit these terms, did not escape the vicious circle. Indeed, when they wanted to define the possible, they included in its definition either the impossible or the necessary. And when they wanted to define the impossible, they included in its definition either the necessary or the possible.[54]

The three modalities form, as it were, three circles that implicate one another and are all bound together (in a manner that is somewhat analogous to the weaving together of the real, the symbolic, and the imaginary in the Lacanian schema). It is impossible to separate one of the modalities from the others without dissolving all three of them into inconsistency. Just as Lacan grants a certain primacy to the real among the three circles, Avicenna considers the necessary dimension of being "the one that must be represented as primary." This comparison of the two schemata is not arbitrary. In his way, Lacan is a distant heir to Avicenna. But he is a very unfaithful heir, and willfully so: the real, which in a certain sense has primacy over the symbolic and the imaginary, is more analogous to the impossible than to the necessary. In the Lacanian schema, the real is analogous to the impossible, the symbolic to the necessary, and the imaginary to the possible.[55]

Giving priority to the circle of the real over the two other circles involves a decision concerning being that is opposed to Avicenna's decision (a decision that governs all of Western ontology up to Leibniz and Hegel). It is an attempt to put an end to the Avicennian moment I am outlining here.[56] I say this in order to emphasize Avicenna's decision, to underline its tremendous importance. For Avicenna, the necessary is first. It is what we must begin with, and we will define it without appealing to other terms, quite simply because the necessary designates "the firm instantiation in existence" (*ta'akkud al-wujūd*).

This remarkable expression must be examined closely. The verb *ta'akkadah*, in the fifth form of the root *'-k-d*, is a passive reflexive; it means "to be convinced, to be assured" of something. The second form, *akkadah*, means "to assure, to confirm." *al-Ta'akkud* is the act by which one assures oneself of the reality of something, a sort of convincing oneself, an act by which one attests for oneself, in the fullness of the evidence, to the truth before which one finds oneself. It is a confirmation of truth for oneself; it is, therefore, also an assurance of reality and a firm instantiation, an act that is not far removed from what is designated by the derivatives of another root, *q-w-m*, particularly the verb *qāmah*, to stand upright, to arise. This is the root of *al-qiyam*, the fact of holding oneself upright, of rising into being or existence; of *al-qā'im*, what is erected or is maintained in existence; as well as of *al-mustaqīm*, what is straight – which characterizes the "straight path" mentioned in the first sura of the Qur'ān, the divine name *al-Qayyūm*, the provident, the one who founds in being, and the set of terms designating resurrection, the resurrector, and so on.

There are several overlapping semantic fields here; they have in common that they signify the necessary density of existence that is translated by the following fact: "existence is known through itself."[57] Existence is in itself its own proof and manifests its presence to itself (even before being attested to for another); it is the evidence for itself and becomes certain of itself from itself. Avicenna's remarkable expression formulates existence itself as the act by which existence becomes certain of itself from itself. Nonexistence, says Avicenna, is always known, in a certain mode, through existence, and not the inverse. We find this unity of existence and knowledge again in Sadrā; at best, it expresses another unity, that of existence and necessity.

All existence is necessary, in a certain way, since it establishes itself in the real, is the real, and knows itself and is assured in itself as real. That is why the modality of the necessary need not be defined by the possible or the impossible. In its fundamental essence it expresses the very act of existing. In the gradual order of causes, and as a result of the intellectual abstraction that, for us, has its point of departure in material things (in the substances of the sublunary world), we begin with the possible and go back from there to what is necessary by itself. In the effective order of being, however, the necessity of the necessary existent – God – grounds the derived necessity of possible existents, such that existence is never in itself a contingency, even if it remains contingent for a quiddity to exist, since existence is not constitutive of the essence of the possible existence.

The deep logic of the "Avicennian moment" thus leads to an evacuation of all contingency in the effective order of hierarchies, Intelligences, souls, and bodies. Sadrā's work completes this movement and eliminates all traces of contingency.

It would be useful, in following this movement of the reduction of contingency, to trace the development of two types of causality that play a great role in Aristotle's physics: chance and spontaneity.[58] It is necessary to show how substances composed of matter and form are subject to chance events that raise the question of divine prescience: Does God foresee chance events? Or, in the manner of Leibniz, does the notion of each individual envelop the ensemble of events like so many predicates of a subject? How do chance and spontaneity enter into the network of causality (they are effective causes and not a suspension of causality, a sort of blank page or blind spot in the book of causes) in order to liberate the radical contingency of the future? Finally, how is the contingency of the future combined with the providence integral to God?

These questions gradually came to be organized into a structure that formed the labyrinth of freedom and necessity. In Avicenna, they are not posed in relation to the long history of free will, for one very simple reason: the power of deliberation proper to the rational animal is not conceived of in the terms that will be taken up in the modern debate on free will and the subjugated will, and *a fortiori* in the Christian framework of freedom, original sin, nature, and grace. These questions are sketched out within another problematic framework: What does divine science know? How does God, whose science is one with his will and life, know particular existents? How does he know not only what I will eventually decide — I who am rational — but also what will happen, as an accident that is nonessential to a particular substance of the sublunary world (it being understood that the spheres and what moves them are ruled by a flawless necessity)?

Avicenna maintains that God knows all particulars, but with a universal knowledge, and that he knows their quiddities. Sadrā says that divine science extends to all of the most minute determinations of our existences, and that God knows existents not only with a universal knowledge but also with a particular providential form of knowing. It is thus, no doubt, that this profound necessity of existence, this spontaneity emanating from divine necessity, accounts for, in the end, every space of contingency, if by contingency we mean all of what God foresees without necessitating it absolutely — for example, the share of nonabsolute conditional necessity, and the share that falls to the future, to deliberation, and to chance.

We see that the "contingency" of the possible existent expresses, at best, only the fragility of its existence, the relative weakness of this reassurance in being that its being itself is. The modalities of being designate not the space of a contingency and a freedom confronted with a necessity but a gradation, a variation of intensity or weakness, a position of priority or posteriority in the logic of causes. The consequences of this are great for the status of freedom. Freedom must be thought completely otherwise than as a conciliation of free will and providence, completely otherwise than as a compossibility of divine projects and the infinitely free will of human choice. Freedom must be thought of as an intensification of existence, as a realization of the decree and of predestination, as the trace of divine freedom in the intensity of an existence insofar as it knows itself. Islamic philosophy, culminating with Sadrā's work in a completed ontology of Islam, approaches salvation in a way much like Spinoza, rather than Descartes or Leibniz. It is a spiritual salvation and an ever greater affirmation of necessity at the heart of the possible existent.

Therefore, the question of freedom in Sadrā rests not on the idea of arbitrary free choice but on a doctrine of the will. Free will is present, but subsumed by the question of the will: who wills what I will? Sadrā writes: "Your movement and your rest occur through your will except that your will is not through your will but through the decree and the predestination of God. If it were not so, this will would need another will, and so on to infinity."[59] Here we are indeed within the Avicennian universe of causes, a universe that merges with the theological space of divine decree and predestination. Since one cannot conceive of an existent without a cause, the will needs a cause. But causality cannot go back to infinity (since no existent is able to see its sufficient reason recede to infinity). Therefore God is the cause of the will, but this will does not cease to be my own. Moral responsibility and abandonment to divine decree are one. This provides confirmation – if such were needed – that the philosophy of the act of being in Sadrā has no relation to the modern Western philosophies of existence, conceived of as pure ungrounded act.

In this moment of truth Sadrā will find the origin of his own questions: How can we conceive of the unity of being if we begin by radically distinguishing what a thing is, its quiddity, from the act through which it is assured and positively affirmed in reality, from the actualization of its act, that is, existence? How to reconcile what one previously had to split apart according to the norms of the intellect? How to deal with the strange assertion claiming that existence "comes" to quiddity, that it is an accident of this quiddity, while also being inseparable from quiddity, without being intrinsically constitutive of quiddity? What are we to make of an existence that is at the border of the intrinsic and the extrinsic, that is not completely internal to the existent, since it always comes to it "from outside," but that is not completely foreign to it either, since the existent, as soon as it exists, cannot be perceived in its effective essence, without being perceived as "existent," as receiving existence, which will henceforth go together with it, and will be implied in it?

What we translate as "concomitant," a rather ugly technical term, is the Arabic *al-lāzim*, literally "inherent, adhering." The verb *lazimah* means to adhere, to be inseparable from something, but also to persevere, to be maintained in something, or along with something, and to be required, indispensable. Existence is not an accident of quiddity, if by this one means that it could be separated from this quiddity in concrete reality, since it perseveres in being the very actualization of this quiddity in the real. Existence is, therefore, an accident that is quite difficult to grasp. For the essence in question, it is neither really essential – since the essential reality of the thing must be conceived of without this accident – nor really foreign – since essential reality would be nothing without the act of existing that makes it be, whether in the individual or in a thought.

Scholars of Avicenna's work have not failed to meditate on this strange logic and to link this set of questions to those that, for the sake of convenience, could be summarized thus: Must we say that existence is univocal or equivocal? Does "exist" have one meaning or several? When the history of Avicennism is written, it will appear that its heirs' concern was, above all else, to save the unicity of the divine principle.[60] A concern external to philosophy, this preoccupation with the unity of being satisfies the fundamental requirement for revelation, in which there is no being except in God. Existence must proceed from God, and it must also, in a certain way, return to God; it must never be separated from God but must reside in him and through him. This scriptural exigency converges with the logical exigency of a unique ground for the rationality of discourse, and with the metaphysical exigency of a unique ground for the multiplicity of physical causes.

Must we then give existence the tenuous and somewhat ambiguous status of *lāzim*, that is, something inherent that is inevitable but accidental? Must we reverse the relationship Avicenna establishes between this existence and quiddity? We see here the emergence of an insistent question concerning a precise object:

priority – the priority of existence or that of quiddity. One cannot say that this question is present in Avicenna, since no quiddity exists prior to its act of existing. But it is made possible by some of Avicenna's formulations. He says that quiddity as quiddity is "before" existence, and he proposes that we examine the state of quiddity that exists solely by virtue of divine existence, which could be understood as an ontologically prior state, though not temporally primary. This question of priority will be important for Sadrā, partly because it has become a scholastic question.

But the concern for the unicity of being will also result in valorizing questions of univocality or equivocality. Having firmly bound being to God, having identified absolute being with the divine essence (without considering any reflections on the internal movement of the absolute), was it possible to avoid asking what the consequence are for existence?[61] If existence is said in a single sense, it does not matter whether it is a constitutive of divine essence or a concomitant accident of the essences of possible existents.

Whether possible or necessary, the existent has a single existence. Is there not then the risk of an association between God and his creatures, or, as it was awkwardly called, "existential monism"? But if existence does not have the same sense, both in the case of God and in the case of possible existents, how can one avoid the trap of agnosticism? How can one avoid saying that it is impossible even to know that God exists, since we can no longer ascend to a certain apprehension of absolute existence, namely God, beginning from the existence of the possibles, which is where presence is manifest for us? How can we save the unity of being, which is indispensable to the attestation required by revelation? To escape this double trap, Sadrā will amplify and radicalize a discourse that, before him, was most clearly formulated by the great Avicenna scholar Nasīr al-Dīn al-Tūsī.[62]

Here is Tūsī's interpretation of one of Avicenna's formulations in the *Ishārāt*: "But it is not possible for the attribute (*sifah*) of existence to belong to the thing only because of its quiddity – which is not existence – or because of another attribute, since the cause is prior in existence; but there is no antecedent by existence before existence."[63] Avicenna presents two theses. On the one hand, existence is an attribute, and this attribute cannot belong to the thing only because of the quiddity of the thing, since existence is not constitutive of this quiddity. Quiddity does not account for the existence of the thing. On the other hand, the cause of this existence cannot be found in another attribute of the thing, since the cause must exist before its effect, and the attribute that is the cause of the existence would have to exist prior to the existence that would be its effect. But nothing can be prior to existence through existence.

Nasīr al-Dīn al-Tūsī examines this "priority" of existence within the framework of the Avicennian theory. His commentary is important, because he places us at the center of the interrogation of "priority" – the antecedence of existence – that will provoke the Sadrian revolution. But it is also important because it preserves something that Sadrā will radically call into question: the status of existence, seen here too as an "attribute" of the thing. Sadrā says that existence is not an attribute like the others. There are attributes that can very well be causes of other attributes, so that difference can be the cause of the proper. For example, the difference of the human species, rationality or being-rational *(al-nātiqīyah)*, is the cause of what is proper to man, astonishment. As an attribute that is proper to man, this capacity to be astonished can be the cause of something else proper to man, laughter. But this is not the case with existence. What distinguishes existence from all the other attributes "is that the other attributes exist only because of quiddity, whereas quiddity exists because of existence."

This is a very important statement; it announces all the Sadrian propositions. But it is still trapped in the Avicennian metaphysics that, as we have seen, is not reducible to a "metaphysics of essences," but makes possible a reflection that will reach the threshold at which the causal priority of existence can be thought. Existence is indeed an attribute, but this attribute has the astonishing power to make something effectively be, to realize quiddity in its entirety. The exteriority of existence with respect to quiddity—or at least what we have called its "border" situation, between internal and external—authorizes existence to be the cause of the act of being of quiddity (*al-māhīyah tūjad bi-sabab al-wujūd*).

What, then, is the status of this existence? Nasīr al-Dīn al-Tūsī takes on his illustrious predecessor, Fakhr al-Dīn Rāzī, who, according to him, "is troubled in this passage by a certain confusion."[64] Rāzī maintains that existence is "a single thing," in short, that it is understood in a univocal manner, and that the existence of the Necessary (God) is "equivalent" to the existence of the possibles. The consequence of Rāzī's thesis, according to Tūsī, is that since existence is an accidental reality for the quiddities of the possibles, and since existence is understood univocally, then for God, too, existence is an accident. The quiddity of God is thus other than his existence, and God loses his fundamental unity and simplicity. Whatever the relevance of the attack, what is important is the solution Tūsī proposes, a solution that will have great consequences for Sadrā: existence occurs by analogy (*bi-l-tashkīk*).[65] Existence comes to different things not equivocally, univocally, or identically (*lā 'alah al-sawā'*), but "by analogy."

This question concerning existence, the manner in which it comes to things emanating from God, the univocality or equivocality of its signification, its unity and diversity, thus lead to the notion of *tashkīk*, analogy, which allows one to escape the double trap of associationism and agnosticism. But this notion, in turn, allows one to examine the causes of the mutual differentiation (*ikhtilāf*) of existences. If existence is both like itself in all existents and different from itself according to whether it constitutes the divine ipseity or happens to possibles, this differentiation must be generalized to the entire arc of existences, from the principle to the limit of first matter. It is necessary, then, to state the three types of differentiation of existence, the three modes of hierarchization that will form "the set of differences" brought together by existence.

The first mode of differentiation is that which is brought about by priority and posteriority. Continuity thus comes to dimensional extension before coming to the body possessing extension. Corporeal extension in general is continuous, and this continuity is prior in the hierarchy of existents to the continuity of a singular body belonging to extension. Therefore, the existence of the continuous in extension is prior to its existence in a body, and this relation of order hierarchizes and differentiates the two existences.

The second mode of differentiation is that which is effected by primacy and by the absence of primacy. It is thus that oneness is attributed first to what fundamentally cannot be divided, and second to what can be divided but from a certain perspective is one.

Finally, the third mode of differentiation is thought in terms of intensity and weakness. Nasīr al-Dīn al-Tūsī's example is the attribution of white to snow and ivory, snow being more intensely white than ivory. The whiteness that we grant as a predicate to snow and ivory is attributed to each one not in a univocal way but by analogy. It seems, then, that Nasīr al-Dīn al-Tūsī does not place analogy at the heart of univocality; rather, he thinks of it as a concrete structure of existence escaping from the pair univocality-equivocality. The whiteness of snow does not exist in the same way as the whiteness of ivory exists, since it is more intense; but it does not exist in another way either, since it is, in both substances, an accident called whiteness.

Between synonymy and homonymy, the whiteness of ivory and snow varies not according to the notion but according to the intensity of the act of existing. It is not quiddity that varies or is differentiated. Rather, it is an external, concomitant, or separate accident. In the case of snow and ivory, for example, what undergoes a variation is not the quiddity of one or the other, nor even a part of their quiddities, but whiteness, which is a concomitant accident, inseparable from them, certainly, but coming to them from outside their nature. This color, whiteness, can exist in infinite degrees, and these degrees are all given the same name, whiteness, although they vary infinitely among themselves, from the most intense to the weakest. We speak of red and black in the same way as "white," but there are, potentially, infinite reds, whites, and blacks.

Likewise, "the attribution of existence relates to the existence of the Necessary and to the existence of the possible." And what we call "the possible existent" is just like color. Like color, it does not possess detailed names, whereas it has potentially infinite variations, through intensity or weakness, such that in actuality we are dealing with infinite and hierarchized series of possible existences.

At the heart of the Avicennian schema, a very important notion emerges: *intensity*.[66] Existence, conceived of as a concomitant of possibles, not as constitutive, is determined by its degree of intensity. The consequence of this is that every grade of beings will be intuited according to a movement of increasing or decreasing intensification, according to a relative intensification or a relative weakening. The concept of intensity will have an ontological value, but it will also have an ethical and perhaps a political value.

Conceived of by analogy with the status of a predicate (color), the notion of an intensity of existence will make it possible to think the analogy of existence. We can already see that this is a forced analogy: we pass from a predicate of essence to a predicate of existence. But the important thing is indeed the appearance of this notion of intensity and, through it, of intensification, which will lead Sadrā, from the very heart of the Avicennian moment, to radically modify the status of existence. Ceasing to be a concomitant of quiddity, it will fully become the act of being whose variable intensity will determine its place within the continuous flux of what he will call substantial motion: the origin will be located at the maximum intensity of the divine being, and the lowest degree will border on the nonbeing of first matter.

Chapter Four

Freedom and Intensity

Activity and Substantial Movement

The act of being is not an accident but the constitutive principle of things, "that through which the thing becomes one among all concrete realities."[1] It leaves the periphery of the existent to be instantiated at its center; for this existent, it is the real center and focus of its reality.[2] It determines the concrete becoming of the thing and cannot be confused with the abstract universal concept of being. The abstract concept of being in general represents an existence that is merely thought and that the mind attributes to an essence as a concomitant, without ever being able to reach living spontaneity through this addition of abstractions. If the act of being is the generative center of the ensemble of events organized in relation to a singular thing, not only does our doctrine change, but so does the very mode of our perception of being.

The antinomy between "points of view" – between the intellectual primacy of quiddity over existence and the real primacy of existence over quiddity – vanishes when we privilege the knowledge of the act of being in the increasing intensification of an actual reality, and when we cease to represent abstractions arising from a mental distinction between quiddity and existence. Sadrā was able to leave the terrain of Avicennian metaphysics (by which he was deeply influenced, as we have seen) because he abandoned the logic of essence and existence to return to effective reality and its movement according to the intensive freedom of the real.

The act of being is entirely in its activity (*nafs al-fi'līyah*).[3] Identifying real being with the energy of activity, Sadrā wants to remain faithful to the Aristotelian perspective. The possible existent passes from potency to act; it deploys a certain energy whose final term is a full actualization in entelechy. That is why potentiality is relative nonbeing. Being can be ascribed only to what presents a certain actualization (*husūl*, corresponding to the Latin *actuatio*), an actualization translating itself into a manifest occurrence (*wuqū'*). Reality is never completely stabilized in any particular existent; rather, it sets the existent in motion, in its substance, toward higher thresholds of perfection. In Sadrā, the notion of actualization or of actualizing intensity determines a doctrine of substantial motion whose importance for the palingenesis of the soul we will see below. Being is permanent metamorphosis, not stasis or definition; it can never be reduced to *what* a thing is. Conversely, what each thing is expresses a degree of actualization, a provisional station that tends to be fixed only by thought. We are mistaken when we hypostasize the act of being by representing it with a verbal noun (*ma'nah masdarī*). Real being is an act and is contained entirely in this act; it is not the name of the act that expresses the being that comes to be completed by actualization. Being "is the very reality of the occurrence," and it is in this actual occurrence that its goodness resides.

How could abstract being be a pure good? The good is an object of desire. It must be effective and real, for desires, nature, will, and natural disposition do not turn toward the mere fictions of the understanding. Nothing and no one seeks, with the intimate desire at the heart of one's nature, a mere abstract signification. No one aspires to possess a first intelligible. In his philosophy of resurrection, Sadrā will say that the effective salvation of the soul would be derisory if it were a question of the intellect possessing knowledge of a few conceptual generalities. If there is a desire for eternity, and if this desire encounters its object, it is necessary for eternity to be an effective reality, a concrete state of being, an experiential truth.

Thus we can begin to elucidate the relationship between the

effective being of a thing and its quiddity. Quiddity is inseparable from the act that makes it be as a concrete individual. But it is secondary with regard to the act of being, and the beingness of quiddity (*mawjūdiyat al-māhīyah*) emerges into being only through the effectivity of the act of being that grounds it. The "reality" of a pure quiddity fades away. Prior to the attestation of an essence, it is always necessary to perceive the effectivity of a divine, concrete, or mental reality.

In actualizing itself, the act of being of an individual grounds the manifestation of a quiddity through actuality itself. The rose is not first a rose that then receives concrete existence; it is an inflection of the real, a divine rose enveloped in the secret of divine names, an intelligible rose, an imaginal rose, a sensible rose, according to the more or less intense modalities of its act of existing, and it thus makes its essence exist. This modalization of the rose will be its concrete becoming in the hierarchy of the universes, from the proximity of God to the shadowy composite of form and inferior matter. Existence does not precede essence but constitutes it at a certain degree of freedom, spontaneity, and subtlety, or, on the contrary, at a certain degree of opacity and material constraint. At each degree of this expansive movement, the quiddity of the rose expresses the relative limitation of its act of being.

The quiddities therefore have no reality by themselves, since their beingness is actualized through the beingness of the thing itself, the concrete individual.[4] When thought conceives of them, it grasps only an abstraction, a representation, which requires in the intellect a mental existence communicated by this intellect and by the act of cognition. But these quiddities "eternally breathe the fragrance of being": they proceed from the "breath of the Merciful," from the existentiative expansion by which the divine unity deploys the expression of its names and attributes.[5] We asked whether this allusion to Ibn al-'Arabī contradicted Sadrā's approach. How is it possible to reconcile the fundamental nothingness of quiddity and the existence of eternal essences? How could Ibn al-'Arabī's Platonism harmonize with a doctrine that accords the real of all reality to the act of existing? By ceasing to split the act of being from quiddity.

Sadrā receives the acknowledgment of this split from the Avicennian tradition, and his point of departure is located where the split between existence and quiddity demands a reconciliation. But he in no way reverses the priority of one over the other. In posing the question of the priority of existence over quiddity, he does away with the question itself. He reverses the problem that arose in the Avicennian moment of thought. He says that "the qualification of quiddity by existence is an abstraction of thought."[6] One ought no longer to ask whether one is prior to, posterior to, or contemporaneous with the other. Quiddity and existence are one; essence *is* existence.

This is the point of rupture between Sadrā and his master, Mīr Dāmād. It is striking to observe that the latter does not grant any real importance to the questions we are addressing in these pages; he proceeds as if they went without saying. Indeed, he maintains that "existence, in the thing itself, is the firm establishment of the thing (*thubūt*) and its real effectuation (*tahaqquq*) within its own limits, and not through the operation of the intelligence in any aspect whatever."[7] What is important to Mīr Dāmād is to affirm that in God existence is identical to essence. But the consequence, according to him, is that in the possible existent, existence is always added to quiddity.[8] Mīr Dāmād wants to distinguish radically between the status of the divine essence and the status of the essences of possible existents. How is it possible to do this if one does not distinguish between the status assigned to the existence of God, on the one hand, and the possibles, on the other? The commentary on the *Book of Burning Coals* (*Sharh Kitāb al-Qabasāt*) by Mīr Dāmād's student Ahmad al-'Alawī illuminates this point: God is singular through his very existence, which is not the case for any merely possible existent.[9] In him, singularity, existence, and essence are one, whereas there is no possible whose existence and whose quiddity are one. In this sense, existence is added to the quiddity of the possible existent.[10] This is precisely the scheme that Sadrā rejects.

The fundamental identity of being is always threatened by the abstractions of thought. Sadrā does not attempt to make the original unity of essence and existence the result of an effective dialectical process; rather, he treats it as the immediate given of the *presence* of the thing, for which thought irresistibly substitutes an abstract division, an imaginary split. "The existence of each existent is this existent itself *in concreto*."[11] Given the identity of the effective existent with its act of being and the immanence of the act of being to the reality of the existent, it follows that quiddity is inessential. Essence is no longer thought in terms of the fixity of quiddity. The identity of essence and existence is an identity of existence and the existent, such that quiddity becomes expendable and must enter the realm of shadows. The existent is a limited light, projecting its share of shadow, if it is a possible existent; it is pure light if it is the existent that is necessary through itself. "But to reflect the light / Bespeaks another half of shade."[12]

In Sadrā, the ontology of Islam reaches its completion. But it is not completed in the synthesis of the concept; rather, it is fulfilled in the return to the luminous essence, identical to the act of being of light.[13] Sadrā definitively orients the ontology of Islam toward immediate presence; he translates the immediate given of Islamic consciousness, which is the grasping of reality in the scheme of *appearance*. All things are appearance, because to be real is to appear, and because all that appears is an appearance of the real. Appearance and veil, light and shadow, exteriority and interiority, manifestation and effectivity: these are the categories of an aesthetics of the absolute.

The Luminous Essence

It is by being pluralized that the light of being receives its qualifications. This plural definition expresses the intensity of luminescence, which is the potency of effectivity (*shiddat al-nūrīyah, quwwat al-wujūd*). Intensity, or potency, is revealed, accompanying the luminous effusion of a continuous enshadowing. The multiple's conversion back toward the one is an intensification of reality, a liberation from limits, a return to the free source of instantiation. The series of processions is a continuous degradation of the infinite intensity and initial freedom of the real; it translates into an ontological deficiency, down to the degree of dense and opaque material bodies. The most manifest is also the most difficult to perceive: the very intense act of being, the immaterial luminous realities that are "at the extreme limit of the potency of being and of luminous intensity," which elude our inferior knowledge and the authority of our judgments.[14] Conversely, we easily perceive sensible bodies within the process of our natural growth, but these bodies extinguish their truth in the shadow of their deficiency.[15]

Intensification increases all the way up to the light of lights. It is significant that Sadrā takes up Suhrawardī's concept for his own purposes, designating the source of all illumination in order to think the absolute act of being, the real of realities or of the monads of existence (*wujūd al-wujūdāt*). This maximal intensity is the integral manifestation of the absolute and necessarily remains withdrawn from all perception of the mind. The mind grasps the revelations of the light of lights in derivative acts of being, in appearances by what is most apparent – light itself. But this aura eludes its own perceptive grasp. The most real world in our eyes, in our natural life, is also the most unreal; it is the one in which the real is veiled by the perishable existent, "tinted with the color of different quiddities." Our ambient world has the colors of the unreal; in it, the effective singularities of light are veiled beneath abstract generalities, and we perceive sensible bodies naively, for we are unaware that in perceiving them we perceive something imaginary.[16]

We call "necessary being" the act of being at its maximum intensity. It is the light that illuminates but not the supreme light; radiant light but not the highest radiance of light. It is therefore not a "being" – the supreme being – but the real of every being. It is absolute immanence in absolute transcendence, the generative source of all the intensities that are inferior to the infinite: the infinite is at the center of the finite. The perfection of necessary being is equivalent to the maximal evidence of its light, whereas the derivative lights are established at a greater and greater distance from their source. Opaque bodies seem to us to be *here*, whereas their effective reality, the source of their light, is very distant. The pure presence of necessary being, the cause of their causes, fades away from them and becomes absent, so that it *seems* transcendent in relation to the world.

When spiritual knowledge has inverted the relationship to light, in our third "birth" or growth, it can finally appear that the absolute act of being is the most manifest of realities: "Because of the weakness of our intelligences, and because they are submerged in matter, from the fact that they are closely related to the realities of nothingness and the shadows, it is difficult to know necessary being and impossible for us to intelligize it as it is in being."[17] Here below, we are without remedy, distanced by our shadows from the "mines of light and manifestation," unless we practice the repeated techniques of purification on our souls. Morality serves the exegesis of light, and light purifies conduct and morals to appear finally as what it is.

In the effusion of reality, the quiddities are similar to the tints of various colors in the refraction of light:

> Observe the hierarchical degrees of light that emanate from the sun, this image of God in the world of sensible realities. See how the pieces of glass are colored by the tint of the colors. There is no difference between them, except in the intensity of the colors or in their weakness. Someone who goes no further than the pieces of glass and their color, no further than the veiling they cause in relation to the real light and its real degrees of emanation—for such a person the light is hidden from him. He is like those who profess that the quiddities are effective realities, firmly implanted in being, whereas the realities of the act of being are abstract things, things of pure thought.[18]

This is an astonishing reversal of Suhrawardī's thesis, accomplished through a meditation on light that claims to be faithful to the philosophy of illumination and to the *Oriental* wisdom of Suhrawardī. The value granted to the quiddities is an optical illusion. Fascinated by the epiphany, we no longer see what is epiphanized. But this passage has more than a polemical value. It situates the aesthetics of epiphany within a gradual process that allows one to accede to the light of the real. Each thing is an epiphany, because its reality is constituted by the light refracted in it. Perception indirectly grasps this light by way of the special tint it has taken on. The optical illusion begins when we isolate the epiphany from its source and privilege the color of the thing, its shape, its delineation in reality. We isolate it, and we think irresistibly that it is what it is by virtue of *this (thing) that* it is, its quiddity, and not by virtue of this (thing) *that it is*, the very fact of existing. We no longer see what appears in it, the splendor of the real; rather, we are caught in the veils of that which carries the thing into nothingness.

Sadrā's Platonizing aesthetics are not an exaltation of epiphanies for their own sake, just as the Platonic approach accords value to beautiful things not for what they are but as signs that must be interpreted. Their splendor must lead back to the source of all beauty — the beautiful in itself, according to Plato; the source of light, according to Sadrā. The aesthetics of the real is an exegesis of our gaze, which goes from the revealed to that which reveals itself. Such is the force of the epiphany that it tears us away from itself in order to let pure light be mirrored in it. It is the effective origin of love and the ground of its spiritual virtue.

The contemplative man privileges the point of view of the real. For him, what appears is light itself. He knows the monadic degrees for what they are: manifestations that are pluralized according to their aptitudes and particular receptivities, just as the colored tints translate the receptivity of the glass. He perceives so many "flashes of effectively real and necessary light."[19] Existents are led back to their veritable essence: they are revelations (*zuhūrāt*). The perception of epiphany is a vision of light that traverses things and constitutes them as a mirror of this effusion. At the same time, these epiphanies must be manifest at the rank imposed on them by their dimension of receptivity. They take the form of quiddities and "are tinted with the colors of quiddities made of the mere possibility of being."

The singularity of each existent is inflected according to two aspects: that of its fundamental necessity, derived from the necessary light, and that of its relative potentiality. It is, on the one hand, a divine, necessary ipseity, a surging of intensive light, and, on the other hand, a quiddity, a form intrinsically united to it, in which it is colored and veiled. The creative activity of the real thus requires sites of manifestation (*mazāhir*). It is a theophanic operation, and every effusion of a monad of existence is accompanied by the manifestation of a divine name. It is impossible to conceive of the quiddities in which realities are colored without attaching them to the operations in which the divine attributes and names are epiphanized.

This effusion, which is the existentiation of existents, is the production of monads. Quiddities are the receptacles or the supports of their development, and the effusion takes place upon the quiddities. What, then, is the being of quiddities? It is the act of being that projects its ray of light onto them, that is reflected against the dark ground of the mirror, and that constitutes it as a site of manifestation. It is the capacity for being an epiphanic site (*al-mazharīyah*). The being of quiddities is entirely in their epiphanic function. Thus we can resolve the apparent contradiction between the nonbeing of quiddities and their quasi being, thanks to the theophanic scheme of existence.[20] All the forms that are enveloped in divine science are mirrored forms. The substances and their accidents are not being but the mirror image of being. This is not to say, however, that this image of being differs from the being reflected in it. Indeed, "there appears in the mirror only the act of being itself, which is reflected in it." The real is the other of the image, but the reality of the image is the real itself.

The Mirror of Appearances

There are two points of view regarding quiddities that will make it possible to generalize the model of the mirror. According to the first point of view, quiddities are the mirrors of the act of being of the divine real, of its names and attributes. According to the second point of view, the act of being of the real is the mirror of quiddities, since they appear in it, as the concomitants of its names and attributes. The divine principle is the mirror in which quiddities are manifest; they have no other epiphanic site than the real itself, no other being than the act of being. But quiddities are the mirror of the principle, since they are the epiphanic sites of its names and attributes. According to this generalized model, the mirror is a mirror of mirrors, and being is the reflection of itself onto itself, the epiphany of epiphanies, a mirror that gives back the image of a mirror in which its image is reflected. The principle, the real, is this unique point, a pure intensity, which is the blind spot of all manifestation. As soon as we are situated at the level of its revelation in the names and attributes, we enter a universe of images, a network of mirrors. Islam is the world in which reality is always speculative, because it can only be speculative, and in which all things, from created beings all the way to God, are revealed. Each is a light reflected within another light, suspended in a realm of shadows and appearances in which dreams are premonitory and the most vivid action quickly returns to the world of dreams.

The mirror of the real finds its own mirror in the real. The fully contemplative man is the witness of the three "births," the one here below and those of the imagination and of the intelligible. He contemplates both these mirrors — the creaturely world and the world of the imperative, the mirror of forms and the mirror of the real — in their unity, with no dissociation or differentiation. The dialectic of unity and multiplicity is converted for him into a specular exchange.

Philosophy is exegesis because it is always sustained by a relationship to the revealed text of the Qur'ān or to the prophetic illuminations and inspired teachings of the imams. But it is also exegesis in another sense. It raises our inner gaze from one plane of existence to the higher degrees, from an appearance to its source, from an image to a model, according to the play of the mirrors of being. Philosophy is an optics of the real that explores the sites of appearance. Its guiding principle is that everything that appears possesses a "hidden" dimension; it is a principle of generalized esotericism. But why speak of the apparent and the hidden? Because we must always return to the essence of the phenomenon. Sadrā perceives all things as phenomena, without the slightest remainder of a "thing in itself"; the thing is constituted entirely by its act of appearing, which is its act of being, its effectivity. But what would an appearance be that had no correspondence with anything "hidden," with a higher plane of being to ground its surging forth into reality? It would be a mere phantom, a figure (*shabh*) that would contain no spirit.[21]

It is necessary to save the "world of form" from being a form without consistency, a purely spectral play of mirrors. It is to this demand that exegesis responds: "God created no thing in the world of form that does not possess a correspondent in the world of signification, and he instantiated no thing in the otherworld that does not possess a correspondent and a spirit in the world of principles and of the return." The three "worlds" – that of sensible material forms, that of imaginal significations (the otherworld), and that of entirely immaterial spiritual principles in which all things return to the final term of the substantial motion of elevation and intensification – correspond with one another, and the last one grounds the two other, inferior worlds. This gradation corresponds to the triple correspondence of effective reality (*haqīqah*), which devolves to the intelligible spiritual world; inner signification (*bātin*), which corresponds to the imaginal world; and appearance (*zāhir*), which corresponds to the sensible world.

> The lower is an image and an apparitional form of the higher, and the higher is the effective reality and the spirit of the lower, and thus proceeds what is still the most eminent, until it is completed in the

> reality of realities, the mystery of mysteries, the light of lights, the act of being of acts of being. All that resides in this world is a figuration; they are receptacles of what resides in the world of psychic spirits, just as these psychic spirits are the figuration of what resides in the world of immaterial and complete intelligible spirits. These latter are, in turn, the figuration and the sites of manifestation of what resides in the world of eternal divine essences.[22]

Bodies make souls appear; souls makes intelligences appear; each degree of the world of the soul is psychic spirit; each degree of the intelligible world is pure immaterial spirit. All the various degrees lead back to the eternal essences, which express the breath of the Merciful. The physical, psychic, and intelligible worlds are all three apparitional forms (*ashbāh*) of these essences, which are the epiphanies of the divine names. Each corporeal form is the specter of a psychic spirit, which is the specter of an intelligible; the three worlds are the specters of the essences, and there is nothing truly real except the divine names, which are one with the divine essence.

Only God is real, whereas his epiphanies are mere specters, according to the meaning of the Arabic word *al-shabh*, plural *al-ashbāh*. These specters are silhouettes, and often Sadrā recognizes in them a reality that he distinguishes from the cast shadow: thus the act of being is to quiddity what the silhouette is to the shadow. But he also makes it the equivalent of symbolic realities (*rumūz*) that owe their meaning and their being to what they symbolize. Finally, and above all, all things are passing away, and only God subsists.[23]

In Suhrawardī's visionary experience, the "apparitional forms" bear witness to the world of supersensible realities. Let us quote this admirable passage from Book Five of *The Philosophy of Illumination*:

> At times they contemplate the forms of what is, and at times they see human forms of great beauty addressing the most beautiful words to them and conversing with them in confidence about the invisible

> world; at other times these forms appear to them like those figures created by the most delicate art of the painters. Sometimes they appear as though in an enclosure; sometimes they see forms and figures "in suspense." Everything that one perceives in a dream — mountains, oceans, and continents, extraordinary voices, individuals — these are all so many figures and forms subsisting by themselves.[24]

Such are the visionary dreams, the prophetic visions, the imaginal perceptions, and the sensations, scents, musical sounds, and paintings that emanate from the higher world. Specters populate the world of truthful appearances and thus fashion the aesthetics of prophecy. Sadrā preserves this power in the forms of appearance. And here form is used in the Aristotelian sense of the substantial form of each existent, its specific form. But it has undergone two major modifications.

Since the act of being determines the degree of intensity of the concrete existent, substantial form is no longer the center of this existent. It expresses henceforth the generative activity that deploys it. But this activity changes the forms that it animates, following a movement that Aristotle probably would not have accepted. The moving form is perceived as an appearance of the light of being that actualizes it, sets it in motion, and transports it from world to world. Sensible form is converted into a form of the imagination, which is converted into an intelligible form. It is similar to a movement that goes from the crudest and most shadowy to the most concrete, the most vivid, and the most luminous. It is the movement carried out by the painter of miniatures when he stylizes bodies in order to place them within the graceful space of the image. The painter realizes the exegesis that the philosopher describes with his awkward words. Form ceases to be a mere conceptual given and is instead grasped by simple perception. Ontology becomes aesthetics.

Form is the appearance of the divine in the sensible, in the imagination, or in the intelligence; it is never an abstraction of the understanding. But it is indeed also an appearance, since its provisional fixity is wrought by a nostalgia for what cannot appear in it, for what is veiled as soon as it is perceived, and which alone remains: the creative imperative of the Painter par excellence, who is God. The world of essences is a world of epiphanies, an ascendant world of infinitely numerous degrees, which carries in itself, within the hierarchy of its degrees, the feeling of what it has lost.

At the end of Balzac's short story "A Passion in the Desert," the hero, a young soldier of the Empire who has become an old *grognard*, says: "In the desert, you see, there is everything and there is nothing.... it is God without men."[25] The worlds are shades of one another, and in their totality they are doomed to disappear and to return to the plane of divine names, which are the face of God revealing itself to its own creation. The divine names are the highest manifestation of the act of being: in them alone is reality truly real, and it is toward them that the exegesis of being must be oriented, in order to see its effective reality unveiled.[26]

The Act of Being Is a Subject

We know that it is possible to cognize the effective reality of the act of being if one is disposed to welcome it in an immediate illumination of its presence—that is, if one carefully distinguishes this presence from the cognition of substance, composed of matter and form. The ipseity of the act of being is absolutely simple and is not the result of bringing together different parts, as matter and form would be.[27] More generally, it is impossible to represent the composition that would affect the reality of the act of being. Nothing precedes it in its pure spontaneity, and the effectivity of the being, before establishing itself in being, possesses nothing—it depends on nothing in order to be, and nothing is doubled or reiterated in it. The act of being is always primary; no nonbeing precedes it, and it is the product of its own foundation. It is established through itself, and it is the act of being itself (*wujūd dhātih*). The act of being is a subject; it is the principle of all subjectivation, in that it is this "self" that is reflected immediately in itself, this existence that is first and foremost existence of self, needing nothing else in order to be itself. Without a ground, with no origin other than its own effusion, the act of being is a self, expressing itself, in its pure freedom, in multiple series of manifestations, without anything previously determining or causing it.

Sadrā says, "The act of being is bound to no other reality by virtue of its own self," which justifies the negative path discussed above.[28] The negative path eliminates every necessitating link on which the act of being seems to depend. The effective reality of being is an ungrounded freedom, a freedom that is in itself instantiation. The whole of determinate existence, according to the hierarchy of possibles, originates in this first freedom, which is the sole ipseity of the real. We can distinguish the act of being in itself—which is pure detachment, freedom or spontaneity of being without determination or composition—from the manifestations of this freedom in concrete determinations. From there, the act of being then proceeds to its own limitations, which are the consequences of its position in the emanating flow. This flow leads from the absolutely immaterial degrees down to the prison of first matter and nonbeing.

The real movement of effusion animating derivative existence —the movement of "descent"—prepares the movement of "reascent" or the "upward return" of conversion, which in man recapitulates the totality of its "stations," up to the greatest proximity with the divine essence. The divine essence, as pure existence, remains out of reach—even though it is also the origin of the descent and the destination of the return—because it is more than perfect and is superabundant in being and in reality. The conjunction of all the degrees, the ranks of the existent (sublimated in man) and of God (pure act of being), will be, simultaneously, the ecstatic final term of being in its substantial movement of intensification, and a term infinitely distant from any complete union. It will be the pure limit, the maximum steepness of the existent's "upward return" toward its origin, a pure spontaneous freedom of existing that can be approached by a transfigured angelic existence, but that can never be appropriated by this existence because of its eternal status as created freedom.

The movement toward being is infinite and interminable, and the act of being that effuses from God is gathered into God without ever reaching the full reconciliation that would be translated by a final stasis. In the various degrees of emanation, the freedom of the act of being is subject, through its own limitation or relative shadow, to accidental determinations, from which come multiple attachments to all that falls under the categories of quiddities, substances, relationships, places, and times. The history of being is infinitely open-ended.

In itself, the act of being is the pure and detached real, without foundation, even through itself. Free from all that belongs to substances, it is not characterized by any of the four causes: it has no matter, no substrate, no form, no finality. Being is not *causa sui*; "it has been unveiled that it has no cause at all, that there is no cause through it, no cause coming from it, no cause proceeding outside of it, and no cause for it within it." One thinks its nature in the radicality of the negation that preserves the pure detachment of the act of being, in the mirror of its multiple examples in concrete things, in the variable and moving communication of its spontaneous surging forth and of its affirmation, which is the real itself. These examples are the manifestations, but also the inevitable veils, of finite existence, whereas in its principle of freedom there is unveiling, pure light. Sadrā remains strongly influenced by the Aristotelian and Avicennian conception of the divine act of being. While conceiving of the real as pure detachment, pure spontaneous freedom of effusion of self, he defines the act of being as pure good and the ultimate finality. That is why he can say that the act of being is the agent of agents, the form of forms, the goal of goals.

To the extent that Sadrā follows Avicenna and distinguishes the act of being from everything that falls into one of the ten categories, he can give a foundation to presential knowledge: presential knowledge receives its evidence from the act of being, whereas conceptual reason is incapable of this. There are no concepts or rational definitions that do not fall into a category, whether substance or accident. This is the meaning of the critique aimed at every doctrine that makes the act of being a concomitant of essence, since such a concomitant will be conceived of, *nolens volens*, as an "accident" and will threaten to fall back into the logical field marked out by the categories. But "the act of being's way of being (*kawn al-wujūd*) is not, in its essence, a substance, or a quality, or another [category], and this by virtue of the fact that its mode of being does not consist in the fact of being universal."[29] The categories designate universals. It is enough to be named under the heading of a relationship – paternity, for example, or the being that writes – in order to fall under some generality. Then the act of being, which is pure singularity, fades away.

From its affirmation in itself as pure indeterminate freedom to the final term of its effusion in the examples of its determinations, the act of being is always a singularity. The entire procession of acts of existing, united with the accidents of the quiddities and the universals, is distanced from pure self-presence at its source and passes through the multiple individuations of its originary simplicity. To make the real a pure freedom, to identify the real with the self-grounding spontaneity of existing, is to identify the real of each existent with the generative source of its singular existence, from which it proceeds and which remains immanent to it. This generative source is a reality of existence.

The realities of existence (*wujūdāt*) are therefore monads constituted by pure existence, living singularities at the center of concrete existents and of the essences of these existents. Their irreducible singularity is shown insofar as they are concrete ipseities individuated through themselves. The order of what is effectively concrete (*'ayn*) is the order of the monadic one, expressing the ineffable and unqualifiable unity of the act of being; it is the regime of concrete monads or the concrete unity of the freedom of existence. The monadic deployment of the freedoms of being is subject to the progressive determination of its own pluralization, according to the points of view regarding being, and it receives the accidentality of the quiddities based on divine decree, which is free and creative spontaneity. Thus decree and predestination are not opposed to the effusion of freedom and singularity, since they are the very order of this effusion. In them, the necessity and the freedom of the existent find their first unity, their common origin.

The individuated concrete ipseities are not subsumed under a universal concept of essence (*mafhūm kullī dhātī*). They fall under no generic or specific definition. The monads of existence cannot be thought as if they were in any way accidents for quiddities. It is not even possible to say, as Avicenna does, that the quiddities subsist through the existence that comes to them. Being is not something that can be abstracted by the understanding; the act of being is not abstract, intelligible being, a pure verbal noun (*al-intizā'ī, al-'aqlī, al-masdarī*). This verbal noun, "being," is conceived of as the accident common to all existents. It is as empty as it is general. It is the being that turns into nonbeing, since it is not affirmed in the simplicity of its singularity. Sadrā critiques the earlier metaphysicians because they all think of existing on the basis of judgments of existence: substance *is* (possesses being as a property attributed to it by the intellect), and quality, quantity, and relation *are* through the being of their substrate, and so on. Existence, in this case, always needs a substrate in which it is thought, in which it resides: existence *of* the flower, of the soul, of the Intelligence.

And yet, in truth, the flower is a flower of existence, a flowering of a monadic degree of being, a flower of intensity and of spontaneous freedom. The act of being is not an accident that happens to quiddity, because it is not the being of quiddity in the sense that it could ever be separated from quiddity; it is quiddity effectively existing, or rather the generative source of this quiddity when it exists, when it manifests as real.

The generative source of a thing can be detached from it only by an operation of the understanding that converts it into an empty abstraction (the "being" of substance, the "being" of the accident), whereas the act of being of the accident is the accident itself *in its realness*; it resides in the accidentality of the accident, and not through an accidentality added to that of the accident. The accident expresses its act of existing by being this accident, by affirming itself in the real as the accident that it is, not by receiving an accident of existence, an adventitious act added to its nature as an accident. Likewise for substance: "We choose to say that the act of being of substance is substance through the substantiality of this substance, not through another substantiality."[30]

Being is manifestation, pure shining forth of the existent; it is the revelation of this existent in the intensive space of the hierarchized worlds. This is what justifies borrowing the lexicon of light from Suhrawardī and the Ishrāqīyah. The act of being is similar to light, not in the general and abstract sense of a "light-being" (*Lichtwesen*) but concretely, in individuals. It is manifest through itself. Sadrā identifies being with the *apparent*, which is Suhrawardī's point of departure in *The Philosophy of Illumination*: "If there is in being something that needs neither to be defined nor to be explained, it is the apparent (*zāhir*). And there is nothing that is more apparent than light."[31] Like light – and because it *is* light – the act of being knows no internal differentiation except through the degree of intensity or weakness, which is also the degree of priority or posteriority in emanation.

Sadrā thus turns the analogy of being into something completely different from a logical solution to the problem of the predication of existence. We have seen that Nasīr al-Dīn al-Tūsī maintained that existence is predicated *kbi-l-tashkīk*, "analogically," from the existent that is necessary through itself and of the possible existent. This is not a purely logical thesis, if by that we mean that it is of interest only in the order of discourse. For Tūsī, this "analogy" of existence was already something quite real. The difference between existences occurs, indeed, he says, on the basis of intensity or weakness.

The Skepticism of Being

The term *al-tashkīk* is derived from a root whose principal meaning is to suspect, to entertain doubts. Literally it means "skepticism," a suspension of belief. But, as Cécile Bonmariage rightly points out, "the root *sh-k-k* also has the sense of 'arranging in a series.' A term is qualified as *mushakkik* when the reality it corresponds to is susceptible to modulation, this modulation being most often understood in a sense of gradation."[32] It seems to me that both registers of meaning—that of doubt and that of gradation—ought to be preserved. The act of being is animated by a movement that robs it of all permanence in each of the ranks or degrees of existence that it traverses or instantiates. It thus *places in doubt* the reality of these provisional stations to which its impetus has carried it. It establishes them and disestablishes them all at once, since it is fundamentally simple and univocal. The necessary plurality of its emanations must be gathered together in its fundamental unity, and, reciprocally, this unity must always be established beyond any of its expressions.

This skepticism of being places into doubt the truth in and for itself, the separate, fixed, and definitive reality of each degree of its expression, and that by which this degree tends to be consolidated in a reality distinct from the unique act of being that has its source and its truth in God alone. The movement of being, its "restlessness," as Corbin quite aptly puts it, is the very freedom of being, always producing, beyond any one of its expressions, a more intense expression, ceaselessly surpassing the finite in its infinite perseverance. But it is also the engendering of a gradation, which "modulates" continuous being along an infinity of degrees and differentials.[33]

The real is always made intensely present in an effective act and determined at a certain level of the hierarchy. What one conceives of as being (*mafhūm al-wujūd*) is conceived of according to analogy. The plurality of gradations and the unity of being implicate one another, such that one must say that being "is predicated on what is below it, in an analogical manner."[34] This analogy of being concerns our perception and our discursive activity. In presential knowledge, the act of being is made manifest by the simple insistence of the real. But in discursive knowledge, we treat being as the most common concept, and we make it the most general predicate of the existent. But the act of being is never, in itself, a generality. This generic attribution of being must therefore correspond, in the concrete, to a simple analogy. Absolute being is characterized by its priority.[35] Through this priority, it is the maximum of intensity (*al-ashaddīyah*). Being is always more intense than that on which it is predicated, because it is prior to it. It is more complete and more potent than what comes to be. This *primaritas* is the principle of the analogy of being and of the hierarchy of existents.

The immaterial existent *is* more intensely than the material existent. The analogy thus grounds the most essential relationship to existents: the relationship of priority and posteriority, which is a relationship of power (as potency) and weakness. These are the two constituents of the realities. One monad of existence is always more or less potent than another; it is constituted by its rank, not by an extrinsic determination. If we eliminated this hierarchy, being would then only be ascribed to a single existent, and it would be impossible to represent its residence and its occurrence (*wuqū'*) in another degree, prior or posterior. The scheme of nature, consisting of the mineral, vegetable, and animal kingdoms, would disappear. According to Mullā Sadrā, this is completely faithful to the Aristotelian scheme, the priority of nature over first matter, and the priority of form in relation to matter: it is not a question of quidditative priority. This priority concerns the act of being itself. Aristotle, in meditating on the substantial priority of nature or form, guided the mind toward the gradation of the acts of existing; he founded the principle of analogy and the variable intensity of existents.

The History of Being

Thus there is a history of being. The temporality of the existent is a property of what the existent is in its most intimately constitutive moment. It is an internal temporality that in turn grounds the external temporality by which movement in space and the movement of increase are measured. It is a purely intensive temporality that attests to the internal movement and the priority of certain substantial states, and that in turn brings certain accidents with it. Priority and posteriority are not first of all mere extrinsic relations measurable in natural time. Rather, they delineate the order of the ipseities, whose reality consists in being-prior, being-posterior. That is the processive movement in which each monad of existence is continually renewed and continually disappears. Renewal does not take place through some external thing, as we say that a body is moved by the effect of another body.[36] We must distinguish that *in which* there is anteriority (external time) and that *through which* there is anteriority, the concrete history of the real. It is through their ipseities, not through an adventitious relationship, that perfection and deficiency, power and weakness, priority and posteriority, constitute existents. The father comes before the son, and his being, as father, bears its temporal position within itself.[37] More generally, we can be prior to ourselves, or, on the contrary, we can become lower and degrade ourselves, such that we will be our own epigones, the decadents of our own history.

Freedom and Connection

Mullā Sadrā interprets the distinction between being that is necessary through itself and being that is merely possible according to the intensive hierarchies of the effectively real act of being (*al-wujūd al-haqīqī*). The possible act of being is necessitated in being by the eternally necessary act of being from which it proceeds. Thus, taken together, the necessary and the possible are the source and the effusion of a single processive series; they are a single act of being, which is said univocally. But since the Necessary is an infinite source, without cause, instantiated through itself, it is distinguished from the possible, which is necessitated by its effusion and is consequently "in connection" or "attached" (*ta'alluqī, irtibātī*). By itself, the act of being is indeterminate freedom, whereas its expressions are subject to a certain degree of connection, attachment, and limitation of intensity. This gradation translates their dependency with regard to the principle and with regard to more eminent existents. Thus they are called "possibles," that is, they are "possible" in relation to what their existences are as "bound realities." The necessity of these realities expresses only their connection to the real and to the fundamental freedom of the principle.

Not free of the principle, the existences of possible existents are determinate and "modulated" manifestations of infinite freedom at the limit of their own expressive power. The ontological significance of their potentiality is completely different from the potentiality of the quiddities. The latter are affected by a lack in being, a constitutive negativity. By themselves, they have only a fictive, general, abstract reality. They have being only through the act of being of which they can be the accident, according to a degree of intensity or weakness – whereas the acts of being that effuse from the Necessary are all affirmations connected to the real by the linkage of (always effective) modulated stations. Existences modalize the necessity and the freedom of the One. Possible existence is the restless epiphany of the absolute real.

The divine essence is imparticipable and entirely unbound from all manifestation. There is no doubt that in distinguishing the plane of essence from the plane of attributes and operations in the analysis of the Necessary Being, Sadrā wants to preserve a transcendence for the generative source of existence, in the sense that this transcendence is pure freedom, nonconnection, nonrelation. On the plane of the attributes – the divine names – and on the plane of revelation, the unbound ineffable One of the real is manifested and engenders the various "modulated" series of connections between bound realities, in which each determinate expression of a possible being assumes its share of light from the generative source. The Real-One that is beyond all bonds is revealed in the One-Being, the principle of all the generative connections and of the living expressions of his most beautiful names.

Having established that the nature of each act of being is its own epiphanic potency, we can distinguish this potency – the effective act of being – from general "being," which is merely thought by our understanding. "The act of being is, in each thing, an effectively real reality (*amr haqīqī*), which is different from abstract being, mere 'beingness' (*mawjūdīyah*), whether it is a question of the beingness of being or the beingness of quiddity."[38] This is a distinction, therefore, between the abstract beingness of the being and its real being – between a logical concept and a concrete effectivity. But it is also a recognition of their connection, like that between "humanity" and an actual man, between "whiteness" and an actual instance of white. Quiddity is bound to the act of being, as "whiteness" is bound to snow. In this case it is an accident of the concrete body, an event that the understanding abstracts and renders falsely autonomous.[39]

This analysis shows that Sadrā, like his predecessors, the philosophers of illumination (Ishrāqīyah), owes an important debt to Stoic logic, which is here substituted for Aristotelian logic: "The principle of the effects and the effects of the principle are only effectively real act-of-being realities (*al-wujūdāt al-haqīqīyah*), which are concrete ipseities (*huwīyāt 'aynīyah*) existent through themselves, not abstract kinds of being that are intellective realities with no act of being *in concreto*. They are not quiddities whose essences are obscure, and which do not breathe by themselves, and in their definitions, the fragrance of being."[40]

In what way are act-of-being realities existent through themselves, even though they are connected with the Necessary? In what way, even though they are possibles, do they express the necessity of the principle from which they proceed? To understand this, we must grasp the meaning of instantiation in being. The instantiated is pure effect or manifestation of the principle, conceived of as instantiative freedom. On the plane of divine names, the real in its attributes becomes a principle of effusion, the instantiator of being (*al-jā'il*). The bond between the instantiated and the instantiator is simple, independent of quiddity; it is an expression of the absolute Singular within the derived singularities. The instantiator is not distinct, in its essence, from its own effusion in the instantiated, but "insofar as it is instantiative, it is nothing other than a hierarchical rank (*martabah*) of being."[41] Moreover, it is not one of the quiddities.

A thing of pure nothingness, with no other "reality" than that of an abstract being of thought, would be unable to prevent itself from being reduced to nothingness (*in'idām*). And, a procession of quiddities would be not a real procession but the abstract shade of real instantiation. Only that to which effective reality is properly given can "prevent" nothingness. The greatest error therefore consists in claiming that being is an abstract, intellective reality, lacking all effective concrete reality.

Quiddity and the act of being to which it is united do not possess separate realities, as if the existent were the unification of two existents that precede it in being. This would make it the abstract unification of two abstractions. The existent is entirely through and in its act of being alone. Sadrā identifies the existent entirely with the act of being: "The existent is the effective act of being."[42] What sort of unification will this be, between a quiddity that is nothing (outside its concrete act of being) and this act of being, which alone constitutes the real of the existent? Sadrā explains that the unification (*ittihād*) of quiddity and act of being, in a concrete man, is not a third term, an abstraction supplementary to the abstraction that a quiddity, independent of existing, would already be. Not only does quiddity have no other being than the act of being that actualizes it, but the unification between the act of being and the quidditative accidents is the act of being itself.

The same is true for the unification of the "animal" or of "whiteness": the fact that man is an animal, and the judgment that denotes the predication of animality – the unification of the first and the second substance – is not the pure and simple logical copula. This copula, the verb *to be* in the judgment "this man is an animal," is an abstraction, which we conceive of in the place of the reality that is expressed in the judgment. The reality is, rather, a fundamental and primary unification of this man in the concrete act of being. When we say that a man is white, the unification of man and whiteness is the real act of being of the singular man. Whiteness is an accident of this act of being, and it is therefore by accident that it is united to the act of being. It is part of the accidental modifications of the act of being in the movement of substance.

Our judgments still take the form of a synthesis between a subject and a predicate through the copulative link. In the order of these judgments, the unification of quiddities with the act of being is understood in an abstract sense, as a simple manner of thinking (*i'tibār*). However, in the order of the concrete existent, the quiddities indeed appear as what they are, abstract things of pure thought, whereas the act of being is real. The truth of judgments that say "this man is an animal" or "this man is white" do not consist in this man's entering into universal classes that exist by themselves. Rather, the predicate is only an aspect of the act of being of the subject, a "point of view" on the limits and determination of its being-bound. The terms species, genus, and accident refer to certain qualifications of quiddity, which is only the shadow of the act of being of essence. The judgment of attribution should always come back to a statement of existence: this man exists, having received humanity or whiteness as an accident of the existence that determines his essential reality. All predicative judgments should be converted into experiences.

Quiddities are "points of view" on this absolutely simple flow of monadic existences. These existences are therefore quite real, but they are real in the concrete act of existing. On the other hand, they are conceived of under the heading of copulative abstract being. From this abstraction and, as the inevitable consequence of language, the existent receives a "point of view" and enters universal classes. Language grants the existent with a "purely intellectual reality," a conceptual and common reality, like "thingness," "knowability," "universal possibility."[43] We thus say that the existent is "something," a "possible," and so on. Unlike in these language games, in which the existent becomes the particular of a common universal, there is pure concrete effectuation in the act of being.[44]

And yet, the addition of the accidents of the quiddities is not indifferent to the act of being. Each act of being inevitably actualizes a certain quiddity, which reveals the "point of view" taken by this act of being regarding absolute being. In the position of an act-of-being monad, quiddity is distinguished in its proper actuality. Before the event of creative flow, quiddities persist in their obscure reality of nothingness, which is precisely the most difficult to imagine: what is this quasi reality of quiddities in their obscurity, their nonrevelation? It can be nothing other than matter.

Matter, prior to every act, is the "site" of the quiddities, their fundamental shadow. But this is matter conceived of as the indistinction of the "primordial cloud," which Ibn al-ʿArabī teaches us to recognize in the effusion of the "breath of the Merciful." It is there that the eternal essences dwell before their affirmation, like so many limits to the acts of existing, ready to modulate and intensify the unique flow of divine expansion.[45]

The quiddities are "hidden" in this first matter and are revealed only in the singular and concrete act of being — which alone is manifestation, since, by itself, it is light. It is apparent (*zāhir*), and in this sense it is the center of manifestation (*zuhūr*) and the site of manifestation (*mazhar*). "It is through it that the quiddities are manifested, and it is for it, with it, and by way of it."[46] The whole of existents is the self-revelation of the act of existing, whereas "the quiddities, as we know, because of what they are and their definitions, are deprived of the act of being and of manifestation; hence the act of being and manifestation descend upon them; according to their definitions, they are passing away in their essences, are made of nothing in their realities."[47] Their only "being" is their shadow; they exist only in the full light of the constitutive act of being that falls upon them.

Mullā Sadrā counters the possible objections to the absolute priority of the act of being. Some of these objections claim that the act of being, if it is actual *in concreto*, would itself need an act of being, and so on to infinity.[48] These objections are based on Suhrawardī's thesis that the existent alone is concrete but existence is a simple abstraction of its luminous reality. To identify this existent with the act of being would, according to this thesis, lead to hypostasizing existence, transforming it into an essence that, in turn, needs an act of being.

Sadrā does not accept the objection, because "the act of being, and the fact that it is existent, is through itself the fact of its being an act of being; it is the beingness of the thing *in concreto*. The act of being does not have another act of being. No, it is rather the existent as existent."[49] The other doubts consist in making the act of being a qualification of the existent, an accident that needs a substrate. How, in that case, could the existent not be prior to existence? Sadrā answers that, first, existences are concrete ipseities singularized through themselves, and therefore they do not enter into a universal essential concept and are not qualifications of the existent; second, the act of being is not an accident in the sense of subsisting through the existent quiddity, in which the act of being would be inherent to quiddity; and, finally, the act of being of the act of being is identical to the act of being of quiddity and not to the act of being of some other thing.

Conclusion: The Schemes of the Real

Mullā Sadrā identifies the real with being, and he wants to be faithful to the intuition of the fundamental unity of the act of existing (*wahdat al-wujūd*). He thus belongs to the great family of spirits inspired by the ontology of Ibn al-'Arabī. The following text attests to this; in it, he gives a summary explanation of "the modality of the flow of the reality of the act of being in existents whose singular realities are determinate."[50] I will quote him at some length, for the sake of greater clarity:

> Know that things have three degrees in existentiality:
>
> First degree: Pure being, whose act of being is not attached to anything other than itself, the being that is not connected by any linkage. It is this being that the mystics call the mysterious ipseity (*al-huwīyat al-ghaybīyah*), the absolute *mysterium* (*al-ghayb al-mutlaq*) and the One essence (*al-dhāt al-ahadīyah*). He it is who has no name, no determination, to whom no cognition or perception can be attached, since everything that has a name and a description is a concept among concepts existing in the intelligence or in the estimative faculty. And anything to which any cognition and perception can be attached is bound to something other than itself. But he is not so, since he is prior to the entirety of things. He is identical to himself in the definition of himself without alteration and without transport; he is the pure *mysterium*, the absolute unknown, unless he be known through the intermediary of his concomitants and his effects. Because of his supereminent essence, he is not defined or linked by any determination, nor is he absolved [from a determination],[51] for

the consequence of this would be that his act of being would be conditioned by linkages and properties, as differences and singularizations are. The consequents (*lawāhiq*) of his essence are only the conditions of his manifestation, and not the causes of his act of being, for that would imply deficiency in his essence. He is exalted beyond that by a very great eminence! This absolution (*itlāq*) is a simple negation (*amr salbī*) that implies the negation of all qualifications, statuses, and determinations, from the depths (*kunh*) of his essence; it is the absence of linkage and of definition in a description or a name, a determination, or anything else, to the point of negating these negations themselves, insofar as they are things that express only a point of view of the intelligence regarding him.[52]

Second degree: the existent connected with something other than itself.[53] This is the act of being that is linked by an added description, and characterized by definite statuses, as are Intelligences, souls, the celestial spheres, the Elements and the composites, among men, beasts, trees, minerals, and the other particular existents.

Third degree: the extended absolute act of being[54] whose generality is not comparable to universality, but has another mode of being. Indeed, the act of being is purely and simply actualization (*tahassul*) and activity (*fi'līyah*), whereas the universal, whether natural or intellective, is confused (*mubham*) and requires, for its actualization and for its own act of being, the addition of a thing that actualizes it and makes it be. Its unity is not numerical, is not the principle of numbers. It is a reality that extends over the temples of the possibles and the tables of the quiddities. This extended act of being is not restricted to a particular description; it is not encircled within a determinate limit, which falls under the eternal or the eduction into time, the prior and the posterior, perfection and deficiency, causativity and caused being, substantiality and accidentality, immateriality and incorporation [into some matter]. No! Because of its own essence, without the addition of anything else, the extended act of being becomes determinate through the entirety of effective act-of-being determinations and concrete actualizations. Or better, the effective concrete realities proceed from the degrees of its essence, from the modes of its effective determinations and of its

> modalizations. The extended act of being is the foundation and ground of the universe, it is the heaven of life and the throne of the Merciful, the real through which the created is (*al-haqq al-makhlūq bi-h*) – to use the vocabulary of the Sūfīs – and it is thus the reality of realities. It is multiplied in number at the heart of its very unity by the numeric multiplicity of existents that are one as to quiddity. It is eternal with the eternal, temporal with the temporal, intelligible with the intelligible, sensible with the sensible. In considering this, people have gotten the idea that it is universal. But that is not so. The points of view by which one attempts to explain its expansion (*inbisāt*) over the quiddities, and its power to envelop existents in itself, fail – except in a figurative way and by assimilation (*tashbīh*).

This passage, if analysed dogmatically, might permanently dissuade the reader from engaging with the philosophers of Islamic Iran. It appears as if these philosophers state, rather dryly, what the poets and painters of miniatures expose infinitely more gracefully: the epiphany of the unknown real in the appearances that make up the universe. What is conceived here is the epiphanic structure of being. It forms a scheme whose terms are borrowed from the doctrine of Ibn al-ʻArabī, then systematized by Sadr al-Dīn al-Qūnawī. It must be recalled that, in Iranian mystic poetry and visual art, this doctrinal scheme became something of a spontaneous feeling.

It is in fact impossible to isolate this ontology, whose language is so cold, from the tragic and ecstatic experience of Rūmī, from the transfiguration of the universe in the poetry of Hafez, or from the intense melancholy that seems to imbue the Persian soul. When one reads these lines, one must keep in mind that the aesthetics of being are expressed above all in the practices of desire. These practices, in return, bring together all the teachings of metaphysics. The West, land of history and of God-made man, and the Islamic East, land of desire and of the unknown real, shimmering in the brilliance of fugitive lights: this travelers' commonplace is not without some truth.

The "three ranks" that Mullā Sadrā lays out in this passage

form not three types of existents or three types of separate things, but three moments in the constitution of all reality. Each body, soul, or spirit possesses in itself, like a series of concentric circles, these three immanent degrees of existentiality.

The first, and the most central, is the source of its act of being, pure being. I translate *al-ghayb* as "the *mysterium*," to create an echo with the theosophy of Jakob Böhme in Western literature. For here there is indeed the idea of a real that is absolutely withdrawn from nomination, from all positive statements — a real that is removed from its own determinations. It resists intellective cognitions and perceptions. It is not even "absolute," if by that we mean that it would at least be liberated from all attachment. Its generous and threatening freedom seems to be "absolved" from all bonds only if we negate in it every kind of limit and restriction. But this "reality of negation," and the negation of this negation, are still only approximations, legitimate from our point of view but inadequate to the real. Contrary to Western ontology as it is completed in Hegelian metaphysics, in which the negation of negation grounds the reconciliation of the identity of the absolute and the multiple moments of its revelation, all revelation separates us from this degree of the absolute. Its "absolution" says nothing complete, because it cannot be said completely, cannot be fully revealed, cannot be incarnated without remainder in what effuses from it. A perpetually renewed negation, the intuitive grasp of pure being is doomed to silence.

This intuitive grasp is reversed in the third degree, the expansion of being. The negative path never produces the universal; the universal is "confused," which we can take to mean that it mixes and obscures distinct things under terms that efface the singularity of their existence. But the expansion is "general" because, in an irresistible movement, it spreads over all substances, which it overwhelms and submits to an intensive metamorphosis. Sadrā's great discovery, on the basis of these dogmatic positions from the theosophy of Ibn al-'Arabī, was the intuition of substantial motion. We are familiar with the movement affecting the accidents of substances, their quantities, their qualities; but here is a movement that renders their very substance malleable and ductile, apt to change its nature. An energy that carries it from kingdom to kingdom, transforming the mineral to vegetable, man to angel.

The expansion of being will be an existential revolution (*inqilāb wujūdī*).[55] The expansion of being is the breath of the merciful, the real from which beings are created, according to the vocabulary of Ibn al-ʿArabī. It is no longer the unknown real, withdrawn into its solitude and its ineffable unity, but rather the real creating itself, creating a multiple work of creation, "eternal with the eternal, temporal with the temporal." The expansion is epiphany. It is the "primordial cloud" that, in the vision of the Andalusian master, is homologous to the absolute imagination. It is the movement by which the hidden real is revealed and is completed by the activity of the divine imagination, in which the form of every existent is configured. The world of apparitional forms is an epiphany because it is a world imagined by God, because God imagines himself in his creation, which is the created God.[56] The expansion of extended being is a synthesis, a gathering together of the "sides," the "right side," the "Yeman" of being, and its opposite pole in mercy and wrath, with a preeminence given to mercy. It is "theophany giving itself free rein."[57]

This epiphanic operation is realized in the hierarchy and the order of existents, constituting the "second degree" of existentiality. The determination of the freedom of the real is then translated by the totality of interlinked realities – in which we find again the traditional cosmology – from the elements of weakly informed matter, the minerals, vegetables, animals, and men, up to the superlunary world of the heavens, moved by the desire of the elements' souls under the influence of the Intelligences. This is a hierarchy that Sadrā has rethought following the scheme handed down by Plotinus, which describes the triadic movement from nature to the world of Intelligence, through the mediation of the world of the soul.

The intelligible, psychic being, and natural being are not compartmentalized regions and worlds with no communication between them. Sadrā thinks of them as stations in the flow of the expansion of being, and as stages in the conversion of all the existents toward the most central source, pure being, which they strive toward with all the force of their desire but cannot reach. At the heart of the movement of their substances reigns a desire that responds to the expansion of being that passes over them, a desire for an unfathomable and unconditional freedom. Perfect obedience to the order of the created God is fidelity to the imperative freedom of the hidden God. This complete reversibility of total obedience and infinite freedom is the meaning of Sadrā's eschatology. Sadrā warns that the degrees of being must never be confused. What is pure freedom in the first degree, in the generating source of being, is manifest in the obedience of extended being. Thus the response to the freedom of the *mysterium* is the epiphany of its spontaneity in the perfect man, whose only form is obedience without reserve, which mirrors the angels who circle the divine throne in perpetual adoration.

Hegel's ontology expresses the Western synthesis of the freedom of God with the determinations of men in the guise of love and in the formations of world history. The age of love is the age of spirit, realizing in spirit the promises of God's son. But it is also the final harmony of the historical spheres, with no contradiction between earthly existence and spiritual existence. Mullā Sadrā, fulfilling the expression of the ontology of Islam, says something completely different: love is the experience of a tension, of a never-completed motion, of an elevation without a final term. He mobilizes existents and the degrees of existence (natural, psychic, intelligible) introducing restlessness into the epiphany of the real. The hidden real remains inaccessible, ineffable, ceaselessly fomenting an intense existence, withdrawing from all final reconciliation, except in the ecstasy of the extinction of self. The history of being cannot reach its supereminent principle. It carries within it the melancholy of its loss and the joy of its presence. God "appears in that He is hidden."[58]

Part Two

The Existential Revolution

Chapter Five

Essential Motion

All existents, except God, are in a process of becoming. Coming into being, changing, metamorphosing at every moment, then returning to nothingness: do these immediate givens of experience lead the mind to conclude that movement has a destination? Must they be treated as mere appearances, in which the stability of effective realities is veiled? Or must we rather consider the metamorphoses of bodies and souls real, without giving them any final term or any meaning? These questions provide a schematic overview of several ways the ancients tried to think becoming. It can be said without much exaggeration that becoming was *the* question for Greek philosophy. The being of beings was interrogated in order to provide a satisfactory answer to this question, born from the most ancient astonishment: Why do things move? Sadrā situates himself, in turn, within this program of physical investigations; he emphasizes and develops Aristotle's fundamental idea that motion is essential to natural beings, and nature and becoming must be thought together.

For Sadrā, it is essential to give a metaphysical validity to the prophecies that announce the end of the world and the overturning of all stable reality. The becoming and ruination of created things is for him a matter of revealed truth. So are their transmutation and salvation in a future retribution that not only compensates the faithful but also offers all existents – from the simplest of elements to Intelligence – a proximity with the divine that will consecrate their superexistence in the otherworld. The philosophy of motion prepares the way for the doctrine of corporeal resurrection and spiritual salvation. Conversely, no theory of salvation can be satisfied with a weak conception of motion that does not grant it all its power by situating it within substances themselves. Thus, a way of thinking becoming is necessary for the exegesis of the Qur'ān and for the prophetic promises. A theory of intensification and growth requires that being be thought intrinsically in the guise of becoming.

The Birth of the World

The most general property of the universe is the *event*:

> The entire world eventuates in time, since everything in it is preceded, in its act of being, by nonexistence in time and is constantly renewed, in the sense that there is no ipseity, no individual – be it celestial or elemental, simple or composite, substance or accident – but that its nonexistence precedes its act of being in time and its act of being likewise precedes its nonexistence in time. In general, every body and every bodily thing, everything whose act of being is in any way connected with matter is constantly renewed in its ipseity and is impermanent in its act of being and its singularity.[1]

Every reality instantiated in matter – every body, but also every soul, insofar as it is united with a body – "eventuates in time." The word *hādith*, which means "occurring," "eventuating," "constituting an event," implies an eduction into being (*hudūth*) that characterizes the world itself.

The world is not eternal (*qadīm*). Motion and time are first intuited in this anteriority of nothingness in relation to being and this posteriority of nothingness in relation to existence, which are the translation into each instantiated reality of its potentiality, its ontological poverty. If the heavens are as perishable as the least vegetable composed of matter and form, it is because, like the vegetable, they carry in themselves this precariousness, this instability of being.

How to reconcile this with what we know of the act of being, with its fundamental necessity, its positive potency? In itself, the act of being is affirmation, presence; it always translates the effusion emanating from the being that is necessary through itself—that is, God, whose act of being is "above the infinite." Is there a contradiction between this essential positivity of being and eduction into being, which seems to carry in it a certain power of nothingness? If being is affirmation, how can one not be Parmenidean? How can one submit the entire world, in its very substance, to becoming? This is an old question, one that was taken up by Plato in particular, and that Mullā Sadrā encounters in his own way.

The remarkable commentator on our text Shaykh Ahmad al-Ahsā'ī is perfectly aware of this when he writes, concerning the expression "the essential motion of existence":

> According to his own discourse, his statements contradict each other, for the act of being is necessary by itself! And yet an accidental deficiency is attached to it here, because of what is attached to it in the linkage of procession. The eduction of the act of being, according to Sadrā and his disciples, indicates the bond of this act of being with the quiddities and with the accidentally concomitant deficiencies, and not the very essence of being. But since the act of being is necessary by itself, then it is not true that there is a linking of motion with it, since *motion* designates the movement of ontological need and ontological poverty.[2]

In other words, if the act of being of the world and what is in the world is intrinsically in motion, if it is affected by a movement that is essential to it, how can we explain that it is necessary by itself? How can we reconcile the essential necessity of being—down to existents necessitated in being—with ontological precariousness, and consequently with potentiality and nonnecessity? One could respond that this precariousness of existents is due to the limitation of the act of being through a certain dimension translated by quiddity. Granted. But this link with deficiency, or limitation, ought to be merely accidental rather than essential. How can one speak of an essential *motion* of existence? How is the procession of existence from the divine generative source in itself "motion"?

The solution proposed by Shaykh Ahmad assumes that Sadrā's thesis, according to which the quiddities do not have their own existence, has come to ruin. According to him, "quiddity is existent through an existentiation that is proper to it." This existentiation proper to quiddity is hierarchized according to the existentiation of the act of being. Existentiation subsists in concrete beings only through a certain quiddity. God first creates the quiddities and then, secondarily, confers an existence on them in an accidental mode. Shaykh Ahmad interprets the Avicennian legacy in a direction diametrically opposed to that of Sadrā. Quiddity thus has its own proper movement, toward its divine principle, because of its nature. The world can pass away, not because being, in itself, is affected by an essential movement of eduction, but because being *can* be granted to quiddity by divine action.[3]

Sadrā obviously does not think this way. For him, the reality of an existent is more or less intense, that is, more or less real. The real that has emanated from the divine principle is modalized along an endless hierarchy of degrees whose upper limit is located at infinity in the divine instantiative real. The fundamental positivity and necessity of being do not contradict this gradation of intensities; rather, they found it. It suffices, consequently, to conceive of the relative weakness of every corporeal act of being in order to deduce its temporal production.

This eduction of the world into time, its beginning as well as its end, refutes the Aristotelian model of the heavens. The universe is not eternal. The essential movement that affects all bodies does not spare the celestial spheres. But it does not come to an end with the cessation of the sensible world. On the contrary, it brings all bodily existents into an intensification that metamorphoses them and carries them to a higher degree of intensity. Essential movement is at the heart of Sadrā's eschatological metaphysics, because it leads from the sensible to the intelligible and because it unites the three great regimes of being: nature, the soul, and the intelligence. It converts the temporal into the eternal and leads from the multiple back to unity; it is the history of the act of being, oriented toward maximum unity. Far from betraying a weakness, it is the redemption of all finitude. The world is evanescent, because it is involuted into the otherworld and into the ultimate stability of the divine names. Natural motion is the incomplete quest for perfection.

Movement and time are still always the index of a precariousness in relation to the act of being, since they "belong to things that are weak in existence, things whose being is interlaced with the nonbeing that belongs to them, and whose activity is mixed with potentiality."[4] Here Sadrā follows Avicenna, for whom motion concerns all things that pass from potency to act. Being that is absolutely actual is absolved from this motion. At the lowest level, first matter, as pure potentiality, is not a thing of any kind and undergoes no motion. Motion is conceived of not according to sheer mathematical measure, as it will be in modern science, but in the intuition of a thing's eduction from potentiality to act. That is why physical investigations are always haunted by a properly metaphysical question: how does motion affect the various categories (*ma'qūlāt*) of the existent? The ten categories are determined by the passage from potentiality to act: the actual man comes after the potential man (substance), and it is the same for quantity, quality, relation, "where," "when," *situs*, possession, action, and passion.[5] It is on this doctrinal basis that Sadrā constructs the doctrine of essential motion.

The eduction into being (*hudūth*) is identical to fading and passing away: this is the fundamental thesis. It expresses an intuition of motion, a grasping of what it is in its reality: the identity of being and nonbeing—not their distinction but their fundamental community in all reality endowed with a certain potentiality. Each "part" of a movement entails the nothingness of another part, or, "better: It *is* the nothingness of this other part." Motion is indissolubly both disappearance, one thing after another, and eduction of being, one thing after another. In becoming, being and nonbeing are reciprocal terms; one ceaselessly passes into the other. There exists a first unmoving mover, but everything that is caused by its activity is, in its very substance, in a process of becoming.[6] Its act of existing unfolds in the rhythm of annihilation and manifestation.

One might object that Sadrā's stubborn refusal to grant the slightest status to positive nonbeing renders his concept of becoming incomprehensible. That is exactly what Shaykh Ahmad says. It seems to me that there are two responses to this. The first is simple: the analysis of natural motion conforms with Aristotle's physics, and nonbeing is the privation of the act that affects the potential existent. Nothing here contradicts the full positivity of the existent as existent. The second response is more delicate: motion, in essence, is a passage from nonbeing to being and from being to nonbeing. But this passage is fundamentally positive, because it is confounded with the emanating flow of extended being, expressed in the matter that makes up natural receptacles and psychic substances. But the flow of the act of being is existence, and entirely so, such that potentiality and privation express only its limits, in the sense of the limits of an algebraic function. Dynamics would then prefigure something like a differential calculus.

True, the feeling of the world that animates Sadrā's thought is accompanied by a belief in the vanity of the natural world, a belief born from Qur'ānic revelation and far removed from the Aristotelian perception of nature and the Greek vision of the cosmos. The tension arising from these two versions of the world renders Sadrā's task rather difficult. The concept of essential motion is both a symptom of this tension and the theoretical solution to the problem arising from the inevitable confrontation between Greek physics, which postulates an eternal world, and monotheistic revelation, which affirms its final disappearance and its illusory density.

That is why motion is not understood on the basis of the simple motricity of the thing. It is, rather, the very "renewal" (*tajaddud*) and "expiration" (*inqidā'*) of the thing.[7] The concept of renewal is something quite different from the representation of motion in space or quantitative increase. Identifying motion, by definition, with a certain metamorphosis of the existent amounts to justifying expiration, in the sense that one says of a state that it "comes to an end" through a change of form. Renewal is innovation, and becoming has an end; it is the desire for this end, for the actualization of perfection. Renewal is the effective positivity of the existent.

With the concept of renewal, motion is thought of as an intensification and conversion to the world in which there is no more need for metamorphosis, that is, the divine world. The movements affecting the categories that correspond to accidents of substance originate in a first, fundamental motion, the motion of substance itself. The eduction of potentiality to act, which Avicenna said was motion affecting substance, becomes a motion *of* substance, substantial motion (*haraka jawharīyah*) or essential motion (*haraka dhātīyah*).

Substance in Motion

A decisive theoretical event can be located here. We know that all metaphysics after Aristotle took up his teaching of the fundamental stability of the substantial substrate: "Substance, it seems, does not admit of a more and a less. I do not mean that one substance is not more a substance than another (we have said that it is), but that any given substance is not called more, or less, than that which it is. For example, if this substance is a man, it will not be more a man or less a man either than itself or than another man. For one man is not more a man than another, as one white thing is more white than another."[8] This man can receive contrary accidents and be ignorant or learned, young or old, but he will always be identical to man. Substance must always be what it is, such that becoming, the passage from potentiality to act, may be possible. Sadrā, however, maintains that this becoming implies the tranformation of substance itself, and that a man becomes more or less a man according to whether he actualizes certain potentialities, such as intelligence or virtue, or not. His humanity is renewed, from the stage of bodily existence to that of imaginal existence and finally to that of intelligible existence. Man is caught up in becoming, like every other natural reality.

Why does Sadrā reverse such a venerable doctrine of substance? He does it for metaphysical reasons, which we will examine later. But one might think that he wants first to respond to the demands of religious revelation and the gnostic interpretation that he gives them. More precisely, he claims that annihilation, the precariousness of all things except God, does not spare substance. If "all things will perish except his own face,"[9] then this "perishing" must change all apparent stability into a continuous fading and passing away, which so well characterizes the images reflected in mirrors. In the mirror in which God is reflected, no substantial form exists except through the revelation that God effects, of himself and for himself. God, the absolute, revealing himself in the forms of manifestation, is the only real subject of being. The subject that receives this manifestation – created substance – must be transient and in flux. Sensible or psychic manifestation unfolds the stable unity of the real in the multiple movement of its forms.

On the other hand, men have a destination that recapitulates all the destinations of the universe: man is a microcosm enveloping the seminal reasons of the macrocosm. His substantial renewal both fulfills and encapsulates the renewal of all natures and all souls. He has a moral responsibility, a duty to intensify his own act of being, in a liberation and a return: a liberation from the chains of the passions and animal desires and a return from the lands of exile in the material modes of existence.

Sadrā lives in the belief that a man is never a man once and for all, that he does not receive humanity as a natural form that he must actualize naturally, through a simple growth of forces. He largely adopts the Aristotelian doctrine of the virtues, but he inscribes it in the eschatological motif of Shīʿite Islam: one becomes a perfect man, or one tends toward being the perfect man (the Prophet, the imam), through an imitation of his moral perfections and his intelligible virtues. When a man lives the life of intelligence, both practical and theoretical, he becomes other than what he was at his corporeal birth. He must choose between an animal destiny and a truly human destiny, that is, an angelic destiny. He can become a tyrant over himself and others, or a free man reflecting the spontaneity and the light of God.

How is essential motion possible? It must have a cause: "The proximate agent of motion must be stable as to quiddity and self-renewing as to its act of being."[10] This agent is nature (*al-tabīʿah*), the constitutive principle of the body that actualizes the species, "the first perfection of the natural body insofar as it is an actuated existent." Even if the body is stable from the point of view of quiddity, it is ceaselessly renewing itself in existence, and its ipseity is in flux.[11] In order to understand this, we must return to what we know of Sadrā's doctrine of the act of being and of quiddity. The act of being constitutes the existent in reality; it is its generating source, and quiddity expresses the limit or the definition of the existent, and is a concomitant of the act of existing. It is its shadow. Sadrā is careful to maintain that the substrate of motion must necessarily be a reality stable in itself, but this "stable" substrate is nothing other than the substrate understood according to quiddity, that is, according to the shadow of the act of being, which has no reality by itself. From this point of view, it is not subject to renewal. But this is not true for the act of being — the ground of reality — which is subject to permanent renewal.

Nature is not the principle of motion in the sense of being external to the renewal of the body. Nature is identical to the essential renewal of the body; it is in flux because it consists of the effective flow of bodies in motion. Matter and form are not abstractions isolated from each other. The reality of matter is potency and availability; it is the potency of the multiplicity of forms. Natural form possesses "the eduction of renewal"; its actuality consists in this innovation or actualization, always open to a future of unknown presents.

Matter is the availability of the body for this innovation in natural form. At every instant, it has *another* form, for which it is available; it tends toward this alterity, which it summons and prepares for, whereas each form has *another* matter that it necessarily implies. This newly actualized potentiality is, in turn, ready for another form. Form is prior to matter in essence, and matter is prior to form in time: if we combine these two priorities, we obtain movement and renewal, the remarkable plasticity of matter and form, the one preparing other forms, the other actualizing other matters.

This is not a vicious circle; rather, it is the law of the renewal of the body, of the eduction of its essential nature. The form of the body seems unique and stable, but this is an error. It is unique only according to the definition we give of this body and the signification that our intelligence produces from it, in a simplification that completely disregards the indefinite multiplicity of successive forms taken by this body in renewed matters. The numerical unity of the body — no more than its abstract definition — says nothing of the concrete effectivity that is the constant renewal, at every moment, of the real body. Each one of us is a multiplicity of continuous forms, unified by the essential movement itself.

The multiplicity of the states of substance thus governs the totality of accidental movements, such as movement in space, change, and growth. It is not endless, although it might be analyzed into an ever-divisible series of enumerations. Enumeration, the counting of discrete moments, is derived from an intellectual analysis, whereas the continuous flow of renewal is a concrete thing. The body is guaranteed, in its relative unity, from location to location and from one state to another, by the very principle of its movement. This unity, beneficial to the body, is the active potency subsisting in it, which is called nature. It subsists through the body, and all the accidents follow from this subsistent form, nature. It is both one and unifying, mobile and flowing. Ipseity, the "self" of all bodily reality, is — through and in this unity — the subject of its own renewal.

Essential or substantial motion is a motion of ipseity, of the "self," because it would be unintelligible to say that what is renewed (the body) proceeded from something that was stable. Avicenna saw this clearly: a nature that did not change could not be the cause of motion. But he maintained that change was in a way added to nature by, for example, seeking the renewal of degrees of proximity or distance from the end in natural movements that tend toward an end (location in nature); the renewal of different states within compelled motion; or the renewal of particular acts of will and particular desires born in the soul.

This is quite an understatement. The final term (and therefore the cause) of the renewal of these states is what is called nature. Sadrā, like Avicenna, maintains that all compelled motion leads back, in the last instance, to the condition of natural motion. Thus, every renewal is caused by the nature of the body. But then it must be argued that the renewal produced in all bodily changes implies the renewal of nature itself.[12]

Avicenna foresaw and vigorously refuted in advance any doctrine introducing motion into substance: "If we say that there is motion in substance, our statement is entirely metaphorical, for this category is such that motion does not occur in it."[13] His argument is based on the definition of substantial form, which determines the quiddity of the concrete existent and can never abandon its identity and its fixity. To the extent that the existent is grounded in being what it is by its substantial nature and by its form, how could nature and form undergo any intensification or an eventual degradation? The nature of a being that is subject to generation and corruption comes to existence or is corrupted all at once, not gradually. For example, when a child is born, when it begins to grow, its substantial form is already what it will cease to be only in death. Growth and degeneration will bear on the accidents of substance, not on substance itself.

Between being in potentiality and being in actuality there is no median perfection: "If it received intensification and decrease, substance, which would be at the median degree between intensification and decrease, would have to remain identical to its species, or else it would not have to. If it remained identical to its species, then the substantial form would absolutely not change. Only the accident of the substance would change." To be intensified or to decrease, it must, in a certain way, be annihilated, since the prior state disappears for the sake of the subsequent state. But substance, by definition, cannot undergo annihilation. Either it is, or it is not; if it is, it is fully, although it may increase or decrease with respect to its accidents. Substance and negativity are mutually exclusive.

According to the hypothesis that substance does not remain identical to its species, the intensification of substance would provoke the acquisition of another substance. There would then be two substances for a single existent, which is absurd. "It is clear then that the matter stands quite to the contrary. Substantial form disappears and comes to being all at once. Between its potential being and its actual being, there is thus no mediation that would constitute movement." The rest of Avicenna's arguments here are based on the impossibility he has indicated, namely that there could be several substances for a single existent, which would result from a substantial motion. This line of argument is remarkable. It vividly confirms a conception of substance and specific form in which no becoming can be imagined. If the being of substance is identified with the species, which is stable and fixed, how indeed can one conceive of any becoming of substance without falling into absurdity?

Mullā Sadrā is perfectly familiar with these arguments. He radically displaces the question of substantial being. Its quiddity is indeed fixed and stable, since a man remains a man and a plant remains a plant. It is not a matter of anything like an evolution of species.[14] If substance, as such, undergoes increase and intensification, it does so within the framework of the species itself. It reaches higher levels or degrees of being, from the sensible world to the worlds of the soul and the intelligence, in such a way that the species itself comes to possess higher or lower levels of existence.

What becomes necessary here is Sadrā's profound revision of the notion of substance. Substance is determined in its real act of being not by its quiddity but by the degree of intensity or weakness of the act of being. Quiddity expresses this degree of existence; it is what it is according to this degree. Consequently, the stability of its definition is subject to the instability of its act of existing. More profoundly, being is one; it is an effusion of the divine creative unity, and its variable modalizations are translated into monads of existence that constitute the generative centers of the substances. These monads are in themselves life and potency, and their activity does not exclude movement but integrates it into the totality of its differences. The negative is introduced, from a certain point of view, into substance itself. Substance authentically becomes subject.

We have seen that Sadrā refused to grant the slightest effective reality to negation, nothingness, or negativity. It seemed contradictory, then, to posit substantial motion, which implies a nothingness in substance itself and, in the same thesis, refuses all positivity to this same nothingness. But Sadrā was able to respond to this difficulty. Nonbeing has no effectivity, if by nonbeing we mean the privation of a good. But the negativity that we are describing here is not privation; it is the impetus of perfection in essential motion, the surpassing of prior states marked by a relative weakness. Extinction is the prelude to a superexistence.

If nothingness really became this negativity of substance, Sadrā would be another Hegel. But that is not at all the case. The fulfilled metaphysics of Islam is not identical to the conclusive ontology of the Christian West. The way taken by Islamic Neoplatonism leads to this intrepid proposition by Sadrā: substantial motion exists. But the negation implied by this motion is not equivalent to the negation that Hegel locates within a fully elaborated interpretation of Neoplatonism. In an authentically Muslim framework of thought like Sadrā's, it is unthinkable that the divine real would die *for* a resurrection on the third day. The absence of any death of God thus compels him to envision negativity in a completely different way from Hegel. What dies here in order to be reborn is substance, the created essence, not the creative Essence. Essential motion ceases at the threshold of the divine, stable, and eternal imperative.

Theory of Nature and of the Multiple

The concept that authorizes Sadrā to think the "renewal" of the thing is nature:

> Certainly, there exists a thing whose reality (*haqīqah*) implies renewal and flux. In my view, this is nature, and according to the common view it is motion and time. But all things possess a certain stability and a certain activity (*fi'līyah*), and that which effuses from the instantiator is only a mode of its stability and of its activity. When the stability of a thing is the stability of its renewal, and when activity is the activity of its potency (*fi'līyat quwwatih*), there can be no doubt that what effuses from the First upon this thing is precisely that mode of stability and of activity, just as each thing possesses a mode of unity that consists in its being continuous in existence. When its unity is identical to a certain multiplicity, whether potential or actual, what effuses from the One, the real, is the unity of the multiple. And, among existents, that which has a stability identical to renewal is nature. That which has an activity identical to potency is matter. That which has a unity identical to the multiple in actuality is number. That which has a unity identical to the potency of the multiple is the body and what there is in it.
>
> Nature, insofar as it is stable, is bound to the stable Originator, and insofar as it renews itself, the renewal of the things that are renewed and the temporal eduction of the realities that occur in time are bound to it. Just as first matter, to the extent that it possesses a certain activity, proceeds from the active Originator by the adjunction of form, according to a given instantiation, and to the extent that it is potency and potentiality, it reveals itself thus as eduction and expiration, destruction and extinction. These two substances [nature and matter], through their essential destruction and renewal, hold the middle ground between eduction to being and disappearance in corporeal realities, and through these two the bond between the eternal and the temporal is actualized and the matter of formal perfections is fully completed.[15]

It is true that the emanative effusion proceeding from God instantiates only stability and actuality. Nature, therefore, is stable. But its stability is nothing other than the permanence of its renewal, of the duration that constitutes it. It is a duration that is a becoming other, a permanence that is impermanence: nature is the unity of contraries. In this case, it is not alone: the activity of matter resides in potency; the unity of number is identical to multiplicity; the unity of a body is unfolded in an actualized multiple. Nature is fundamentally median and mediating. United with form-receiving matter, it is the mediation between the eternal and the temporal.

The ontological scheme that governs this definition of nature comes directly from the Neoplatonic exegesis of Plato's *Parmenides*. Let us recall its broad outlines. The first hypothesis corresponds to the pure or ineffable One, which Sadrā calls the real or the divine essence, the act of being that is necessary through itself, the one and unrevealed essence. The second hypothesis corresponds to the multiple or entirely intelligible One, in which Sadrā recognizes the plane of divine names and intelligible lights. The third hypothesis corresponds to the One-and-multiple, or the mediating soul, which in Sadrā is the world of celestial, human, animal, and vegetal souls. The fourth hypothesis corresponds to the unified or entirely empirical multiple, and this is the rank of nature. Finally, the fifth hypothesis corresponds to the pure multiple or pure matter.[16]

Nature is renewed; it is substantial motion because it is multiplicity. It is stable because it is a unified multiple. As Plotinus expresses it, "For nature, to be what it is means to produce [*poiein*]."[17] This production or, we might say, this poetics of nature is a contemplation, for nature proceeds from the soul and is an effusion of the soul. The ceaselessly moving activity of nature is a weakened contemplation of the intelligible. Substantial motion expresses this degradation of pure *theoria*, illuminating the existence of immaterial realities in a mobile production of material beings.

Thus the feeling of the world is made up of several intuitions that do not all have the same origin. Sadrā draws from the Qur'ānic revelation the notion that the world has a beginning and an end, that the poetics of nature does not engender a universe that is held together and maintained forever. In this sense, he is not faithful to Plotinus's view of the cosmos. He would not agree with Plotinus's statement that "it would be absurd to believe that the soul, if it is able to hold the universe together for any length of time, however short, would not do so forever."[18] But he does agree with Plotinus that "the universe has a body that continually flees and flows."[19] Nature is stable; it is "at rest" because "it is an image of another contemplation," a contemplation that is "silent and somewhat blurred," Plotinus says,[20] and it is movement because from this silence it gives birth to the splendors and graces of the corporeal universe.

Substantial motion is a spiritual motion. The sensible universe is the image of the intelligible universe of the divine names, but it is this image in time, just as time is the mobile image of eternity. Intelligible life gives birth to another life, which is natural motion. The identity, uniformity, and permanence of the intelligible seem to be opposed by the ever-differing change and activity of nature, which proceed from them, as the image proceeds from its model. Sadrā could use these words from Plotinus for his own purposes: "Instead of indivisibility and unity, an image of unity, that which is one in continuity, and instead of an infinity that is a whole, a continuous progress toward infinity."[21]

The divine instantiating (or founding) essence is indeed thought here in Neoplatonic terms. It conforms with what Plotinus writes of the One: "It is the productive power of all things; if it did not exist, neither would all things, neither beings, nor intelligence, nor first life, nor any other. It is above life and is the cause of life; for the activity of life, which is all things, is not first but itself flows out, so to speak, as from a spring. For think of a spring which has no other origin; it gives its water to all the rivers."[22]

Life begins in the intelligible whole. For Sadrā, the Intelligences are the sparks of divine light, the originary multiple expressions of the divine names. Sadrā exempts them from substantial motion, because the divine names are one with the divine essence they reveal, and because they cannot be the bearers of any potentiality. We will examine this delicate problem later, in a close study of the world of the divine imperative. It remains true, in any case, that intelligence and the intelligible world translate the divine origination, its revelation in emanated being. To understand substantial motion, we must situate the perception of nature within the framework of a text that Mullā Sadrā has constantly in mind, the *Theology of Aristotle* — that is, Plotinus again, more or less recomposed and glossed in the Arabic version. Here is a passage that seems to me to govern Sadrā's entire conception of motion:

> We say that the motions of the Intelligence are substances, and there is no substance after the Intelligence that does not proceed from the activity of the Intelligence. The Intelligence makes substances by its own motion only because it is the first activity of the first true Agent, and therefore it has such power as nothing else has. The Intelligence moves in substances, and the substances are a consequence of the motions. The Intelligence moves only in the arena of the real and does not need to go outside that arena.... Its motion is intelligible, and the motion of the other substances completes all the substances. Every substance and every life is of the motions of the intelligence. The substance of the intelligence preserves all the substances that are below it, and the life of the intelligence preserves every life below it, and every traveler there, whether he is intelligence or life, travels a living journey, and his way passes the things of life. And just as the traveler on this earth travels only an earthly journey, and the things he passes are all of them earthly, even though they be many and diverse, so the one who travels on that living earth travels the journey of life, and the things he passes are life too, and the living thing travels on that living earth.[23]

Avicenna refuted — in his *Physics* at least — the idea of substantial motion. Sadrā accepts it, because he adopts a conception of substance that is inspired entirely by such passages as the one just quoted. Substances are affected by motion in their very ipseity (a motion that does not concern only their accidents) because they *are* motion. They are motion because they proceed from the activity of the intelligence. This activity, originary life, is the divine imperative deployed in the flow of the act of being. The act of being of substances expresses the originary motion. In these substances, it is always intelligible life that produces what is most inward, the source of existence, which is intrinsically motion. Essential motion is a motion of essences because essences are motion.

Substantial motion takes place in the "arena" (*midmār*) of the intelligence. There is no life other than intelligible life, in souls and in natures. But in the latter, life is silently degraded to the threshold of matter, metamorphosing from pure knowledge into sensible corporeal action and operation. However, this procession always takes place within the intelligible circle and is itself circular, since it is complete not at the end of its "descent" but at the end of the movement of "upward return," the movement of conversion of all existents, from threshold to threshold, toward the pure intelligible.

On the plane of the divine names, the motion of all realities is maintained, and this motion will be called the spiritual resurrection of all things. The end of the passage just quoted alludes to the spiritual earth, the archetypal living earth, a notion that will find many echoes in the Islamic Neoplatonists. Sadrā identifies it with the imaginal world, with the corporeality of the events of the soul. Here, the earthly journey follows the living being's journey, his essential pilgrimage. The movement of souls in this world — the movement of natures involving material bodies — leads to the movement of psychic life in the otherworld, "the living journey on this living earth" of the imaginal world, on its way to the supreme destination, the intelligible world and proximity to God.

The soul and nature are movement. But the soul is stretched between two demands. On the one hand, it directs its gaze upward, toward the intelligible; on the other, it pours the superabundance of its being downward. It is thus that the poetics of natures, seminal words, inform bodily matter: "When the soul is filled with light and power and other perfections, it cannot remain at rest in itself, because of these perfections within it that desire activity. It journeys downward, not upward, because the intelligence does not need any of its perfections, since intelligence is the cause of its perfections."[24] Nature is intelligible and sensible; it is the soul come from the body. The soul is the last of the divine substances, and it does not refuse its perfections to sensible nature, in which the natural world begins. It only refrains from mixing in inferior, blameworthy states.[25]

The concept of nature has a long history, which I can only briefly evoke here. Sadrā is not far from the Plotinian conceptions of origin that were current at the time, expressed, for example, in the definition presented by the Brethren of Purity: "Nature is only one of the powers of the universal soul, instantiated by it in all the bodies under the sky of the moon, flowing out upon all their parts."[26] Sadrā, however, attributes the power of nature to all bodies endowed with any materiality whatever.

Nature was conceived, at bottom, in terms of a mediation between the world and the soul, particularly in the Ismā'īlī literature on the subject. Thus the demiurgic, artisanal action of the soul in the body of the world becomes intelligible: "Natures, proceeding from the universal Soul, exist in this universal body; the proof of this is that there are two orders of conformative realities: natural or artificial. As for the natural conformative realities, these are mineral, vegetable, and animal substances. The artificial conformative realities are the artisanal powers of man and of man alone among the animals."[27] One is eager to emphasize the stability of nature — whose persistence grounds that of the beings it engenders — and the eminent dignity of nature, closely united with the eminence of divine power.[28]

Sadrā nevertheless does not think about nature according to this strictly Platonic scheme of the soul of the world and of universal nature. He remains Platonic, as we will see; but he is much more in dialogue with Avicenna, who transmits to him the concept of nature. It is through Avicenna that the Aristotelian conception of nature comes to be mixed, for Sadrā, with the Plotinian scheme (from which it is not absent, in fact).

In his properly physical analyses, Sadrā conceives of nature by disengaging it from all reference to any "world of the soul" that would be the soul of the world. At this point, we see a true divergence between the completed metaphysics of Twelver Shīʿite Islam and that of Ismāʿīlism; Sadrā begins with bodies in motion and with the potencies that exist in them and that are the principles of their effects and their operations.

He divides them into four categories. First, there is natural potency, from which activity and alteration proceed in a unique manner, without the participation of the will. This is nature, which, for example, makes the stone fall and come to rest in the midst of the whole. No body is exempt from it; it is an unconscious nature that can be conceived of without a bond – or the absence of a bond – to a soul or an intelligence. The second category is the celestial soul, which acts like nature, but with a will added to it. The third category is the vegetal soul, whose activity is diverse, but without will. The fourth is the animal soul, which is expressed in sensibility, concupiscence, and wrath. It is diverse in its activity and accompanied by will. According to this Peripatetic scheme, soul and nature are conceived of according to two criteria of discrimination: the unity or diversity of activity and the presence or absence of will.[29]

Mullā Sadrā distances himself from Avicenna in the dispute over the universal rather than the definition of nature. He maintains that nature is sometimes particular and sometimes universal. Particular nature is nature proper (*al-tabīʿah al-khāssah*), while universal nature exists in a separate immaterial ipseity. The link between the second and the first is the link between the root and its derivatives. Universal nature is not universal quiddity, for the latter does not exist independent of individuals. Universal nature is not an abstraction but "an intelligible form that is separated, both in its act of being and in its signification, from particular matters."[30]

Avicenna, however, denies the existence of Platonic Ideas, and as a consequence he cannot maintain the existence of a separate universal nature. Sadrā responds to this with his doctrine of substantial motion and the increasing intensification of existents. In other words, nature explains the motion of bodies, but in order to be grounded in turn, it requires the comprehensive conception of the essential motion of being. Indeed, each existent intensifies its act of being in the hierarchy that runs from the sensible to the intelligible. Particular sensible nature thus returns to its origin, to its intelligible root, which is its most intense mode of being.

That is why Sadrā does not need to justify — over and against Avicenna — the existence of separate immaterial realities. Rather, he sees a weakness in Avicenna, linked to the theory of quiddity and common nature:

> It is very surprising that the Shaykh admits that particular natures have finalities and that the finalities, in the succession of individuals, are the permanence of the species, and that he says that the universal is sometimes universal according to the species and sometimes universal absolutely speaking, and that he maintains that these two universals have no existence *in concreto*, except in mental representation, and that they have no existence except in individuals![31]

What is the meaning of the well-known statement according to which perishable individuals find their finality in the persistence of the species, if this species is only a mental concept, if it does not reside — like an authentic living being, like the archetype and the concrete finality of the individual — in the science of God? We may remark in passing that Sadrā does not believe that Avicenna makes pure quiddity reside in a sort of existential permanence in God; he quotes this passage from Avicenna: "It is impossible for there to be in the divine essence a reality that is foreign to the divine essence." Sadrā's consistent Platonism is opposed here to Avicenna's no less consistent Aristotelianism — if we admit, with Sadrā, that the solution evoked above, namely the existence of quiddities in divine science (a solution inspired by Avicenna's metaphysics itself), is insufficient.

Death and Transfiguration

Such is the conceptual framework inherited by Mullā Sadrā.[32] He explains motion by saying that "the nature of each substantial individuality is in flux, in renewal. It also has a stable, permanent reality that is linked with it the way the mind is linked to the body, for the human mind is permanent through its immateriality, whereas the nature of the body is always in renewal, flux and dissociation (*dhawabān*)."[33] A few points about the Sadrian doctrine of spirit should be clarified. More generally, motion must have a natural cause, which is of the order of an event and is not sedentary. This cause must come from within a nature that is renewed in its essence, and it must have a constitutive mover that is a stable reality, an intelligible mover.[34] The act of being of natures has a series of gradations (*tadrījī*), because natures are material, spatial, and temporal, whereas the intelligible act of being is permanent. The immaterial constitutive principle from which flowing nature proceeds is the "separate Platonic form."

Sadrā thus returns to a doctrine of the Platonic Idea, which he rescues from the Avicennian critique by identifying it with the contents of divine science. Each substance therefore has two "states," two acts of being: "the act of being of the world below, which is perishable, transitory, temporal (*bā'id*), impermanent, destined to oblivion and extinction (*dāthir*)"; and "the act of being that is not destined to oblivion, for it is false to say that anything at all disappears from divine science." The ascent from one of these states of existence to the other will be the essential motion of being.[35] Natural motion in this corporeal world is only the first stage, and it is the image – Sadrā says the "metaphor" – of essential integral motion. This motion assumes the extinction and disappearance of the world and is thus a prelude to its permanence, that is, its integral return to the site of the "Platonic" archetypes, the site of the most intense acts of being in the science of God, on the plane of the divine names.

The intelligences that are entirely separate from all matter are not in motion. But souls move; their acts of being "are subject to transformation." Souls are of the order of events and have a history. In the sensible world, they are "imprinted in matters," and the mode of their existence is the "connected being" (*wujūd ta'alluqī*) that is transformed along with the body. Nature is the inferior dimension of the soul. At the final term of physical becoming, the soul's metaphysical becoming begins, leading it to the threshold of the intelligible world. The intelligible dimension of the soul then becomes dominant, and the soul makes its pilgrimage toward the separate light.[36]

It is in order to ground this scheme that Sadrā quotes the *Theology of Aristotle*, combining its teachings with the other "confirmations" of renewal of natural substances, namely the verses of the Qur'ān, the traditions of the imams, and the theosophy of Ibn al-'Arabī. Indeed, he cites two passages from the "first master of Greek philosophy": "It is impossible for any body, be it simple or compound, to be stable and subsistent if the power of the soul does not exist in it. And this is so because it is of the nature of the body to be flowing and to disappear. And if the whole world were a body containing no soul and possessing no life, then things would disappear and perish."[37] And:

> If this is so, and if the soul is a body belonging to the realm (*hayyiz*) of bodies, it is indisputably disappearing and flowing. Indeed, it will flow as bodies flow and will disappear into matter. And if all bodies disappear, being ceases, for all things go toward matter. And if all things decline toward matter, and matter has nothing to give it form, which is its cause, then being will be brought to nought. And if being is brought to nought, then this world too will be brought to nought, if it is purely and simply body, which is absurd, for the whole world is not brought entirely to nought.[38]

It is clear that Sadrā makes the Plotinus text say the exact opposite of what it says. Plotinus and the *Theology of Aristotle* maintain that the world is eternal because it is not purely and simply a body devoid of a soul. The nature of the body is to flow away, to disappear. The body is always in motion. But the activity of the soul of the world saves the world from the disappearance that would follow from its flowing nature alone. Sadrā mobilizes an impressive number of Qur'ānic verses to support the opposing notion that the world is produced temporally and must come to an end. He points to the phrase "nature of the body" (*tabīʿat al-jirm*) and the word "disappear" (or disappearance, *fanā'*). He takes up for his own purposes the Plotinian intuition of essential motion, borrowing even more directly from Plotinus the old Platonic and Heraclitean conception of the flowing away of things in becoming. The Greek term *rheos* (river, stream) has an Arabic equivalent in the notion of *sayyalāni* (flowing away). But Sadrā is faithful to a certain Platonism, particularly that of the *Cratylus*, the *Theaetetus*, and the demiurgic action in the *Timaeus*, which is at odds with the "Aristotelian" cosmology that maintains the Plotinian conception of the universe (since for Sadrā, let us not forget, the *Theology* is a text by Aristotle). Sadrā's commentary on the first citation confirms the impression of a misunderstanding here: "That is what he indicates. This confirms that according to him [Aristotle, alias Plotinus] corporeal nature is a substance in flux and that all bodies are, in their essence, fading and passing away, whereas the intelligible spirits remain, as we have indicated."[39]

Sadrā is right when he finds elements of a doctrine of corporeal flow and a mobile conception of corporeal nature in the *Theology*. But he reads this within the framework of a faithful exegesis of the Qur'ān, and thus within a cosmology that has no place for the eternity of the world. This is not an "error" on Sadrā's part, but rather a striking example of the most common way of producing new conceptions of the world in philosophy. This metamorphosis of Greek wisdom into the Islamic practice of philosophy, and the infidelity he shows toward the works he cites is the very practice of the concept.[40] There is no philosophy that does not have an imaginary relation to philosophy's past, in a history that is truth because it is a succession of "errors" and miscalculations.[41]

We have seen that the concept of essential motion is based on a differentiation between acts of being: every corporeal substance, celestial or elemental, is inflected according to two levels of substantiality, corresponding to the sensible world and the intelligible world. There is substantial motion because existence changes in substance, having at its root a stable intelligible substance whose "derivation" is a substance and whose act of being is transformed. "And the link between this intelligible substance and this corporeal nature is like that between perfection and deficiency, like that between the root and the derivation."[42] At the origin of the existent there is God, who "is closer to us than all that is close." The intelligible substances are the forms of all the existents that will enter the world of generation. They are all present in divine science, and they radiate from it; "they have no free existence by themselves for themselves, but they are only acts of being bound in their essence to the divine real, and archetypes of these forms of knowledge that exist in our thoughts."[43]

In the lower world, the images or derivatives of these intelligible archetypes are the natural forms. Here motion involves not only quantity or quality but also substance. To explain this, Sadrā draws an analogy between what happens in quantity and quality and what happens in substance itself. Quantity and quality are both stable and unstable. They are particularities determined *in the permanence* of the natural body from a certain aspect, but not from another. The body is the substrate of motion and quality or quantity and is permanent in that it is determined to a certain degree (for example, the body has a certain degree of blackness). But what changes in this substrate are precisely the particularities of the determinate definitions of quantity or quality (blackness is variable). Blackness can be intensified between the two limits, according to a unifying and continuous process. It is this process of intensification of blackness, this movement of quality, that is stable and permanent. Between the origin and the maximum term of blackness, an infinity of degrees is possible.

Qualitative motion is not limited, however. The black body is the substrate of this movement and the unity of the degrees of blackness; it is being-black. "What produces motion in blackness must necessarily be a black body and nothing else."[44] There are, says Sadrā, infinitely potent and particularized limits of blackness between two extremes: the intensification of blackness is a hyperbolic curve whose asymptotes are the minimum and the maximum of quality. We see how important the concept of the limit is: each intensive degree is a limit in a curve of gradual perfection (*istikmāl tadrījī*).

Formal substance has an analogous curve: from one point of view, it is one, temporal, and stable; and from another, it is continuous and gradual, the integral of differentials. The permanence of the individual is both a unified and a temporal continuity: substance is the temporalization of its own temporality in that it is the unity of the continuous motion of its gradual perfection. The continuous has indeed *one* act of being, even if it unfolds in the potential infinity of its degrees. Its unity comes to it from its intelligible ground, of which the multiple sensible expressions, the successive limits of gradation, are the shade and image.

This stable and permanent ground (in the science of God) "is determined through itself, and it has stations (*maqāmāt*) and degrees (*darajāt*) through its very ipseity and its very unity. In relation to each station and each degree, it has essential universal attributes, which for it correspond to its unity, in differentiated significations abstracted from it and unified with it in a sort of unification."[45]

Embodied Time[46]

Bodily individuals undergo becoming in the transformation of particularities and the accidents of their substances: change of time and place, modification of quantity, situation, and so on. But this transformation is only a consequence of the one affecting the act of being itself. Sadrā clearly saw that when bodies move, grow, and undergo all the effects of generation or corruption, they do more than pass through adventures or journeys from which their substance is preserved. The body that is displaced does not simply change its location; it does not remain the same as it was, merely coming to rest at a new stopping point. Rather, its fundamental being, its effective reality, has been metamorphosed; it undergoes a "revolution of existence," and this revolution involves movement in space.

Thus time does not let us remain ourselves. We change from day to day because our act of being is transformed, such that we create, through this interrupted revolution of our existence, the possibility of a temporal life. It is as though time, far from being the mere external framework for the unfolding of this life, is engendered by this life itself. Time is a consequence of the intensity of our substantial motion; we are not "in time"; rather, time is a consequence of the sensible act of being and its own metamorphoses: "And the transformation of dimensions, colors, and places necessarily requires the transformation of the singular, substantial, bodily act of being. That, then, is movement *in* substance, just as the act of being of the accident is an accident."[47]

Each individual is a mode of the act of being. It is singularized through itself. Its concomitants, Sadrā says, are born from it as rays of light are born from the source of light. The individual is a singular monad of existence that, as such, has no quiddity. That is to say that the set of differences by which one designates it are indeed real differences, which we name through logical differences (thus man is a rational animal). But these real differences simply express the originary act of being, the source of light from which they emanate. Likewise for time, place, quantity, situation: the categories of the accidents are radiations of substance. But the substantiality of substance is the act of being. Changes in space, quantity, quality, and so on express the motion of the substantial act of being. What Sadrā calls substantial motion is the metamorphosis of the individual act of being, expressing itself in the light rays of accidental movements.[48]

Time is the measure of motion, according to the classic definition in Aristotle.[49] It is eternal, since there cannot be a time prior to time.[50] Its eternity is its mutation, since it is the permanent renewal of the celestial sphere, which has a synthetic unity and a continuous multiplicity of places and situations.[51] Substantial nature, the form of the body, is flowing, is passing away. The eternity of time is this continuous passing away; its measure is the discrete marking out of this renewal. Thus the continuity of nature is motion, whose measure is time.

But what is the cause of time? It can only be the stable ground of all the derivatives and the limits of bodily movement. It is a matter of the "one agent substance, possessing infinite modalities." Essential motion determines all accidental movements – movements of place, time, and so on. It is a potentially infinite modalization of the substantial unity of the immaterial agent. This immaterial agent is not a soul, because the soul is attached to the body and it therefore has the status of material nature and of bodily form subject to transformation. The cause of time is not the soul.[52] "Consequently, the cause of time, and of the ever-renewed temporal realities, transcends time in its freedom (*'alah al-istiqlāl*)."[53]

Time effuses from divine freedom, through the mediation of the supreme imperative called the agent Intelligence and the Spirit. Time expresses an imperative and ungrounded freedom, the creative spontaneity of God, who is manifest in the person of an intimate angel and envelops numerous angels who are the divine hosts. Motion animates the world of creation and is determined by divine decree; it is made up of bodily realities and of natures occurring in time and graduated in their acts of being. It is a world that proceeds from the world of the free and intelligible imperative, which is the world of the intimate angels. Time is the verb of the angel. The whole of creation is a movement celebrating the angelic liturgy, which pronounces in time the modulated response addressed by the revealed God to the hidden God, since the angelic hosts are the revelation that God effects for himself in the mirror of the intelligible. Time is thus the expression of a singular, living, and personal reality, the angel of revelation. There is no "impersonal" time, neutral and devoid of signification.

What is meant by the statement that time is the measure of motion? If time exists, it is through a continuous interval crossed by a movement. Motion is therefore the reality that parses time, in the sense that motion causes the anterior and posterior parts of time. But, conversely, time is the number of motion, since motion is measured by time. It is also thus for number. Ten men, concretely existing, make it so that the number "ten" has a reality.

But their "being-ten" comes from their being counted as ten, which assumes that the "ten" is a ten by itself. Since there is a real of number, there is a real of time.

The real of time and the real of motion, together with that of the interval crossed, are one. Only our intelligence abstracts them and isolates them from one another. The continuity of movement in the concrete is the continuity of the interval, and time is the measure of this real continuity. The cause of the existence of time is not only the continuity of the interval but also its continuity through the mediation of the continuity of motion. Because the interval is continuous, insofar as it renders motion continuous, time can exist.[54]

In a difficult passage of *The Wisdom of the Throne*, Sadrā apparently distinguishes the purely abstract concept of motion from the concrete reality of this motion, which is renewal itself.[55] He maintains, moreover, that there is no cause of temporal eduction and renewal except the very essence that is renewed in essential motion. But we have seen that this flowing nature is grounded in a stable and intelligible root. Sadrā invokes "the philosophers" who claim that the ipseity of time is, in itself, something that is continually renewed and fading away. However, he distinguishes time, measure, and motion from the motion that renews itself.

This is a logical distinction, since, in the concrete, it is the same act of being that moves and temporalizes. Shaykh Ahmad, in his commentary, understands clearly what is at stake: "God creates the thing; he does not create its concomitant through a creation and an existentiation added on to the existentiation of the thing." He cites Suhrawardī, who says that God creates not the apricot apricot, but simply the apricot. God therefore creates the body in motion, but not, in addition, motion and time. Shaykh Ahmad protests nonetheless against the Sadrian proposition that renewal has no instantiator. Here he does not understand clearly that Sadrā in no way denies the imperative action of God, but rather claims that it is entirely immanent to the essence of the body in motion.

Shaykh Ahmad writes:

> Perhaps the argument of the philosophers who say that the ipseity of time is renewed through itself, is that the instantiator made it as something renewing itself *through* itself and not that its renewal would occur by accident through the renewal of its accidents. They did not mean that the renewal occurs *of* itself, without any principle of renewal! That was rather the argument of the first among those who were in the school of the prophets and who gained wisdom from them!

He says later that this principle of renewal is the action of God, the subsistence that is emanation. Faithful to his thesis that quiddity is the first fruit of existentiation (in opposition to Sadrā), he says: "Time is motion itself, not according to its act of being, but according to its receptivity to the existentiation that is its quiddity and that is a part of its quiddity in the secondary sense, i.e., a part of its ipseity." Substantial essence is immutable, whereas the "states" of things can be transformed according to the movement of the act of existing. If one did not make this distinction between the essential stability of quiddity existentiated by God and the mutability of the act of being, affecting only "states," Shaykh Ahmad argues, the promises of revelation would collapse.

We see where Shaykh Ahmad wants to take these arguments: as conceptualized by Sadrā, substantial motion, by affecting the act of being that is the very reality of the existent, becomes the mutation of the substantial essences themselves, and threatens the Qur'ān's promise that everyone will receive a reward for what he is. We will see that, on the contrary, substantial motion, affecting not only the states of substances but also the substances in their essential act of being, founds the doctrine of resurrection.[56]

We have mentioned the numerous confirmations that Sadrā draws from the Qur'ān.[57] He elaborates a doctrine of essential motion in order to support this Qur'ānic exegesis. The Qur'ān is not used to reinforce Sadrā's Plotinian intuition; rather, it is what evokes and orients this intuition. Sadrā carries out the exegesis of the Qur'ān by way of the theoretical framework of the *Theology of Aristotle*, but in response to the demand of revelation, he refuses the eternity of the world. The renewal of natures has an ultimate end, the finality of finalities, the return into God.

The physics of motion is governed by eschatological metaphysics. It is impossible to dissociate Sadrā's exegetical attitude — his attachment to an esoteric reading of the holy book — from his meditation on substantial motion, which is the motion of the creaturely act of being. Here is a testimony to this, which I quote from a passage that should be given in its entirety, the "spiritual testament" that closes the *Treatise on Resurrection*:

> Thus, in the Qur'ānic verses we find an indication of the disappearance of the world here below, and of the extinction of all those who populate it, all that is on the earth and in the heavens. As well as an indication of their transferal, by the essential lightning flash, to another birth, the return of the All, and the complete effacement in the One, the Living, the Subsistent, and He is the origin and the end.[58]

The verses Sadrā chooses express the vanity of the world. For example: "What is the life of this world but amusement and play? But the home in the otherworld, that is the true life, if only they knew!"[59] They also say that creation has meaning and that the futility of this world is outweighed by the destination of the return to God: "See they not how God originates Creation, then repeats it? Truly that is easy for God. Say: Travel through the earth, and contemplate how God did originate creation, so will God create another birth: for God has power over all things."[60]

We are thus led back to the passage from *The Wisdom of the Throne* that was mentioned above:

> According to the proof that appeared to us from God through reflection on several verses of his book, like the verses "They are in confused doubt of a new creation" (Qur'ān 50:15), and "And we are not to be forestalled, in that we will renew your likenesses and give you rebirth in what you will not know" (56:60–61), and "You will see mountains, and think them firmly fixed: but they will pass away as

> the clouds pass away" (27:88), and other verses besides these which indicate the constant renewal and destruction of this world, and which point to the passing and fading away of this world here below and its brutal end, like this verse: "All that is on [the earth] is passing away, but there remains the face of your Lord, he of majesty and glory" (55:26–27), and "And the heavens are rolled up in his right hand" (39:67), and "He will bring forth [in your place] a new Creation" (14:19), and: "Verily we shall inherit the earth, and all beings thereon, and to us shall they be returned" (19:40).[61]

Exegesis passes through the heart of the Qur'ānic text, weaving together verses abstracted from their context, bringing out their real, effective meaning by gathering them together in a single text, where they illuminate each other. The meaning that arises from the mutual contact of literal expressions is meant to provide proof for the philosophical discourse on nature. Sadrā continues:

> This proof is taken from the continuous renewal of nature, which is a substantial form flowing in the body and the principle of its motion and rest. There is no body that does not have in it this formal substantial nature flowing in the entirety of its parts. It is the immediate principle of each body's inclination, whether it be an inclination in potency or in actuality, circular or straight, and if straight, toward the center or away from the center. It is eternally changing and transforming itself and flowing according to the substance of its essence.[62]

Nature is the principle of desire that moves all bodies. Forced motion and voluntary motion do not differ, in this sense, from natural motion. All motion is ultimately the expression of a desire, whether it is the motion of the celestial sphere or that of a sublunary body, whether downward or upward. The Avicennian conception, inherited from Aristotle, is here framed and interpreted according to the fundamental concept of *self-transformation*.

This concept has ethical and eschatological resonances: it is necessary to transform oneself, to carry out a revolution of the self, in order to be faithful to the nature of motion, which is the motion of nature, and which expresses this renewal spoken of in the holy book. The man who takes care of himself, not by preserving himself but by changing himself in the direction of maximum moral perfection, the man who does not maintain a merely vigilant rapport of self with self but always introduces into his desire a concern for God and for the teaching of the prophets and the imams – such a man cultivates natural desire. He is the man of desire, as all creatures, celestial or terrestrial, are creatures of desire. Nature is not the other of history; rather, it is history itself, the history of all creation, of which man is the summation, stretched toward the return, toward his finality, which is extinction in God, superexistence and divinization. The doctrine of substantial motion is the philosophy of history required by the text of revelation. It is a messianic philosophy, if it is true that the man of God, the imam, carries within himself the effectuation of the ultimate ends.

Spiritual Physics

Essential motion is the motion of the concrete act of being, and of the reality of the existent, by which nonbeing is expelled from it. The temporal eduction from nonbeing to being is the instantiation of the concrete existent. Only the intuition of presence reveals essential motion. The abstraction of the understanding cannot reach it. Reciprocally, the presence of being in the created existent is motion. The very word *presence* is deceptive when one hears it in the language of a "philosopher of presence," where the object is unveiled in authentic experience in the guise of identity, permanence, or stability. The "thing," quite to the contrary, is self-movement. Concrete presence is flowing; only the intellectual abstraction is fixed.[63]

It is remarkable that the great commentator Shaykh Ahmad understands the Sadrian distinction between the effectively concrete and abstraction in the following way: according to him, Sadrā distinguishes the renewal of essential motion (*tajaddud al-harakah al-dhātīyah*) and the renewal of time (*tajaddud al-zamān*). The renewal of motion is the renewal of the state of what moves but not of its ipseity, whereas the renewal of the ipseity of time does not follow from the renewal of its state, "for its ipseity, by itself, is renewed by the changing present, which is not the case for bodies, in Sadrā's opinion." According to Shaykh Ahmad, the renewal of essential being, through essential motion, is only a renewal of its state. He wants to claim that "the *state* of ipseity is renewed, not that *ipseity* itself is renewed." When a substance is animated by the essential motion of its act of being, it changes state, but not ipseity.

Shaykh Ahmad's interpretation is ingenious. He says that no thing, other than God, is free from a certain "ontological need" — an ontological poverty in which its possibility, its nonnecessity, is expressed. Nothing has ontological stability except God. Otherwise, the creature would be eternal. All things subsist, therefore, through divine existentiation, through the subsistence originating in the divine emanative flow. That is why the being of a created thing is its renewal, which is a renewal of state and not of ipseity. Shaykh Ahmad argues that the renewal of fixed stars, formal substances, and essential being is similar to the mutation of shadows, to an "accidental shadow being," a being "of pure thought," as the shadow on the wall makes the light of the sun appear reflected on it.[64]

It is true that, according to Sadrā, created existents are precarious, although they are necessitated in being. And it is true that they are beset by desire because of their ontological need, and that they are shadows of the divine light. Motion, says Sadrā, signifies the thing's renewal of state, its passage from potency to act. But this movement metamorphoses the essence of the thing by making it pass from a lower, sensible degree to a higher, imaginal or intelligible degree. Substance changes worlds, and in so doing, changes its world.

Quiddity is the shadow of the act of being. It varies with its intensification, being both stable in its intelligible ground in divine science, and unstable in its mutations and successive growths. A man never ceases being a man, and his quiddity will never change. But he will be more or less a man according to whether his act of being is that of sensible, psychic, or intelligible man: so many degrees or limits along the curve of essential motion. Ipseity is one and multiple, unity is the unity of the intelligible generative source (intelligible man), and multiplicity is the modalization of this monad of existence. Stability is regained only at the final term in the movement, in intelligible superexistence, which is a unification with the divine light.

Sadrā's physics of motion is in no way a material physics. It is a spiritual physics, in the sense of spiritual exercises. It is remarkable that Sadrā uses all the arguments derived from Aristotle's physics to bring the conception of causality to its culmination in a physics of lights, in which the cause of phenomena is systematically attributed to a spiritual reality. This takes place at a time when, in the West, the decisive rupture that would lead to the conception of extension and material forces was under way. The breach between the two worlds is already evident.

Sadrā is reluctant to grant the slightest importance to material causalities in his examination of natural bodies. If he does so, it is in accordance with the classical doctrine of secondary or elementary matter. He prefers to explain motion – using the vocabulary of Suhrawardī's illuminative metaphysics – in terms of the power of spiritual lights. He writes, for example: "If you examine the things that are in this world, among natural bodies, you will find that what preserves them, what supports them and moves them toward their natural sites, is nothing other than a sort of light."[65]

The celestial bodies, men, and animals are moved by a separate reigning light. The other physical realities owe their properties to sensible light. Psychic light and sensible light belong to a continuous and graduated flow that is fundamentally spiritual, even though sensible light is more dense. Sensible light is, first of all, the rays of light from the stars, the causes of heat. The stone's natural downward movement cannot be explained solely by the nature of the stone. Nor can rain or snow be understood solely by the nature of these phenomena. All movements find their ultimate ground in light. "As for bodies, whether celestial or elemental, what carries them, moves them and preserves them from destruction, has its ultimate ground in an intelligible light. As for the heavens and the stars, the explanation is that each one of them possesses a reigning light of the soul that moves it by desire toward its principle, and another, intelligible light that moves it by desire as the loved one moves the lover." Illuminative Avicennism inspires here a physics of desire that owes nothing to quantitative analyses.

At the final term of essential motion the ecstatic encounter of immaterial forms occurs. "They are the forms of that which resides in the science of God and the veils of divinity, the pavilions (*surādiqāt*) of his grandeur." The model for the ascent to the intelligible is the heavenly ascension of the Prophet who is carried toward the veils of light where the divine essence is revealed and hidden. Without any screen against these ultimate stations of divine manifestation, "the splendors of the face of God (*subuhāt wajhih*) would consume all that is in the heavens and on the two earths," as the well-known *hadīth* of the "veils of light" says.

The intelligible forms, however, do not have existence through themselves. Sadrā refuses to join the debate opposing philosophers and theologians, a debate in which some, like al-Fārābī and Avicenna, affirm the hierarchized existence of ten Intelligences possessing existences of their own, while others deny them. The intelligible essences "are effaced and submerged in the ocean of unity." The link between these forms and the unity of the divine essence cannot be imagined; it is experienced in another way. These forms protect the souls that return to them, while also giving them a superexistence, and they confront these souls with their necessary extinction in God.

There is an image for this annihilating unity with the highest existence: *l'amour fou*. The intelligible forms, in which the monads of existence are carried to their culmination by essential motion, are not intellective abstractions; they are not the secondary substances in the Aristotelian tradition. They are subjects of a passionate love; they are mad with love (*al-muhayamūn*) and "never regard their own selves, because they have passed out of their ipseities and because the shapes of their existences have been leveled." But they are also "rays and flashes of intelligible light from the first light, subsisting through its (self-)subsistence and not through its act of giving any preservation."[66] Passionate love thus resolves the logical problem of the unification of the multiple, which is insoluble at the level of the concept. It governs the personal ethics of the faithful, the "true supporter of unity, the practitioner of spiritual unveiling." In other words, of the faithful Shīʿite who is truly inspired by personal experience and the teaching of the imams. An esoteric Islam, culminating in a practice of love: such is, indisputably, Mullā Sadrā's universe of thought.

Chapter Six

Births of the Soul

It was from Aristotle and his commentators that Muslim philosophers inherited the essential aspects of their questions concerning the soul: What is the nature of the soul? How should its various powers or faculties be envisioned? Does it disappear with the body? How can one heal one's soul? Is there a difference between the destiny of the animal and that of man because of man's intelligence?[1] Sadrā is largely faithful to the Aristotelian perspective; he emphasizes its most salient features, taking from it a fundamentally vitalist conception of the soul that culminates in a history of the successive births of the soul in a movement of increasing intensification.

What is the human soul? It is "the first perfection of an organized natural body possessing life potentially, from a point of view that perceives universal realities and carries out rational actions."[2] Sadrā adopts the Aristotelian definition of the soul in general: "That is why the soul is an actuality of the first kind of a natural body having life potentially in it."[3] He adds to this the specific difference of the human soul: intelligence. The soul is the perfection of the body, and when it is human it is rational.

Providence and Life

Sadrā situates these somewhat dry definitions within a science of the soul that embraces its entire becoming, "from corporeal matter to the final term of its stations and its return to the most distant finalities."[4] Sadrā's intention is dynamic; it can be understood only within a movement whose spirit is rendered by his general prologue of the "science of the soul": "Know that the providence of the Creator benefits everything that can be existentiated from the holy effusion according to the gradation that passes from the most noble, then from the even more noble, until it reaches the lower degree of simple realities and their most humble rank. In his providence, there can be no interruption in the gift that it gives, within a limit beyond which it would not go."[5]

Unlimited effusion – the flow of existence – is communicated to all the realities emanating from providence (*'ināyah*, equivalent to the Greek *pronoia*), that is, divine science indissolubly united to God's will and power. The lower term of this procession is the degree of shadows, maximal density, and cold. But this first matter continues to receive perfection, in a more and more intense existence. The operative action of God is similar to that of the sun, which tempers matter and makes it more subtle. The living being must have two things to make it living: an active principle, which balances and harmonizes the internal temperament or organization of the body, and a passive potency, which receives the increase of life. The forms of living beings testify to a hierarchy in the effects of divine wisdom and providence.

Thus the first concept is life. The living God communicates life to all the degrees of existence that proceed from him. Life is structured by three different degrees that determine the stages and the "births" of man, recapitulating all living beings in him: the life of nutrition, growth, and reproduction; the life of the senses and of movement; and, finally, the life of knowledge and discernment. The notion of the soul designates the form of perfection for each of these species of life, and through this form the effects of the life in question will effuse upon matter through the powers in its service: "We call this form a soul. The lowest is the vegetal soul, the median degree of the soul is the animal soul, and its highest degree is the thinking soul."[6]

Sadrā knows that the soul is understood in several senses, as either a potency, a perfection, or a form. He is in no way troubled by these distinctions, which are abstractions: the soul is a unique effective reality whose various properties are expressed by the concepts of perfection, potency, or form. Nor is he unaware of the difficulties engendered by the Peripatetic concept of the soul: how is it possible to think that it is a perfection of the body and a material form, and yet to preserve its proper substantiality?

Avicenna had seen very clearly the need to acknowledge a certain ambiguity concerning the soul. This ambiguity can be explained in two senses: "The definition of the first sense is this: the soul is the first perfection of a natural body possessing organs and having life potentially in it." The soul is form; it enters into composition with a determinate matter, which is to it what potency is to act. The soul is the principle of life and of the various operations of the organized natural body. "In the other sense, the soul is an incorporeal substance, a perfection of the body, moving it by a choice that comes from a rational, that is, an intellectual principle, actually or potentially. The potential principle is the specific difference of the human soul, and the actual one is a difference or a property of the angelic soul."[7]

There is indeed an ambiguity. The soul is not a notion that helps to distinguish a homogeneous type of existent. At any rate, the question of its unity must be posed: the form of the body (its first perfection) is just as foreign to the material intellect (the substrate of the intelligibles) as the fully corporeal (whose existence is inconceivable without composition with matter) is to the fully incorporeal (which uses bodily organs as instruments that do not affect its own intelligible essence). This mutual foreignness of the corporeal and the incorporeal is reflected in the hierarchy of living beings: there is a division between two types of kingdoms, and man is located precisely at this division.

On one side, plants and animals have a soul in the first sense of the term; on the other side, there are men and angels. Men also have bodies, whose form is the soul, and a potential intelligence, whose actualization will project them into the realm of the angels. But if they neglect virtue and contemplation, they will regress back toward the animal. The Sadrian program is clearly laid out: to save the unity of the soul by accepting its multiplicity; to situate man within the intensive continuity of the psychic generations; to reform Avicennism; and to restore the authentic significance of Aristotle. Above all, what Sadrā owes to Aristotle and to Avicenna is a recognition of the human soul—the ruler of the body—as a *soul*, not as a separate intelligence whose subsidiary functions are linked to the body accidentally. They make it possible for him to confront a difficult question, in which the ambiguity of the soul is expressed: Is the soul a substance?

Avicenna's Problem

At the very least, this particular point in Avicenna's doctrine is rather complicated. For clarification, we must keep in mind that Avicenna carefully distinguishes two types of examination: one dealing with the soul as a perfection, and one dealing with its quiddity. We might think that these are the same, since the soul is defined as the perfection of an organized natural body. And it is true that the soul is understood through the concept of perfection, when this soul is defined in *relation* to the body that it brings to its perfection. But this does not prevent us from asking what category the absolute concept of the soul should be placed under, and whether that category is *substance*. Relation and substance do not exclude each other, even if these two categories express two distinct perspectives.[8]

Certain operations of the soul, such as motion, show it to be purely active, while others, such as sensible perception, indicate that it is receptive. The two dimensions of activity and potentiality would exclude each other if the soul did not organize and transcend their opposition. The soul is one, and its unity resides in the perfection it actualizes. To define the soul through perfection dispels confusion, whereas defining it as a potency obscures the matter.[9] The supposed ambiguity of the soul does not undermine the concept of perfection: "The soul separated from matter is a perfection, and the soul that is not separated is also a perfection."[10] But souls, the principles of life and of motion for determinate bodies, come under the category of relation. For sublunary bodies, they do so in three aspects: the soul is potency with regard to the operations that proceed from it; it is form with regard to the process of perfection that takes place through it, from genus to an actualized species;[11] and finally, it is perfection. Potency, form, and perfection can only be posited in relation to some other thing, and "for us there is no doubt that this thing is not a substance."[12]

The soul is not a substance, neither in the sense of a material substrate nor in the sense of form within a composite of matter and form. If someone claims that the soul, being a form, cannot fail to be a substance, let us not argue with him. To say the soul is a substance because it is form amounts to saying form is form or man is man: it is pure ratiocination. To be sure, the perfection of the organized body is in its material substrate different from an accident, but this does not entail that the soul is a substance, for accidentality differs from the accident.[13]

Avicenna writes:

> When we know that the soul is a perfection ... we do not yet know the soul in its quiddity, but we do know the soul insofar as it is a soul. And the name soul applies to it not insofar as it is a substance, but insofar as it rules over bodies and is relative to them. That is why the body is included in its definition, just as, for example, the act of building is included in the definition of a builder, even if it is not included in his definition insofar as he is a man. That is why the investigation of the soul belongs to physical science, since the investigation of the soul as soul is the investigation of the soul insofar as it has a connection with matter and motion.[14]

The word *soul* necessarily attaches to the word *body*. The soul thus signifies *that which animates* the animal body or *that which vegetates* the vegetal body, entirely within its constitutive relationship to the body – in that the soul is what makes secondary matter come to being. But it could not have any ground for living outside this constitution of which it is the formal principle and the full completion. Here, the name *soul* designates not the ipseity of the soul, what it is in itself, but rather the constitutive activity in which this self is exercised. Nor does it designate a mere function of the soul, for the constitution it exercises is the soul entirely, not a mere attribute of it. The word *soul* names the soul insofar as it is animative; it expresses its deployed energy.

The other perspective is that of the ipseity of the soul, its point of origin, its own indiscernible center of constitutive expansion—the real of the soul. What is this soul if one grasps its quiddity not in the course of the operations it authorizes, but as the source of this instantiation? It turns out that a vegetal or animal soul brings into existence, in actuality, a particular composite of matter and form, and "the soul is a substance because it is a form."[15]

For the rule it exercises there must be a principle, and this principle can only be the soul itself: the soul is substance before being in relation to the body it animates, according to a sort of ontological priority. True, the soul is not a substance if one considers it a form relative to a matter. But from a different perspective, if one considers the form a *principle* of the instantiation of a certain matter in positive, concrete existence, then the soul is a substance in that it is a form. Form is then understood not in relation to a matter but absolutely, since matter is pure privation of being as long as no form brings it into actuality in a corporeal composite. As formative, the soul is relative, it is relation, whereas it is substance because it alone is responsible for giving actuality and reality to the matter it informs. It is substance as the generative source of the material living existent; it is a relation to the body that it governs and perfects.

These categorical questions are not empty "scholastic" investigations. They determine the framework in which the subject, its becoming, and its destiny can be thought. Must substance be renounced, and with it a certain freedom of the soul grounded in its identity? Or, on the contrary, must the necessary unity of the soul and the body be reconciled with the originality of the soul? If the soul is a relative form, its relation to the corruptible body threatens to ruin the supersensible destiny of man, which is indispensable to his salvation. If it is substance, how is its composition with the body to be imagined? Sadrā grants substantiality *and* relativity to the soul. He maintains that the human soul is immaterial in its origin, corporeal at the beginning of its becoming, and intellective at its term. The soul is the substance that best manifests essential motion: its substantial becoming integrates the moments of the lowest materiality as well as those of the most glorious intellectuality, such that the soul is almost nothing in its first birth, but draws near God at the end of the journey.

The Soul Attached to the Body Is Corporeal

For the soul, the fact that it is a soul – its "psychicity" (*nafsīyah*) – is not a mere accident foreign to its essence, like the father's paternity or the writer's writing. The soul does not rule the body the way a builder builds his work. Its being a soul is a mode of its singular act of being; its entire existence is implicated in an activity and a union that are essential to the body: "The quiddity of the soul does not have another act of being according to which it is not a soul. But after the gradual perfections and the essential transformations that come to it in its essence and its substance, it becomes an agent intelligence after being an intelligence in potency."[16] Sadrā claims that the soul, when it is the form and perfection of a natural body, is fully what it is, even if this means undergoing the essential movement of intensification that will metamorphose it into another "birth," into an absolutely immaterial agent intelligence.

This amounts to abandoning a naively Platonist image of the soul, which would first make it an intelligible substance, separated from all matter, and then imagine it leaving the world of intelligences in order to apply itself to elementary matters. This conception confronts the persistent difficulty of thinking the union of two realities, one immaterial, the other material. However, if one posits the link between the soul and the body – expressed in the soul's reign over the body – as an essential reality for the soul, this relation no longer takes place after the fact but constitutes the soul as such. The soul does not cease to be a substance; rather, it ceases simply to be a separate intelligible substance.

This is the correct interpretation of the relationship between the receptivity of first matter and natural form.[17] "Therefore the soul's act of being, because it is the form of matter, entails for it that it be a relation to the body, just as this entails for all form a relation to matter. But it does not follow from this that the soul falls under the category of the relative. It does not belong among the accidents."[18] The relationship between the soul and the body is the expression of the soul's mode of existence. It is the very act of giving subsistence to the body, and it is the body's gradual perfection. The soul is *substance*, in that it makes the body subsist. It is the body's generative source of reality and growth; it is the body's own life. The substance of the soul is no longer opposed to its relative being but is expressed in it. It is the first perfection of the body, even if the secondary perfections are not actualized, as an engineer is already an engineer in actuality, even if he is not carrying out his surveying work.

The soul is not like a pilot in his ship, or a king in his city. The whole that is formed by the metaphorical ship and captain is not a body or a substance, a single reality. In Sadrā's account, however, the first perfection of the natural body and the body itself are one. Sadrā repeats many times: "What has no unity has no act of existing." Unity and existence are one. The body whose organs (suitable for life, sense, and movement) the soul makes subsist is therefore the generic body and not an already informed material body to which the soul is added from the outside.[19]

The Flying Animal

This intrinsic union with the body might suggest that the soul is *fundamentally* material.[20] We have seen that it is not an intelligence falling into a material receptacle. Rather, the animal soul presents all the signs by which to recognize the fundamental immateriality of the soul.

Sadrā does not hide his deep affection for animals, or his desire to assign them a destiny within the return of all creatures to God. Indeed, he proposes a remarkable analysis of the animal soul, which is also the soul of men when they do not exercise their intellective potency. The living animal remains identical to itself; it possesses a permanent individuality in all its states. Moreover, beasts have a certain consciousness of themselves. They flee that which causes displeasure, and they seek that which gives pleasure; they flee the pains they know are painful *for them*, and this implies that they have a certain cognition of themselves.

But whoever speaks of knowledge as cognition (*connaissance*, *'ilm*) necessarily speaks of separation from matter (*tajarrud*). Indeed, an animal's knowledge of its own self is permanent and is not acquired through the senses. It is an immediate knowing that needs neither proof through reflective thought nor the testimony of the senses. The animal is not deprived of this pre-predicative knowledge of itself, this presence to itself and to its individual act of existing. Such a knowledge thus attests to the immateriality of this self.

In support of this analysis of subjectivity, Sadrā cites, almost verbatim, Avicenna's famous text on the so-called flying man.[21] The mental experience Avicenna attributes to a man falling in the void or in open space, without feeling the density of the air, is staged by Sadrā in reference to an animal. Imagine, for example, a flying cat. With its paws spread, it would feel nothing of the qualitative realities and would remain unaware of its own external or internal organs. And yet it would have the certainty of its own existence. But this "self" would have no dimension, no length, no width. What it would know would be independent of all its bodily organs, and thus pure subjectivity.[22]

Sadrā's use of the argument of the flying man illuminates what Avicenna meant by it: not that the soul is a *res cogitans*, not that it becomes conscious of itself in the reflexivity of a thought in which it knows that it is pure thought, but that it has a knowledge of its existence independent of all proof that would come to it from what it is not, from its senses or even from any internal or external perception.

This knowledge is the experience of the immateriality of the soul, that is, more rigorously, of the fact that the "self" is not constituted by some property of matter. It is an experience that is proper to the living being, to the extent that this living being possesses a knowledge of self that is one with its existence as a living thing. The animal is the great witness to this luminous presence of the self to itself, of the emergence of self-knowledge (self-cognition), and of the affirmation of the singularity of the self. This knowledge is a cognition without concept and without representation, which is the dawning of all cognition and its originary condition. United in its substance with the body, the soul — from the point of view of its psychic nature itself — is "a spiritual fire" (*nār maʿnawī*), "the fire kindled by God, which penetrates hearts."[23]

The ipseity of the soul, the immediate and generative "self," is the subject's act of existing. In the "self," existence, unity, and originary cognition are one and the same reality. Such is the origin of the multiple ramifications in the organs of the body, which are called powers or faculties. The theory of the faculties is so deeply inscribed into rational psychology and the discourse of physiology that it offers an unvarying framework for all the thinkers of the Islamic tradition. There is nothing surprising in this, if we think of its continued presence in the Western discourses that modified and attacked it, without entirely renouncing all its concepts.

The Monarchy of the Soul

Sadrā preserves the Avicennian doctrine of the faculties.[24] He hierarchizes the vegetal soul, the animal soul, and the human soul. Each is the perfection of an organized natural body, considered from a certain perspective. It is not stable and immutable but possesses various degrees of perfection and deficiency. The perfection of the body is in a constant process of internal perfection. The doctrine of the faculties is a doctrine of the essential motion animating the faculties with increasing intensification, from degree to degree of potency and activity, corresponding to the intensification of bodily life. Vegetative, animal, and human life thus form a continuous flow that reaches perfection in intellective activity.

The vegetal soul branches into three faculties: nutrition, growth, and generation. The animal soul governs locomotion and perception. The faculty that incites movement has its ultimate cause in the faculty of desire, which is united with the imaginative faculty. Sadrā gives the greatest importance to desire and wrath— the two animal faculties exercised in seeking pleasure and avoiding what is harmful—because they are allies to the imagination. Without the control of the intellect, they misdirect the living being, leading it far from the divine world.[25] Necessary for the survival of the animal body, these faculties are also veils that conceal the presence of the otherworld and its authentic finalities.

The perceptive faculty is divided into external sense and internal sense. The animal perceives. The Arabic term *al-idrāk*, which designates the perceptive grasp, encompasses all forms of grasping, from the most lowly sensation to the highest contemplation. This is to say that what is intensified and perfected in the human soul begins with sensation, and that the freest intelligence, the most liberated from material constraint, is still a form of grasping.[26] The sensible is an inferior moment of a process that will always preserve some element of sensibility, without which there would be no knowledge: the act of giving and the act of grasping.

"External" grasp and "internal" grasp. The external senses are diversified to the point of being threatened by excessive pluralization. One of the weaknesses for which the theory of the faculties is often reproached is its loss in endless ramifications. Touch, for example, threatens to lose its unity, for one species of touch distinguishes hot from cold, another hard from soft, a third rough from smooth, still another wet from dry: where will the enumeration end? Avicenna responds: the fact that they all occur in a single organ makes us think that they are one in essence.[27] The evidence of the body is the sign indicating the synthesis of the different species of touch. Such a solution does not satisfy Sadrā, for whom all cognitive synthesis demands more than bodily signs, since the unity of organic activity expresses the unity of psychic activity.

The faculties of perception are differentiated according to whether they perceive particular realities or universal realities.

The external senses have only particular objects. The internal senses are likewise destined for particular objects. Either the internal sense limits itself to grasping its object, or it grasps them and freely acts. If it only perceives them, either it perceives the particular *forms*, or else it perceives the particular *significations*. There is a grasping of particular forms when the soul is present, for example, the form of Zayd. There is a grasping of particular significations when one grasps that a certain individual is just and that another is unjust. The faculty that perceives the particular forms is common sense, which assembles the forms grasped by the external senses; the faculty that perceives particular significations is called the estimative faculty. There is a storehouse specific to each. The storehouse of common sense is the imagination; the storehouse of the estimative faculty is memory.

This doctrine of the faculties is a sort of politics of the soul. Sadrā evokes several times the conception of the *pneuma* (*rūh*), spreading through the brain, to which the external sensible forms are given in their entirety. He discusses and challenges it. But he claims that one can compare the faculty of common sense to a king's vizier.[28] The king represents the hegemonics of the soul, the center of governance and sovereign decision, which is identified with the intelligence. The minister is the common sense, for whom the external senses act like spies, bringing news from every direction – as if the soul grasps the forms of things the way a spy collects information on potentially undisciplined subjects.

Cognition is not a passive receptivity but a sort of permanent investigation that reinforces the central power of the intelligence. Psychology is constructed within the horizon of the monarchy of the soul. We need a history of this monarchic politics of the soul, which has become foreign to us since Hegel deprived consciousness of all originary unity. Perhaps it is still at work in the Kantian doctrine of the subject. It governs Sadrā's vocabulary in a completely explicit manner, influenced as it is by Suhrawardī's polemical lexicon and the givens assumed by the doctors and physicists whom he criticizes from another perspective. The soul is free because, at bottom, it is sovereign, and the grasp of the external world is an attentive espionage, an instructive paranoia, by which the internal prince keeps himself in power.

The Critique of Organicism

Sadrā denies that perceptive forms are impressions embodied in a certain region of the brain. They subsist only through the soul, in a subsistence that is neither an embodiment (*hulūl*) nor an impression (*intibā'*). Forms occur in the soul like the reflection on the surface of a mirror. This Docetist conception of cognition can be linked to the rejection in Islam of every "incarnationist" doctrine of the divine word, as Henry Corbin often pointed out. But it results above all from a critical analysis of the crude materialism of the physicists. How could a cognitive form enter and imprint a trace in a material organic body (*jirm*)? The brain is needed not as a substrate of perceived forms but as a substrate of potency, of the potentiality for a possible eduction of form. The brain brings the disposition of the soul into conjunction with the form-giving principle (*mabdā' al-taswīr*). The brain is to the soul what the material substrate of potentiality is to the actualization of forms received from the agent intelligence. Sadrā justifies his thesis by referring to the nature of imaginative forms, which do not exist in the corporeal world, since they have no bodily localization. They are the index of the fundamental incorporeality of all cognitive forms.[29]

Mullā Sadrā tirelessly insists on the unity of the human soul, and, more importantly, he deduces the necessity of the thinking soul (*nafs nātiqah*) by demonstrating that this soul is indispensable to the operations of the animal soul, namely perception and movement. If man's faculties form a composite, and if the lower faculties undergo the unifying regime of those immediately above them, this is because the thinking soul is unlike the top floor of a building, which is so well protected from the lower floors that it remains unaware of its inhabitants and their ways.

The human soul in its entirety is conceived as a subject. Not in the sense of a simple substrate of representations, but rather as the generative source of all the operations of life. The soul is the perceiving subject, the subject that intelligizes, the subject that tastes, nourishes, moves, desires, and so on. The operations that multiply in relation to different organs exist only through the unified activity of this subject. Self-consciousness, and the representation of intelligible and imaginal forms, do not need the mediation of any organ.[30]

Sadrā proposes a phenomenology of perception. When particular forms are actualized by the senses, the perceiving subject is not the bodily organ. For perception to take place, a subject that receives the presence of what is presented to the senses in some mode of presentation must be admitted. But only the soul, independent of the bodily organs, can actualize the presence of the object of this presentation. Every thing, insofar as it is perceived, is a configuration (*tasawwur*) of the soul. The soul is configured in the object and the object is configured in the soul. All cognition is cognition in interiority (*fī dimn*).[31] Such a grasping cannot take place by virtue of the body. It is therefore established that the thinking soul designates the principle of actualization of this presence — the subjective principle of all perception and all activity — and that the various faculties are so many expressions of this single principle.

The perception of particulars must no longer be absolutely separated from universal perception. It is true that there is a gradation, that the thinking soul is more intensely itself when it is an intellectual soul, grasping intelligible realities in their illuminative act of presence. But it is already itself when it grasps particular sensible forms. Sensation, imagination, and intellection characterize three distinct degrees of cognition and belong to different "births" of the soul. However, they communicate in the same subjectivity, as degrees of the internalization of form. "In man, the thinking soul is the subject that perceives particular realities and universal realities together, and to it falls the task of judging the universal according to the particular, and the particular according to the universal."[32]

The Intensive Unity of the Soul

Man therefore possesses "a single, unified ipseity." Increasing intensification gives this ipseity an internal motion with various stations (*maqāmāt*): "Its act of being begins, at first, at the lowest degree, then it rises little by little to the rank of the intelligence and the intelligized." The connection between the soul and the body is, consequently, a unifying connection (*ittihādīyah*), in the sense that it does not join the soul to the body as one reality to another, pre-given reality; rather, the reality of the body and of the soul are, at bottom, one and the same, from the point of view of concrete existence. The soul unifies the body. It lives, first, in its purely corporeal station and is one with the body that expresses its operations. But it is also purely immaterial in its essence, and it perceives according to modes that are fundamentally immaterial. This is Sadrā's major intuition, one that we must explicate and understand, for it seems paradoxical, to say the least.[33]

The connection between the soul and the body is neither contingent nor adventitious, and the soul is not reducible to the body's temperament. Sadrā's target here is the legacy of Galenic medicine, in which the soul, reduced to temperament, is deprived of a higher principle. This type of medicine is inappropriate for thinking the soul as subject. It is therefore also inappropriate for thinking the unity of the body itself, which cannot be reduced to the balance of the mixture but is a totality in which each mixture is always subordinate to the unity that authorizes it. The multiple is always dependent on the one, without which no multiplicity could emerge from the indifference of first matter.

Now, all unity has its root in the low degree of the immaterial world, in the Malakūt. "Consequently, the human soul, in its proper state, is a holy substance from the root of the Malakūt." The true sense of the Aristotelian tripartite division of the soul into vegetal soul, animal soul, and human soul is a dynamic conception that assumes the originary simplicity of the soul. The soul possesses different parts not in the sense that it is composed of them "but in the sense that it has to do with the perfection of its substantiality and the full completion of its act of being, as well as with the totalizing power possessed by its ipseity with regard to these hierarchies of forms." The faculties have no separate existence. They exist only within the unity of the human soul, which is expressed, to a very weak degree, in the lower stations of the reproductive faculty, vegetable growth, and nutrition: "That is why the operations of the faculties all exist only through a single act of being in the soul, but in a simple and subtle aspect that is connected with the subtlety of the soul."

At their origin in the soul, all the faculties are immaterial. At the empirical beginning of the individual, in the body, they are all material. The transcendent origin ("the root in the Malakūt") and the empirical beginning are to each other as the one is to the multiple, as the subtle is to the dense. That is why all sensible perception is at once internal to the soul and external to the body. The real aspect of perception is in interiority. But at the degree proper to the sensible body, it is expressed as if it were external: the world of external nature is a moment in the unfolding of the internal soul. Reciprocally, at this moment of its growth, the human soul cannot do otherwise than cause its perception to be unfolded in the exteriority of dimensions and extensive magnitudes. When the soul is thus rendered foreign to its own subtlety and simplicity, through the necessity of its own growth in connection with that of the body, it is divided into various faculties. The thinking soul, potentially intellective, is then a growing vegetal soul, a remembering animal soul, a moving soul, and so on.

"In general, the human soul proceeds from the superior rank where it is immaterial, down to the level of nature, sense, and the sensible." Its single power envelops all the lower powers, which at this lower level develop and express it, in the same way that the notions of the physical species – vegetable or animal – are found again in an originary and unified way in the angelic intelligence, once they have been elevated to this more eminent rank. "And just as one finds all the natural species in the intelligence in a more eminent and more elevated mode, likewise do all the natural, vegetative, and animal faculties exist through the existence of the soul, and in the mode of a higher psychic existence, more eminent than their existences in the other substrates."[34]

The Journeys and Struggles of the Soul

The ramified faculties, their integration into a human soul whose origin and finality are an intelligence, and the successive births of the soul—these are the major schemes of Sadrā's psychology. They owe their central concepts to Plotinus and Avicenna. The long elaboration of these theses must be submitted in turn to a work of exegesis. The spiritual significance of the doctrine of the faculties is the internal struggle waged by God in man, the moral war that justifies the creation of man and reaches completion in the distribution of heavenly or infernal retribution.

The births of the soul do not follow the calm trajectory of a substance passing through the sensible, imaginal, and intelligible worlds, as if a simple vital movement were enough for it to grow in perfection. They mark out the stages of a tumultuous journey in which man shows his fidelity to the divine commandments and his resistance to satanic suggestions. On the horizon of this other scheme we discover three great dramaturgies: one imposed by the Qur'ān on the faithful, one taught to the inspired disciple by the traditions of the imams, and one quietly maintained, at the heart of the inherited spiritual discourse, by the most ancient dualist teachings of the religions of Iran. Man is not born in order to pass peacefully into eternal life, or for a natural movement toward perfection in which the mere power of existing suffices for salvation, but for an incessant war of the spirit, whose stakes are expressed in moral discourse.

Ascetic morality provides a way to synthesize the revealed dramaturgies, according to what Sadrā calls "the method of those with inner vision" (*ahl al-basīrah*). To explain this method, he brings together a vast body of references, including the illuminative philosophy of Suhrawardī, the *Epistles of the Brethren of Purity and the Comrades of Faithfulness*, the theosophy of Ibn al-'Arabī, and the anthropology of al-Ghazzālī. It is remarkable to find that al-Ghazzālī, the greatest theologian of Sunnī Islam, provides Sadrā with a theoretical framework that satisfies the demands of this moral exegesis of the psychology of the faculties.

The powers of the human soul are armies mobilized by God, armies "whose essential reality is known only to him and whose number he alone can analyze."[35] To support this, al-Ghazzālī cites the verse "None knows the armies of your Lord save himself."[36] The faculties are the armies commanded by the heart, which is the spiritual organ par excellence.[37] It designates what the philosophers call the thinking soul. This homology is important, since it signifies that the intelligible synthesis of all the human faculties, their generative source, is not simply the faculty that enables them to abstract universal forms and to cognize them, but is also the "heart," the spiritual organ, and the leader of the armies that wages war on the path of God. At this level of exegesis, the entire process of knowledge is interpreted in terms of war, rule, government, and destiny.

The visible army, the organs and the bodily members, is accompanied by the invisible army, the faculties and the senses. Body and soul are commanded by the heart, one serving in external combat, the other in internal combat; both are "models of the heart's obedience." The major concept around which this spiritual psychology is organized is obedience (*tā'a*), in opposition to the concepts of rebellion and deviance. God creates man obedient in his original nature, and man responds to his call ("Am I not your Lord?") by recognizing the divine lordship.

The original covenant between man and God, which founds the relationship of the Lord to his servant, is also the condition of possibility of the revelation of God in his creature, his anthropomorphosis into the perfect man.[38] It is this scheme of divine revelation, the passage from God's withdrawal in absolute transcendence to his manifestation in the perfect creature, who recapitulates in his essence the whole of creation, that governs Sadrā's reference to al-Ghazzālī's doctrine of the heart.

In the text cited from al-Ghazzālī, this eschatological background remains implicit. al-Ghazzālī explains the meaning of the native obedience of the heart, which is expressed in the power of mastery the heart exercises over the body's members and the soul's faculties. Completely devoted to serving its Lord, the heart is no less capable of imposing its imperative leadership on the body and soul. Both obedient and imperious, the heart submits itself all the more to God in that it submits the armies to its enlightened guidance "so that when the eye receives the order to open, it opens, when the feet receive the order to move, they move." The submission of the organs and senses to the heart is similar to the angels' immutable and undeviating obedience to God. This comparison is not simply a metaphor; it illuminates the angelic destination of the human heart.

al-Ghazzālī also cites the Qur'ānic verse "I have only created jinn and men so that they may be obedient."[39] Why does the heart need armies? Because human life is a journey, and in the course of this journey man will have to combat himself and the satanic suggestions within himself.[40] "This journey is toward God and the heart hastens toward his proximity; it is for this that hearts are fashioned." The vehicle is the body; the traveling supplies consist of knowledge. With the help of these supplies, man accomplishes the just and beautiful action (*al-'amal al-sālih*). This is what justifies — over and against a Sūfism that extenuates the body — a dietetics in which the care of the body (*ta'ahhud al-badan*) prepares the way for the care of the soul. Man needs both the great animal faculties, desire and wrath, as well as the spiritual organs that exercise these faculties. Knowledge, for its part, requires the internal army of the five senses. The armies of the heart are organized into three species: those belonging to the will (desire and wrath); those belonging to potency (the other faculties); and those that perceive and govern, the famous spies (*jawāsīs*) that keep watch on the outside world.

The armies of the body belong to the "world of the Mulk and of manifestation," an inferior and external world. The armies of the soul are invisible, and Sadrā locates them in the worlds of the Malakūt and the Jabarūt, higher worlds bordering on divine proximity. The monarchical model of the soul is combined with the angelological model; the dominance of the thinking soul, the heart, over all the faculties is similar to the angelic liturgy around the central source of revelation and existence, the Lord (*al-Rabb*) – not the unknowable divine essence, but the Lord revealing himself to his highest creatures, who eternally sing his praises.[41]

Man is properly endowed with knowledge and wisdom. His perfection, his happiness, and his salvation depend on his proximity to divine perfection and glory. The science par excellence is therefore the science of God, of his attributes and operations. The body is the frame of the soul. When al-Ghazzālī recalls this, he is clarifying the doctrine of the substantial motion of the soul. It was from his own conception of the act of being that Mullā Sadrā derived the idea of the movement of perfection and the successive passage through the corporeal and imaginal births; what he owes to al-Ghazzālī is the spiritual anthropology and the moral tonality that are inseparable from this substantial motion. al-Ghazzālī writes the following, which Sadrā quotes in his commentary on the Qur'ān:

> Man, in the beginning, is located at a rank between the beasts and the angels. . . . He who engages his faculties in knowledge and in action makes himself similar to the angels, he is constituted by the fact that he is connected to them and, to use the proper terms, he is called "angel" and "lordly," as is said in the verse: "This is none other than a noble angel!" Whereas he who diverts his spiritual energy and follows bodily pleasures eats as the herds eat, and he sinks then to the base horizon of the beasts; he becomes voracious like the bull, gluttonous like the pig, rapacious like the dog, stubborn like the camel, vain like the tiger, crafty like the fox, or he even has all this within him, like Satan.[42]

The becoming-animal of the man of passions, who plays such a large role in Sadrā's eschatology, is announced by al-Ghazzālī's moral analysis. When a man conducts himself like an animal, he becomes an animal; he enters into the rich bestiary just evoked. Based on his eternal decree, God makes predominate one or another of the animal faculties in such a man and the heart is unable to discipline them. Carried away by wrath, man becomes an aggressive, hateful tyrant driven to violence and abuse. Carried away by concupiscence, he becomes gluttonous and greedy and gives himself over to sexual liberty. On the other hand, if he is dominated by the mind, which is a divine imperative – "the spirit comes by the command of my Lord," says the Qur'ānic verse[43] – he establishes a balance within and outside himself, thanks to his wisdom and knowledge. He sees in himself the actualization, in the first case, of the satanic essence (*shaytānīyah*) and, in the second, of the angelic essence.[44]

Hence man is not a homogeneous reality. There are four human potentials: pig, dog, sage, and Satan. Here the pig and the dog are not external forms but complexes of passions: greed, enraged thirst, violent desire (the pig), wrath and ferocity (the malicious dog). It is within the interiority of man that these animal destinies are realized.

The soul's imaginative perception grasps this interiority when the soul is separated from the body after death. The four human realities then determine, respectively, the four types of visions – demonic, bestial, ferocious, and angelic – that assail man in his tomb. The real tomb is not the grave dug in the ground, in which we have nothing more to fear or to suffer, but the theater of the soul, concentrated in its imaginative activity, a theater of the tomb's punishment or reward. Here is one image that Sadrā gives of it:

> You know that death is a reality, and that the end of the natural existent is an exit from this world, and that is when the return to God begins. Therefore, know this: when the mind is separated from the natural body, and when a certain connection to the body persists and remains with it – not through its material parts, as all the Moderns think (the vanity of their opinions have been discussed elsewhere), but through the totality of its body – when the soul, then, is separated from the body and the imaginative faculty (*wahm*) carries within it particular significations and bodily forms, due to the work of the imagination (*khayāl*), then the power of imagining is independent in

> its act of existing, and it remains and persists, after the death of the body. If you follow our path, you know this. Thus, when the imagination is separated from the material body, it perceives the forms of particular realities and material realities, just as it perceived them in this world. When a man dies, he imagines their realities separated from this world, and he imagines the man himself, the one who is dead, the one who is buried and who died, according to his form. His body is in the tomb. And his organs perceive all that happens to him in the way of sensible punishments, according to what the true commandments of religion have prescribed. Such is the punishment of the tomb. If the soul is happy, it imagines the rewards foretold by religion, in a form that is fitting for it according to its due, and that is thus determined for it—the form of the Garden, of streams, orchards, young boys, and houris, in a just proportion for this soul. Such is the reward of the tomb, as the Prophet has said: "The tomb is a garden among the gardens of paradise or a grave among the graves of hell."[45]

The sage is made in the image of the intelligence. He weakens the chain of Satan, al-Ghazzālī says; he outwits the demonic temptations, the specious suggestions. Oriental light (*nūr al-mashriq*) is not only, or not principally, the faculty of gnostic illumination unveiling the supersensible realities; it is, rather, the spiritual power of moral discernment. It functions less to unveil the secrets of God than to remove the disguises donned by the passions. The sage plays the passions off each other: he breaks the gluttony of the pig within him with the dominating action of the dog; he weakens the violence of the dog with the dominating power of the pig. He thus submits the whole to his own internal politics (*siyāsah*). The result is a golden mean, an equilibrium, which is justice in the realm of the body. Peripatetic ethics, the medicine of the humors, meets Platonic psychology. An entire complex of convergent knowledges thus develops a moral illuminism. The gnosis of the soul is a politics of the body and the passions, a ruling and controlling of contradictory drives resulting in equilibrium and justice. Medical equilibrium and moral justice are the expressions of wisdom (*hikmah*) and angelic knowledge.

The Two Forms of the Soul

The soul and the body are bound by a "connection" (*ta'alluq*) that presents some difficulties. It seems that we are caught in the following dilemma: either the soul is immaterial, intelligible, and essentially separated from this sensible world, and its connection to the will is purely external and adventitious; or the soul's connection to the body is essential to the soul, and we must renounce its immateriality and its spiritual destiny. Put in the starkest terms, there is a choice: Platonism or Aristotelianism. Sadrā refuses to choose. He accepts the Aristotelian doctrine of the soul and pushes it to its most extreme limits while integrating it into a scheme that satisfies the fundamental demands of Platonism.

According to the common notions of the philosophers, the soul is connected to the body for the sake of perfection and the acquisition of perfection. It first becomes a soul, in possession of a rational faculty, and then is connected to the body. Sadrā shows that such a mode of connection is the weakest of all. The body becomes the instrument of the soul, which is like an artisan. In this case, an accidental, purely external connection is unacceptable. The soul's connection to the body is natural and essential.[46] This will be demonstrated with reference to the necessity of the body and the imperfection of the soul in the initial stage of its becoming.

At the beginning of its first "birth," the animal or human soul is still devoid of every attribute of perfection and existentiality; it borders on nothingness. The perfections will be actualized for it in its ontological growth through the multiple organs of the body, divided into different operations: various sensations and desires, wrath, and so on. If these organs and their corresponding faculties were not differentiated, all the perceptions of the soul would be confused (which is not the case). Moreover, cognition must begin with the senses, for "the loss of the senses means the loss of cognition." The higher faculties of the animal soul become differentiated: common sense, the estimative faculty, the imagination.

Sadrā adopts Aristotle's scheme to justify the notion that the essence of the soul necessarily possesses, in its first birth, a substantial connection with the body. Contrary to the perceptions that begin with the senses, intelligible perception is the existence of things in the intelligence, where things possess a unique and unified act of being, the intelligible act of being. This intelligible mode of being belongs to all objects of perception, beginning with the objects of the senses — smells, tastes, sounds, colors, heat, cold — when they are intensified to a more eminent and noble degree than the sensible mode of being here below.

The authentic intelligible is not a mere abstraction of form from matter but an immaterial existence given to the sensible itself. It is the unification of the sensible in the intelligible. In other words, it is the eternal archetype of the sensible. At this degree, corresponding to another birth of the soul, there is no more differentiation, and therefore no more corporeal connection.

Sadrā believes that he has taken this scheme from Aristotle, but in fact he has taken it from the *Theology* — that is, from Plotinus! And it is Plotinus who, in general, makes it possible for him to adopt an integral Peripateticism in his conception of the connection between the soul and the body in the first birth of the soul. Plotinus also allows him to affirm the immateriality of the soul in the actualization of the intelligible, the mode of being superior to the sensible:

> It will be understood that the soul, in the beginning of its becoming, is like first matter, devoid of all formal perfection, all sensible, imaginative, or intelligible form. Then it initiates its becoming, it becomes an *agent* of form separated from matter, whether particular or universal, and there is no doubt then that these forms are more noble and more eminent than the forms here below that are subject to generation and corruption. What an unsurpassable imbecility on the part of those who imagine that the soul is a single thing in its substance and its essence, from the beginning of its connection with the body all the way to the end of its existence![47]

For support, Sadrā cites the Qur'ānic verse "Was there not a time in the life of man when he was not even a mentionable thing?"[48]

One objection to this doctrine of the becoming of the soul might come from the Peripatetic definition itself: if the soul is the first perfection of the natural body, if this perfection is one with its form and can be distinguished from it only from an abstract point of view, how can one maintain that the soul, at the beginning of its fundamental nature (*fitrah*), is stripped of all form?

The only way for Sadrā to respond to this is to distinguish two forms in the soul. The soul is not one single form but a hierarchy and succession of two forms, a "material form whose act of being is that of a divided, partial, dimensional reality" and "a form unmixed with matter." The first has unity only through its receptivity of the multiple, has stability only in renewal and expiration, and is form only insofar as it is subordinated to matter: it is the multiple, material act of being in uninterrupted revolution. It is, in its beginning, neither sensible nor imaginative nor intelligible. In short, the first form has no perceptual being.

The second form, however, "has a formal immaterial perceptual act of being." It is this form that is sensible, when it exists in relation to an epiphanic site, a sensible mirror in which it is manifest; it is this form that becomes imaginative and intellective. At the beginning of its odyssey, the soul is merely the material form of the body; it belongs to the world of nature. When its eduction into being (*hudūth*) is complete, it arrives at the end of this first natural birth. Its existence overcomes bodily weakness, and the soul becomes the second, perceptive form of a spiritual essence and is inflected along the three degrees of perception – sensible, imaginative, and intelligible – since all perception is spiritual.[49]

Prior Existence of the Soul

The great problem that orients the readings of the ancient and modern philosophers is tremendously simple: do souls exist prior to bodies?[50] In favor of the eternity of human souls, there is Plato, who is confirmed by two prophetic traditions: "I was a prophet, while Adam was between the water and the clay," and "Spirits are mobilized armies, and those who believe in them are our companions, those who deny them are our adversaries." Following these traditions, it seems impossible to deny the existence of the soul before its connection with the body.

Our reason is divided between contradictory arguments, each as powerful as the others. In favor of the eduction of souls, their temporal birth caused by the eduction of bodies, there are two observations: souls change and are renewed "from the lowest substantial states to the highest." The soul needs the organs of the body to erase its initial deficiency. Seen as eternal, the soul is necessarily perfect. On the other hand, if the soul were eternal, there would not be a multiplicity of individual souls.[51] If an existent's act of being consists not in availability, movement, matter, and passivity, if it is rather eternal and intelligible, then its species is one with its individual existence. The angel is the individuation of its own species, since the entire species is in the individuation of the angel. As opposed to this spiritual unification, there is specific unification, that is, the unification of the individuals included in a species in this world. Since it is patently obvious that there are several souls belonging to a single species, the soul is not eternal. These two arguments have the advantage of emphasizing the consequences of the soul's initial precariousness and its pluralization in the sublunary world for the soul's reality.[52]

The Platonists make three arguments against this claim. If souls had a beginning in existence, they would be material, which is false. If souls came into being temporally, they would be dependent on the birth of the body. But the number of past bodies is infinite, which means that the number of past souls must be infinite. But souls persist in being after the disappearance of bodies. There must then be at present an actually infinite number of living souls, which is incomprehensible. Finally, if the soul came into being, it would have no persistence, for everything that is subject to generation is subject to corruption.[53]

Sadrā accepts none of these arguments, and he rejects the grounds on which they are made. He sees clearly that they all have the same presupposition: that eternity is an infinite time, that it is the privilege of indefinitely enduring substances. The antinomy of eternity and time is the product of an illusion of ratiocinative thought, which sees the priority of the soul as an immeasurably extended segment of physical time preceding the birth of the body. This illusion presupposes another: that the soul knows only one world, only one condition of being, which renders insoluble the conflict between the evidence of its imperfections and the certainty of its essential perfection.

To understand Plato's argument, one must relinquish such a naive question. Indeed, it is absurd to maintain that because of particular determinations here below (time and space), human souls exist before the body. It deprives the soul's powers of their operations and posits a human soul that is not the ruler of the body and is unable to exercise animal perceptions or vegetative actions. This is a pure abstraction that denies the attributes necessary for the very psychic existence of the soul. A soul without a body is a soul dispossessed of itself.

What the prophets reveal, and what clarifies Plato's argument, is the hierarchy of worlds and conditions of being: they speak of the priority of the *principles* of the acts of being of souls in the world of divine science, principles belonging to separate intelligible forms, which are themselves the divine models (*muthul ilāhīyah*) Plato calls forms or Ideas.[54]

There are, then, three conditions of being for the soul, one prior to nature, in the divine science; the second in nature, as a corporeal condition; and the third, *post mortem*, in the reascent toward the intelligible principle. The soul undergoes these three conditions in an odyssey moving it from world to world, from the eternity of its intelligible principle to a return to the permanence of divine science. The correct interpretation of the prophetic message of the Platonic teachings therefore rests on "the establishment of what is most intense and weakest in substance, and on the emergence of the movement of intensification in material substances, as well as the confirmation of the principles and the final goals, for the ends of things are their origins."[55] This is why the objections referring to the impossibility of an actual infinity are invalid: "Even if the souls separated from matter are infinite, they are not hierarchized according to a natural hierarchy or according to a place. The falsity of numerical infinity could be proven if souls were hierarchized and gathered all together (which is false according to the scheme of substantial motion)."[56]

Among the philosophers who denied the anteriority of the soul to the body, Sadrā focuses primarily on Suhrawardī, whom he both quotes and refutes at length.[57]

Does the existence of the soul before its corporeal mode of being entail a belief in the transmigration of souls? Is the essential motion of the soul a transmigration from body to body? The question of the soul's transmigration and its palingenesis is an ancient one. Once Plato made it the keystone of his doctrine of justice and retribution it was it has inescapable: it has haunted philosophers and mystics of Islam ever since.[58]

Sadrā does not believe in *tanāsukh*, or transmigration of the soul. But he does not overlook the weakness of the arguments used to refute it. For example, Abū al-Barakāt al-Baghdādī maintains that our souls cannot have been in another body. If they had, he says, they would now have some awareness of their previous states. This argument fails. It is possible, in fact, that the states and the awareness of a previous life have been wiped out by oblivion. There could remain in the soul only traces and dispositions, which could explain the differences we observe between them, since some are more stupid, while others are more intelligent and more apt to learn. Sadrā, like Plato, explains the diversity of actual souls in terms of their previous states and the consequences these have for them. In this sense, there is nothing absurd about the transmigration of souls.

Moreover, we must not think that the existence of souls prior to their corporeal birth is in any way contradictory to their psychic status. It is correct that the soul, as such, must be connected to the body. But nothing prevents the soul from having another birth and another mode of existence either — in the intelligible act of being, which is superior to its psychical being, or, on the contrary, in an inferior natural mode of being.

The soul goes through all the stations passing from the most material state to the intelligible state; it is a mobile substance, and the doctrine of transmigration poorly interprets this substantial motion from birth to birth, which, for its part, is true:[59]

> Know that the difference between the return (*maʿād*) and transmigration (*tanāsukh*) is that the return signifies the transferal (*intiqāl*) of the spirit from the sensible world to the supersensible world.... Transmigration signifies the transferal of the spirit, and its coming and going in this world, from one material body to another. The transferal from a human body to another human body is called reincarnation; to the body of an animal, zoomorphosis; to the body of a plant, absorption; to the body of a mineral, solidification. Transmigration, in my view, is radically impossible, whether one conceives of it as a descent, as the author [Suhrawardī] says the Buddhists and other Easterners do, or whether one conceives of it as an ascension, as others have represented it, and as the Brethren of Purity have tended to do; or whether, as another school professes, souls are caught in a perpetual coming and going in material bodies, without ever being able to escape to the world of Light.[60]

What is absurd is not palingenesis itself, but the naive doctrine of palingenesis.[61] What is unreal is the coming and going of souls and spirits in *this* world from one material body to another. But if one puts forth the hypothesis of other bodies in other worlds, such as the bodies configured by the imagination, the doctrine can make sense. The question, says Sadrā, has divided earlier philosophers. It is difficult because it is believed that the soul has one determinate rank in being and that it is like the other existents, which all have a fixed station. It is difficult to conceive of the truth, the plasticity of the soul, the differentiation of its stations and its degrees. The soul is nothing other than the sum of its metamorphoses, and it always has another form when it undergoes a new "birth" into a new world.

Multiple States of the Soul

The traditional conception of the soul cannot escape some inevitable contradictions. It is inconsistent: the soul is defined first through perception and motion, which are animal faculties: "What the common people conceive of the reality of the soul is restricted to those things whose act of being depends on the body and its accidents." As for the permanence of the soul after "its rule over the body" has ceased, it is reduced to being only the substrate of cognitions. The essential simplicity of the soul derives from the simplicity of consciousness, and grounds the immateriality of the intellective soul. According to Sadrā, such is the limit of a form of knowledge that engenders its own theoretical difficulties: the contradiction between the intelligible simplicity of the soul and its temporal eduction into being; the contradiction between the spiritual nature of the soul (*rūhānīyah*) and its attachment to the body and the corporeal passivities (health, sickness, pleasure, pain).

The *unity* of the soul is the most deceptive representation, especially when it is based on the unity of the quiddity of man, on the definition of the human species. Indeed, the primacy of quiddity, and the unification of the soul through this quiddity, prevent one from thinking the true unity of the multiple, which is the unity of the act of existing. The soul is one because it unifies the multiple flows of the states of its existence, but its unity is not that of a single *definition*. How, in this case, could the soul be differentiated into various modes; that is, how could it be transformed according to sensible, imaginal, and intelligible modes of being? In order to journey and to be modified in its essence, from the beginning of its connection with the body to the supreme degree of separation, the soul must change form. It must manifest intensive degrees of existence in which its plurality expresses the unity of a becoming. The substance of the soul is a generative center of modes, not the individuation of an abstract generality.[62]

We must therefore give up trying to define the soul through the quiddity of the species or through the composition of this quiddity and the body – a sensing soul for the animal, a thinking soul for man. Genus and difference never lead to the effective reality of the soul, and it is impossible to reach its concrete effectivity through them. It is at this point, and not in the doctrine of the faculties, that Sadrā breaks with Peripateticism. He sees very clearly that he can save the corporeal functions of the soul only by granting the soul the full rights of its corporeal birth, and he can save its imaginative and intelligible functions only by granting the soul in its full rights an imaginal mode of existing and an intelligible birth. To avoid the perpetual conflict between "Platonic" and "Aristotelian" demands, it is necessary to break with the entire metaphysics of the quiddities and to understand the soul in its essential motion, a motion that is one with its essence or, in other words, its act of being.

If one begins with an abstract concept of the "rational" or the "sensible," one conceives of merely logical differences. One then applies these logical differences to the derivative differences that are the specific forms of natural bodies (for example, the sentient soul). The body is then conceived of as the genus to which difference happens. How to imagine, in this web of abstractions, that the rational soul could be separate from matter while also being the form of the body? The union or composition of the soul and the body, the separate faculty of the perception of intelligibles, cannot be conceived of in the logical unity of a form produced by the play of difference within a genus.

This logical scheme must be replaced by the concrete scheme in which form is doubled, animated, mobile, in which it is corporeal in its eduction into being and spiritual in its intelligible superexistence:

> This is one of the proofs that establish intensification in the category of substance, as in the categories of quantity or quality. It is thereby possible to represent what is required both by the eduction of the soul and by its permanence after the natural state. Whereas the common notion among the philosophers does not understand this principle [of intensification].... And you will see them becoming confused about the states of the soul, its eduction, its superexistence, its separation from the body, its connection with the body, since some of them deny the separation of the soul, whereas others deny its existence after the body, and still others swear by the

> transmigration of souls. Whereas those who are experts in science find themselves in agreement, based on theoretical examination and demonstration, on the one hand, and spiritual unveiling and intuition on the other. According to them, the soul has multiple conditions and modes of being. Although it is simple, it has various modes of existence, some of which are prior to nature, while others are contemporary with nature, and others are posterior to nature. They maintain that human souls exist before the body, by virtue of the perfection of their cause. The perfect cause entails that, like it, what is caused is also perfect. Therefore the soul exists with its cause, for its cause is perfect in its essence and complete in its gift of the good.[63]

The mode of existence prior to nature is the act of being of souls enveloped in the intelligible grounds of divine science. The mode of existence contemporary with nature is the first birth of the soul; it begins with its eduction into the greatest potentiality and precariousness in the imperfection of the body, of which the soul is then the form. The availability of the body is then one of the soul's conditions of existence in this moment of "birth."

The first birth of the soul is a process of perfection, but as a whole it is characterized by need, deficiency, potentiality, and ontological poverty.[64] The soul exercises its rule over the body, governing and dominating it as well as it can. This difficult sovereignty, however, confers no authentic autarchy, no wealth, no necessity. The soul's reign over the body is not spiritual; it does not consist in the impossible conjunction of an intelligence and a material reality. No doubt it is luminous and immaterial, because nature is still an *agent* light. But the entire exercise of the soul in and by the body is corporeal, such that the soul exists in a corporeal mode of existing.

Conversely, when death takes place and the soul is separated from the body, the second birth of the soul begins. It is not the case that an intelligence is extricated from the prison of the body. Rather, the soul begins a new growth; it sets out on a new journey. It becomes the matter of the spiritual body, and the gradual process of its ascent is completed on the plane of the intelligible, where its act of being is freed from all precariousness. The second birth of the soul is a new process of perfection whose final term is spiritual salvation, the third birth. The end of the journey of the soul is the same as its origin.

Death is a provisional term, the initiation of a second birth. It can be conceived of only at the heart of the movement of desire that carries all existents toward the otherworld and toward the otherworld of holiness.

> The body, like a camel or a ship, carries the soul away in the journey toward God, over the land of bodies and the ocean of spirits. When growth here below has attained its perfection, and this camel has lived a long time, the soul leaves it behind and encounters a second birth; it enters into another dwelling, closer to its principle and its end. Thus does it gradually progress in self-perfection, in the construction of its inner reality, and in the strengthening of its act of being, with the help and providence of God.[65]

Death is the natural passage to the otherworld; it is the abandonment of the perishable body, so that the soul may assume the matter of the spiritual body. The corruption and destruction of the physical body are an accident without being an evil, since the essential aspect of death is in essential motion itself, in which it appears as a necessary event, an inevitable and fortunate inflection. Death delivers the soul — as birth delivers the child from the enclosure of the womb — "into the space of the otherworld."

The natural body has a contradictory status: it must be protected and nourished, the way one cares for one's frame. But it must also be combated and disciplined, so that it will make itself discreet. The body ruled by our soul is, in itself, "subjected and perishable, apt to disappear."

> Whenever souls are more noble and more powerful, the bodies placed under their rule are weaker and have less reality, are more deficient in act of being. Inasmuch as the soul devotes its efforts to

> power, life, and perfection, the body devotes its efforts to weakness, death, and disappearance. When the soul reaches its goal, which is independence (*istiqlāl*), the body is annihilated in its totality and disappears.[66]

The body always tends toward its own death, because the matter that constitutes it is made from the extinction of every act of existing. That is why the passions, which abandon us to the body, are bad and are a desire for death. The drive of life is what moves the soul toward its perfection. When we practice true ascesis, the life of contemplation, we weaken our body, which is itself our weakness. Physical death completes this disappearance of disappearing nature. Physical death accomplishes nothing that spiritual death to this world does not realize. Sadrā quotes this formula: "Death is an effect of the epiphany of the real." When the divine world is manifested in the soul at the end of its effusion of ardent love, the physical dwelling place dies. The epiphany kills the body of the one who receives it; it is at once the happiness of the soul and the terror of the lower existence. "The mountain of the body's existence is flattened." That is why the light of epiphany can shine forth only in the world of the Malakūt, when the soul is firmly bound to the spiritual world and fully possesses spiritual existence. It then abandons the dimension of bodily existence, that of the lower world, the Mulk. We thus begin to sense that the life of the soul is a struggle, since the relation between the Mulk and the Malakūt is adversarial: "This world and the other are like the two plates of a tilting scale, where the strength of one means the weakness of the other."

The spiritual body, the body of the soul in the otherworld, does not have this status. The life of the soul, whose act of being is entirely perception, is essential life, not the accidental life of material bodies here below.

The death of the body fulfills the love for being:

> By the necessity of his wisdom, God established in the nature of souls a love for the act of existing and of superexisting (*mahabbat al-*

> *wujūd wa-l-baqā'*). And he established in the nature of the soul an aversion to disappearance and to nothingness. And that is true, since you know that the nature of the act of being is pure good and pure light, and that its superexistence is the very goodness of the good, the luminescence of light. Now, there is nothing that nature accomplishes that is a mere nothingness, and to the extent that we dwell in nature, we have a goal to which we are subordinated and to which we tend as toward our own end. We thus know that the love souls have for superexistence, and the aversion they have to death, exist only in relation to a certain wisdom and a certain finality, which constitute their being under the most perfect conditions and in the most perfect existences. Consequently, the fact that souls are naturally disposed to the quest for superexistence and to the love of permanence is the proof that they possess a mode of being from the other world, subsisting always. This is so because the permanence of the soul in this natural birth here below is destined for annihilation. If there were not another, permanent birth for the soul, toward which it will be transported, then the love of eternal existence that is implanted in the soul and that resides in its nature would be futile and miserable. But nature does nothing in vain, as the metaphysicians have said.[67]

The natural desire to exist and the nostalgia for eternity are proof of the soul's resurrection and birth into the otherworld. Hatred of death is a sign of immortality, and the death of the body, far from sealing its destiny, fulfills the desire for immortality, since the natural body contradicts this desire. Nihilism is a misapprehension of the nature of the soul, a forgetting of self and one's desire. When the soul becomes immortal, it does not give up on its desire.[68]

The soul therefore has three principle states and three "births." First, there is its original state in divine science, an existence that is intelligible in essence and through the essence of the divine instaurator. This act of being prior to the natural existence of the soul is a manifestation of the science of God that expresses the unfathomable unity of the divine essence. It is the being-intelligence of the soul, submerged in the divine unicity.

The soul-intelligence then descends into the corporeal world. There it is born for the first time; it passes from the rank of eternity to that of temporality. It is no longer stable; rather, it becomes: it undergoes the destiny of generation. The soul is then a lower form, a natural act of being, the mover of the essential motion that perfects the body and perfects itself according to its control over the body. This first birth is the second state of the soul, in which it is truly a "soul," no longer pure intelligence.

At the end of this journey in the evanescent sensible world, the higher faculties of the animal soul – memory and imagination combined – survive the decomposition of the material body. They enable a retribution of the good and bad actions of an entire life, collected in the body constituted by the "lesser" resurrection. This is the reward or punishment of the tomb. From the shadowy depths of the grave, illuminated by the terrible lights of hell or the sweetness of heavenly visions, the soul is called to complete its second birth.

If it is faithful, if it has perfected its moral existence here below, if it has cultivated contemplation and intellective knowledge, its intelligible mode of being is led to the end of its return to God, in a spiritual and angelic state of unification that finally rescues the soul from its exile and leads it back to its true homeland, the native dwelling of superexistence.

However, if the soul allows the attributes of the beasts and wild animals to take root in it, its aptitude for contemplation is destroyed. The effects of the immaterial spirit are extinguished in it; its humanity disappears. Indeed, Sadrā thinks that man is man not solely through his mortal finitude but also "through his immaterial spirit and the angelic destiny that is potentially in him, not through his shadowy body and his animal soul."[69] Hell is a paradoxical existence, where there is neither death nor life. The soul lives without living and dies from not being able to die, in an agony in which the only activity of the soul is the persistence of its passivity, and in which punishment is the distress of passion. The condemned "remains prisoner of the anguish of hell, burning with the fire of desires, whipped by serpents, as the verse says:

'And when their skin is burnt up and singed, we will give them a new one so that they may taste the punishment.'"[70]

This story of the human soul owes a great deal to the gnostic sense of life staged by Suhrawardī in his mystical narratives, particularly *The Narrative of Occidental Exile*, which aims to continue the revelations provided by Avicenna's visionary narratives.[71] The notion that the soul is at the center of a drama of light and shadows is derived from Suhrawardī. Sadrā, however, contradicts the "master of illumination" on two major points: the nature of the link between the soul, a luminous essence, and the body, a shadowy substance, and the question of the soul's preexistence. Those he disdainfully refers to as the "common" among the philosophers are Suhrawardī's disciples, the lineage of the Ishrāqīyah, who were unable to disentangle the threads of the eduction of the human soul and of fundamental atemporality.

Sadrā cannot understand how Suhrawardī could have followed the Peripatetics in their denial of the soul's preexistence to the body. He comments in detail on the pages of *The Philosophy of Illumination* in which this denial is supposed to be demonstrated.[72] He takes the opportunity to write an important gloss, the substance of which he reproduces in *al-Asfār*. In this commentary, he provides the exegetical and theoretical elaboration necessary for the complete exposition of the doctrine of the "substantial revolution."[73]

Sadrā does not agree with Suhrawardī that souls are unified as to species, "in the sense of being the individuals of a single species," distinct in existence, but parts of a single reality, dependent on a single quiddity and according to a specific unity.[74] He refuses every notion of an intelligible unity of souls reduced to the abstraction of a quiddity ("rational animal"). According to "certain eminent philosophers" — that is, according to Sadrā himself — intelligible substances are not universal quiddities, but pure monads of existence without any quiddity. The only difference for these monads of existence consists in the gradations of intensity and weakness rather than the difference of the part and the whole, or the individual and the universal. The law of differentiation through intensity determines that something is more intense if it includes within itself the models (archetypal realities, *amthāl*) of the weaker. The most intense is that which grounds the hierarchy of the weaker individual's multiplicities. The hierarchy of the intense and the weak is a hierarchy of monads, in the sense that one envelops the others, in the same way that a more powerful unity envelops weaker ones. We never leave the realm of the singular.

Thus the state of souls before their descent into the body is the monadic state of intelligible singularities. Souls can be considered prior to bodies because they are individuated in the intelligible and not through accidents consequent to their quiddity. Individuation is effectuated not by matter but by the form of the soul itself, a form characterized not by a modification of quiddity but by a degree of intensity or weakness, in the act of being itself – that is, in the individuation of intelligible existence. Unity, existence, and the intelligible are one.[75]

The unification (*ittihād*) of human souls depends on the status of their birth. "Souls, in this corporeal birth here below, come into being to the extent that each one of them is attached and united to a body in a natural unification."[76] The soul has another type of unification that one can call supernatural, according to the perfection and the separate intelligence it has attained in its intelligible birth. Essential motion, which draws the soul from one birth to another, leads it from pure unification to natural unification.

When the soul descends into the physical world, it rules over the body with which it is unified. Better still, it renders it singular, since "the body is singularized only by the soul."[77] But because of this, the soul undergoes an inevitable multiplication, since "the substrate of what is one by nature is multiple in its parts." The descent of the soul from the intelligible to the natural state corresponds to the first phase of the movement of being, which is the production of the multiple on the basis of the one being [*l'un étant*], the intelligible. Whereas its ascent (*su'ūd*) "from this birth to the birth of the intelligence entails the unification of the multiple. And there is no multiplication of the one and no unification of the multiple in what is connected with the spatial dimensions and the body, as Suhrawardī thinks, since this would mean that souls are dimensional and corporeal."[78]

The movement of being is not a spatial movement but a degradation or intensification of the soul in which the body, in its materiality, merely plays the role of a receptacle, a potentiality. Natural birth itself does not have its formal and final cause in a particular necessity that comes to the body; inversely, the multiplication of corporeal singularities — in which the soul is the form and perfection of the natural body — is the emanation of a primordial unification that comes to be degraded in multiplicity.[79]

The Fall of the Soul

It is important to understand exactly what the descent of the soul is. The Arabic term for it is *al-hubūt*. It means "the fall." Does Sadrā think of this "fall" as a disaster and a tragic event, as it is represented in some of the gnostic myths? Not exactly. He summarizes quite faithfully the dualist Mazdean dramaturgy,[80] but he does not cite the Manichaean gnosis, and even less the versions of gnosticism that criticized Plotinus. He places himself under the authority of Plotinus in order to integrate the Mazdean myth into the long history of the fall of the soul, which according to him cannot be a disaster, but is a necessary phase in substantial motion and a prelude to the reascent toward the intelligible.

In this sense, there is a profound difference of feeling between Suhrawardī and Mullā Sadrā. For one thing, the world of bodies is truly a shadow world, made of night and death; it is the place of "Occidental" exile, resisting with its positive nothingness the effusion of the intelligible lights. Spiritual life is less a struggle than the exercise of the soul's harsh government over the "citadel" of the body. This government is a prelude to the soul's uprooting, as it leaves behind the Occidental region and moves toward the Orient of lights.

For Sadrā, this scheme of the journey persists, as does the thematic of government by the soul. But paradoxically, Sadrā can only reactivate the theme of mortal combat and place it at the center of his theoretical scheme because he resists interpreting the fall of the soul into the corporeal world as the arrival of light in a universe entirely foreign to it.

The body is a mode of being of the soul; it is the state in which the soul is completely and fully a soul and in which it exercises its formative activity. It must therefore combat the lower powers in order to prepare for the later phase of its journey toward the intelligible birth, where its becoming intelligence will begin. It is less an uprooting than a victory, less a repatriation than a purifying ascesis. The gnostic duality that so strongly inspired Suhrawardī's thought is replaced in Sadrā by a Neoplatonic scheme. The Suhrawardian soul does not struggle: it escapes. The Sadrian soul rises up because it is the site of a struggle.

It is true, however, that the fall of the soul is revealed by traditions that must be interpreted in philosophical terms. This is the goal of a *story*. Sadrā summarizes the leitmotif of the story of the fall (*hikāyat al-hubūt*) thus:

> Know that the story of the fall of Adam's soul — a fall from the world of holiness (*'ālam al-quds*), which is the native land of his sacred father, down to this world, the native land of the corporeal nature, which is like the cradle and the native land of the animal soul, which is like its mother — the story of this fall is told according to what emerges from many revealed pages that have come down from the heavens, parables of the prophets, indications of the friends of God and eminent sages.[81]

The sacred father here is no doubt the *nous patrikos*, the "paternal" intelligence. In the Plotinian tradition, the expression also designates God, the principle of emanation, and in this sense the Sadrian scheme of the fall is faithful to its Plotinian configuration.[82] We also find here a trace of the Suhrawardian conception of the natural species, guided by its angel, the "mother of the species" (*umm al-naw'*).[83] Is there a distant echo here of the Manichaean notion of the "mother of the living," or rather of the Peripatetic conception of the "maternal" and feminine receptacle of form? I think one should focus not on the homology between the natural receptacle and the feminine creator as the theophany of the holy spirit but rather, more simply, toward the representation of the nuptial union between the immaterial intelligible agent and the psychic patient as a "sexual" (*nikāh*) union, a metaphor that appears often in Sadrā.

For his interpretation of the fall of the soul, Sadrā constructs a *ta'wīl* whose structure is exemplary. It incorporates the story of the fall, according to the Qur'ānic verses;[84] the prophetic traditions; the statements of the "prince of believers," the first imam, 'Ālī ibn 'Abī Tālib; the *Theology of Aristotle*; the symbolic narratives: Salāmān and Absāl, the story of the dove that brings a necklace in *Kalīla and Dimna*, and Avicenna's story *Hayy ibn Yaqzān* and his *oasīda* on the soul;[85] and the sages of ancient Greece.

In this remarkable order, which hierarchizes the holy book, the person of the Prophet, that of the imam, the Greek philosophers, and mystic literature and poetry, Avicenna occupies a select position. The unity of revelation, philosophy, and "literature" is organized around the prophetic and imamic exegeses.

The main idea suggested by the quotes from the Qur'ān is the following: the fall of Adam out of the world of paradise is the effect of a divine command ("Fall!") whose consequence is "strife," which for Sadrā means the multiplicity and chaos inherent in material reality. This strife will come to an end by means of divine guidance, which will illuminate certain men, whereas others are "bound to go astray." The fall prefigures the image of the end of time, the bodily and spiritual retribution of the chosen and the damned.

A prophetic tradition states that "men are mines, like gold or silver mines." According to Sadrā, this designates

> the anteriority of the existence of souls in the mines of their essences, among the separate intelligences which are the storehouses of divine science . . . just as external concrete particular things have subsistence in the prior divine decree and are there preserved from alteration, effacement, and establishment, whereas here they dwell

> in generation and corruption, effacement and establishment, as in the verse "God blots out or confirms what he will: with him is the mother of the Book" (13:39). This means: the well-guarded tablet of alteration and change.

With this spiritual exegesis, Sadrā gives the letter of the prophetic text a hidden meaning, which is nothing other than the doctrine of the two states of the soul. On the one hand, there is the intelligible state in the science of God, a state common to souls and to the archetypes of all creations, an eternal state. On the other, there is the state subject to essential motion and its effects, the corporeal movements. The divine decree is one with the intelligible world, the science of God commanding "what he will." The fall is the emanation of all things, particularly of souls, by a free divine decision: this is an astonishing synthesis of Neoplatonic Emanatism and the imperative freedom of God according to Qur'ānic revelation. The world of the souls will be the world of the well-guarded tablet or predestination. The entire passage from the intelligible state to the natural state is homologized with the descent of the holy book from "the mother of the Book."

This scheme is confirmed by certain sayings of the first imam: "God shows his mercy on any thing known beginning from 'where,' in 'where,' and to 'where.'" These three "wheres" designate the three states of the soul—before, during, and after generation. The imam also says: "May his intelligence make its presence manifest, and may it be among the sons of the otherworld, because it will be given a priority from the otherworld, and it is to the otherworld that it will bring its revolution." For Sadrā, these words attest to the soul's movement of revolution (*inqilāb*) toward the intelligible world and its angelic condition. Only one who is engendered by the otherworld will return to the otherworld, which echoes with the teachings of Christ: "Verily, verily, I say unto thee, except a man be born again, he cannot see the kingdom of God."[86]

The imam clarifies the nature of the soul by revealing that it is the manifestation of God in the mirror of his creation. Elucidating the status of the soul means not only responding to the demands of a philosophical discipline, but also showing man in his true nature, which condenses all the universes together and testifies to the unfathomable mystery of the divinity, for it is through him that this mystery enters the path of manifestation. The human soul unfolds within itself the entirety of what is, from the origin to the final term. The human form par excellence is that of the imam, a perfect man, whose person signifies the "straight path" announced by the holy book, which takes the faithful to paradise and the unfaithful to hell: "Know that the human form is the greatest proof of God in his creation, it is the book that he wrote with his hand, it brings together the form of the worlds, it is the summary of the well-guarded tablet, it is the witness of all that is hidden, it is the straight path to every good, and the path that stretches between paradise and hell."[87]

The *Theology of Aristotle* makes it possible to interpret the fall in terms of a procession that does not harm the soul.[88] Contrary to many gnostic schemes, Sadrā's intention – which is faithful to Avicennism in this sense – is to preserve the fall of the soul from indignity. The fall is not fundamentally a misfortune, even if its bodily condition is an occasion for suffering and sin. By coming into the world of nature, the soul learns about evil; it will learn how to avoid it, and so it will have acquired something and will have undergone no loss. The process of moral perfection that the soul will have to engage in, with the instruments of the body, is a paradoxical progress that assumes its descent into this world. The fall is a manifestation of power and knowledge of self rather than a loss; it is the condition of memory and of the return to self.

The same moral tone and the insistence on the purification of the soul are present in a gloss by Avicenna that perfectly agrees with the following statement by Sadrā:

> If the soul is pure, it succeeds in quickly separating itself from its [terrestrial] world, because it has realized its perfection, because its nature is joined with that of the intelligible principles, and because it is cleansed of the impurities that, after the dissolution of

> the corporeal composite, prevent it from reaching the intelligible world. Insofar as the soul hastens its arrival at the degree of being that is prior to it [in dignity], far from suffering harm from its descent, it rather gains from it.[89]

The movement of the soul is not a disordered vertical fall but a circular movement, the sensory image of which is the apparent course of the sun. From the intelligible Orient to the corporeal Occident, then from this Occident to the Orient of its origin,

> all this indicates that the soul has a certain mode of being prior to the body and an act of being in the higher divine world, that it has a return and a conversion back to what it proceeds from, that in its Occident an ascent belongs to the sun of its essential reality and to the stars of its power, and that in its Orient it may be resplendent in its firm uprightness [*droiture*], or else eclipsed, reversed, and darkened.[90]

The circular movement encompasses the entire sky of the soul. Its final term depends on its moral uprightness and its fidelity to revelation, without which the soul is eclipsed. It is therefore not the fall from the Orient to the Occident that is harmful but the wanderings on the path of return to the Orient. There is often an inclination to identify Sadrian psychology with Suhrawardian or gnostic dramaturgy. But here, the entirety of moral knowledge does not teach the tragedy of the fall but rather the tragedy of the reascent, the return, which assumes that the soul, as Avicenna puts it, is "cleansed" of the impurities it gains from knowing but from which it must free itself.

The intelligible principle of the soul, its "intelligible and holy father," would not be what it is if it did not provoke the procession of the soul. The sole meaning of the fall of the soul is in this procession (*sudūr*). Sadrā mobilizes the ancients in support of this exegesis. They help one understand the essence of Adam's sin and the meaning of divine wrath. It is remarkable that Mullā Sadrā erases all tragedy from a story that seems to reveal a separation between the soul and its creator, a separation that betrays man's original freedom for evil, the consequence of which is original sin and a hopeless human condition.

Nevertheless, with Sadrā we are as far as possible from the inspiration at work, for example, in Kierkegaard. Adam's sin is certainly the cause of the soul's deficiencies, and it accounts for our ontological poverty. Adam and his descendants fled divine wrath. But this sin, like its consequences, must be understood precisely on the level of intellection and cognition. This sin is a matter of misapprehension, an incapacity to understand. We experience this, says Sadrā, whenever we wish to examine a theological question but have to give up on the problem because we become preoccupied with the realities of this world.

Sin is a breakdown in the endurance of knowing; it is a forgetting and a veiling. It is absorbed into the soul's descent once the soul has left the intelligible place. But all the techniques of gnosis will help to efface forgetting by actualizing, at ever greater lengths, the contemplation and the testimony of being. If "your brain is inflamed when it is captivated by the intelligible manifestation of divine reality," this can only happen because the latter is veiled. As a *felix culpa*, sin maintains the distance that the Prophet himself had to suffer, that of the seventy veils of light separating him from the divine essence during his celestial ascension. "If they fell away, the splendor of the face of God would scorch everything that turned its gaze to it," the tradition tells us. Adam's sin is the human condition itself, its creaturely ontological weakness.

It remains true that the fall is indeed a fall, and that it punishes a blindness and a shadow that must be defeated at the end of the struggle. Sadrā quotes three passages from Plato,[91] as well as this thesis attributed to Empedocles: "The soul is in the high and noble place, and when it sins it falls into this world, and it comes into this world only by fleeing from divine wrath. But when it comes down to this world, help comes to the souls in which their intelligences are mixed."[92] To reinforce his argument, Sadrā presents several long passages from the *Theology of Aristotle*.[93] These passages attenuate the negativity of the fall and sin: "The soul must not be blamed and censured for having left the intelligible world." By falling, the soul loses its simplicity and is divided: "it receives the divisibility that divides the body."

In the origin narratives, Adam's sin and what surrounds it are only symbols, functioning within what is apparent (*zāhir*); they are not the true and hidden meaning:

> It is no secret that a number of the ancient philosophers maintained, in agreement with the prophets, that they founded their discourse on the symbols and the parables of wisdom.... They did not say that the soul had sinned and fallen while fleeing the divine wrath bearing down on it. They and those like them knew that in the world of holiness one cannot conceive of any sin occurring or any disobedience being perpetrated, and that none of the effects of motion have any sway there. No! By the soul's "sin" they meant what I myself indicated when I spoke of the dimension of potentiality of the soul and its actualization on the basis of the principle, its ontological deficiency, which is made necessary by its attachment to the body, or its being in potentiality. The natural crime of the soul is the weakness of its substance, and its fall is its procession from the intelligence that has become separated from it because of its corporeal attachment, and the fact of the soul's being a potential intelligence — in other words, the fact that the theoretical power does not have enough strength to dominate something whose condition of being is that it proceeds from this force, except after a certain time in which it will mobilize the practical potency in its animal and psychical operations. Consequently, the soul turns its face away from its sacred father, because of a certain corporeal attachment. And this attachment is one belonging to its mode of existence. The flight from God's wrath is that natural desire to govern the body through its love for the perfection of its own essence, so that this substantial weakness will disappear from it, thanks to the substantial perfection of its act of being, which consists in its separation from matter.[94]

Since Sadrā refuses to grant any effectivity to nonbeing, the latter must be thought in terms of privation or potentiality. Sin and disobedience are thus only the inadequate symbols of an ontological deficiency made necessary by the soul's descent into the corporeal world. There is no original sin, any more than there is a fundamental freedom for good or evil. When the soul turns away from its "sacred father," this gesture of denial is an act of disobedience, but it is also a positive and necessary act in the becoming decreed by God.[95]

When man is driven out by divine wrath and flees from his heavenly sojourn, he does not suffer the consequences of his decision, which in a single moment has made possible all future free decisions. He has distanced himself from God only to exercise again, in corporeal nature, the spiritual power that comes to him from God. The soul, having proceeded to the rank of nature, is far from its principle. This distance is poverty and natural desire (*shawq tabīʿī*). Desire, at the heart of nature, produces love, which is the love of self-perfection. The government exercised over the body is useful to this loving perfection of oneself, in which the soul experiences a return to substantial perfection, to the intelligible act of being that will be, once again, the proximity of its principle.

This exegesis owes its coherence to Neoplatonism and, more precisely, to the concept of substantial motion. One of the main consequences of this debt is the rejection of any imaginary representation of a rebellion or an irruption of freedom linked with the possibility of evil in the intelligible world or the world of the divine imperative. This world must remain faithful to its own identity with itself and to its luminous essence. Sadrā's intent to formulate the constitutive ontology of Islam is made clear in the fact that he wants to preserve the real essence of God — his manifestations in the pleroma of divine names, the epiphany of his most beautiful names in primordial man — from any hint of an internal rupture or a brutal negation that would break up the reign of this identity. It is in this important doctrinal point that any possible comparison ceases between the theoretical disposition of the spiritual philosophy of Islam — or at least of the Avicennian lineage that comes to completion in Sadrā's reforms —

and the philosophy of German Idealism in the West. In the text just cited, there is no echo at all of the disquiet of Friedrich von Schelling, who was an heir to the theosophy of Jakob Böhme. Sadrā dismisses every form of exegesis that gives divine wrath any positivity whatever or is grounded in a freedom conjoined with evil at the very heart of the divine. Evil, the pure impotence to act, is left on the lower frontiers of the creaturely world. Nor is there anywhere in Sadrā a scheme of becoming that would carry within itself, as its mover, a freedom consisting of a split between unity and principle.

Between the divine essence and its manifestation concentrated in primordial man, only peace can reign. This peace can indeed create a distance, a degradation, and a progressive deficiency, but it does so with the best in mind, leading to the return and the process of perfection. The inner meaning of the drama of creation is the circle traveled by the intelligible, descending into the precincts of shadow in order to climb back up to the precincts of essential unity. The One leaves its unity in order to rejoin the One, and the history of the soul is the narrative of this positive history of the power of the One, of peace and order.

We have said that this scheme grounded the thematic of moral struggle. We have also said that in his own way Sadrā made use of a certain form of duality, an irreducible opposition between light and shadow, which he owes to the meditations of Suhrawardī's *Philosophy of Illumination* and to the teachings of the imams of Shī'ite Islam. There is no contradiction in this, but there is certainly a tension between radical ontological monism and a pronounced ethical dualism. The domain in which this dualism is expressed — without any rupture in the fundamental unity of being — is the imagination.

In his long critical commentary on Suhrawardī's theses, Sadrā corrects what he sees as the miscalculations and misunderstandings that might result from this philosophy of unity.[96] If being is identity and unity, the acts of being are both hierarchized and different in their essence. The soul possesses two separate acts of being (*wujūd mufāriqī*). One in the world of intelligence, and another one that is connected (*wujūd ta'alluqī*) to the world of bodies.[97] That is why all the refutations of the soul's priority are futile, for they do not take into account the following: we are not speaking of the same soul when we speak of one or the other of its acts of being. We wrongly assume that the soul, as a soul ruling over the body, has an intelligible essence (which is contradictory), while at the degree of the intelligible the soul is intelligence, is not the soul ruling over a body, and has no concern for the body.

It seems that the most solid argument is based on taking the nature of infinity into consideration. Sadrā finds here an opportunity to elaborate on a remarkable thesis: numeric or temporal infinity must be distinguished from *infinity in intensity*. The intuition of intensive infinity is at the foundation of the doctrine of the births of the soul, and Sadrā leads us in this direction in the demonstrations that we will now analyze.

The intelligible principle of souls, says Sadrā, is infinite "as to potency, dimensions, and existential qualifications." It does not exhaust its potency of effusion in the production of a given number of singular souls; it is an infinite monad. There always remains in it the infinite potentiality to produce a new psychic existence. In this sense, the intelligible principle is pure potency, *analogous* to the pure potency of first matter. However, this analogy does not allow us to ignore what is revealed by the "vision of the heart": that there are three degrees of existence. A thing exists in its agent —just as here the principle of the soul exists in the intelligible agent. This act of being of souls "in their intelligible principle" is a necessary, undivided, simple, and noble existence, that is not separated from the principle. A thing also has an act of being through itself which makes it simply possible. Finally, it has an act of being in the receptacle (here, the soul connected to the body), which is a more degraded act of being, predisposed by the material potentiality of bodily attachment. This act of being is weaker than the preceding acts of being, which are the necessary and pure act of being, and the act of being according to pure quiddity.

That is why we find meaning in the concept of existential revolution: it does not signify that the quiddity of a thing is transformed into that of another thing; rather, it means the intensification of the act of being through the gradual perfection of the substantial form, "until it becomes subsistent through other essential characteristics, different from what they were at first."[98]

> The act of being is prior to quiddity; it is the root, and quiddity comes after it. Do you not see that natural forms are perfected and intensified until they separate from matter and change into an intelligible form existing in the higher intelligible world in the mode of unity and immateriality? Conversely, souls are likewise in the mode of intelligence, as a single thing, a simple, unified, intelligible substance. Then they are multiplied and they descend into this world; they become the likenesses of natural bodies, through the weakness of their substantiality, dwelling in inferior dwellings.[99]

At the corporeal degree of being, the soul is a likeness to the body, it is indissociable from the potentiality and the existential weakness of the body.

This is true for all quiddities, all "specific and conceptual realities," such as man, earth, sky, water, and so on. Their being is mobile, subject to a revolution that consists in a variation of the act of being, such that each reality possesses four modes of hierarchized existence: the act of being in the divine decree, the intelligible act of being, the psychic act of being, and the natural act of being. Existence in the divine decree is the very existence of the divine names when they are still enveloped in the simplicity of the essential unity of God. The three "births" correspond to the effusion initiated by the "breath of the Merciful," according to the three degrees (intelligible, psychic, natural).

It is thus that an intelligible sky and earth exist, as well as a psychic sky and earth and a sensible sky and earth. Each mode of being of the sky is such that I perceive it with either the intelligence, the imagination, or the senses. It is not a simple representation of one and the same sky. The two forms I imagine and intelligize are as real as the one I see, if not more real. An injunction that could be expressed as "to be is to be perceived" must be taken literally. Not in the sense that the degrees of perceived existence are mere phantoms of the mind, but in the sense (closer to the true sense of George Berkeley's maxim) that the act of knowing reveals and unveils an authentic act of existing.

The Avicennian tradition resists imagining the essential of motion of revolution because it maintains that such a motion would prevent one from knowing what constitutes the being of the thing, its signification (*maʿnah*) and its quiddity. But the true theory of knowledge claims that "the knowledge of hidden things designates the act of existing of their congruent form in the knowing subject. This form of the thing is either intelligible, imaginal, or sensible, according to the degrees of potency of the knowing subject."[100]

The knowing subject is not homogeneous. It undergoes the same variations of existence as the known object. When it is constituted by a weak act of being, it perceives only the corporeal sky. When its act of being is intensified, it intensifies its perception to the imaginal or intelligible degrees, because it is an imagining or intellective subject. The fundamental unity of the subject and the object is based on the unity of the act of existing shared by the object and the subject. One perceives only at the level of the horizon unveiled by one's own act of existing, and one reveals in the perceived object this same level of intensity. The more intensely I exist, the more intense and real is my perception, and the more the perceived object reveals an intensity and potency for existence. That is why the intelligible mode of being is the perceiving subject's and the perceived object's most concrete mode of being.

The "perceptive homelands" (*mawātin idrākīyah*), or sites of perception, correspond to the existential "births" and are one with them.[101] Thus, the imaginative power corresponds to the "psychic essences existing in the world of silhouettes and models," a world of "imaginal forms." In the hierarchized totality of forms, each form is congruent with the others, according to a process that integrates the multiple into the one. The soul therefore has degrees or successive births, corresponding to the four degrees mentioned. Its divine root effuses its intelligible degree of being, which Sadrā identifies as its "perfect nature." He cites the dialogue between a soul and its alter ego, in which the soul asks: "Who are you?" The other of the soul responds: "I am your perfect nature. And you, my friend, if the reascent to the degrees of your existence is unveiled to you, you will then see numerous ipseities, differentiated as to their act of being. Each one of them is the perfection of your ipseity, and no part of you is deprived of them. It is through me that each one of them is designated. And it is the same as in the well-known symbol: you are me and you come from me."[102]

The Hermeticist reference invites us to see in the intelligible root of the soul's becoming a living monad with the "personal" life of an "ego." But this "ego" is revealed to the subject as its true subjectivity, corresponding to its root in the revealed divine ipseity. It is therefore the one to whom one addresses oneself at the beginning of knowledge, a "you" to whom one asks the question: "Who are you?" Thus the soul's act of existing is manifest in the fundamental alterity of the major respondent, the one to whom desire is addressed. This formulation evokes the entire Hermeticist tradition, and the thematic of initiation, which is common to both Suhrawardī and Mullā Sadrā. Sadrā is able to play off of this similarity in thinking in order to refuse Suhrawardī's rejection and to propose the concept of intensive infinity.

Intensive Infinity

The existence of souls prior to the body is impossible, according to Suhrawardī, since it would imply "infinite reasons" in the separate substances – in other words, an infinite number of intelligible substances prior to the souls connecting their bodies. But, Sadrā says, this neglects the essential difference between the act of being in the world of intelligence and the act of being in the sensible world. The fact that souls exist in an entirely separate mode of being, before the stage of their corporeal becoming, does not entail an actual numerical infinity, which, for all our authors, would be an absurdity.

On the contrary, "a radical distinction must be posited between infinity in intensity and temporal numerical infinity" in order to understand that the unified intelligible form from which the open multiplicity of souls proceeds "has an infinite potency of effectuation and activity, and I mean this in terms of intensity." It is absurd, Sadrā explains, to claim that there exist infinite dimensions in the intelligible principles that are analogous to the dimensions encountered in the material sensible world: multiplicity, number, potentiality. The intelligible monad is one, and its unity is not that of the quantitative one, the first term in the series of numbers.

The intelligible monad's potency is not the potentiality of substance deprived of perfection. Its infinite potency is that of the substantial unity that is most intense in perfection. It is the producer of the series of multiple states, a pure necessity. However, "the dimensions of the good and of necessity" are infinite in intensity, whereas the dimensions of deficiency and potentiality are finite in intensity and number. They have definite durations and distinct spatial dimensions.[103]

This deduction of intensive infinity depends on the distinction made between number, understood as quantity, and the monad, understood as necessity and intensity. The intelligible one, root of all souls, is not a quantity; it is not the one that totalizes a multiplicity. Thought is not forced to choose between one model of the existent that culminates in the presentation of a closed totality and another model that situates the existent within the horizon of the infinite. The existent, when we know it in its intelligible reality, is infinite. But it is so while still being a totality, and without losing its intensive potency to engender a hierarchized totality of sensible emanations from its own intelligible essence, which is its eternal and necessary act of existing. From the perspective of its eternity, each living thing testifies, in its form and its provisional finitude, to this immanent infinity of intensity that animates it. This infinity is the generative center of each thing, the principle of its essential movement toward its divine destination, and the true name of its freedom.

Chapter Seven

The Imagination

> When I awoke in a new world everything that I found there was perfectly familiar and near to me, so much so that I felt more at home in it than in my previous surroundings and manner of life, which, so it seemed to me, had been only the reflection of my real life. It was a different world but one in such perfect harmony with me that I felt as though I had returned to my natural surroundings. I had been born again in a world which was ancient but which at the same time was closer and more natural to me than the other.[1]

Sadiq Hidayat's novel orients us toward the second birth of the soul as envisioned by Sadrā. This birth is governed by the ancient division between the light of Ohrmazd (the Avestan Ahura Mazda) and the shadows of Ahriman, and it assumes that hell and paradise are the retributions the soul brings on itself in the exercise of condemnation or excellence, from which it fashions its own space and its own body. The novel brings to life a woman who is all the more dangerous and real in that she has arrived in the world of the imagination, populated for Hidayat by monsters rather than angels. It is a demonic imagination, whose atrocious details are distilled by Sadrā,[2] or an angelic imagination, which takes its figures from the Qur'ān: not a world of abstract symbols, but a sensory, effective, immediate world, whose significations are immanent to their signs, full appearances screaming with truth, and yet semblances, in which the real is endlessly mirrored.

No concepts of the philosophers or mystics of Islam have had as much resonance as those of the imagination and the imaginal world. The use of these two notions has become so widespread that they are often cut off from their birthplace and exported into the varied domains of psychoanalysis, literary analysis, and spiritual practices foreign to Islam. Readers attempt to find traces of this "imaginal world" in every work by a Muslim philosopher or mystic, a notion that, Hegel would say, has become the shibboleth of all knowledge.

Henry Corbin cannot be blamed for this. When he demonstrated the importance of the imagination in the theosophy of Ibn al-ʿArabī, and when he proposed the expression *monde imaginal* [imaginal world] as a translation of *ʿālam al-mithāl*—with as much felicity as he had proposed the adjective *historial* to translate a major concept in Heidegger—Corbin opened a new path. What he saw in the importance Islam grants to the world of imaginal forms was nothing less than a master signifier with which to decipher the meaning and the destiny of this vast continent of the spirit, which contrasts with the relative coherence that characterizes the various Western forms of knowledge. But he never ceased warning hasty readers, and he tried to prevent the concept of visionary imagination from being confused with either psychologism or analogous notions in non-Islamic literatures.[3] He foresaw what has in fact happened, namely the separate use of the adjective "imaginal," the loss of the systematic coherence of the discourses in which the concept of the imaginal world has a precise meaning, and a forgetting of the functions effectively assumed by this concept. Henceforth, all comparatism was doomed to fail, and the magic word "imaginal"—to the chagrin of Orientalist scholars, to the exaltation of the nonspecialists—became a source of ecstasy and no longer a source of knowledge. Such is the destiny of every discovery: it is bound to be travestied in a web of misunderstandings.

It is not my intention here to carry out the work necessary to reestablish the concept in its rigorous validity. This would require a separate study, one that would trace the concept's genealogy. It will suffice to demonstrate that Sadrā constructed a doctrine of the imagination with a precise, concrete goal: to support the spiritual exegesis of prophecy and the final retribution announced by the Qur'ānic revelation. The *agent* imagination has a *prophetological* function, a *moral* use, and an *eschatological* role.

The Writing of the Intelligence

The imagination is a power of the soul that produces a certain mode of knowledge. It is the power of representation, the source not of an illusion or an "imaginary" but of a *form*. To be sure, we can imagine things that do not exist, and we can wrongly judge that they do exist. But the imagination is not defined by this poorly dominated freedom. It belongs to the process of cognition, and in order to understand it, we must trace it back to the essence of cognition. There is nothing surprising about this philosophical decision, since it remains faithful to a conception of the faculties of the soul that goes back to Aristotle.[4] When the imagination is understood as a capricious invention of the mind, it will have broken the bonds that united it with the other faculties of knowing (common sense, estimative faculty, intelligence), and the Aristotelian scheme will have been outlived. This is not the case in Sadrā, and even less in his predecessors in the Muslim world, particularly in the Avicennian lineage.

If imagining is a mode of knowledge, what is knowledge? "It seems," writes Sadrā, "that knowledge is one of those realities whose existences are one with their quiddity."[5] What knowledge is can be unveiled only in the concrete existence of this act of knowing. It is impossible to define it through the play of logical difference within a universal genus. All knowledge is singular, and "nothing is more known than knowledge, for it is the state of existence of the soul." It is the state in which the soul feels itself, the immediate attestation to its existence.[6] Knowledge is pure manifestation; it is one with the act of existing and is not definable by a quiddity whose general terms are prior to the experience one has of it. Thus, each thing that becomes manifest to the intelligence makes manifest the existence of this intelligence itself through the knowledge the intelligence has of it. Knowledge is nothing other than the act of existing of this intelligence, since the activity of the immaterial faculty of cognition is one with its existence. This will also be the case for the imagination.

Error is always an error of judgment. Sadrā remains faithful to Avicenna on this point. Our judgment that "an existent on a par with the Creator is impossible," or that "the union of contradictories is impossible," is true. The judgment that asserts the existence of a golden mountain or an ocean of mercury is false; we call it a fiction. The imagination has nothing to do with these false judgments.[7] The false judgment bears on something that is not necessitated in being. There is a maxim claiming that "the thing that is not necessary does not exist." If one assigned an existence to the representation of the golden mountain, this existence would be pure nothingness.

It is necessary to distinguish the consideration of quiddity from that of quiddity *insofar as it effectively exists*. The representation of the golden mountain is a thing of pure thought; it has a purely mental existence, which, however, is a non-negligible existence, since for the soul that imagines this golden mountain, the mountain in some sense "exists." Whether I invest any belief in the existence of this mountain or not, I must represent it; it must have a meaning for me. The golden mountain has a certain mental existence. But whether the golden mountain is possible or impossible is a question that engages a concrete judgment of existence. The possibility of error resides in the affirmation or negation of concrete being.[8]

It appears here that the cognized form is not the form existing *in concreto*. It is a form whose concrete existence is not self-evident, although its mental existence is undeniable. The form of sensation, for example, is not the object external to sensation:

> The form of heat exists in the organ of touch, but is not itself something "touched." Likewise, the form of taste, like that of the intense sweetness perceived by man through the organ of taste (the body of the tongue), does not belong to the external objects of taste, other-

> wise this form would be tasted by what this tongue tastes in its singular way; no, the form is not some thing among the realities that remain through the senses, unless it is through the psychic qualifications that belong to the accidents of souls, not to the accidents of the body.[9]

The heat that is sensed and imagined is not the same as concrete, external heat. Coldness in thought or a color in thought are accidents of the soul. A sound that is heard subsists in and through the soul, not in the vibrating or expelled air, although it is necessary to possess an organ of hearing, an unobstructed auditory canal, in order to hear it. Thus Sadrā demonstrates that the sensibles themselves have a nonsensible act of being — an effective mental existence — that belongs to the soul, as a psychic sensation destined to be metamorphosed into an imaginative existence, then into an intelligible act of being once the soul has acceded to its own intelligible birth. The status of the imagination as an act of cognition is situated within the scheme of births and depends on this fundamental distinction between the form of cognition and the specific, concrete form that exists in the flesh-and-blood individual.

The agent imagination is also inscribed within the framework of Sadrā's cosmology, which governs the theory of knowledge. If one does not keep the cosmological scheme in mind, this theory becomes a simple play of concepts, devoid of concrete substance.

The first of the worlds is that of the intelligence. At its center, the universal intelligence, "sun of the world of intelligences," is the caliph of God and his image (*mithāl*). Sadrā unites Qur'ānic exegesis with a formula that repeats a famous statement by Plato: the sensible sun is the image of the intelligible sun. The Qur'ānic verse invoked is this: "It is he who instantiates creation; then repeats it; and it is easy for him. To him belongs the loftiest *semblance* in the heavens and the earth: and he is all-powerful and wise."[10]

This is a very important quote, since this verse has often provoked anxiety for commentators: how can God have a *semblance* of himself if he is beyond all knowledge and all representation?

Sadrā chooses to give the word *al-mathal* its fullest sense, and to isolate the phrase, "To him belongs the loftiest *semblance* in the heavens." Henceforth, the scheme of universes, like that of the modes of knowing, will be governed by this manifestation of the mystery of the divine essence in its intelligible *semblance*, in the primordial theophany. When we encounter the expression "imaginal world," *'ālam al-mithāl*, we are dealing with a median degree proceeding from this first *semblance*, from this configuration of the image of God in the intelligence. Far removed from those readers who disregard the letter of the holy book, Sadrā saves the literal expression, which authenticates theophany and – in the precise context of creation and return, and in the complete curve of each thing's essential movement from its origin to its end – reveals its proper mode of permanence in God.

The intelligence, the image of God, is identified by Sadrā, as by Suhrawardī, with the archangel Bahman (Vohu Manah) in Mazdean theology.[11] Thus the Qur'ānic lesson, the recollection of ancient Persia, and the Platonic scheme of the Idea of the Good are joined together.[12] The intelligence enables one to know why "in the act of being there is only God."[13] God is constitutive of all existence because all existence, in its first reality in the intelligible world, is the face of God, his *semblance*. Sadrā quotes the famous verse "All things will perish except his own face" to justify the theophanic nature of the intelligible world, which is at once the caliph of God, the mother of the book, and the Muhammadan reality, the pleroma of the fourteen immaculate ones (the Prophet, Fātimah, and the twelve imams).[14] The intelligible world and the knowledge grounded in it make up the eternal praise addressed by the image of God to the mystery of his essence. Knowledge (cognition) is this original and permanent praise, since praise is fundamentally an act of knowing.

The face of God will not perish. The intelligible *semblance* remains. It is not a mere copy. When it is configured in the world of the imagination, it descends to the threshold of the perishable world, the world of nature. The imaginative *semblance*, the similitude perceived by the agent imagination, configured by it and living from the matter of the soul, will have its reality in the intelligible from which it proceeds, and its permanence in the reality of the soul after returning to its root in the Malakūt. The imaginal forms will never be mere copies, for they will be the embodiment of the truth of our souls, revealed at our death. Before death, in the first growth of the soul united with the body, appearances are condemned to disappear, and they can be a mixture of metamorphosis, truth, and deception. The imaginary is the product of the body and its constraints; it arises from the trouble that the body causes for the soul obliged to take care of it, and not from the soul alone, in which every imagined representation has its source in a particular impression.

The witness of the intelligible is stripped of human corporeality and is united with the intelligible *semblance* of God, and this intellection strives to devote itself to God. The true witness ("martyr") is the one who effectuates this totalization (*jam*ʿ), for which the intelligible world is the model. The most perfected type of this "pillar of wisdom" is Plato.

In the passage I will quote, Sadrā gives no other example. This is because Plato founded the doctrine of Ideas, archetypes or eternal models, which Avicenna rejected, but which Sadrā reestablishes in order to support, in metaphysical terms, the entire structure of hierarchized worlds:

> What bears witness to these worlds is the totalization effected by the pillars of wisdom and those who draw the lights of knowledge from the tabernacle of prophecy, like the great Plato, who possesses authority and light. And we others, we reinforce his path and revivify his wisdom, with the help of God, with his grace, his inspiration, and his teaching—and through the establishment of an intelligible substance and an archangelic and spiritual model, held in God's hands, for every corporeal species. This model is the Lord of the icon of this species, it is what gives the body its subsistence, it is the mediation between his creation and its existentiation, and the preserver of its permanence.[15]

To know is to grasp the mediation between the divine existentiating act (*ījād*) and its effect in the creatural condition (*khalq*), a mediation that passes through the manifestation of the divine imperative in its intelligible *semblance*, the Idea. This Idea is the universal archetype of individuals and the intelligible individuation of this universal, the lord of the icon of the natural species.[16]

Knowledge of essential reality belongs to the intelligence, not the imagination. The active force of the imagination will never make it superior to the agent intelligence.

If the properties of the Idea entail that it necessarily exists before the sensible being that corresponds to it, then the Idea will exist necessarily.[17] But the Idea is more noble than the sensible; it is necessary, whereas the sensible is possible; it is the form of the existent instantiated in the world of the divine decree, and it is known essentially, whereas the sensible is known only accidentally; it is simple, whereas the sensible is composite; it is "intense because it has been stripped of matter," whereas the sensible is subject to the bonds of space and time; its existence is entirely free of any nonbeing; it is perfect and the species in it is a single intelligible individual, whereas the sensible is imperfect as to existence and in need of a substrate in order to be. The essential reality of every sensible is not sensible but intelligible; the intelligible is pure light, whereas the sensible is pure shadow; sensible perception is complete only through the intelligence, whereas the intelligence has no need of the senses.[18]

Necessity, unity, stripping away (*tajarrud*), perfection, intensity, light, freedom – these are the characteristics of the intelligible, which are opposed to the corresponding characteristics of the sensible: possibility, accidentality, subjection to material conditions, spatiality and temporality, shadow, weakness, constraint.

If the intelligible is prior and superior to the sensible, the cosmos reproduces a similitude of the intelligible archetypes. One single existence thus proceeds from the most luminous and the most subtle to the most dense and the most opaque. Light gradually decreases. Knowing means taking the opposite course, from a sensation heavy with shadows and devoid of intensity, to the intelligible conjunction bathed in light.

In the order of material realities, we observe this gradation of lights: fire is "chief" of the elements, because it is the most luminous and is placed above the others; the sky precedes the earth, and it is mentioned before the earth in the Qur'ānic verses. God creates light and existence first, not shadows. Light is existence itself, and witnessing being means contemplating light. Light is the intelligible, not an abstract representation of the intellect on the basis of the sensible but a reality stripped of matter, one and unified, prior – in the order of reality – to all multiplication, to every shadowy burden that will deprive it of its simplicity in its sensible images or emanations.

It is thus that the verse must be understood: "God is the friend (*walī*) of those who believe, and leads them out of darkness into light."[19] God "leads the faithful souls – the souls that have authentic knowledge (*'irfānīyah*) through the effusion of the essential realities of knowledge upon their ipseities – out of the shadows of the sensible world into the light of the intelligible world."[20] The birth of the thinking soul is one with the illumination given to its ipseity by intelligible knowledge. The gift of existence is the gift of knowledge. The thinking soul is created by the act that actualizes the intelligible light in it. That is why Sadrā can affirm that knowledge is existence itself:

> Knowledge is not a negative reality, as would be the mere separation from matter; it is not a reality of relation, but an act of existing. It is not every act of existing, but rather an actual and not a potential act of being. It is not every actual act of being, but a free (*khālis*) act of being, unmixed with nonbeing. The intensity of its being-knowledge is given by reason of its freedom from any mixture with nonbeing.[21]

The intelligible is the act of being at the luminous center of worlds. Evil occurs only along certain *margins* of being (*hawāsh*). Enveloped in this intelligible center is that which will be accompanied by shadows and relative baseness when deployed. The intelligible is the place of return and of the passage from sensible servitude to divine freedom:

> Do you not see that the form of the sensible, whose act of being is in matter, becomes intelligible when one assumes that it has been stripped of matter and is independent in the act of existing (*istiqlāl fī-l-wujūd*), and do you not see that it becomes subsistent through itself? We know then that intelligible existence (*al-ma'qūlīyah*) is the freedom of the act of being (*ghanā' al-wujūd*) and that sensible existence is the poverty of the act of being (*iftiqār*).[22]

In Sadrā's conception of the world, freedom is the independence from need that characterizes the intelligible. The human quest for freedom is the quest for intelligence, the quest for God and obedience to God – an obedience that responds to the imperative act of existentiation, in a knowledge effusing from God in the free act by which God existentiates the intelligence of the one who truly knows. Freedom is primary, and poverty and constraint are secondary: "In the act of existing, the free is prior to what is poor."[23]

The exercise of this freedom, far from excluding the divine decree, absolutely implies it. The agent intelligence, the *semblance* of God in the intelligible world, is the becoming of the human soul. It is the divine decree itself. God decrees each thing in the necessitating freedom that he confers upon it. The independence of this act of being expresses the infinite power of his decree. This decree is not an arbitrary contingent, even if it has its source in an unfathomable imperative. It is one with the intelligible. The emanation of things as a whole, in the various worlds, is a form of *writing*:

> All that comes to be in our world, among the essences, the attributes, and the operations, comes from the first real through the medium of the intelligence, since it is the pen (*qalam*) of the first real, and since our spirits are like tablets. Our actions are written by

> its contraction and its release, and the pages of our souls are written by its withdrawal into the secret and by its deployment. The records of our itineraries are kept by means of its liberation and its retention, for it is held in the very grip of the Merciful. The entire earth is in his hand and under his government. Thus, through the justice he does and through the balance he establishes, our souls are printed in the ink of his seed, and the carpet of deployed forms is unrolled over the extended expanse of first matter. The intelligence is the science of the Qur'ān and of faith, according to the verse: "Read! For your Lord is all-giving, he who taught by the pen, taught man what he did not know."[24]

Justice, balance, and the gift of being are the productions of God the merciful, as he reveals himself in one of his most beautiful names. They are the writing of the intelligible, a writing that creates souls before their first material birth and that turns the soul toward its intelligible source. This entire world is like an unrolled carpet, presenting the splendor of its designs and geometric figures to the mind. The verse, which reveals the nature of prophecy and divine revelation on the path to fulfillment, founds the destiny of man, which is to be united with the agent intelligence in order to become this agent intelligence. What is written must reascend to the hand that writes, which maintains or releases the pressure of its fingers, like the scribe over his tablet.

This intelligible writing is expressed in the world of souls and in the world of bodies. Souls proceed from the universal soul, the second world, that of the faithful mind, the preserved tablet (*al-lawh al-mahfūz*).[25] It is the water on which the throne of God the merciful rests. In this world of the soul, prophetic events take place and the noetic function of the imagination — a function that consists of common inspiration (*ilhām*) and properly prophetic inspiration (*wahī*), for these two inspirations are often combined in one and the same act — is justified. It is the world of revelations obtained in sleep; it is also the world of the effusion of natural existences from the source of the water of life. There is fresh and limpid water for those who join with the real (*al-wāsilūn*), scum and foam for those who are forgetful and negligent (*al-ghāfilūn*).[26]

The third world, that of bodies, is organized according to the cosmological model of the nine heavens. It is delimited by the encompassing heaven, called the limit heaven, which determines spatial and temporal dimensions.[27] Thus one goes from throne to throne: from the heaven that is the throne of the world of the soul to the soul that is the throne of the intelligence, and finally to the intelligence that is the throne of the merciful. This tier-like structure of the various degrees of the divine majesty defines the thresholds of knowledge.

The Prophetic Imagination

Intelligible knowledge is a decipherment of divine writing. The imagination receives these letters traced by the pen onto the tablet of the soul, and it fills in and develops the forms of this inscription. The imagination is thus essentially prophetic.

The prophet Muhammad has three properties, three types of power, attached to his mind, his soul, and his sensibility.[28] The spirit is the intelligence, the soul is associated with the imaginative power, and the sensibility consists of all the external senses. These three powers legitimate three concrete powers and three exercises, ordered according to the three "births," which the substance of the prophet integrates to perfection.

Indeed, the "substance of the prophet" is not a single individuality but "three eminent individualities." Because of his spirit and his intelligence, the prophet is an angel among the intimate angels. Because of "the mirror of his soul," he is a "tablet preserved" from Satan's attacks. Because of his senses, he is one of the greatest kings. The Prophet has three levels of existence; he participates in the three worlds – the world here below, the otherworld, and the world of lordliness.[29] His substance recapitulates all three of these births; it possesses three perfect faculties: the senses, the configurative faculty (*al-mithālīyah*), and the intelligence.[30]

The prophetic imagination is the power to actively produce *semblances* (*amthāl*) in which the divine intelligible world is reflected. It is distinguished from the power that abstracts from forms on the basis of common sensations. Unfortunately, the term "imagination" is inappropriate for distinguishing the significations of these two ways of producing images; hence the difficulties of a theory of knowledge that combines them. Indeed, how could the imagination – the faculty of forms derived from the sensible – also be the faculty that receives influxes from the higher world? How could this reversal take place?

This is a problem that Sadrā will be obliged to resolve. He will have to save the empirical process of abstraction, which passes from the sensible to the intelligible via the forms of the imagination – a process defined in Aristotle's terms. But this process only enables one to understand the production of the formative faculty (*al-musawwira*), not what takes place in the soul when it becomes the mirror of intelligible effusion (*al-khayāl*, *al-mutakhayilah*). The reconciliation of these two competing schemes requires two theses: on the one hand, the affirmation of the fundamental immateriality of the soul and its rootedness in the Malakūt; on the other hand, a psychology that is not simply a physics of the soul but also a discourse on the internal world of the soul able to justify the claim that the soul's representations, beginning with the sensibles, come from the soul itself, according to its degree of existence and the "birth" at which it has arrived.

The two theses are linked. If the imagination defines the soul itself, prior to its fall, at the median degree of the descent that leads it toward the origin of its first birth, then it is prior to the soul's corporeal destiny. Conversely, then, the imagination can define the second degree of the soul's reascent toward God, the second birth. But all cognition takes place in and through the soul, since the cognitive forms are not made of the matter of natural substances. Formal cognition, like the configurative imagination's cognition of divine *semblances*, thus belongs to the same register of inner revelation and cannot be explained in relation to any abstraction of forms from impressions in the bodily organs.

If, on the contrary, we adopt an Aristotelian perspective, it is impossible to bring together the imagination of sensible forms here below and that of prophetic or eschatological semblances. Here the confusion between the imagined and the imaginal reaches an extreme. That is why all the discussion about the independence, validity, and truth of the semblances perceived by the soul must be disengaged from the traditional interrogation of the imagination's gnosiological function, understood in the sense of an abstraction of forms derived from empirical sensation. That said, let us return to the lessons of prophecy.

Men in general know only the inferior world and trust only their senses; they are subject to the veils and imperfections of the "homeland" here below, which justifies the exercise of the Prophet's royal power. The only ones to escape from this lowest condition are those who believe and act righteously, the small number who are able to accede to the higher births, through practical and noetic intelligence and in imitation of the actualized perfection of the Prophet.[31]

The real believer is not someone who merely obeys the commandments reiterated in the letter of revelation. He is not someone who submits immediately to the injunctions of prophecy's royal power within the restricted domain of the sensible. Here is Sadrā's definition of the real believer (*al-mu'min al-haqīqī*):

> He is among those who believe in the *mysterium* (*al-ghayb*) and in the world of the lordly Malakūt, who commit in heart and mind to the birth in the otherworld. Strictly speaking, they are none other than the gnostics (*al-'ārifūn*). The others will be on the side of the Satans (*hizb al-shayātin*) and will be the faithful among the armies of Iblīs, if they do not blamelessly imitate the heartfelt adherence of the people of religion and the masters of certainty, those who follow the [straight] path.[32]

We recognize here the Shī'ite definition of the "true believer," he who does not abandon himself to the sole consideration of the letter and the legalitarian religion but adopts the imitation of the inspired master, the imam, in a "second birth" leading to the lordly Malakūt, the third intelligible birth. The gnostic, the true man of knowledge, is not an expert jurist but an assiduous practitioner of the wisdom leading to inwardly experienced certainty. The Prophet integrates the three degrees in his substance: the lower degree, necessary but insufficient in itself for exercising sensible governance; the middle degree of birth to the otherworld, to which corresponds the power to configure the symbols of religion; and finally, the intelligible knowledge that is the source of true faith. Sadrā will distance himself from both fundamental esoterism (similar to that of Ismā'īlī Shī'ism) and fundamental literalism (that of the Hanbalīs or those who claim a single external sense for the scriptures).[33]

The most noble prophetic power is knowledge through intelligence, which allows the Prophet to receive, by divine inspiration, the divine sciences (*al-'ulūm al-ilāhīyah*) and a direct knowledge of the essential reality of things as they effectively are. The Prophet accedes to the essence (*haqīqa*) of things, to their act of being, and does not stop at their concomitants or their veils, which include the quiddities. He exercises the two higher powers of the soul, noetic intelligence and practical intelligence. He is the ideal of the contemplative man. But he also possesses the perfection of the imaginative power. This is the "internal faculty" (*al-quwwa al-bātina*) "through which the essential realities are configured for him beneath the clothing of the forms of appearance, the symbolic *semblances* (*al-ashbāh al-mithālīyah*) in the 'intermediate world.'"[34] Imaginative power is the capacity to make an intelligible reality appear in a determinate figure. This is not what Aristotle or Avicenna called "the imagination" in the process of empirical cognition.

In the case of the Prophet, the power of symbolic figuration reaches the point where the "silhouette" of the angel becomes manifest in this world. The Prophet then sees the angel "with his own eyes." The intensity of vision in the intermediate world of *semblances* is such that this inner world is reflected in the world of the senses.

The third prophetic power is that of force, "the considerable capacities by which the Prophet victorially dominates the obstinate and the deniers and prevails over the enemies of God and the friends of Satan." This power is exercised in the sensible world, and it is bound to the inferior status of this world. But it is suffused with moral virtues—patience in misfortune, mastery in the preparation of armies, prudence in struggles.

The imagination is situated between this power of political leadership and the power of pure contemplation. It derives its meaning from its place in the structure of the three births and also in that of the three types of men: kings, when their *himma* is very powerful; the practitioners of divination and the ascetics living a monastic life; and the friends of God and the philosopher sages (*awlīyā'* and *hukamā'*).[35] These correspond to royal power, the power of the diviner or the hermit, and the power of the imam or the complete sage, the man invested with *walāya*.[36]

The configurative faculty is part of the substance of the Prophet; it participates in the formation of the "divine caliphate" and loses all meaning outside the triad of prophetic powers and functions: legislation, message, and prophecy. The sensible birth and the power of the legislating prophet (*shāri'*) correspond to the inferior world and to the necessity of a royal authority; the birth of the otherworld and the power of the messenger prophet (*rasūl*) correspond to the world of median semblances; the intelligible birth and the intelligible world correspond to the prophet's power strictly speaking (*nabī*), in the ultimate perfection of his substance. The power of the imagination configures the divine science in visible forms, and it authorizes the transmission of these forms to those who hear the Prophet. The imagination is *information*, in two senses: it is the configuration of an intelligible form, and it is the power of the message (*risālah*). It corresponds to the median degree of the celestial sphere (*falak*), between the sublunary world and the world of the angel.

The situation of the imagination in the prophetic substance is clarified further if one is aware of the deep harmony between the holy book and man. The Qur'ān is similar to man, and man is similar to the Qur'ān, in that both are divided into an "evident sign" and a "secret" (*sirr*) sign.[37] Without the esoterism of the

Qur'ānic reading, without its homologation with a spiritual anthropology, there would be no place for any symbolic imagination. The book unfolds according to three registers, known as the apparent (the tangible printed letter), the esoteric (perceived by the inner sense, *al-hiss al-bātin*), and finally the esoteric of the esoteric. The same is true of man.

The inner sense corresponds to the alliance linking imagination (*khayāl*) and memory. Better yet, it is the unbreakable bond of recitation, reading, and memory that preserves and protects the hidden sense. The imagination is the storehouse of the memory characteristic of the "readers" of the Qur'ān (*qurrā'*) and those who "recite from memory" (*huffāz*). The meaning of the book is configured in this memory/imagination, not in its intelligible purity, but with all the additions and all the veils left by the various concomitants of substantial truth – quantity, quality, place, *situs*. The imaginative form is certainly separable from the sensible, but it is still a form linked together by the connections of the inner senses. It is the spatialization of the intelligible and the temporalization of the eternal.

What are the prophetic senses? They are inner senses, belonging to the soul: an inner hearing, taste, sight, touch, and smell. They are the perceptual grasp at work in the world of the imagination. The Prophet's hearing of the angel's "ordered logos" and the vision of forms in which spirits are embodied – for the prophets, these were moments of unveiling. The inner sense carries out lordly conquests (*futūhāt rubūbīyāh*), such as the inspiration of the "divine winds" or the drinking of the milk of science. (The Prophet said: "I saw that I was drinking milk until it flowed from my nose, then I understood that it was knowledge.") It captures a vision of "his Lord in the most beautiful form," a vision had by Abraham, to whom God showed the Malakūt of the heavens and the earth.[38] Perception then occurs through the spiritual senses, and engenders from itself an understanding of the intelligible world, the unveiling of the "lordly reality" configured in this sensible *semblance*.[39] The prophetic imagination is the strength and force of the prophet's soul when it animates its own sensibility.

The esoteric of the esoteric has two gradations: access to the world of the imperative, and access to what is above both the world of creation and the world of the imperative. The world of the imperative and the world of the creation correspond here, respectively, to the purely intelligible world and the sensible and imaginal world. The "secret" of the Qur'ān and of man is essential, intelligible reality – the signification entirely stripped of every accident of place and time, quantity and quality. It is the synthetic unity of multiple manifolds. The spiritual organ that perceives this unity is the thinking mind or the soul. At this "station of the imperative," the mind perceives the meaning of the holy book in the imperative unity of its truth, as it proceeds from its principle agent, the divine science. For that reason, it must be stripped of every attachment to the world of the creation. This intellection is a unification of sense and a conjunction with the angelic condition.

Beyond this angelic condition is access to the supreme degree of meaning, which characterizes the nature of the Prophet. "As for what is above creation and the Imperative, that is veiled by the senses and by the intelligence together." This is the supreme stage of the word of God (*kalām Allāh*).

> No prophet has seen it and approached it except in the station of divine unity, after being stripped of his two conditions of being, that of the world below and that of the otherworld, and after having climbed and entered the two worlds [the creation and the mperative], as the most perfect of the prophets [Muhammad] has said: "For me there is a time with God, in which I am understood by no intimate angel and by no messenger prophet."[40]

Sadrā understands this famous tradition in the following way: Muhammad is given a station, a rank, where he has been stripped of imaginal vision (corresponding to the *risālah*) and of intelligible perception (the angelic state). He expresses the superiority of the prophetic man over the angel. He accedes to the word in its state prior to the two manifestations corresponding, respectively, to the imperative or the "well-guarded tablet" and the creation or the "tablet of obliteration and reestablishment."

This scheme, borrowed from the Sūfī tradition and from Ibn al-'Arabī in particular,[41] sets up a gradation from the "secret" of the revealed divine unity (*al-wahdah*) to the sensible world. The imagination has its place in this gradation, midway between the letter and the spirit, between the sensible condition and the intelligible condition, between creation and imperative.

The hierarchy of the letter, the esoteric, and the esoteric of the esoteric is found again among the faithful in the hierarchy of the common, the elect, and the elect of the elect. The "common" among the faithful receive the letter and its imaginative explication, which provides the guidance that brings one out of the shadows of impiety. The elect are led out of the shadows "of the psychic and corporeal attributes" into "the lordly spiritual light." This light takes on spiritual attributes and abandons its psychic attributes. Through its cognition (*ma'rifah*), the soul of the faithful is thus illuminated with the light of recollection, and the heart realizes its powers of contemplation and purification. The ethos of the faithful is deeply altered, eliminating blameworthy desires, becoming habituated to praiseworthy conduct. This is the condition of the soul's tranquility, according to the famous verses: "O you tranquil soul! return to your Lord, well pleased and well pleasing him; enter then among my devotees, enter then my heaven!"[42] The elect of the elect leave the shadows of eduction into creatural *and* spiritual being, "through the annihilation of the act of being," all the way to the light of theophany, in which arises the manifestation of the divine attribute, "the eternal" (*al-qadīm*). This is the place where the faithful superexist by way of their very annihilation, at the point of coincidence between superexistence (*baqā'*) and annihilation (*fanā'*).[43]

The Immateriality of the Imagination

The prophets justify us in granting a truth to the imagination. Sadrā's doctrine of the three births grounds this truth in the gradual procession of worlds. Henceforth it must be situated within the framework of anthropology. To the prophetic function of the imagination will be added its eschatological role and it moral use. The imagination will be a form of knowledge, as it appears to be in dreams or divination, and it will be a power — the soul's capacity to sort through its actions and its habits, to divide them up into distinct modes of being, to envision its own hell or its own paradise. If it is clearly understood, it enables us to escape the dilemma confronted by the exegetes of divine retribution: whether to condemn to nothingness — after the death of the body — the souls of those who do not reach the degree of intelligence, or whether to have them sojourn in the world of the celestial spheres, in a mode that seems futile to Mullā Sadrā.[44] As for those who prefer to think of this destiny in terms of the transmigration of souls into elemental, vegetal, animal, or human souls, they are mistaken.[45] The goal of Sadrā's doctrine of imagination is therefore to destroy the doctrine of transmigration and to restore the literal sense of the Qur'ānic promises of an effectively lived paradise and hell.

The crux of the question is the immateriality of the imagination. If we agree with Alexander of Aphrodisias that the soul has no activity if it is not combined with the body, and if the representation of forms always assumes this combination, then the soul will have no power after its separation from the body.[46] The intelligence's superexistence would then be ruined. Sadrā's intention, however, is to preserve not only the immaterial existence of the soul's intellective activity, but also the separation of the "animal faculty of perception from internal sensibles" — its separation from this inferior world and its belonging to another world.

The immateriality of the configurative faculty will consist in a separation not from every kind of body but from *this* external material body (*badan*).[47] The imagination is an inner sense, and this inner sense is the birth of the soul in the median degree between its sensible birth, the form of the natural body, and its intelligible birth. In the scheme of successive births, the imagination becomes the soul's mode of existence when it is a "middle soul," occupying the middle between carnal realities and the angelic mode of being. This soul is separated from the external body, but it remains attached by "the attachment of attached bodies." Its status as an animal soul destines it to the "land of retribution" (*dār al-jazā'*), the place of election or punishment. Thus the "otherworldly region" is animal life itself, which is one with imaginal life, according to Sadrā's interpretation of the Qur'ānic verse "What is the life of this world but amusement and play? But the region in the other world is animal life, if only they knew!"[48]

The power that deploys the *semblances* (*al-khayāl*) does not differ in essence from the one that stabilizes forms, configures them on the basis of the givens of the common sense (*al-musawwirah*). According to Sadrā, the two Arabic terms indicate a single faculty, which is immaterial in two aspects: its objects are stripped of the matter of the empirical bodies they represent for the soul, and the imaginative subject, the substrate of imaginative activity, is itself immaterial.

In his dialectical demonstrations, Sadrā shows that the imagined forms cannot reside in a material substrate — in the brain, for example. Thus, the image of the limit-sky would be too vast to dwell in the narrow space of the brain. The form of this organ is a natural form. Like all nature, it is ruled by constraints inimical to our freedom. However, we can vary the dimensions of the sky that we imagine at will.[49] Our perceptive faculty is therefore not bound by a constraining relation to this form imagined by us. More radically, the imaginative configuration is not a relation between something with a localized existence and another thing that is also localized. The imagination does not itself fall under the category of place when it figures places and dimensions.[50]

The immateriality of the imagination is also demonstrated in Plato's proofs of the immateriality of the soul in its entirety.[51] Can it be, then, that the intelligence is responsible for imagined representations? Does the immateriality of the imagination identify it with the intelligence? Such a thesis runs up against conclusive objections. On the one hand, the active intelligence, united with the intelligibles, does not perceive imagined forms. It is immersed entirely in the intelligible. On the other hand, the imagination presents particular forms. It suffices to look closely at the phenomenon of imaginative configuration to be convinced both of the immateriality of this form and of its distinction from intelligible forms. Consider black and white, two colors that can only be imagined as particular. They cannot be found at the same time in one and the same corporeal substrate: a body is not both black and white. Our imagination, however, can represent them together; it is, therefore, not made of the matter of bodies. But, on the other hand, the subject that perceives imaginative forms perceives particular forms that absolutely cannot be universal: the white that I imagine is participated in not by an indefinite multiplicity of bodies but by this body that I am now actually imagining. The imagination is therefore entirely separate from corporeal matter, while also always forming particular figures, colors, and degrees of hot or cold. The imaginative form is particular *and* immaterial. This disjunction of immateriality from universality is the imagination's great contribution; it grounds the real status of the immaterial particular.[52]

The imagination must also not be confused with the common sense. The latter receives forms, whereas the imagination preserves them. This proves again that the imagination is active. Just as one speaks of an agent intelligence, we must also say "agent imagination," which is of the order of necessity and activity, whereas the common sense, like flowing water, receives forms only to lose them just as quickly. Receptivity is passivity and potentiality.[53]

Sadrā saw clearly that the imagination is related to habit. Our soul cannot perceive the objects of its contemplation whenever it wants, without first seeking them out and then appropriating them. The senses are indispensable to the imagination in its first growth, and intellection itself becomes familiar to it through an intellective habit that becomes actualized after numerous perceptions. Whence does the habit of thinking come to the soul? How is it that the soul preserves and repeats perceptions, to the point of creating a stable form within itself, from which it can pass to a perception of the intelligible? The power of habit cannot come to it from the senses, whose testimony is unstable and fleeting. This power is therefore an intelligible light, stable in its act of being, emanating in the soul from the principle. It is a substance located above the soul but below the agent intelligence.[54]

The power of recollection is indeed immaterial. The power of habit, as imagination, must therefore be distinguished from the receptivity of common sense. "Establishing the difference between common sense and the imagination – this is one of the tasks in the foundation of wisdom that we should by no means neglect."[55] The difference between the two is not that one is less perfect than the other. Rather, there is a rupture between worlds: the imagination "is a substantial inner faculty, different from the intelligence and the external senses. It has another world, different from the world of intelligence and from the world of nature and movement."[56] It is remarkable that this power of habit is also the power to preserve the trace of our habits, and to give rise to the events of our *post mortem* life. This future of the soul, our retribution, will be made from the sum of our sedimented habits. The imagination will be that in which "the states of the tomb and the retribution of the soul are effectuated, as well as its punishment and the states of the *barzakh* and of the body's resurrection." The resurrectional body is the very form of our habit.

Avicenna and Imaginative Vision

In his conception of the imagination, Sadrā owes an undeniable debt to Avicenna. The separation or the stripping away of imagined forms is discussed by Aristotle and, after him, by Avicenna: it is not a total and complete stripping away, since the imagined form of the individual still possesses the dimensions of width and length, a certain position, a place, colors, a set of sensible qualities. In the imagined form, the specific form is still affected by accidents that do not belong to essential quiddity, that is, to the universal form of the intelligible.[57] Something of the material concomitants received by the essential form remains in the imaginative perception. But this incomplete stripping away will be rethought in very different terms by Sadrā, when, instead of speaking of the presence of corporeal dimensions necessitated by the matter of the lower world, he refers to the internal dimensions of the world of the soul, where the very matter of imagined representation is distinguished from the concrete matter of external bodies. Everything happens as if Sadrā accepted the legacy of the Avicennian doctrine of abstraction in order to use it in a new way, for the sake of a resolutely Neoplatonist scheme.

Sadrā privileges the *visionary* function of the imagination, eminently actualized by the Prophet and revealed to us in dreams, premonitory visions, and many other common experiences. Avicenna himself was not insensitive to this, having been directly influenced by a more ancient tradition.

The imagination is the formative faculty (*al-quwwah al-musawwira*), since the form of sensible realities is constituted in it: this is the fundamental thesis of Avicennian psychology. It is a constitution that mobilizes common sense, which sends to the formative faculty what was sent to it by the senses. We have seen that the imaginative constitution of form prevents the unified sensible from being dispersed and lost; it is essentially conservative. According to Avicenna, far from putting forth some image foreign to the surrounding world, it exercises the power of the guardian of a storehouse; it deposits the received form and constitutes it in a form destined to be stripped away and put into play by the estimative faculty and the intelligence in the storehouse of memory.

The imagination is memory recording the world of the senses. Descartes will note the fundamental conservatism of the imagination.[58] It not only seems to condemn the imagination to the passivity of things seen, which might explain why the imaginative memory does not liberate us from the past world, but instead encloses us in it. It also condemns the imagination to its own rich abundance, that of a storehouse of knowledge with no possible escape. This hoarding activity leads to a knowledge of essences, but it cannot escape the realm of essences realized in their natural forms. Sadrā will open it onto another world by identifying the internal space of the imagination with the infinite space of the soul.

It would be a mistake, however, to neglect what this memory contains and stabilizes. In fact, it includes only what we perceive through the common sense, but in principle, it captures the endless set of forms manifest in individuals. The imagination is the first mirror of the world; it extends as far as the soul itself and populates the soul with its forms. It probably produces nothing new, since it borrows from the sensible, but it epiphanizes essences in a form that is dimensional and imperfect but revelatory. This is what Sadrā will draw from Avicenna's reflection.

What world does the soul mirror? Avicenna would say the sensible world, insofar as intelligible universal forms, possible quiddities, are actualized in it, that is, in matter. For Sadrā, as we have seen, these forms have no *sui generis* existence; they are not Plato's forms. At the same time, Sadrā reestablishes the existence of the intelligible world as such and rehabilitates the Platonic Idea. This changes everything when it comes to Sadrā's treatment of the scheme found in Avicenna, particularly his understanding of Avicenna's analyses concerning what the soul receives when it is not occupied by the external senses.[59]

The cogitative faculty, says Avicenna, employs the forms that are in the formative faculty, analyzes and combines them, because for it the preserved forms are like substrates. This can happen either through an act of thought or the imagination, or by virtue of something that belongs among the celestial configurations. A form, then, is configured in the formative faculty, and a *semblance* (*mithāl*) takes shape there. For such an event to take place, thought (*dhihn*) must be absent or at rest and the consideration of any object must cease. If the soul is never absent from itself, thought can make itself absent and suspend its activity without the soul ceasing to be active. It is remarkable that when a *semblance* comes into the imagination, it results not from hyperactive thought but, on the contrary, from the suspension of thought.

The form that then emerges can be configured in the common sense by borrowing its powers, and we see the *semblance* as if it were an external body: this is indeed the situation of the prophet, the diviner, and even the daydreamer or the dreamer in the grips of a truthful dream image. This is not to say that the form comes from an "imaginal world." Sadrā inherits a fully elaborated doctrine of such a world, but in Avicenna it is still only a theoretical possibility with no explicit confirmation, at least not in the psychology of the *Shifā'*.

The suspension of thought is the repose of the intellective faculties, the indifference of the estimative faculty, a sort of liberation of the imagination. The formative faculty of the *phantasmata* (*al-musawwira*) and the higher imaginative faculty (*al-mutakhayilah*) then have the power, says Avicenna, to carry out their specific operations, their properly configurative operations, with no direct connection to the work of knowing and intelligizing. As the pure configuration of a *semblance*, this activity then occupies the soul entirely. This is because the soul is single and unified, and if there is a pause in thought, then the entire soul will configure the received *semblance*. The soul forgets external things so that the imagination can give sensible form to the *semblance* that has come to it.

Avicenna describes in detail the medical conditions caused by the soul's disengagement that are favorable to the emergence of the imaginative form of received *semblances*: sickness, fear, and sleep. Ordinarily, the soul is awake. It takes hold of the imaginative faculty and places it at its own service. It diverts the imaginative faculty away from imaginings that do not coincide with real, external existents. It rejects them, declaring them illusory. The imaginative faculty cannot then impose the image of these illusions and represent them to the soul with intensity. The imaginary is always less intense than the sensible.[60]

This weakness of the imagination ceases when the soul is weak, when it ceases to exercise its vigilance, and when the preoccupations it imposes on itself are removed. In sleep or in sickness, the soul is distracted from intellective activity. In fear, the soul forgets itself and the imaginative grasp is strengthened; it directs its object toward the formative faculty and mobilizes it. The union of the imagination and the formative faculty produces a form that appears in the common sense: if we can still speak of an imaginal form (which would be to abuse the term), this form populates the realm of madness, fear, weakness of the soul, and sleep, "and for that reason, whatever the mad, the fearful, the weak, or the enfeebled see, they see as subsistent forms, as what they see in reality when they are in good health."[61]

The examination of the imagination and its visionary power thus falls within the domain of spiritual medicine, which evaluates the relations of force between the faculties. Certain subjects have visions in the waking state that others have in sleep, because the mutual play of the faculties makes them prone to it. The first condition is the discretion of the external senses: the senses do not take hold of the imagination or occupy it with their impressions. In order for the imagination to receive an "engraving," an "inscription" (*naqsh*) originating in the domain of realities hidden to ordinary sense perception (the "mystery," *al-ghayb*), "sensible preoccupations must be diminished so that only a small number of preoccupations remain."[62]

A weakness of the senses combined with a weakness of the formative faculty that unites and conserves the forms received in the common sense liberates the soul from the constraints imposed on it by the lower world. Sickness and sleep are states in which the body can be forgotten, in which the functions of the soul closest to the external corporeal world are weakened or silenced. The weakness of these powers is caused by the dissolution or the dissociation of the *pneuma*, their organ. Thus liberated, the soul escapes, "journeys," "runs," "goes," "flows away," takes a vacation from the world.[63] In this vagabondage, the imaginative soul is drawn toward the higher world where it can receive warnings and omens. The term that refers to these "omens," *al-sānih*, plural *al-sawānih*, is rich in meaning: it is the bird of augury whose flight must be interpreted; it is the mystical inspiration of the heart, as in the title of the work by the great poet al-Ghazzālī.[64] The imagination receiving these "warnings" proceeds, without fatigue and in a single stroke, toward the supersensible realities. As for the soul, it mobilizes the imagination in all its movements and operations.

The second condition is the force or strength of the soul. Ravishment will provoke imaginative inscription, or even the sensible apparition of the imagined form, only if the soul is a strong soul. Its substantial force gives it a greater capacity to embrace the suggestions coming from the otherworld. The soul's rapture is then the effect of a greater intensity rather than an insufficiency. And we see where the division lies between the visionary states specific to sleep and illness, and the raptures of the soul that take place in a waking state. In the morbid state, the flight of the imagination is the result of an absence of the senses, a dysfunction of the *pneuma*, in short, a disturbance of the connection between the senses, common sense or fantasy, and the formative faculty.

It can happen that, in dreams, the truth speaks; the dream image becomes truthful. The case of Heraclius is remarkable in that the truth of his dream is interpreted for him in another dream. The imagination, freed from the grip of the senses, carries out by itself the deliverance of its own truth. It deciphers the symbols that it presents by means of new symbols, which, in turn, require yet more interpretation. Does this mean that dreams are prophetic? Certainly, if the Avicennian doctrine of dreams can be included within the vast literature of oneirocriticism. But it would be in the sense in which Michel Foucault says that "the analysis of dreams was one of the techniques of existence."[65] To receive traces of invisible reality is to receive instruction on what one is, on what one should be, on a world in which the essence of things is more clearly revealed than it is here below. It does not mean that dreams reveal the forgotten past. The imagination can indeed be the storehouse of past representations, but is not the staging of repressed events that we listen for in our dreams today.

Dreams are an object of interest not because we need to know whether they tell us of our past or future but because they offer the rebus of our subjectivity, written in the higher world of divine decree. The modern debate and the Freudian approach are not relevant here.[66] Dreams, like waking visions, are situated in a vertical vagabondage, which is not given to everyone in the same way. The signifying dream is distinguished from the nonsignifying dream. It signifies in relation to the dreaming subject, to the singularity and particular intensity of this soul. The truth of the dream image is the reward for an elevation and a freedom that the dreamer owes to the intensity of his imagination and to that of the soul mobilizing the imagination, free from external suggestions.

The force of the imagination, the force of memory, and the nobility of the soul all favor the appearance of a *semblance* (*mithāl*), such that an apparitional form, a silhouette (*shabh*) is configured for the one who imagines. The imagination reflects this first imagination: the one who receives it imagines that it is an address, a message (*khiṭāb*) coming from the apparitional form. The vision suggests an entire discourse that has been preserved and related, just as the prophetic vision reports and preserves the words of the angel.

Thus we come to the most remarkable case, which is not the sick person or the dreamer but the human soul in its full visionary activity. This activity is explained through the structure of the universes:

> We say therefore that the essential significations (*ma'ānī*) of all realities subject to generation and corruption in this world, whether they have been, are, or will be, are existent in the science of the Creator and of the archangelic Intelligences (*al-malā'ikah, al-'aqlīyah*), and that this is so in a certain way. And we say that they are existent in another way in the celestial angelic souls (*fī-nafs al-malā'ikah al-samāwīyah*).[67]

This is what confirms a certain mode of existence for the essences in the divine science, in the Intelligences, and in the celestial souls.

Men, says Avicenna, have a more intense relationship with the angelic souls than they do with the archangelic Intelligences, because their souls' adherence to corporeal matter hinders their ascent toward the intelligible and the stripping away of essential forms in the human intelligence. Visionary activity corresponds, then, to the process that strips away and purifies the soul, which thus ceases to be submerged in the world of bodies and renounces the attraction to "the lower way." It demands a turn toward the two angelic worlds, the Malakūt – the world of celestial souls – and the intelligible world. It attests to a greater proximity with the divine world. Imaginative contemplation is actualized when there is no more distance, and it delivers souls from the veils associated with bodily receptacles.

This brings us back to the status of illness and the necessity of spiritual medicine. For the soul, the manifestations that come from the Malakūt represent, in a certain way, the essences present in the divine science. It is in this sense that they are true. But they are liable to be confused with all kinds of imaginary manifestations and phantasms. In order to discern them, one must practice a dietetics of the imagination, which prepares for the ascesis and elevation of the soul. One must distinguish the vision from the phantasm, of which Avicenna gives a remarkable analysis. In the phantasm, and in it alone, the imagination is an expression of concupiscence that provokes the expulsive force of the sperm. The imaginative form surges forth as a desired form and sets off certain processes in the *pneuma*, provoking erection and ejaculation. To this imagination of desire must be added the vast circle of nonrevelatory imaginations, the dreams of the poet, the impostor, the wicked, the drunk, the sick, and the afflicted.

Everything depends on the force of the soul. In the privileged case of authentic vision, the effect of being ravished by the form coming from the Malakūt is maintained in a waking state, because it "descends all the way to memory."

> Sometimes it becomes master and illuminates the imagination, provokes a certain bright illumination, and the imagination takes the tablet of common sense by force [and attracts it] toward itself. Then the imagination draws out what is originally imprinted in it, and the thinking soul gives its assistance, diverting nothing away from the imagination, as would the estimative faculty in the sick and the bilious.[68]

The effect will be an exclamation of joy, or – if the power is even greater – a steady *semblance*, a discourse composed in verse, or a vision of sublime beauty.

The border between illusion and truth is indistinct; the poet can err, just as he can bear witness to an authentic vision. It seems to me that Avicenna poses the question of the imagination at the intersection of two great disciplines: medicine and metaphysics. There is, on the one hand, a dietetics of the imagination, the examination of healthy or morbid states, and on the other, the structure of the universe, the corporeal world, the celestial souls, the archangelic Intelligences culminating in the outer regions of divine science. At the center stands an entire morality of the soul, a series of purifications and processes of stripping away, without which the soul would not be capable of employing the natural force granted to it.

In his commentary, Nasīr al-Dīn al-Tūsī bears witness to this proximity between medicine and the metaphysics of revelation. Here is what he writes on the imaginative form that takes possession of the "Oriental" (*ishrāq*) illumination, the configuration that is then imprinted into the common sense and remains there:

> There is also what the prophets have reported, the revelatory manifestation of the angels whose words become audible. Of course, something like this happens with the sick and the bilious, whose estimative faculty has been corrupted and whose fantasy is indisposed and weak. And this occurs among the friends of God, because of their holy, noble, and powerful souls.[69] For them, vision is more eminent and more true than for the sick. The impression in the common sense differs in weakness and intensity, such that what comes from it as a revealing manifestation is an authentic form (*wajh*) or merely a veil.[70]

For the sick man, the friend of God, and the prophet, distinguishing the nature of the vision means distinguishing its force, its intensity and the visionary power at its heart. But for Tūsī, the forms of beauty are authentic: they reveal "the face of God," and his word, without intermediary. The imagination is then the soul's face-to-face encounter with God, who reveals himself to the soul.

Citadels in Suspense

If Avicenna's psychology lies on the distant horizon of Sadrā's doctrine of the imagination, the inspiration of Suhrawardī's illuminative philosophy is something that Sadrā wants to preserve while also correcting and criticizing a number of its theses. It is remarkable that there is no trace of an *imaginal world* in Avicenna, although the elements necessary for the elaboration of such a concept can be found in his work. The imagination provides access to the essential significations in the median degree of apparitional forms, insofar as these are present in the celestial angelic soul. We will see that Sadrā does not conceive of the imaginal world as external. But if there is one philosopher whose disciples constructed this concept of the imaginal world, it is Suhrawardī. Sadrā will take up this construction for his own purposes, modifying it in order to rethink the imagination, not as a vehicle to the imaginal world, but as the human soul surviving the death of the body and becoming the matter of the resurrectional body. He will internalize the imaginal world within the process of the soul's growth and increase.

Suhrawardī's thought on the imagination is presented in a chapter of *The Philosophy of Illumination* that discusses both the forms reflected in mirrors and the imaginative forms.[71] It is not possible that the forms are imprinted in the eye or in some location of the brain: "The truth about the forms reflected in mirrors and the imaginative forms is that they are not imprinted but are suspended citadels that have no substrate." The Shaykh al-Ishrāq forgoes the medical approach and the doctrine of the impression, which played such an important role in Avicenna, as we have seen. The mirror is where the forms that we see in it appear, and the imagination (*takhayyul*) is a mirror, so to speak; it is the site of epiphany for the forms of the imagining faculty (*suwar al-khayāl*). Suhrawardī does not refer at this point to the imaginal world, but his commentators do so, particularly Qutb al-Dīn al-Shīrāzī and, before him, the great thinker Shahrazūrī.[72]

The structure is simple: the forms received in the imagination are *suspended citadels*, corporeities without substrates. They cannot have their substrates in our thoughts, and they no longer exist *in concreto* or in the intelligible world. The two types of substrates assumed by Avicenna in existentiated forms – thought and empirical matter – are inadequate to the imagined forms. It is therefore necessary to suppose that what they have is not a substrate but a type of existence that Avicenna was unable to represent. It is clear that on this point the two commentators must abandon the Avicennian theoretical framework in favor of a deliberately Platonic scheme. Without any substrate, the forms of the imagination will dwell in "another land," and this land receives the name *imaginal world*, whereas their manifestation occurs in the apparitional site (*mazhar*) of the imagination. Shahrazūrī alerts us to the significance of this matter: "Most philosophers have forgotten it, but it belongs among the mysteries maintained in secret and the hidden sciences; we will devote to it an esoteric elucidation."[73]

The imaginal world responds to a double exigency: to give an ontological status to imaginations, and to guarantee that they have no inhesion in a substrate, which makes them resemble the forms seen in mirrors. Like these mirror forms, imagined forms have no existence in matter; they appear and are limited to appearing. Their being is entirely within their appearing. But both have an irreducible substance; their appearing is a being and is not pure nothingness. It is therefore necessary for both to have an origin and a ground. The imaginal world serves as the ground of this being of appearance.

Of course, this type of existence presents certain difficulties. Mullā Sadrā will maintain that there is nothing concrete and effective about it, that the Ishrāqīyah have given a name ("imaginal world") to something that possesses no effective act of being, and that they undermine their own efforts to ground the reality of the imaginative representations.

The form reflected in the mirror is often larger than the mirror.

This trivial observation leads not to any laws of mathematical optics but to the statement that since what is large cannot enter what is small, reflected forms must not have their site of existence in the world of the senses. The same is true for the imaginative forms. They are not pure nonbeing, for in that case one could form no representation of them. "Consequently, it is patently clear that they are existent in another world, which we will call the imaginal world (*'ālam al-mithāl al-khayāl*)."

The impossibility of a doctrine of the impression thus leads to the following canonical statement:

> This world is of a higher degree than the world of the senses and lower than the world of the intelligence. Consequently, it is a median world, intermediate between these two worlds, and all the apparitional imaginative forms and the dimensions of the body and of what is attached to them, among their movements and rest, their positions and aspects — all this is existent in the median world, which is that of *semblance* (*al-mithāl*). The forms reflected in mirrors all subsist by themselves in that world, and mirrors are their epiphanic sites. These forms are suspended, they are not in a place, they are not in a substrate. As for the forms configured by the imagination, they are not in the brain, but the cerebral *pneuma* is the epiphanic site, and these forms are suspended, subsisting by themselves, not in a place or a substrate.[74]

Closer to us, Jorge Luis Borges meditated a great deal on the enigma of mirrors:

> The fact that I know you without seeing you,
> Adds to your horror, you magical thing that dares
> To multiply the number of these things
> That we are and that envelop our fate.
> After I am dead, you will copy another,
> And then another, and another, and another, and another...[75]

The creative magic of the mirror does not evoke horror for Suhrawardī; rather, it invites him to perceive new existents, appearances of a world that remains hidden to the senses when they are applied to material bodies, but that appear to the senses when they turn toward these images without a subject. The mirror "multiplies the number of these things," as Borges writes, evoking the prohibition that forbids the creature to simulate creation. It is a simulacrum of the real creator. The image robs us of our existence by depriving us of the belief that it is unique. The mirror, in its indifference to us, gives to the other the existence that we will lose; it makes things visible when we are blind; it imposes a real that does not depend on us. Specular reflection does not found our relationship to the ego or produce the mirror stage, in which we delight in identifying with our image. It is pure strangeness. In that sense, it is well suited to the imagination, which does not comfort us either but tears us out of ourselves. The strangeness of the reflected image, the form of appearance, indicates a separate world, because for us it indicates only separation and isolation:

> Whoever has had the vision of this station experiences the intimate certainty that there exists a world different from the world of the body. This is the imaginal world in which forms and figures exist "in suspension," and there exist ruling angels who choose the theurgies and forms through which they speak and become manifest. Impetuous forces and a victorious domination emanate at times from these theurgies, mediated by imaginal forms and marvelous voices which it is not in the imagination's power to reproduce. What is astonishing is that, when he isolates himself, man can hear this voice — because then he is attentive to it, and his imagination also finds it by seeking to hear it.[76]

If the forms of our imagination are the apparitions of the suspended citadels, if they constitute a separate world, they provide souls with enjoyment or sorrow, before and after their death. The domain of pleasures is not based on empirical things or intelligible representations. Pleasure pleases itself with mirrors, with appearances that seem to have no solid consistency and to be held up by nothing, free from attachments. "In suspension," the body of desire consists of seductions, threats, lies, and metamorphoses.

It rewards and it disappoints, so that the sage may learn to live beyond all desire. The imaginal forms are the initiatory road leading to the world in which one no longer desires, in which the signs of enjoyment no longer appear.[77]

Perfect men do not imagine anymore. But those who have acquired merits without leaving the sphere of desire receive their retribution in figurations of their own desire, so that nothing is lacking. If the imaginal form disappoints desire here below, it fulfills it in the beyond. The imaginal world is the land of complete enjoyment. This land must therefore be located, even though it would have no place. It is populated with unlocalized forms, in a paradoxical space not governed by any dimension. Our imaginations, mirrors of the forms of such a world, reflect the large in the small, and the distant in the near. Every caprice is rendered actual and living, because these dreamed or figured bodies have no space that could be their substrate. Their only space is that of the mirror of our soul.

Suhrawardī's construction of a theory of the imaginal world is inseparable both from a cosmology of hierarchized celestial spheres and from the interpretation of the scriptural statements on future retribution. It is a question here not of a rational psychology, and much less of a mere "theory of knowledge," but rather of a theory of happiness.[78]

Suhrawardī distinguishes degrees of advancement in spiritual progress. The "moderately advanced" differ from the perfect, whose status is defined by pure illumination, the "direct vision of the world of pure light." After the death of the body, these perfect ones become mirrors reflecting the illuminations they receive from the light of lights, the source of all existence, in an infinite enjoyment.[79] All the archangelic and ruling lights, which are reflected in each other, project light onto the soul, and "these are spiritual circles of light in whose striking beauty both the contemplation of the light of lights, and the illumination that emanates from it, are continually increased."[80]

The "moderately advanced" do not reach this supreme degree of purity and illumination. They correspond to the rank of ascetics who have "acquired moral purity," who are perfect in practice but not in contemplative knowledge.[81] These latter "escape toward the world of suspended images whose site of appearance is in certain higher *barzakhs*. Their souls have to make the images exist, and they have the power to do so. Thus these souls make present for themselves certain delicious foods, beautiful forms, exquisite sounds, and so on, just as they desire." The reprobates, on the contrary, undergo the effects of a demonic imagination, which after their deaths projects "certain shadows of the suspended citadels" for their souls.[82] The sweetness of heaven and the tortures of hell are images, luminous or shadowy, that reflect certain suspended citadels from the imaginal world into the imaginative soul of the elect or the reprobate. One can therefore speak of an imaginal salvation, an imaginal damnation, and an interpretation of Qur'ānic retribution according to the existence of the median world of suspended images.

We know that with the term *barzakh* Suhrawardī designates the body, in its substance as a "bearer of night and death," a substance made of shadows. The body does not form a composite with the luminous form but comes to be governed by it and by the victorial domination when light is reflected on it — that is, on a surface that has now become a mirror whose density is a barrier to light rays. At the death of the body (which in essence is already a bearer of death), and on its separation from the ruling soul, the soul rises up to higher bodies, to the higher *barazikh*, the bodies of the celestial spheres.

The soul freely activates heavenly images whose sites of appearance are the celestial bodies, just as mirrors are the epiphanic sites of sensible images and the cerebral *pneuma* is the site where the image was reflected in terrestrial life. The degree of clarity and splendor of images reflected on the celestial bodies, illuminating the souls of the "moderately advanced," depends on the subtlety of these bodies, whereas the weakness of our images here below is a result of the weight and the opacity of the perishable material body. The spiritual body, the suspended citadel, is accessible only in its mirror reflection, and the purity or impurity of the mirror determines the degree of clarity of the imaginal projection.[83]

The soul purified in this world by moral practices enters the world of the spheres and the celestial souls and is raised from heaven to heaven; it stays for a time in the heaven of the moon, then attains a clearer vision in the heaven of Mercury, and so on up to the supreme heaven.[84] The commentators examine the power of this median soul, and the effects of the continuous purification received during the journey from heaven to heaven: is there a way for it to pass to the world of pure light, the archangelic intelligible world, or does it remain bound to the limit heaven? If the passage is possible, as the authors of the *Epistles of the Brethren of Purity and the Comrades of Faithfulness* believe, then the imaginal world, hierarchized according to the gradation of the heavens, leads to the higher world. It functions as a sort of instrument of visionary purification, leaving the reprobates in the lower stage of the nightmare vision, while filling the elect with visions of happiness that guide them in regaining the luminous homeland of the soul in the intelligible place.[85] The imaginal soul is inseparable from the structure of the system of worlds, and it has its own internal gradations. This is explained by Shahrazūrī in his commentary on an important passage of *The Philosophy of Illumination*.[86] The first world is that of intelligible archangelic lights that are not attached to bodies. "These make up the armies of divine holiness, the reigns of intelligible lights of the divine lordship; they are the angels of God, the intimate angels, his very pure servants." The second world is that of the ruling lights of the celestial spheres and of men, called Espahbod Lights, from a Persian term for the equivalent of the Stoic *hegemonikon*.[87] The third world is the sensible world, the celestial spheres, the stars, the elements, and composite elementary bodies. The fourth world is the imaginal world: "It is there that the suspended forms bearing light and shadow reside. The forms bearing light are those in which the blessed find their reward, and the forms bearing shadows are those in which the damned receive their punishment."[88]

How can it be that the imaginal thus includes both luminous

and shadowy forms, if the shadows are condensed in the world of bodies? In *The Philosophy of Illumination*, Suhrawardī explains that jinn and demons are produced by suspended images and the ruling souls of the damned. Suspended images are engendered by the world of the souls in order to be received as epiphanies by the elect and the damned, and to appear and disappear from our imaginations and mirrors. They are ranked according to the order of the elements – the hierarchy of the mineral, vegetal, and animal species. The imaginal world is organized according the model of the land of light, populated by the luminous archetypes of the sensible world:

> All the living beings of the imaginal world and the men of that world have thinking souls. Some of these souls are the bodies of the imaginal world, forming a certain rank among the ranks of the imaginal world. These are human souls whose attachment with these bodies here below was broken, so that later they will be attached to the bodies of that other world. If the psychic modalities and habits have a middle degree of perfection, souls become attached to the human bodies, which are at the highest levels. If these modalities and these habits were blameworthy, the souls become attached to bodies that correspond to their customs, among the brute animals, which are at the lowest levels. It is possible that some of the souls receive an effusion from the intelligence whose mode of effusion is singularly appropriate to the imaginal world. The greatest number of souls have the ability to reach the world of the intelligence, gradually rising through the sensible world and the imaginal world toward the highest of these degrees, until they reach the world of pure intelligence.
>
> As for the elements of the imaginal world, its minerals and vegetables, they have no soul. For them, there are "lords of the species." Among these suspended spiritual forms and these souls that are attached to them – among the souls of the inhabitants of that world – there are the jinn, the Satans, the ghuls, and so on. Their sites of appearance are in the world where they are manifest and alive, according to their receptivity of celestial movements. And it is

> in the imaginal world that the blessings imagined by the medially advanced take place. When we hear from the ancients that there are two worlds endowed with extension, they are not speaking of the sensible world and the intelligible world. Jābalqā and Jābarsā: these are two of the cities of the imaginal world. Each one has a thousand gates.[89]

This long description of the imaginal world allows us to distinguish its essential properties. First of all, it allows us to discern the meaning of the word *al-mithāl*, often linked with the world *al-khayāl*. Here it does not seem to designate a symbol, a form of expression that must be elucidated to reveal its meaning. The imaginal world is not a symbolic world, a world of expression linked to archetypes or representations. It is a region populated by bodies whose matter is the form adequate to the projections of the soul's desire. As an embodiment of each desire's final aim, the imaginal body is the presence of enjoyment. Whereas the natural body is an obstacle to my desire, and whereas it separates me from myself and from enjoyment, the imaginal body is union, conjunction, and totality. All enjoyment is imaginary, and real enjoyment therefore requires a site where the imagination becomes real, a real mirror of imaginal bodies.

The technical term *al-mithāl* designates not symbols but, according to Shahrazūrī, silhouettes that receive some consistency through the effusion of "imaginal" celestial movements and illuminations from the intelligible worlds.[90]

The silhouettes of the imaginal world are the effects of a theurgy, a divine operation that consists in the activity of light being reflected and condensed at the level of the ruling souls, an activity that is fully manifest at the level of the celestial spheres and under their influences.

This theurgy is the property of the archangelic lights, which Suhrawardī calls the "lords of the icons" (*arbāb al-asnām*). These lights grant life and permanence to the natural species through the projection of their luminescence onto the shadowy bodies. This vivification is not conceivable according to the Aristotelian scheme of the composition of form and matter, since Suhrawardī rejects the hypothesis of such a providential composition, just as he rejects the Aristotelian concepts of matter and form. Therefore, he must represent the activity and life of natural living beings as the effect of a spiritual operation, analogous to that of the god animating the icon that represents it. Thus the earth is the theurgy of the archangel Esfandārmoz. Each body is the theurgy of an Espahbod Light, its ruling light, which possesses an imagination proper to it. The imagination is therefore a power of the ruling soul, of the light that projects its vivifying action onto the body; as such, the imagination itself is light. We can understand, then, why Sadrā cannot accept Suhrawardī's hesitation in conferring full and complete immateriality on the imagination, as he himself will do. He writes: "The imaginal world, which delineates a more subtle state than the sensible world, also contains a multitude of heavens, stars, elements, and nativities. This requires that its cause be immaterial lights even more noble and more eminent than the causes of the sensible world."[91]

Concerning the "moderately advanced," Suhrawardī writes: "Their souls have to make images exist, and they have the power to do so."[92] Sadrā comments on this "power," seeing in it a sign of bodily resurrection. When the soul is separated from the body, all its faculties are concentrated in the active imagination, which has the power to configure freely. Imagination then becomes sensible perception, and through these imaginative senses, man feels the punishment or reward of the tomb.[93]

Divine theurgy and astral theology – these are the foundations of the imaginal world. The reference to the Brethren of Purity thus takes on all its importance. The place that astrology occupies in their system, as well as in Ismāʿīlī cosmology, is well known. It should be recalled that the authors of these epistles brought their astrological science to the theology of the Sabians.

Let us read a passage that Yves Marquet quotes in one of his articles. Speaking of human souls as they are fashioned by their comportment, the text presents the Sabian doctrine and explains that it distinguishes bestial souls, good only for populating the sojourn here below and for perpetuating the human species, "from souls that can be raised to the celestial spheres, inhabit them, and—if they are healthy—experience pleasure through and in these spheres, and who can also come down from them and inhabit a body and attach themselves to it when they are ill, experiencing pleasure or being tormented by it or in it: these are human souls."[94] This text does not yet speak of an imaginal world, but it does speak of a sojourn of enjoyment, in which the celestial spheres become the site of retribution. From another perspective, the transmigration of souls and the nature of spiritual beings (*rūhānīyāh*) determines the space in which the destination of man is to be thought.[95]

Shahrazūrī says the constitution of the imaginal forms occurs when human souls are detached from material bodies. These forms are the result of a process in which the death of the natural body is a necessary stage, a rupture that facilitates a new attachment, one that will transform the soul into a body of the imaginal world. Attached to a new body, the life of the soul in this other world becomes metamorphosis. The various conceptions of transmigration are replaced in this fourth world by a mode of transfer in which the soul does not rejoin a natural body but is united to a "suspended citadel." The population of the imaginal world is like that of the lower world, which explains the sense in which it is a world of similitudes (*'ālam al-mithāl*). To be united with what is reflected in the imagination, to be united with the phantom of one's desire—this is happiness. The phantom is not as deceptive as the woman who is transformed into a monster in the arms of the naive lover; it acquires the guarantee of the celestial souls. It becomes a very real angel or demon.

As in this world here below, the elements—the imaginal minerals and vegetables—have no soul but are ruled by the lord of their species (*rabb al-naw'*), by their respective angels. But the living animal beings and the men there are similar to the men of this lower world; they are the souls of the latter metamorphosed into spiritual bodies. A man who conducted himself in a blameworthy way sees his soul transferred to the imaginal body of a brute beast, while a man who lived a moral life becomes an imaginal man and receives the imaginative joys of the moderately advanced. Imaginative perception is their happiness.[96]

The image, the similitude of what lives below in what lives above, is a model to the extent that it expresses and corporealizes the effective interiority of the human soul – more precisely, its moral interiority. The imaginal form realizes a totality of reprehensible or praiseworthy intentions and actions, which are henceforth sedimented in the physical body, from the demonic body to the body of the man whose intelligence, liberated from both physical and imaginative attachments, is raised to the intelligible world.

Imaginal World and Manichaeism

That is why the imaginal world is the stuff of which our dreams are made, the cloth from which our desires are woven. In the suspended space of the imagination, the *longue durée* made up of moral weaknesses or victories unfolds. It is a purifying transition; it is significant that Shahrazūrī, in order to explain it, explicitly cites Mani and the Manichean cosmological myth:

> The sage Mani proposed a symbol for this. He says: When the king of light saw the mixture of light [and shadow], he ordered some of his angels to create this world so that the species of light would be separated and purified from the species of shadows. The sun, the moon, and the stars only purify the particles of light by removing any particles of shadow. The sun purifies the light mixed with the demons of heat, and the moon [purifies the light] mixed with the demons of cold: all the particles of light rise eternally, whereas the particles of shadow go down. The acts of glorification, of proclamation of divine holiness, the Good Words and pious actions coincide with the purification and the elevation of the particles of light. The particles of light are raised, by this means, into the Column of Dawn, up to the heaven of the moon, and they progress from the beginning of the lunar month to its "noontime." Then they escape. Then they are conveyed to the sun, until the end of the month, and

> the sun takes them to a light that is above it. Then [the particles of light] journey in this world until they reach the completely pure supreme light.
>
> This operation does not cease as long as there remain any particles of light in this world, except a certain amount which the sun and the moon cannot purify. During all this time, the angel bearing the earth and the angel bearing heaven rise up; the higher parts of the world fall onto the lower parts. Then a fire begins to burn, and the higher burns over the lower, and what light there is in them is liberated. The duration of the fire is 1,468 years. The king of the world of light lacks nothing in all his land, neither internally nor externally. He has no end, if not for the fact that his land borders on the land of his enemy; the king of the world of light is present throughout his land.
>
> With this symbolic story, Mani recounted the very thing we are speaking of, or something quite like it. It is the truth itself; otherwise, what we are saying would be false.[97]

The Manichaean myth and Mani's prophecy here have the same status as the Platonic myth in relation to the rational truth of philosophy. They are sources of truth, in the way that Avicenna's visionary recitals are a source of inspiration for Suhrawardī and Mullā Sadrā. This is all the more surprising because the Muslim world, Manichaeism "was the sect par excellence, in the most pejorative sense, a group of recalcitrants who secretly spread absurd and dangerously blasphemous fables and doctrines."[98] Within the silence that fell upon Manichaean dualism, whose principles were refuted by the implacable dialectic of the theologians, such a passage makes a thunderous noise.[99]

Such a passage is not completely isolated, since we find a very similar one in Shahrastani's survey of the various systems of belief.[100] But his intention is not to praise the dualists, whereas the Ishrāqī thinker presents Mani as the prophet who announces the truth of the imaginal world.

Mani's story relates to a particular episode in the war between the world of light and the world of shadows. In the beginning, two natures, two substances – light and shadows, good and evil,

God and matter – coexist. The region of the good is in the north, that of evil is in the south. The "dwellings or members" of the Father of Greatness are intelligence, thought, reflection, will, and reason; for the prince of shadows, they are smoke, fire, wind, water, shadows, and an immense legion of demons. The story begins with a catastrophe, the attack of the kingdom of light, which leads to the state of mixture referred to in the text quoted above. Primordial man, the first hypostasis called to combat by the Father of Greatness, is defeated, and a portion of the divine soul is absorbed by matter.

This story is set in a time when the Father of Greatness makes a third invocation, that of the third messenger, the cosmic savior. His task is to organize the mechanism that will remove and carry away the particles of light trapped in matter. The Jesus of Light, assisted by the Virgin of Light, takes his place on the moon, while the Messenger goes to his place on the sun.[101]

The median imaginal world corresponds to the ascent of the column of light during the time when lights and shadows are mixed, after the invasion of shadows into the domain of the Father of Greatness or Splendor. The first liberation of the light imprisoned by the shadows occurs when the living spirit, helped by his five sons, punishes the demonic archons. Three different parts are formed: the light that has not been mixed forms the sun and the moon; the part that has been moderately affected forms the stars; the third part is engulfed in the depths. This triadic scheme also occurs in the division of human souls into the damned, the medially advanced, and the intellective and contemplative souls. During the first two weeks of each month, the substance of the liberated light ascends the column of light – homologous to the perfect man – reaching the moon and becomes full. During the last two weeks of the month, the particle of light is transported to the sun and thereby reaches its celestial homeland.[102]

Shahrazūrī writes: "With these symbols, Mani means the very thing we have mentioned." Not only does such a remark show that the philosophy of the Ishrāqīyah integrates the Manichaean revelation into the heart of Muslim eschatology – which in itself is an event of major importance—but it also offers a key to the interpretation of the imaginal world.

The imaginal world is the site of division and separation, in the sense given to the dividing up of particles in the Manichaean myth. Salvation is the return of the particles of light to their homeland, the end of the time in which they are mixed with shadows. In Ishrāqī soteriology, the division separates two types of forms. On the one hand, there are the spiritual forms bearing the light in which the blessed rejoice: "These are forms of perfect beauty, delightful to eat, to drink, to wear, and the large-eyed houris with whom one mingles, and the boys."[103] Heavenly sexuality and the sensual Qur'ānic promises have their proper place in the suspended forms that are unveiled to embodied souls in other imaginal suspended forms, those of the virtuous. On the other hand, there are "the spiritual forms of the suspended shadows by which the damned are afflicted. These are repugnant and odious forms of darkness, by which souls are afflicted in having to contemplate them, by which they are overwhelmed in their physical contact and intimate relations with them."[104] Visions of horror, sickening contact, and atrocious copulations, or visions of beauty, delicious tastes and sensations, and joyous copulations: the punishment is symmetrical to the reward. There is nothing of the kind, certainly, in Manichaean ascesis. What is added here is the interpretation of what is given in the Qur'ān, which assumes physical enjoyments and must be integrated into the dualist division of light and shadow. This happens through a certain identification of the purifying Manichaean column of light with the cosmic place in which the imaginal dividing up of pleasures and pains occurs. The light of the middle souls is transmuted into an organ of blessed enjoyment, while the shadowy souls enjoy—if we dare call it that—what they have always desired: ugliness and sorrow.[105]

These suspended forms are not the Platonic Ideas. The play of the imagination makes it the site of appearance for forms existing concretely, resulting from the metamorphosis of souls and the effusion of higher archangelic lights. The imaginal world—in which souls with bestial or human bodies, satanic or angelic bodies, are purified and recognize each other – is also the world of *models*. Hence the profound ambivalence of the term *al-mithāl*. It designates the *semblance* that appears in the imagination, but it also designates the form into which the soul of the elect or the damned is metamorphosed. It is the similitude of its moral interiority, and the form that gives the elect enjoyment or makes the damned suffer. Finally, it refers to the archetypal models, the mirrors of primordial archangelic lights. The hierarchy of worlds is established, then, as follows:

The world of signification (*ʿālam al-maʿnah*), of the eternal essence, which is the world of the intelligence and the pure immaterial lights;

The world of forms, which is the world of archetypal suspended forms;

The sensible world of the heavens and of elementary realities. This model is attributed to the ancients, Plato, Socrates, Pythagoras, and Empedocles.[106]

The Vision of the Heart

Most of the ideas just recalled appear in Sadrā's doctrine of the imagination, where they are internalized and made into events of the soul and the soul alone. The imaginative forms are not the result of an abstraction made from the external forms of concrete existents, because the very notion of an abstraction from impressions registered in the bodily organs would be unintelligible. The forms are produced by the imagination itself; they do not exist in this world but emanate from the soul through the imaginative faculty. They subsist in neither the cerebral body nor any other body. The "suspended citadels" spoken of by the Ishrāqīyah are so completely detached from all material substrates that they do not exist in the world of models and similitudes either.[107] It is no longer a question of locating imaginal events in the world of celestial spheres; Sadrā's intention is, rather, to reformulate Suhrawardī's conception of the imaginal world by making it a degree of intensity in the substantial motion of the soul.

The forms do not exist in an "imaginal world," because it is useless to posit the existence of such a world in addition to the world of the soul:

> They exist in the world of the soul, despite their greatness and even though they are immense forms, as great as the greatness of the spheres, as great as wide deserts and immense lands; they exist in a place (*suqʿ*) within that world, since the heart of man is far greater than the throne and what it bears, as Abū Yazīd Bistāmī said of his own soul. They are, therefore, forms that do not exist in this world here below, but the soul sees them with the vision of the heart, and it contemplates them when it closes its bodily eyes, a contemplation more true than its contemplation of sensible material realities.[108]

The reference to Bistāmī's paradox, which holds that the heart contains the divine throne in one of its "recesses," rather than being external to it, requires clarification in terms of Sadrā's exegesis of the Throne Verse. We will analyze this later. For the moment, it suffices to understand how Sadrā justifies the internalization he proposes. It is based on his distinction between forms of perception and forms actualized in matter. He points to eight distinctions between these two types of forms. The material forms are "compact" and do not interpenetrate. They are endowed with sensible qualities, colors or odors, that are proper to them and that do not change. The perceptive forms, however, are not tightly condensed in perceptive existence, and the common sense unifies, or in any case mixes, various perceptions, such that opposing colors or flavors can be given to the senses. At the very dawn of the sensible, it appears that the formal perceptive act of being differs fundamentally from the material act of being. Sensation is not linked with the form inherent to matter but produces a form whose act of existing is completely different. The modality of existence of the phenomenon of perceived form is entirely distinct from the phenomenon of the material form.

In addition, material forms cannot be actualized in smaller matter; "the mountain is not actualized in a mustard seed, the sea does not spread forth in a cistern." But the imagination is able to make present for itself the entire form of heaven and earth together. It confirms what the prophet Muhammad says—"The heart of the believer is greater than the throne"—as well as Bistāmī's paradox—"The throne and what it supports are in one of the recesses of Abu Yazīd's heart." The vision of the heart is homologized with the imagination, which is unlimited and is not confined to any one place. The potential infinity of the act of imagining thus takes on tremendous value, since it refers to the power of vision in the heart, a prophetic vision, the science par excellence of the imams, a knowledge granted to the mystic. This power of containing and internalizing the form of the entire universe shows that the soul and the perceptive forms are free from matter and constitute a distinct world. Or, better, that they are the perceptive form of worlds, the act of existing in the intensity proper to the soul when it reaches a certain degree, where it is delivered from material attachments. Perception is this deliverance itself.

Psychic forms are also distinguished from material forms with respect to intensity or weakness. In the material world, the most powerful effaces the weakest, whereas in the imagination or in intellection, we are free to imagine or to conceive of the small after the large or the less intense after the more intense.

The modalities of material forms are always objects established in a certain determinate place, a certain region of this world. This is not true for the form of perception, which is not, strictly speaking, an "object" (in the sense of something "aimed at"). Nor does it fall under the category of place. Sadrā thus extends to all perceptive forms what Suhrawardī said of imaginal forms: they are from the "land of the nowhere" (*nā-kojā-ābād*). They are not a place; rather, they form their own space.

The form of perception is absolutely singular. Each person is a singular subject through his own perception, and this perception gives rise to his radical singularity, which cannot be communicated to any form of generality:

> A single material form may be perceived by multiple perceptions, by multiple individuals, in the sense determined by their perception. There is a single inscription on which multiple gazes rest, or there is a single sound apprehended by multiple senses of hearing. But this is not the case for the act of being of the perceptive form. Insofar as it is in my imagination, it is impossible for anyone other than me to become aware of it, and insofar as it is in the faculty of taste that is mine, it is impossible for another to taste it. That is why one says that the psychic fire does not burn, and that the burning of the lover's heart is not hot, that the freezing of the snow in his head is not cold.

Material form is like writing deciphered by multiple readers and is subject to their interpretations. All perception is interpretation and depends on the act of being of the perceiving subject, the one who tastes the fruit or the lover undergoing the furor of his passion. The imagination expresses this unique position and pours itself forth in forms that are internally evident. The material form is as unique (despite its multiple perceptions) as the form of perception is multiple, according to the multiplicity of hearts. But this form of perception attests to the infrangible singularity of each of the hearts for which it is actualized.

Material forms cannot come and go, appear and disappear, at will; they owe their eduction to some natural cause. The perceptive forms, however, appear and disappear in the soul, to which they can return without having acquired anything new.

Material form is perfected up to a certain degree: the tree cannot grow beyond the limit allowed by its natural essence. If some natural or artificial form is perfected again after having suffered an imperfection, this happens through the effect of an external cause. The perceptive forms, however, are always perfecting themselves through their own movement of intensification, as in the case of the holy souls who pass through the entire substantial movement leading them from the minimum of perfection to the maximum of intelligible existence. The soul and its perceptions are the active subject of their own progress in being.

We can finally understand the principle of this distinction between material forms and forms of perception and explain the division that separates them, which is also the division between external, constrained, and fixed forms and forms that are reversible, metamorphosed, and free to create their own space. To be sure, we know that the external concrete fire cannot also be called a nonfire, that the body existing in the soul through any given perception of the imagination is not a body. The material body allows no exception to the principle of contradiction, but this is not true of the perceived body, which, after all, is not a body in the concrete and material sense of the term. This does not mean that the imaginative perceptions are illusory. Quite the contrary: in their freedom they are delivered from material imperfections, and they exist, says Sadrā, "in a mode more eminent and noble."

The specification of perceptive forms does not lead us to consider them more or less faithful images of material forms. On the contrary, material forms are the icons (*asnām*) and the receptacles of the separate immaterial forms that are the products of the soul.

> This animal of flesh is composed of contraries and of changing and disappearing forms. It is the image and the shadow of the psychic animal, which is simple, even if the one above it is superior to it. This latter is the intelligible animal, which is simple and one, gathering in its simplicity all the material and psychic individuals and species that are above it. It is their universal model (*al-mithāl al-kullī*), and that is the intelligible horse.[109]

The freedom of perceptive forms is the effect not of their mobility but of their ontological stability. Conversely, the apparent concreteness of material forms, their "confinement," is accompanied by an incessant variation in appearance. Here is the Neoplatonic scheme again. The multiplicity of the material world serves to reflect, like a shadow, the light of the intelligible, through the mediation of the imaginative form. The intelligible world is the world of the authentic model (*mithāl*), and the world of the imagination is that of derivative models, simple but not yet fully unified and illuminated, not yet universal. The imagination is immaterial because it is the production of perceptive forms in their median dignity. The worlds are layered in the soul and the intelligence up to the lower threshold, where the intelligible and the imaginative are degraded into multiple and interlinked material forms. This is where the singularity of the subject is lost, and where its creative spontaneity is impeded.

Are all things merely images of the ego? If the worlds of the imagination and the intelligence are internal, must we speak of a solipsism of the imaginal? Certainly not, if the imagination and the intelligence emanate, as a monad of existence and perception, from the supreme monad, which is God. The world of the imagination is not an external world that we would have to locate, naively, "above" the material world; rather, it is a degree of intensity of the soul, corresponding to a degree in the descent of existence from God and in the reascent toward God. It is an emanation of the divine science, the most objective reality there is, but whose objectivity is one with the greater subjectivity, with the epic of the subject and its wanderings in being.

Sadrā explains our power of imagination in terms we have already encountered: we imagine when we have the strength to imagine, when we have the strength to free ourselves from the ever-multiplying preoccupations (*shawāghil*) of the soul. The multiplicity and density of the forms of sensible perception correspond to the turning outward of our soul as it becomes dispersed in bodily cares, in the exercise of movements and inferior perceptions.[110] In order to imagine, the soul must be concentrated in itself, withdrawn from the tasks of ruling over the body. The position of the perceiving soul depends on the intensity of the *himma*. We have already encountered this important term. Its connotations include certain types of representations, among them the idea of an *aura*. The *himmah* is the force of the soul, its concentration, but also its aura. The aura of imaginative works reflects the aura of the internal potency of the soul.

The internalization of the imaginal world in the process of the soul's growth depends on Sadrā's definition of the soul. Mullā

Sadrā refused to think of the faculties of the soul as separate faculties belonging to distinct quiddities: rather, they are merely modalities of the act of being of the soul in its substantial motion.

> The human soul, since it originates from the root of the Malakūt, possesses a totalizing unity, which is a shadow of the divine unity. In its own essence, it is intellective, imaginative and sensible, growing and moving, and it is a nature flowing in the body, as the Philosopher said, because it possesses three parts: vegetable, animal, and rational. The soul then descends to the level of the senses, according to its perception of the sensibles and the use it makes of the sense organ, and it becomes, for sight, a seeing eye, and for hearing, a listening ear, and so on for the rest [of the sensible perceptions], including touch and the faculties governing locomotion. Thus it rises, according to the perception of intelligibles, to the degree of the intelligence and is unified with it in the mode that is known to penetrating men of knowledge.[111]

The soul is fundamentally one; it has a vegetal body in the vegetative functions and an animal body in the vital natural functions, and it becomes, substantially, an imagination in the imaginal ascesis, before being entirely unified with the agent intelligence. This imaginative stripping away is the very stripping away of the soul liberating itself from its mode of inferior bodily existence, in order to be incarnated in the body that it configures through its acts of imagination. The imagination's eschatological function and moral habits then become its finality.

The power of substantial motion is required here, such that the entire doctrine of the imagination is indeed a doctrine of the *himma*:

> Someone whose soul is firmly rooted, with respect to its *himma*, in the lower region, and whose soul is deficient in its desire for the higher region and is very little turned toward the Right Way of the real and the world of holiness — well, the substance of his heart will not find a path to the acquisition of hidden forms, unless it is

> through the external senses and the conjunction of the corporeal organ and the presence of external matter.[112]

The ethics of the imagination will be an ethics of resoluteness (*al-'azīmah*), concentration, and self-intensification. These practices of the self will offer the subject the power to strip itself of the inferior body, to bind itself again to its *fitrah*, its primordial constitution, and "to learn about particular forms on the basis of its own principial aspects and sources (*ma'ādin aslīyah*), to configure essences (*ma'ānī*) in dimensional forms within the world of forms cleansed of these matters here below."

The imaginal vision is indeed a median degree between sensible dispersion and extreme intelligible concentration. It suspends its vigilance with regard to bodily preoccupations, the governmental guidance of the body. The imaginative faculty, says Sadrā, is the purifying power of the soul that "returns to its world and rejoins its sacrosanct father who is the spirit of holiness (*rūh al-quds*), it goes back to what God wills among sacrosanct spirits." The soul is then filled with knowledge and wisdom by the engraving that results from infiltration or reflection; it is like a polished mirror facing the sun.

The reference to the spirit of holiness is not an empty one. It is indeed a question of the spirit breathed into Jesus that appeared to Mary in the human figure of the angel: "He appeared before her as a man in all respects."[113] The imagination has its model in the prophetic imagination. It is the path to the spirit of holiness, whose manifestation is seen by Mary in one of the most important moments in the history of revelation. Is it forcing things to say that the imagination is the *himmah* of Mary, that it is the power of the Marial soul? The form of the angel is not set down, according to Sadrā, on the "tablet of *phantasia*"; it is not an external sensible appearance destined to take its place in the lower imagination, in fantasy, as the Zāhirīyah, "who have no authority in the science of prophetic things," claim.

The angelic form descends from the supreme world and effuses upon the soul of Mary. But it must not be thought that the form of what is seen and heard is stripped of external material forms, then rises toward the world of imagination and the imagined, and farther to the thinking soul. Sadrā repudiates the psychology of abstraction, maintaining that it is not the form that rises into the soul but the soul that rises into the forms. The soul rises by producing imaginal forms, then intelligible representations: "The soul rises up from the sensible to the imagined, and from there to the intelligible, and the forms subsist in their places and in their respective worlds." The soul rises to encounter the effusion, and it responds to the effusion that makes it rise from its lower worlds to its higher world, entirely internal to it:

> In the vision of the angel and in the hearing of inspiration — a vision and a hearing that are pure and evident — the effusion comes down from the world of the Imperative to the soul, which thus acquires the vision of something from the Malakūt in an immaterial fashion, in no way conditioned by a sensible, imaginative, or estimative faculty. Then effusion occurs, passing from the soul to the imaginative faculty, and to this faculty there appears the form that is joined to speech in the imagination, from the source of effusion and the dwelling (*suq'*) of mercy. Then the configured form and the ordered indication of the imagination and the imaginative faculty descend to the senses that bear witness. Or better yet, the soul descends from the higher world to the median world, then to the lower world, and in each world it perceives what it is given to know and what corresponds to it ... and the soul hears the speech and sees the form in each of its three worlds.[114]

The internalization of what is given in the imagination is accompanied by the affirmation of its effectively concrete reality. The trouble with the imaginal world of the Ishrāqīyah, according to Sadrā, is that it lacks effectivity. It is both naively conceived of as an objective world and deprived, in its very objectivity, of its necessary effectivity. Because of this, the final purpose of the philosophy of the imagination is lost, since salvation and damnation lose their reality.

Sadrā brought together his entire conception of the imagination in *The Beginning and the End* (a book written after *al-Asfār*), in which he undertook a synthesizing meditation on the status of the "realities of the other world," that is, the realities of heaven and hell.[115]

These realities, promised by God, are at the heart of the profession of faith. How should they be understood? What is the meaning of Muslim eschatology? Sadrā responds by distinguishing four levels of understanding (*maqām*). The first is that of the "people of Islam" (*Ahl al-Islām*), those who are content with what is called "blind faith." They believe that heaven and hell are sensible realities, belonging to this world. They are not wrong to demand a sensible effective reality, but they situate it incorrectly by placing it in this world.

At the second level of exegesis, the realities of the other world lose material effectivity. They become *semblances*, like those seen in sleep. There, one conceives of imaginal realities (*umūr mithālīyah*), whose only defect is that they do not exist *in concreto* (*fī'l-'ayn*), since they have no more existence than what a man sees in his sleep. With no other existence that that of a thought, the dreamed forms of the otherworld nonetheless bring suffering or enjoyment. Trapped in a nightmare full of scorpions, the man is tormented. He writhes, he cries out in a dream, he is drenched with sweat and falls from his bed in terror. On the contrary, when he takes pleasure in a dream, his enjoyment has no equivalent in the waking state. The pleasure of the dream is a pleasure in the dream, which is not only the guardian of sleep but also the access to an incomparable enjoyment. The valorization of the dream is not a preference granted to the unreal but a greater satisfaction of desire.

If this were the ultimate truth of heaven and hell, Avicenna would be right.[116] There would be no difference between what one imagines and what one senses: "Such would be the case with the gardens, the rivers, the noble individuals whom the dreamer sees and enjoys in the intimacy of his dream."

Avicenna would be right, and with him al-Ghazzālī, who distinguishes three sorts of pleasures according to the gradations of worlds: sensible pleasures (food, sexual relations), imaginal pleasures, and intelligible pleasures.[117] Pleasure in imagination assumes a perpetual duration:

> Dreams are considered with disdain, because they all come to an end. If a dream were perpetual, one would no longer see the difference between what one imagines and what one senses. Indeed, man's enjoyment takes place because it is impressed in the imagination and in the senses, not by virtue of its concrete existence. If the cause of enjoyment exists concretely, but does not exist in the senses of man through an impression, man has no pleasure. The imaginative faculty has the power to create forms in this world, with the reservation that the created form is then imagined and not sensed, that it is not impressed in sight. For that reason, if the imagination creates a form that is beautiful, with an intense beauty, it may imagine its presence, and contemplate it, but its joy will not be very great, for it will still not see it — which is the case in dreams. If the imagination had the power to configure this form in sight, as it has the power to configure it in the imagined form, then its pleasure would be intense. The form would have the status of forms that exist concretely, and then this world would not be distinguished from the otherworld, in this sense, except by virtue of the perfection of the power to configure forms in sight.[118]

In an admirable analysis of the phantasm, this text relates the drama of the imagination: it is the nostalgia for a power that belongs only to the prophets, for a force in the soul so powerful that it creates what the imagination represents to the soul. The imagination contemplates the most beautiful forms, and its enjoyment is not as intense as that of sight, because it cannot see what it contemplates; it cannot cause to emerge into the exteriority of the real what it fashions in the interiority of the soul. The scopic *jouissance* of the imagination ceases at the gates of reality. How to force open these gates: that is the question.

Intelligible pleasure consists in grasping the models of sensible pleasure and of the various *semblances* that correspond to them. This pleasure leads us to the third station in the interpretation of the states of heaven and hell. Here we find ourselves again in the element of Platonism. Sensible forms are the signs (*ishārāt*) of spiritual intelligible forms, which have their seat in the world of pure intelligences, as Plato taught. The reader familiar with Plato's dialogues will be more than a little surprised to see what populates the world of Ideas. The pleasures have their eternal models there: greenery and vegetation, flowing water, beautiful faces, streams, abundant rains of milk, honey, and wine, trees decorated with precious pearls, rubies, emeralds, castles made of gold and silver, pearl bracelets, subservient boys. In short, all the enjoyments that we dream of and that are announced by the revelation have their place in the intelligible world. Plato would have been quite astonished by this moving exaltation of popular and carnal desires, this taste for jewels and palaces. Rather than being amused by this, however, it is more relevant to ask: who was Plato for Islamic consciousness? How was he changed and represented, so that the world of Ideas attributed to him would thus become entirely a world of intelligible *and* sensible paradise?

The contemplation of these forms is a pleasure allotted to "the people of the gnosis," to the "perfect in consciousness." al-Ghazzālī maintains that the gnostics, who remain "finely tuned thinkers" (*al-mustasghirūn*) of the world of forms and sensible pleasures, receive the subtleties of intelligible pleasures and enjoyments that correspond to them. They delight in abundant food and their concupiscence are satisfied.

The imaginary thus invades the intelligible world, probably at its lower degree, but at a degree that is appropriate to it. If it is heaven, it must have the stability of perpetual Platonic forms. al-Ghazzālī, quoted by Sadrā, gives the best definition of heaven found anywhere: *There, everyone has what he desires.* Heaven is to each according to his desire. It is total enjoyment, not actualized here below, but real in the other world. It is the horizon of desire.

It is impossible, consequently, to deprive the heavenly forms of their effectivity, to reduce them to an abstraction offering no pleasure. From there the fourth station of our progression leads us to the truth of the imagination, or rather of the soul itself, the agent soul, perceiving *in itself* the forms unveiled on the Day of Return, perceiving them no longer in a dream but *in effective reality*. Resurrection opens the gates of reality to the dream of limitless pleasures; it establishes them in an objectivity that presents no obstacle to the most intense subjectivity.

"These realities do exist concretely, and they subsist effectively. They are stronger in existentiality and in stability in being; they are more intense and more durable than the existents of this world." They are real, but they have no relation with the sensible forms of this world that correspond to the first "birth" of the soul, contrary to what the literalists who adhere to the apparent meaning of the Qur'ānic verses think. But because they are real and concrete, they have nothing to do with the presumed "imaginal realities," the "imaginal existents" conceived of by the Ishrāqīyah. Those who adhere to the material sensible, together with the philosophers of the imaginal, are all dismissed without further ado. The imaginal world vanishes, opening the space for the soul's activity after its separation from the body.

The heavenly or infernal forms are unveiled to the soul in their concrete reality at its second birth. They are without doubt announced in our dreams, because the dream is death's younger brother.[119] But, as one prophetic tradition says, "Men sleep, and when they die, they awaken." Here below, the dream is a privileged state, because it depends on the sleep of the bodily senses. It reveals our condition as sleepers, and the world's meager reality. Death is waking: it is an awakening to the only real world, the world beyond. We understand better, then, why Plato was so favored in the Muslim world.

The evanescence of this world is the most immediate feeling of prophetic consciousness. The Qur'ān places the otherworld in opposition to this one and says that this world, in truth, is nothing but deceptive appearance. How could one not recognize this same teaching in Plato, and how could one not then read Plato within the element of this feeling and its fundamental disqualification of all the agitation and restlessness of this world? The ontology of Islam does not reverse this judgment on the sensible; it does not reconcile one to the sensible. Rather, it judges as sensible what we do not sense here below and valorizes the sensible in the extreme, desires it to the highest degree. But that is a sensibility that the body does not offer: an otherworldly sensibility.

The imagination makes way for sensibility. Or rather it is the threshold of heaven and hell, whereas enjoyment and suffering depend fully on an otherworldly sensibility. Sadrā says the interiority of man in this world is the exteriority of the same man in the otherworld.[120] During man's first "birth" and growth, his soul accumulates the traces of his habits, good or bad, within its interiority (*bātin*), within its secret, in the spiritual faculties of imagination, memory, and estimation. Physical death causes a revolution of his act of existing that turns his being inside out like a glove, placing in the exterior (*zāhir*) what was hidden in the secret of the soul. It liberates the internal senses, which become external senses adapted to the forms of the otherworld. The eye of the soul can see its Lord; the ear can hear the revealed verses and the words of the angels, the rustling wings of the birds of paradise; the sense of smell can perceive the perfumes of divine familiarity; the sense of taste can revel in the full fruition of the Garden's succulent offerings; the touch can enjoy the bodies of the houris with beautiful eyes. These, says Sadrā, are the organs of spiritual perception (*al-mashā'ir al-rūhānīyah*) and the internal senses (*al-hawāss al-bātinah*).

The thinking human soul, says Sadrā, is rooted in the Malakūt. Consequently, it has, by nature, the power and the force to create forms (*ikhtirā' al-suwar*). When it descends to the threshold of the first birth, it loses the most illuminated part of this innate force, which explains the already-mentioned fact that the forms that we imagine are weak in existence: what we sense is pale and dim, without effectivity, and we cannot realize what we represent to ourselves, which remains an image.

The imagination is the weakness of our souls here below, but it is their strength in the beyond. There are already some signs of this strength: when the soul escapes from the preoccupations necessary for the preservation of the body, a preservation that involves many hateful things; and when this soul calls for its deliverance, when it abstains from the body, it turns toward the higher heaven, "with a strength that is deep within itself." By nature, or through patient acquisition, the soul then returns to "its Malakūt essence," to the generative source of the forms, "and it creates the forms, it contemplates them with its own senses, which are in its essence, without participation of the body." It then leaves behind the constant renewal and disappearance that affected it, of which its imaginative power was the unhappy witness. The soul is then fully sensible, a subject condensed in the generative source of its internal senses, because it is fully active:

> Man, in the state of sleep or unconsciousness, sees, hears, tastes, touches, and smells, although his external senses are deprived of their perceptive employment. We know that the soul has sight, hearing, taste, touch, and smell in itself, with no need of a body for this. Moreover, these senses are more perfect and more pure than those in the body, since there is no obstacle to their use.
>
> Just as all the senses of the body go back to their single sensing subject, which is the common sense, all the senses of the soul and its powers go back to a single power, which is the very essence of the soul, its luminous essence, the source of effusion. The state of their return from this world to the essence of the soul is a perception of things that is identical to the power of the soul over these things.[121]

Sadrā assembles the principal elements of his doctrine of the soul and of the imagination in one passage at the end of *al-Asfār*, where he says that the human soul perfecting itself in science and in practice becomes like a beneficent and generous tree, bearing the fruits of true cognitions. The tree is rooted in stable, eternal cognitions, and its branches are the realities of the world of the Malakūt and the knowledge of the higher divine world (Lāhūt). Not only does man inhabit the tree of paradise, but he has also become this tree himself, the Tūbā tree homologized with the mystic person of the imam. As for practice—beautiful actions, purification exercises, and moral virtues, taken as a whole – it too has its reward. Thus we verify the principle mentioned above: the interiority of man in this world is identical to his exteriority in the otherworld. There man uses the force of his imagination to configure and create all that he desires, and to make the form of multiple objects of desire appear. Here this form does not exist concretely; it takes on consistency not for sensibility but only in the imagination and in thought, according to a very weak act of existing. That is why the enjoyment we take in objects of desire here below is so weak, whereas in the state of resurrection the soul is liberated from the preoccupations of the body and the effects of the external senses. The interiority of the soul is laid bare, it becomes manifest, and its inward secret is revealed. The soul's enjoyment takes on all its existence and its power of appearance and pours itself out irresistibly, for the sensed forms are similar to concretely existing forms. The otherworld does not differ from this world, says Sadrā, except in the perfection of the human soul's power and strength, its power to configure the forms in the faculty of sense and feeling just as it wishes. This is possible for it in the otherworld, but not in this one.[122]

Having returned to its own generative source of effusions, the soul becomes, in a way, similar to God, for whom knowledge and power are one. It becomes the divinized soul.

> Thus, the soul's cognition is actuality and its senses are potentiality (*qudra*). Every time the soul becomes more perfect in potency, and every time it becomes more potent in substance, and suffers less from strife and the hindrance of its faculties – either because of their languor and their weakness, as with the mad and the sick, or because of its strength, which in turn may be magnanimous, as with the prophets or the imams, or wicked, as with the diviners and sorcerers – its capacity for concrete forms and its contemplation of these forms become stronger; greater, too, are the effects of the act of being, which are determined by their visible forms as pleasurable or painful, even though the connection with the body and with this base world persists. And this is true because of its potency, to the

> extent that it is perfect in both aspects, the external and the internal, the sensible and the *mysterium*. But the *mysterium* is seen only by certain souls delivered from their bodily chains. These are the souls of those who are not attached to the forms of this world, who give no attention to this base world, except with the disdainful gaze that condemns it.[123]

To conclude, I would like to cite a passage from Proust, one that is both faithful to the tempo of the inner melody and close to what Sadrā says about otherworldly sensation:

> Suddenly I fell asleep, plunged into that deep slumber in which vistas are opened to us of a return to childhood, the recapture of past years, and forgotten feelings, of disincarnation, the transmigration of souls, the evoking of the dead, the illusions of madness, retrogression towards the most elementary of the natural kingdoms (for we say that we often see animals in our dreams, but we forget that almost always we are ourselves animals therein, deprived of that reasoning power which projects upon things the light of certainty; on the contrary we bring to bear on the spectacle of life only a dubious vision, extinguished anew every moment by oblivion, the former reality fading before that which follows it as one projection of a magic lantern fades before the next as we change the slide), all those mysteries which we imagine ourselves not to know and into which we are in reality initiated almost every night, as into the other great mystery of extinction and resurrection.[124]

Part Three

Salvation

Chapter Eight

A Philosophy of Spirit

Psychic Man[1]

The soul is the form of the organic body living in this world. But it is also the site of a struggle. The imagination that constitutes the destiny of each man, according to his acts and intentions, configures either heaven or hell, which reveals to him his authentic form. "To cultivate one's heaven" and "to fashion one's soul"—these are not metaphors but descriptions of spiritual movement. The metamorphosis of the human substance, whose root is located in the higher worlds, changes man into what is most profound about him: his act of existing. By practicing the moral precepts, the faithful man does not respect an external law but fulfills the internal law of his spiritual nature. He does not receive heaven as a reward for his obedience; rather, he fashions his heaven and turns himself into his own heaven, just as the tyrannical soul transforms itself into its own hell. As an intensification that is also a return to the origin, the work done on the self animates the soul, which becomes the matter of a precise degree of one's humanity: the psychic man.

The psychic man is the mediation between the sensible man and the intelligible man. He actualizes the intensity of existence proper to the otherworld, situated between the world of substances, composed of elementary matter and specific forms, and the world of pure archetypal intelligible realities. Sadrā borrows the concept from Plotinus: "Within this man made up of the elements, there is a psychic man, who possesses life and belongs to the otherworld. He has all his organs, senses, and faculties. He exists this very instant. His life is not like the life of this organic body, which is accidental and occurs to it from the outside; rather, he has life by his very essence."[2] The reality of such a psychic man is based on the structure of the births and the three worlds and on the substantial movement that passes from one to the other.

The entire structure depends on the reality of the intelligible world. The *Theology of Aristotle* has the merit of affirming the existence of this originary world, endowed with a heaven and an earth and all the real existents of which natural beings are the images. Mullā Sadrā posits this Neoplatonic scheme in opposition to the Avicennian scheme of the Intelligences and substances of the sublunary world, because he believes that the Avicennian negation of the Idea can only lead to the ruin of the intelligible world, which in turn leads to the destruction of the psychic man and his singular world – the world of the soul. This in turn would destroy any rational doctrine of resurrection and lead to the disappearance of the moral construction of the internal man that facilitates resurrection.[3]

Psychic man is not simply a model of natural man. To be sure, he preexists his manifestation in the elemental world, since the soul that forms him preexists the natural body and since the psychic mode of existence is a median degree in the act of being's descent from the plane of divine and intelligible names to the lowest degree of dense matter. But in the order of the return (*ma'ād*) that corresponds to this descent and this procession, the imaginal act of being – that of psychic man – is not realized in the free activity of the subject. Determined in the divine secret, the destiny of psychic man is necessarily what it is. The gradual conversion toward God is no more contingent than the procession was. But the passage from natural existence to psychic existence depends on a separation, a disjunction, a sorting out that takes place among men according to their accomplishments. No moral fatalism can be justified by the omnipotence of the divine decree.

A sorting out, a dividing up: the existence of souls after death distinguishes separate species and human genera, not individuals within a single species. It ruptures the apparent unity of humanity:

> Individual human beings in this world are coincident as to species, composed of a proximate genus ("animal") and a specific difference ("rational"), derived (respectively) from a bodily matter and from a psychic form. But after beginning as a single species, human souls will then become many different species, according to a second birth and a second fundamental nature, and these species fall under four genera.[4]

Substantial motion disunites what the universal form of the human species had brought for a time into a factitious coincidence. To each man it reveals a second nature, which he himself has engendered. Each man will be judged according to this new nature and will find his reward or punishment in the form of his imaginal species. Another scheme is thus superimposed onto the Plotinian scheme, one that comes directly from the Qur'ān and from the interpretations of the imams, valorizing the moral choice between acting well and acting badly.

The philosophers of history have conditioned us to represent the reign of ends as including a demand for universality: universal peace, laws that accord the satisfaction of each and the rights of all, a rational state, the end of classes and class struggles, and so on. These figures of the universal do not repress the aspirations of individuals but are meant to integrate them into a final harmony. The wars that punctuate the movement of historical becoming—as the history leading to arrival of the universal—will be concluded in a final struggle that will put an end to all wars and to the very necessity for man's political existence, and will bring the reign of supersensible ends.

What is revealed by juxtaposing the Sadrian eschatological scheme, based on the growth of psychic man with this very general scheme of the Western philosophers of history? It is symmetrical and inverted. The universal dimension of man's specific nature occurs at the beginning of the first birth of individuals, not at the end of their history. It is then that harmony (*muttafiqah*) reigns, as the inclusion (*jam'*) of all within the single species (that of the rational animal). Shaykh Ahmad al-Ahsā'ī explains this: "By animal we mean the body endowed with growth and voluntary movement, and whose lot is matter. By rational we mean the originary soul of the Malakūt (*al-nafs al-malakūtīyah*), whose lot is the difference that is form." The logical definition of man unifies within it a generic matter from here below and a specific formal difference originating in the higher worlds. It joins a material body and a spiritual soul whose formal essence is constituted in the Malakūt, the threshold of the intelligible world. In the first stage of his substantial motion, man is a universal species, in which one cannot distinguish between prophets, prophets sent with a message, the impious, hypocrites, believers, and the sincerely faithful.[5]

In the state of nature, which is the first nature, the opposite types of humanity, whom revelation will make it possible to distinguish, coincide in a single form. But this "coincidence" or general concordance does not correspond to effective reality. Indeed, as Shaykh Ahmad recalls in his commentary, the People of the House of the Prophet teach that the pleroma of the fourteen immaculate ones (Muhammad, Fātimah, and the twelve imams) introduces a significant difference into the very heart of humanity, since the matter of their existence is the light of eternal Muhammadan reality (*haqīqah muhammadīyah*).

Through a process of luminous effusions, a gradation between human species made of different spiritual materials is established. The living nature and forms shared by Muhammad and the people of the house of the Prophet are superior to the living nature and forms of the prophets of lesser rank. And so on for each rank: believers do not have the same nature as unbelievers, hypocrites, and the like.[6]

This distinction and this hierarchization of species and forms structure the spiritual world according to Shī'ite gnosis. The second birth, as Sadrā conceives of it, corresponds less to a second age in the temporal history of humanity than to a second moment in the vertical becoming of man, in a history that, passing from world to world, is oriented toward a return to God. This history is situated within the framework established by the ontology of "eternal Muhammadan reality" discussed by Shaykh Ahmad, which corresponds to the act of being of the perfect man, the intelligible man – a distant ideal that must be attained and imitated – through a transition that is initiated in the psychic man.

Rather than the temporal history of Western philosophers, a history mutely inhabited by the work of Spirit or freedom, here is a completely different type of history, one authorized by the Neoplatonic scheme of the three men and the three births.[7] It is a history of metamorphosis and distinction, which passes from the abstract universal of the rational animal to the species and genera separated according to spiritual and moral faith, particularly those of the psychic and imaginal man. Motion leads to the absolutely singular monads of the intelligible man, united in the angelic act of being, which is an extinction and an eternal existence in the divine intelligible world.

Contrary to the Western scheme of history, which reconciles the spiritual universal and the temporal particulars, this scheme involves being torn away from the abstract generality of nature and moved toward the singularity of spiritual monads, through the mediation of distinct species of opposed humanities. To a model of temporality whose end lies in a social structure corresponds a discrete and intensive temporality leading from the dense time of natural man to the subtle time of the second birth and on to the perpetuity of intelligible existence. The final triumph of a human singularity reconciled in the universal reign of concrete morality is replaced here by a singular conjunction with the intelligible form, a monad expressive of the divine unity. This end is not a rational state or a rational abolition of the state, but freedom in absolute obedience, an eternal face-to-face encounter between the created unity and the uncreated unity.

Metamorphosis and distinction: our soul is not simply the natural form of the organized body. Because its root lies in the

Malakūt, it has two aspects, which give it two acts of being: one in this world and one in the otherworld; one in the physical man and one in the psychic man. With its first birth, when it has reascended from the depths of matter and begun the odyssey of its return, "the soul is the entelechy for sensible matter, but it is also spiritual matter (*mādda rūhānīyah*) with the capacity of receiving and being united with an intelligible form, and it thereby passes from potency into actuality."[8] Psychic man sees, in the spiritual matter of his soul, the emergence of an otherworldly form in which he will come to know his reward or his punishment. His metamorphosis (which is not a transmigration) is the movement through which the form that had governed the body becomes the sedimentation of various moral habits. This memory of one's acts fashions a spiritual matter that is united with an otherworldly form suitable to it, just as a species is suitable to a certain determinate type of matter. The soul takes this spiritual form, it *becomes* it, in its second birth. It is transformed into a brutish or wild animal, satanic or angelic according to a fourfold structure exemplified through a creative bestiary of the imagination. It is not that the soul imagines its new form; rather, it is united with a new form through the power — more or less intense, corrupted, or active — of its perceptive and practical activity.

> The soul is a form either of the delusive and satanic estimative judgment, or of brute animality, or of a ferocious beast. It is in these forms that the soul will be reconstituted and raised at the resurrection, in another world and not in this world, since the latter would mean the transmigration of the soul and not its resurrection (*hashr*). But transmigration is impossible, whereas corporeal resurrection is a fact.
>
> In this world, therefore, man stands between becoming an angel and becoming a Satan, becoming a brute and stupid beast or a ferocious beast. If knowledge and intensification (*taqwā*) dominate in him, he will become an angel. But if cunning, trickery, and compounded ignorance [that is, being unaware of his actual ignorance] dominate in him, he will become a rebellious Satan; if he surrenders to the effects of sensuous appetites, he will become a brute beast. If

> he surrenders to the effects of violence and fury, he will become a ferocious beast. For the dog is a dog because of its animal form, not because of its particular matter, and the pig, too, is a pig because of its form, not its matter. Similarly with all the other animals: some fall under the characteristic attributes of the appetitive soul, according to its categories, such as the mule, the ass, the bear, the cat, the peacock, the rooster, and so forth; others fall under the characteristic attributes of the irascible soul, such as the lion, the wolf, the snake, the scorpion, the eagle, and the like.[9]

The human species is divided into two major categories, those who adhere to light and those who adhere to shadows, according to a dramaturgy whose origins reach back to the foundation of the dualist religions of ancient Iran and whose inspiration animated the original Shīʿism, in its desire for the eschatological reign of the awaited savior.[10] In Mullā Sadrā's philosophical hermeneutics, this great division operates not within the sphere of eschatological waiting but in a sort of moral psychology that grounds the theory of the resurrectional body. Each soul, according to the faculty it has chosen to emphasize and to cultivate, develops a certain type of imagination or estimative faculty.[11] If it intensifies its act of being, it renounces the animal faculties, tempers them, and prepares the way to its becoming-angel, which is a becoming-intelligence, through the practices of knowledge – that is, through the illuminative knowledge of the esoteric dimension of revelation. If it allows its act of being to weaken by yielding to the deceptions of appetite and wrath, it prepares the way for its union with the brutish or the ferocious animal form. Finally, through moral perversion united with ignorance, it prepares the way for the reception of a satanic form. Four genera of existence are thus manifest in the wealth of the animal world, in the simplicity of angelic life, and in the perverse composition of demonic activity. The psychic man is distributed along three degrees – a salvation in effective existence, a damnation in a deceptive appearance of existence, an intermediate brutish or ferocious status – according to species whose actuality is revealed after death.

Sadrā does not think becoming solely within the element of the collective history of the human species. The community of the elect will be the community of hearts faithful to a teaching and a knowledge whose secret the imams possessed. Sadrā offers a very beautiful representation of this community, derived from his Qur'ānic exegesis. He writes that the Tūbā tree found in paradise is the symbol of the tree of knowledge. Its branches are made of inspired divine knowledge that can be gained not through any sort of acquisition but through the illumination originating from the tabernacle of prophecy, and this occurs through the necessary mediation of the imam 'Ālī and the most eminent among those who are thresholds to the city of knowledge.[12] The Tūbā tree is thus the imamate itself, and its branches are those who remain faithful to the knowledge inspired by the eternal imam. The community of the elect is an arborescence of multiple monads of gnostic perception, whose principle of eternal growth is the mystical generative center, the spiritual person of 'Ālī. It is not a community united by political or juridical relations but a concert of hearts oriented toward the vivifying center of knowledge.[13]

But if it is so with the final community of the elect, the path leading to it is nothing other than the accomplishment of a personal moral habit and a resolutely singular choice. To understand this, we must explicate some passages from one of Sadrā's exegeses of the notion of *spirit*.[14]

The Life of the Spirit

Mullā Sadrā comments on the response given by the sixth imam, Ja'far al-Sādiq, to the disciple who asks him the meaning of the word *spirit*, which is found in many Qur'ānic verses.[15] The imam answers: It means the spirit of God that is created, that God created in Adam and Jesus. By way of exegesis, Sadrā comes back to his distinction between the first birth and the second. Human individuals, he says, are coincident as to species in their first birth by virtue of their common form, the exoteric dimension of their condition of existence. But the esoteric dimension of their act of being, their second birth, is a completely different matter. The becoming of each man is an internal becoming, because it is a passage to the manifestation of its interiority, the otherworldly birth. The otherworld is the esoteric aspect of each individuality, which ruptures the universal uniformity of the natural form. Each man becomes the individual he is through this movement toward his singular otherworld, which is differentiated not through the abstract universal difference of "rationality" but through another specific difference, which is the otherworldly form.

These forms engender individuals who are their own species, according to hierarchized classes: the lowest are the forms of men who have no soul other than an imaginative animal soul (*hayawānīyah mithālīyah*); above that is the class of men whose souls are truly "thinking" and are capable of perceiving the intelligibles. These are the companions of the hearts (*ashāb al-qulūb*).[16] Finally, there is a class of men whose souls are superior: those who reach the station of the spirit, whose souls become a pure spirit, a pure intelligence. These souls reside in the station of the spirit from the origin of their nature (*fitrah*), as in the case of the prophets, or they arrive there after the spiritual pilgrimage (*ba'ad al-sulūk*), as in the case of minor prophets and friends of God, the gnostics, the faithful inspired by mystical knowledge.[17]

The imaginative soul has the power to configure symbols corresponding to supersensible realities; the intellective soul accedes to forms entirely separate from matter. Hearts are the generative centers of the *himmah*, the epiphanic intention, so the intellective activity is accomplished in the heart.[18] Finally, spirits transcend imagination and intellection through a complete unification with the divine manifestation on a plane beyond the intelligible, in the movement of primordial divine instantiation.

The second birth, in which the psychic man comes to completion, is not the end of the internalization, distinction, and metamorphosis of the soul. The imaginal world, understood as the world of the configurative soul, is the first degree, and only the first degree. In this imaginal station dwell the souls whose spiritual matter is united to bestial forms, ferocious animal forms, or satanic forms. Those whose souls take on an angelic form are submitted to a transfiguration that strips them of all matter, whether spiritual or imaginal. They accede to the station of the intelligence, and finally to the station that transcends the intelligible, the station of pure spirit.

Souls are differentiated and hierachized in their most profound substance. To support this thesis, which governs the world of moral purification, Sadrā evokes the discussion between the first imam, ʻĀlī ibn ʻAbī Tālib, and his disciple, Kumayl ibn Ziyād, concerning the essence of the soul. This is a Shīʻite tradition presented as a scene of initiation (*taʻlīm*) in which the master, the imam, carries out an astonishing synthesis of the Aristotelian divisions of the soul and the concepts borrowed from the language of Sūfism.

The disciple makes a request that demonstrates his desire to care for himself by knowing his own soul. It is a problem whose main features were established by Plato: "I want you to help me to know my soul." The master is thus supposed to know the soul of the disciple, what constitutes it for Kumayl and for him alone. But he responds with another question that destroys the disciple's illusion that the soul could be encompassed within a single universal definition: "Which soul do you want me to help you to know?" Then the disciple says: "Oh, my master, is the soul not a single soul?" And the imam responds: "Oh, Kumayl, it is fourfold! The growing vegetable soul, the sensing animal soul, the thinking holy soul, the divine universal soul. Each one has five faculties and two properties." Thus he enumerates the elements of medical knowledge. The vegetative soul has its seat in the liver; the animal soul has its seat in the heart, which here means the physiological organ. The thinking soul has no place of bodily origin, nor does the divine universal soul. The latter has five faculties, which present a number of coincident opposites and paradoxical powers: external existence in extinction, happiness in distress, power in humility, poverty in wealth, patience in affliction. It has two properties: satisfaction and submission (*al-ridā' wa-l-taslīm*).

The purification of the psychic man is the movement that leads, within interiority, from the world of creation to the world of the imperative. Indeed, says Sadrā, "the worlds, even if they are multiple, are included in the two worlds that are creation (*khalq*) and command or imperative (*amr*)."[19] Creation is the sensible world and the external senses that perceive it. It is therefore also the first birth, the physical man. The world of the imperative designates all the degrees of the esoteric, the otherworld corresponding to the second birth and to the psychic man, as well as the world of the *mysterium* (*'ālam al-ghayb*), that of the intelligible man.

The differences among men arise because some have an attachment to the world of creation, while others desire to be delivered from it and to accede to the world of the imperative: they desire knowledge and union with God. The truth for each is manifest in the world of the imperative, not in the world of creation, regardless of whether the supersensible realities are sought, since the soul, the heart, the intelligence, the spirit, and the inwardness of the self belong to the world of the imperative. Heaven and hell subsist in this universe of permanence, as do the supreme realities, the *qalam*, the tablet, and the divine throne.

When the souls are distributed according to the four genera — Satans, ferocious animals, brute beasts, and angels — and when psychic man is diversified into antagonistic species, souls experience their truth by passing from an apparent nature that is bound to illusion and the transience of being into a second nature that belongs to the permanent inner world. The second, angelic nature rises to the second superior degree of the world of the imperative, the intelligible world, and on to the summit of this intelligible world, the reign of the spirit.

The most secret truth of the soul is the spirit. The breathing of spirit into Adam and Jesus shows that spirit is the mediation between the creative act and created man — a created reality, to be sure, but one that expresses the divine creative effusion.[20] The spirit constitutes the origin of human reality as well as its return into God. At the end of the return, the spirit is the satisfied soul, whereas at the origin it is intimately linked with the divine creative act. Does not God say, "I breathed into him of *my* spirit"?[21] Because it belongs to the personal identity of God, spirit reveals the ipseity of God, and it deserves to be called "divine universal spirit." But spirit expresses the divine self in the creative imperative, not at the level of the unknowable essence of God.

> The verse "Say: The spirit is by the command of my Lord"[22] defines the spirit. By that I mean that spirit belongs to the world of the imperative and permanence, and not to the world of creation and disappearance. It is not obscure, as is imagined by a group of people who think that God obscured the knowledge of spirit for creatures and reserved it for himself, going so far as to maintain that the Prophet does not know it. Thus the spirits of the children of Adam are created from the spirit of the Prophet, according to the verse, "We breathe into him something of our spirit."[23] It is the inbreathing of Gabriel and the spirit originating from the spirit of the Prophet linked to divine presence. Because the effective reality of spirit is thus, and because it possesses this nobility, human thoughts are insufficient to grasp it, and the intelligence fails at this, as the light of vision fails to grasp the rays of the sun. That is why it is said in this verse: "The spirit comes from the command of my Lord, and little do you know of this."[24]

There is a prophetic essence of spirit. It does not remain unknown by the Prophet into whom God breathes it, but it is as brilliant and ungraspable to the intelligence as the sun is to sight. It is the very secret of the angel Gabriel. It creates human souls in their fundamental reality, and each man is called to his supersensible nature by the prophetic spirit. Spirit is created, not like the creatures that proceed from it, but like the free and imperative effusion of God that emanates from the Creator. It is in the life of spirit that man wins his freedom, which is an ineffable coincidence with the divine imperative.

This paradoxical coincidence is effectuated in spiritual growth, leading to the intelligence beyond the intelligible, the end of the return to the origin. The history of the soul reaches completion at this point of unification with itself, with the source of its act of existing in the divine imperative. Spirit becomes the spirit of a temporal world not in the way it does in the regenerative world history thought by Western philosophers of history, but in the esoteric dimension of history, since spirit cannot be located in the world of creation, which is always a sign of extinction, evanescence, disappearance (*fanā'*). It resides in a world separate from all dense matter, the world of permanence (*baqā'*), which begins the birth of psychic man and is fulfilled in the prophetic destination of man. This split between creation and command is constitutive of the ontology of Islam.

The imperative spirit (*al-rūh al-amrī*) is the reality of the essence of the prophet Muhammad, the archetype of human reality. The Prophet achieves the self-knowledge that is knowledge of one's lord; he knows himself as he is, the mirror of the imperative of his lord. This station of the spirit (*maqām al-rūh*) fully and properly belongs to him, whereas most men do not attain it, since they lack a knowledge of spirit (*ma'rifat al-rūh*). The split between the temporal and the spiritual is not effaced: "The truth is that, because of its simplicity, and because it is a degree of the effective reality of the act of being, spirit cannot be unveiled to anyone, and cannot be known, except by this divine gift of knowledge, and the ipseity of spirit proceeds from the divine imperative. For that reason, there remains a difference between its eternal being and its being produced in time."[25] Spirit is unveiled only to one who reaches his nontemporal station, and its unveiling is the knowledge of divine presence, which is the act of presence of the absolute act of being in its effective reality. Divine imperative freedom, the pure act of existing, prophetic revelation, and the inbreathing of spirit are one.

All men proceed from the prophetic essence of the perfect man, in that their souls all have their roots in the world of the imperative. Those who choose their animal or satanic destiny turn away from their own origin; they turn away from this effusion of souls out of spirit. The body and the spirit are in relation to each other. It is a relation between the caliph and the one whose prophetic work he maintains. Of course, the caliphal function here is not conceived of in political terms. The caliph (the "successor") is the one who proceeds, secondarily, from a unique first reality, and who displays its multiple attributes while also assuring that these attributes are fully gathered into a unity:

> Know that spirits are all created from a single and unique spirit, which is the prophetic spirit (*rūh al-nabī*). The prophetic spirit is the foundation of spirits, which is why it is called "Mother," that is, "Mother of spirits," just as the well-guarded tablet is the mother of the Book, because it is the base for the inscription of the Book. And just as Adam is the father of humankind and the caliph of God in the world of spirits, the spirit is the caliph of God and the gatherer of the essential divine attributes, such as science, life, power, will, hearing, sight, speech, and permanence. The body is the caliph of the spirit and the gatherer of its attributes.[26]

The historical father of man, Adam, is the caliph of God in the apparent creatural and temporal world, while the spiritual father of man is Muhammad, in the hidden, internal, permanent world of the imperative. The destiny of man is determined by the reconciliation of these two origins, these two caliphal functions. The mediation between them is the mother of spirits, the divine imperative spirit breathed into the prophets.

Does this not call to mind the singular position of Jesus whose life occupies a middle ground between apparent external existence and the hidden, effectively real act of being? The breathing of spirit into Jesus accomplishes an act announced by the angel that testifies to the passage from the bodily life of the divine breath (in Adam) to the fully spiritual manifestation that will be fulfilled in Muhammad. Such an idea is at least suggested by this exegesis.

This interpretation of the prophetic history of humanity seems to me to be determined by the distinction that Sadrā makes within the very unity of spirit. Muhammad's place in the world of the imperative is the same as Adam's in the temporal and historical order. The sons of Adam, in their return to their spiritual origin, must rejoin their mother, the spirit, just as the holy book must be led back to its esoteric archetype, the mother of the book, dwelling in the world of the imperative. This return can be accomplished only with the help of an exegesis of eternal Muhammadan reality, including the luminous realities of the fourteen immaculate ones, which is the fundamental and primary reality in the world of the imperative, the paternity of humanity.

The eternal prophetic reality is in fact nothing other than the eternal Muhammadan reality. The latter is the first reality in which God gives himself to be known, in which he emerges from his secret on the plane of ineffable essence:

> When God created the prophetic spirit, it was God and there was nothing else with him, nothing accompanied by the spirit or with which it was in relation, nothing other than God. No, the prophetic spirit was the first thing to which the pre-eternal power was attached. That is why the nobility of the spirit originates in the ennobling of God's relation *with himself*, and God called it "*my* spirit," just as the first dwelling in which men resided — whose nobility lies in the relation of God to himself — was named when God said "*my* house."[27] Then, when God wanted to create Adam and breathe his spirit into him, that is, some of the spirit connected to himself, this was the prophetic spirit, as the verse states: "When I have fashioned him and breathed into him of my spirit."[28] God does not say "I have breathed my spirit into him," without the "of," and this is the proof that the spirit breathed into Adam is itself the prophetic spirit. But the spirit of Adam is engendered and is the corporeal father of the Prophet and of all other men, whereas the Prophet [Muhammad] is the spiritual father of humankind and of the other prophets.[29]

I have quoted this passage at length because it provides all the elements of the problem of prophetic history, as it came down to Sadrā. It indicates the notion he may have had of a history governed by the exigency of a return to the world of the spirit. All human history is interpreted according to a speculative metaphysics that, as we have seen, owes a great deal to Ibn al-'Arabī. The founding event is an internal relationship of the divine Self with itself, of unity with unity. The spirit proceeds from the divine imperative to the extent that the imperative itself is this relationship of the divine with itself. But this relationship is extremely enigmatic. How can the One, without going out of itself, have a relationship with itself? How does it not engender, *ipso facto*, a duality? The answer is found in the theophanic scheme. The unfathomable unity of the divine essence instantiates its originary manifestation on the plane of the divine names and the essential attributes, without giving birth to something other than the Self. Instead, it effects the immediate relation of the (hidden) Self to the (revealed) self. The act of being located beyond the infinite is manifest in the act of being in the imperative, in the theophanic effusion that thus begins. It begins precisely on the plane of the divine names, which coincides with the eternal Muhammadan reality and with the prophetic spirit. The perfect man is the anthropomorphosis of the revealed God, on the supreme plane where all the divine names are manifest in the fundamental nature of the perfect man. The reflection of God into God occurs thus in the mirror of prophetic humanity, which is itself given as the pleroma of the fourteen immaculate ones.

It is henceforth inevitable that this effusion of the spirit will create a progressive emanation of hierarchized worlds, which reaches from the intelligible world to the sensible world, passing through the world of the soul, as well as a procession of the successive births of man. The expressions of the originary prophetic *anthropos* are deployed in the multiplicity of spirits, hearts, souls, and multiple and successive human natures. We pass from station to station, from the eternal to the temporal. The life of the sons of Adam begins at the lowest level of corporeal nature – which itself begins in Adam, the temporal father of humankind.

Adam receives the breath of the spirit, which remains alive in this hidden interiority. The task of men is to realize the revelation of this interiority of the prophetic spirit, until they join the fundamental archetype, the spiritual father, Muhammad. The historical event of Muhammad's revelation, together with the exegesis developed by the imams, is the fulfillment of this return. The return reconciles the temporal order, governed by Adam's paternity, with the spiritual order, commanded by the anthropomorphosis of the spirit in the original pleroma. But this fulfillment is not temporal. It is a return to the spiritual origin, and it depends on the capacity of the faithful to receive knowledge of the spirit. The temporal passes away, according to its fundamentally evanescent nature, whereas the various degrees of the reascent into the world of the imperative remain – the psychic man, the intelligible man, and the divine spiritual man. Presented here in a condensed form, this intuition of history is specific to the ontology of Islam, which is a liturgy of the spirit and not, as in Western Christian phenomenology, an incarnation within concrete temporal actuality.

Henry Corbin claimed that this scheme was the privilege of Shīʿite Islam as well as the chance for the ontology of Islam as a whole. In a way, this chance has a price. Absolute spirit is destined not to become objective spirit in sensible temporality but to escape from it and to return the point of origin of the divine revelatory act. This is what generates the scheme of human freedom in Islam. It is an imperative freedom, indissolubly united with the knowledge of the eternal condition of the servant, of the *ʿubūdīyah* constituting the primordial *anthropos*, mirror of God and caliph of God.

The price of such a scheme is the ineffectiveness of the temporal world. In his ineffable relationship with himself, God introduces no negation. Or, rather, the negation of essence in the divine names does not have the characteristics necessary to give the temporal world an *effective* status. The split moves – to the point of the annihilation of all creation – between the world of the imperative and the world of creation, between the world of the spirit and the world of material bodies here below. The materiality of natural existents limits the darkening of the theophanic mirrors. Natural time is not able to acquire an authentic ontological dignity. It is the inferior expression of eternity, a moving image of eternity, as Plato and Plotinus said.

It is necessary, therefore, to leave its appearances behind in order to ascend to the effective realities, to move from the image to the model. The destiny in question is not the concrete universal reconciled with temporal phenomena but the universality of spirit concentrated in the sole reality of the act of existing, which transcends all temporality, in order to be unveiled in the eternal instant of divine instantiation. At the terminal point of prophetic history, man is divinized; he is annihilated in God in order to subsist solely from the divine unity. God comes out of himself and is reflected back into himself, and spirit is created from this reflection. The history of spirit is the divine unity's return into itself.

Spirit is the mediation between God and man, between the world of the imperative and the world of creation. It is communicated to man through breath (*nafkh*). According to Sadrā, the inbreathing of spirit consists of the effusion of a superior breath into a receptacle made of an inferior breath. The superior breath, coming from the divine imperative, is the divine spirit. The receptacle that receives it must be subtle, tempered, well ordered. The inferior breath, the vital *pneuma*, receives two effusions, one from the light of intelligence and one from the divine spirit. The mediation between the world of the imperative and the creatural world takes place in this breath where the light from the divine spirit fills the *pneuma*. The *pneuma* is then charged with regulating, ordering, and balancing the temperament and setting forth the soul's effusion upon and rule over the body.

From the body to the divine spirit, there reigns also a single justice, which effuses from the divine imperative, balances the humors of the body, tempers the animal faculties of the soul, and reigns in the light of intelligence and divine spirit. The birth of life is the birth of light from the vital *pneuma* in the drop of sperm. Its cause is not material; rather, it is the source of every act of existing, divine generosity, and generative effusion, conferring existence on all that is capable of receiving it.[30]

Mullā Sadrā is faithful to the Avicennian medical tradition as it was reworked by Suhrawardī and his disciples.[31] If the soul is a light (the Espahbod Light), separated from corporeal matter, free from all incarnation, localization, and temporality, how does it govern the dense and shadowy body? The vital *pneuma* is subtle enough to effectuate the necessary mediation between a material substance and a luminous immaterial substance. Much like Cartesian psychology, the medicine of the philosophers of illumination confers on animal spirits the delicate task of uniting the soul with the body.[32]

The vital *pneuma* is a subtle body, hot and diaphanous, which originates in the subtlety of the humors and depends on their good health. It is born in the heart, because blood is drawn from the liver into the right cavity of the heart, where it produces cardiac heat. The pneumatic vapor is separated from this blood and passes into the left cavity, where it becomes vital *pneuma*, strictly speaking. Since it is subtle and luminescent, it resembles the celestial bodies (the site of the imaginal world, according to the Ishrāqīyah), and it can be attached to the intelligible Espahbod Light. All our animal faculties of perception and movement are sustained by this luminous *pneuma*, which by nature tends toward the higher lights and considers the shadows its enemy.

The struggle against the shadows of the body begins at this very low level of the vital breath, which struggles for life, as our souls rejoice in the lights and the fires shining in the dark night. The *pneuma* rises into the cavities of the brain, where it is cooled. There it obtains the luminous regal power of the thinking soul and is then called psychic spirit. Flowing through the body, this power animates the vegetal and animal functions. Through the real balance it confers, it removes the body from the deadly internal battle. Its diaphanous nature enables the appearance of imaginal forms that subsist through its subtlety. The appearance of the imaginal world takes place in this psychic *pneuma*, according to its equilibrium and its disposition (*isti'dād*).

For the Ishrāqīyah, physiology is dominated by astral theology and the opposition between the world of lights and material corporeality. This physiology attempts to reconcile the functions of governance and justice – the activity of the soul ruling over the body – with the irreducible duality of the two substances. Sadrā reformulated the doctrine of the imaginal world by internalizing it, by absorbing it into the becoming of the soul itself. What he preserves from the Suhrawardian pneumatology is the profound intuition of a luminous and subtle activity, provider of equilibrium and justice.

When the temperament is disciplined by a habit of justice, when customs and mores are regulated, the vaporous *pneuma* is like a throne on which the animal faculties are held in place. The lower *pneuma* offers man this *prostration* of the animal faculties, in a first liturgy that facilitates the second rectitude, the inbreathing of the higher *pneuma*. The lower *pneuma* in the corporeal receptacle is the substrate of the caliphate of God "in the land of bodies," whereas the higher *pneuma* "instantiates the caliph of God in the heavens, the angelic prostration, the uprightness on the throne of the universal thinking soul."

The divine spirit thus makes possible the angelic liturgy performed by the intelligence and prophecy, the effusion of the lights of eternal Muhammadan reality. Man's temporal and spiritual births are homologized with the two breaths, the lower *pneuma* and the divine *pneuma*:

> The light of the sun is the cause of the temporal birth (*hudūth*) of what is correspondingly luminous on earth, although it is weaker. Likewise, divine grace is the cause of the eduction of the light of existence (*nūr al-wujūd*) in each quiddity able to receive the act of being according to its own receptivity. It is given to human matter to be the most proximate of receptacles.[33] One sometimes calls it "my spirit," sometimes "the light of my Lord," as in the verse "And the earth will shine with the light of its Lord."[34] Through these investigations, then, it becomes clear to you that the elevated [divine] spirit has its origin in the otherworld, whereas its site of epiphany and its destination belong to this world. That is why we refer to it as we do. It is in perpetual motion, like the wind.[35]

The wind of the spirit is the essential motion that animates and transforms existences. Human spirits start out vile and miserable in comparison with the angelic spirits, just as their bodies are vile with respect to the celestial bodies. They are then differentiated according to the degrees of their elevation and growth, and some of them reach the angelic degree. The great difference between the hierarchies of the angels and the initial multiplicity of human spirits is the following: the hierarchical order of the angels is such that each rank is occupied by only one singularity. Two angels are never together at the same rank. Each angelic individual is a species, in and by itself.[36] After their ascension toward God and their existential growth, men can still be equal, differing in the aspects and accidents proper to them.

But there is a human spirit that is essentially distinguished from the others and disrupts their uniformity. This is the prophetic spirit, the spirit that animates Muhammad. The prophetic spirit is prior to the temporal creation of man, as attested by a tradition often quoted by Sadrā: "I was a prophet when Adam was still between the water and the clay." It confirms the differentiation of human spirits and the originary anchoring of the essence of spirit in the divine imperative and the world of the imperative. The prophetic spirit thus unveils the ultimate destination of man, higher than all the angelic hierarchies, but comparable to them in the perpetual liturgy and permanent prayer that are the truth of the act of being at the term of its perfection.[37]

Chapter Nine

The Return into God

The Second Nothingness

Resurrection is not the fulfillment of the separate existent endowed with a particular essence. It is the triumph of absolute existence, delivered from all limitation and led back to its originary unity. It is an event for man and for all creatures, but it is above all the ontological event whereby God gathers emanated and dispersed existence back into himself. Resurrection is the final unification of all theophanic reflections within the luminous source from which they proceeded. It is the return of the multiple into the One.

In his third intelligible birth, man is converted toward his origin, his first nature. But this origin was the nothingness prior to creation, since God instantiated creation *ex nihilo*. At the end of time, every particular act of being, accompanied by the shadow of a quiddity, is released from this limitation, and God brings it to a second nothingness (*al-'adam al-thānī*) — that is, to what is nothingness from the point of view of the separate existent. From the point of view of God, though, this second nothingness is the absolute real. This is what is expressed in the verse "All that is on the earth will pass away, but the face of your Lord will subsist, full of majesty and glory."[1] Thus the origin and the return are symmetrical, and the end is the return to the origin.

The origin was the first nothingness, in which resounded the divine question, the question posed to future creatures: "Am I not your Lord?"[2] The affirmative response determined man's eternal obedience, constitutive of his existence. The end is God's answer to the question he poses, not to creatures but to himself, the question of his dominion, which makes him the king of Judgment Day. It is the question of his unicity and dominance.That is when God reflects himself in himself, not in the mirror of his creations; he absorbs all existence back into his existence and completes the perfect circle of the real.

The totality of being is God, whose unity excludes all pluralization, at the end as at the origin. This totality is the superessential One of Neoplatonism, which is adequate, according to Sadrā, to the truth of the *tawhīd*, the revealed attestation of divine unicity. Paradise is this superessential nothingness itself. The first nature of man begins when Adam receives existence. He receives it in the movement of his fall from the first paradise, which was the first nothingness. "The existence that came after nothingness was the fall into this world here below"; the lost paradise was not a figure of the existent but the real prior to any constitution of the finite existent: "It was the garden of our father Adam and our mother Eve." Corresponding to this fall into existence, this fall that is existence itself, is the intensive conversion of the act of being. Its final goal is nothing other than an extinction (*fanā'*) in the real of the divine unity (*fī-l-tawhīd*), a second nothingness and a paradise of the knights of unity (*muwahhidūn*), the real status of the satisfied soul. The procession of the light of being begins in what is symbolized by the night of the decree; the conversion takes place in what is symbolized by the day of resurrection.[3]

This is not a nihilist vision of the real. Sadrā is guided by the Qur'ānic revelations announcing the end of all things. He confronts the reality of human death and the inevitable annihilation of the things of life, which is the inevitable fate of their precariousness and futility. Against the reassuring belief in an eternity of nature, he emphasizes that this belief is remarkably unconcerned with the fluidity of changing substances, or the imaginary vanity of all that is manifest in time. But nothingness does not have any more consistency; it has none at all. We have seen that nonbeing is the pure limitation of the act of existing, such that the first or second nothingness is described as a negation of being only in a very precise sense.

The original or final nothingness is a coincidence between the extinction of existents and their permanent existence in God. We must be careful to maintain the distinction between the *determinate* and "interlinked" existent, and the act of being. The determinate existent possesses a quiddity, which is nothing by itself and therefore cannot exist permanently when the fleeting existent disappears, when the finitude of the existent fades and passes away. The refusal of an ontology of quiddities thus results in a denial of the eternity of nature and of its species or genera. But the annihilation of these quiddities is a redemption of the fall. It negates the first negation, symbolized by Adam's banishment from paradise. It effaces the limitation of the infinite act of existing within the finite and restores it to its maximal intensity. The final nothingness effaces the particular nothingness of the quiddities by effacing what each emanated existent carries with it as a shadow.

Conversion to the Intelligible

In the return to God, the extinction of creation is inextricably linked with the renewal of man. Sadrā explains this in one of the most inspired passages of his *Treatise on Resurrection*.[4] There he presents an exegesis of a number of Qur'ānic verses that announce the end of all things: "Thus we find indicated in the Qur'ānic verses the disappearance of this world here below and the extinction of all those who populate it, of all that is on the earth and in the heavens." But this extinction is the transferal of existence into another birth. The essential realities of creatures have "a fixed term," and God proceeds to a second instantiation, "toward the world of resurrection and toward what dwells next to God among the divine forms and the intelligible archetypes." The second instantiation, presented as a second nothingness, also turns out to be the instantiation of a rebirth in the intelligible forms. The latter are "the separate immaterial forms whose existence was established by Plato and which exist next to God, subsisting through his subsistence. Indeed, they do not come from the world or from what is other than God."

There is a sort of tension in what Sadrā says here between the unhesitating affirmation of superessential nothingness, the final absolute end, and the desire to maintain a status of existence for the acts of existing, in order to save them from the complete annihilation that would ruin the promise of resurrection and deprive it of any meaning. He therefore appeals to the intelligible as conceived of in Platonism, not in order to decipher eternal quiddities in it but to make of it the constitutive element of divine eternal wisdom, internal to God and to the world of the divine imperative – in other words, the divine act of being itself, unfolding in extended being on the basis of its original ineffable unicity. This is the reign of intelligences that manifests the very essence of the divine real, without any mediation between them and the essence, in a full and complete expression.[5]

Resurrection (*ba'th*) is indeed a surging forth, a rising up (*qiyām*), in an end time when man comes out of his immersion (*inghimār*) in the natural world. The tomb whose confinement man breaks is not only his material tomb. Truly, the tomb is the entire natural world, its space and its temporality, from which man, in being reborn, will emerge like the newborn from the womb. He awakens, like someone who has been asleep. His new birth leads him on a pilgrimage toward the divine presence. This resurrection sanctions his desire, his love of freedom or his desire for compulsion, according to whether he goes "free from the chains of the realities that bound him and from the bonds of passion, delighting in himself and joyous in the proximity of God" – for "he who loves the proximity of God loves God for his proximity" – or whether he remains a prisoner of his constraints, gripped with an aversion to the proximity of God and an unsurmountable disgust with existing.[6]

This new birth rewards the lover of God with real pleasure, freedom, and superexistence, as well as a satisfying nostalgia for being.[7] The punishment for nihilist disgust, however, is a torment of the imagination and perpetual imperfection. The task that Mullā Sadrā sets himself is to think through extinction in God and these modes of eternal existence.

Sadrā presents his ontology of the return to God in his exegesis of the Throne Verse.[8] He distinguishes corporeal matter and spiritual matter, and this distinction allows him to preserve the hylomorphic model and ground the existence of imaginal forms and intelligible forms. Corporeal matter is the receptacle of sensible forms; it subsists in them and in the perfection of the animal soul. Its threshold and its limits thus lie in the different affections of the animal soul – appetite, wrath, hope, fear, pleasure, and pain.

Spiritual matter subsists and is perfected only through spiritual forms, through the customs and habits of man. Thus it is verified that man's return to God is governed by the constitution of a spiritual matter, based on the sedimentation of all the moral habits that are condensed in the soul and will receive the spiritual forms. These latter are hierarchized into the intelligible forms (*suwar ʿaqlīyah*) of the objects of knowledge, whose act of being is incorporeal, and the imaginal forms (*suwar khayālīyah*), which are the imagination's imitations of pure intelligible forms.

The sensible forms are the lot of common men, the imaginal forms are the lot of virtuous men, and the intelligible forms are the lot of the gnostics – those who have fully actualized in themselves the unity of intelligence and the intelligible. The soul's movement toward God leads to this last stage, and it determines, in its upward return, the gradation of men and the distinction of their natures.

At the beginning of its growth, the soul is pure matter; it is, properly speaking, *insensate*. The soul is intensified; its matter clothed in the successive forms of its corporeal revolution – spermatic, vegetal, animal, human. The human form corresponds to the rank of the intelligence, the term of the corporeal realities, and the beginning of the spiritual realities. This degree of growth, in which man is capable of receiving the influx of the agent intelligence, is the heart, which is the threshold of the return into God, for it is the "flowing together of two seas," the border that contains in itself the perspective of both worlds (corporeal and spiritual), the interval (*barzakh*) that separates the ocean of bodies and the ocean of spiritual realities. The soul can therefore be conceived of according to two perspectives: in its activity in this corporeal world, it is origin, the unifying center of the faculties. It is the form of forms, the finality of finalities, while remaining corporeal in the sensible "world of manifestation."

But according to the perspective of the spiritual world, the soul is pure potentiality, pure indigence. It is, in the form of the otherworld, what the seed is to the fruit, the drop of semen to the living being. Material intelligence must be actualized *for* the otherworld, if it wants to exist *in* the otherworld, which is why some think that the ignorant have no destiny after death, but are annihilated.[9] The light that emanates from the agent intelligence enables human intelligence to perceive the intelligibles and to be united with them.[10] "This light is the true good and the authentic beatitude. Through it, man becomes an actualized living being and lives with an essential life that does not need matter for its subsistence, because its becoming, which leads it into the permanent and eternal realities, breaks with matters and potentialities."[11]

Beatitude is existence itself, and it is the intelligible knowledge of existence, since being and knowing are one.[12] But the monads of existence, says Sadrā, differ in perfection and in deficiency. Felicity is all the greater when the act of existing is more complete, when the power to act is greater. That is why the first real, God, is pure good: he is pure activity of existing. Pleasure is intimately linked with the power to act. "The act of being of each thing takes pleasure in itself."[13] But it has more enjoyment if the act of being of its cause and its constituent is actualized for it. That is why the enjoyment of the intelligence is more noble and more intense than the enjoyment of the animal powers appetite and wrath.[14] The man who lives the contemplative life has more pleasure than the man who lives like an animal or a ferocious beast.

Sadrā is faithful to Aristotle's analysis: "Pleasure completes the activity."[15] Pleasure resides in "the perfected activity" of each of the faculties, in accordance with its optimal disposition and "in relation to the best objects" that fall within sensible, imaginative, or intellective perception. The hierarchy of pleasures follows the hierarchy of the faculties in intensity. The estimative power engenders shadowy suggestions, which are obstacles to the divine lights, says Sadrā, and they must be resisted through the activity of the intellective power, in an internal struggle.[16]

What we know and love in the sensible world has less being than what we love that is intelligible. The intelligible forms provide our intelligence with its perfection, "its essence becomes their essence," and it enjoys the brilliant and striking beauty it perceives in them, a beauty that dwells in God, according to a unity exemplified for Sadrā in Plotinus's ecstasy: "The conjunction of the cause of this enjoyment [the divine intelligence] and of the one who enjoys [human intelligence] is the most intense and the most penetrating, and this enjoyment resembles the joy that the first emanated being [the agent intelligence] has in and through itself!"[17]

The Aristotelian notion of the contemplative life is interpreted here within the element of the Plotinian experience of ecstasy. The joy of the intelligence does not reach the summit of existence, which is the unfathomable divine essence. Instead, it reaches the rank of intelligence, as if the moment of union with the One remained forbidden, or at least reserved for the ultimate and extreme point of love. True, the union with the agent intelligence, located by Sadrā at the summit of emanation and not at the tenth degree, procures a perfect joy, which is the joy of existence at the height of its power and perfection. Pleasure resides not only in the representation of the intelligible but also in the intellective act of being, since what provides pleasure is the *mode of existence* itself. Pleasure is not a representation, or even the movement of desire toward God, but the effective reality of the act of being, which is the *real beloved* (*al-ma'shūq al-haqīqī*).[18] As a perfect and fulfilled love, the contemplative life is transfigured into a mystical union and an unalloyed pleasure.

The extinction of separate existence coincides here with the maximal intensification of the act of existing. The individual in the true sense is, then, one "whose ipseity has been pulverized."

In a movement that recalls al-Hallāj's doctrine on the union of love, God is substituted for the qualifications of individual essence: he replaces them with the expression of his own essence in his names and attributes. "So that the real one is their hearing, their sight, their hands, their feet, as stated by the famous *hadīth*." Such is the extinction in God, this "immersion in being" that overcomes separate intelligences, angels ecstatic with love, and perfected individuals (*afrād*).[19] The height of individuation corresponds with the most extreme immersion in the divine real.

This ultimate station is reached only at the end of repeated practice in the alchemy of intelligence:

> You see the hot iron and how, through the repetition of practices that heat it with bellows, an incandescent form is actualized for it.... Do not be astonished, then, that there is actualized in the soul, after repeated absorption in the divine principles, a holy light and an intelligible form which intelligizes the intelligibles, just as in the liquid iron is actualized an incandescent power that realizes the action of the fire.[20]

This practice of absorption into the divine *ethos* is moral as well as cognitive. The divinized souls arrive "upon the threshold of God" by means of practical assiduity in imitating divine actions: showing compassion, benevolence, and mercy for God's creatures. Invoking the good for everything that possesses a spirit—for every living thing, the elevation above bodily realities, and obedience to God, the Prophet, and the imams—make up the *homoiōsis* in which the ways of God are substituted for creaturely ways. This occurs in a movement that is at once a repetition of intellection and an endurance in love. The repetition of the contemplations provokes the return to God and the return to self, to the origin of the very form of the soul, to the "intellective Oriental power."[21]

Mullā Sadrā conceives of the "return to God" according to a remarkable synthesis of several schemes: the structure of the intelligence, its power, and the sovereign happiness it gives, as theorized by al-Fārābī; the Avicennian doctrine of the gnostic sage, entirely and uniquely occupied with the divine real; the foundation of spiritual salvation and the authority of the perfect man in "Oriental" illumination, according to Suhrawardī; and the homologizing of the agent intelligence with the world of divine names and with the expression of the "breath of the Merciful," according to Ibn al-'Arabī. This last identification of the intelligence grounds, in turn, the insistence on the "return" as an extinction in permanence, the coincidence of the two opposed states of *al-fanā' fī-llāh* (extinction in God) and *al-baqā' bi-llāh* (eternal existence or permanence through God). The reconstruction of such a genealogy would exceed the limits of the present study, but I will sketch some of its main features.

To be sure, Sadrā takes credit for the doctrine that perfect happiness is found in the union of the actual intelligence and its actual intelligized object. This union of the contemplating subject and the intelligible that is contemplated is the terminal moment of intellection. For him, this doctrine is based on the theory of the essential motion of intensification. Nonetheless, it has its distant origin in the interpretation of the Aristotelian doctrine of the intelligence proposed by al-Fārābī.

al-Fārābī clearly states that the union of the actual intelligence with what it intelligizes is the source of human perfection. The degrees of intelligence – potential, actual, acquired, and agent – must be unified in the person of the complete philosopher or the prophet, since the source of full and integral intellection and prophecy, is divine revelation that comes vertically, from the agent intellect to the passive intellect and the imaginative faculty. This integral knowledge founds legitimate political authority, and the imam of the perfect city unifies in himself sovereign happiness (which he spreads throughout the city), political authority, and real knowledge.[22]

Sadrā attributes these same powers to the imam and the Prophet. But he liberates the perspective of the "return into God" from politics. Clearly, there is no reflection on the beneficial effects of intellection for the community. The examination concentrates personal salvation and the production of the authentic individual. But, like al-Fārābī, Sadrā places the exercise of juridical knowledge at a level inferior to that of the integral wisdom that justifies authority. And he does more than that. His analysis of the "return" profoundly disqualifies all the claims and pretensions of the expert jurist, particularly the Shīʿite jurist, who was a dominant figure of his time.

In effect, these claims go so far as to maintain—first within the sphere of royal power and then against it—that the final term of happiness and obedience to God lies in obedience to the model authority in matters of faith, who is the jurist. But this is what Sadrā vigorously contests, proposing instead the angel impassioned with love, the intelligence intimate with God, as a model for the sage. Because it separates political authority from happiness and intellective union, Sadrā's thought founds not a political theology but a theology of the spirit of holiness.[23]

Avicenna's influence here is significant, in this intimate relationship between progress in contemplation and moral purification,[24] as well as in the constitution of the figure of the sage, the *ʿārif*. According to Sadrā, the perfect sage is the faithful initiate into the light of the imamate. In this respect, he preserves the features of the Avicennian *ʿārif*. The difficulties in translating this Arabic term are well known. Often it is rendered as "the gnostic," which has the disadvantage of confusing our subject with the adherents of the initiatory gnosis traditionally grouped together under the heading Gnosticism. *Maʿrifa*, a knowledge that is intuitive, intellective, and unitive, is no doubt a "gnosis of God," in the sense of a salvational knowledge. But it is problematic in that it must be decided whether this knowledge is a conjunction with the divine intelligence, or a full and complete unification with it.[25] Gnosis (*ʿirfān*) is the living actuality of intelligible knowledge when the object of this knowledge is the divine real and is accompanied by obedience (*ʿibāda*).

Avicenna emphasizes this close link between the grasp of the real and obedience in the *Ishārāt*, where he claims that this link characterizes the *ʿārif*. Avicenna distinguishes the *ʿārif* from the devout believer who obeys God's commandments out of fear or hope, to avoid punishment or to reach heaven:

> The sage (*'ārif*) wants the first real, but not for the sake of something other than him. There is nothing that he prefers to the knowledge (*'irfān*) of this real; he practices obedience only toward him, without any request (*raghbah*) or any fear (*rahbah*) – although requests and fears do exist, such that what one asks for or what one fears is in fact what calls one [to serve God], and such that that is in fact what one is seeking. The real is then no longer the final goal; rather, he is the intermediary for something other than him, which is then the end and the object sought, to the exclusion of the real.[26]

Avicenna distinguishes the *'arīf* from two other types of men devoted to God: the ascetic (*zāhid*), "one who renounces this world here below and its pleasures," and the servant (*'ābid*), who devotes himself essentially to praiseworthy works, fasting, and nightly and perpetual prayer.[27] The *'ibādā* are the forms of service prescribing the ritual obligations to God and the interpersonal conduct that pleases God. As Michel Chodkiewicz writes: "The Law institutes service, orders the *ibādā*, the acts owed to God – whoever the apparent recipient may be – because the *'abd* no longer has any memory of his status. It is through service that he will be led back to the subservient condition in which his servitude becomes evident to him."[28]

Man's fundamental servitude, his very nature as *'abd*, which is forgotten as long as he thinks only of his own status, is revealed to those who practice the ritual acts required by divine law. The *'ābid* is thus the authentic servant of God, one who discovers the law at the very end of the pilgrimage on the spiritual path. His devotion and his acts of adoration are not a middle term in the attainment of truth, but if "repentance (*tawbah*) is the first station on the path, service (*'ibādah*) is the last."[29] The *'ārif*, according to Avicenna, is "one who freely orients his thought toward the holiness of the Jabarūt, unceasingly, in view of the illumination of the light of the real in the inward self (*fī-sirrih*)."[30]

Avicenna does not think that ascesis is enough or that service is the final term in the return to God. As Nasīr al-Dīn al-Tūsī says in his commentary, it is the man of knowledge, the sage, who possesses true perfection, a perfection that integrates the practice of devotion (*ta'abbud*) into contemplation. Contemplation itself is not the final goal, since "the real is preferable to the knowledge one has of him." Whoever is not an *'ārif*, a contemplative man, can practice ascesis and divine service, but he will always be in danger of preferring something over the real, and his preference will be to seek reward and to avoid punishment. The *'ārif*, on the contrary, practices spiritual exercises for the sake of contemplation: true ascesis, which protects him from forgetting the real, is a submission of the body to the soul, which is turned toward the real, such that the entire man becomes a receptacle for the real, for admonishment and love.

Chaste love is a figure of love explained by Nasīr al-Dīn al-Tūsī thus: human love is divided into real love and figurative love, and the latter is in turn divided into psychic love and animal love. Psychic love is the love whose principle is the mutual conformity of the substance of soul of the lover and that of the soul of the beloved. The lover then admires the character of the beloved. The principle of animal love lies in appetite and the search for "bestial pleasure." The lover then admires the physical form of the beloved: his figure, his color, all the lines of his body. According to Tūsī, who uses a Platonic distinction here, Avicenna valorizes the first of these categories of figurative love. Through this love, the soul becomes tender and acquires delicacy and ecstasy. It is separated from the preoccupations of this world, abandons everything that is not the beloved, and indulges in all the ordeals of love (anguish, distress). To this love applies the well-known statement that "he who loves remains chaste, and he who dies... dies a martyr."[31] Chaste human love is therefore a stage on the path of true perfection.

The goal of the spiritual exercises is to acquire the ability to receive the illuminant presence of the real. These exercises clear away everything that hinders or obscures this disposition. They keep one from choosing any object inferior to the real. They submit the imperative soul to the pacified soul and make the animal faculties revolve around the intelligible center; they purify the inwardness of the soul and render it subtle, so that it will be capable of receiving the configuration of intelligible forms.[32] That is why true ascesis, divine service united with the exercise of thought, sweet melodies, and words of admonition, leads to subtle thought and chaste love. In fact, Avicenna maintains the importance of ascesis and divine service as stages of purification. But he inflects them with a tendency toward something else: the purity of the soul's inwardness, the receptacle and mirror of the real. As Tūsī says, the contemplative man, in the exercise of his adoration, has in view nothing other than the real.

We find this Avicennian hierarchy in Sadrā as well. The virtuous man, the ascetic or the servant of God, obeying the necessary commandments of the law, will receive a reward that corresponds to his desire. This will be the pleasure of imaginal rewards, the heavenly feast, the beautiful unions, the drinks that quench thirst without any disturbance. The contemplative man, if that is what the *'ārif* should be called, having passed through these purifying stages and accustomed his inward self to a conjunction with the real through chaste love, will not receive a reward, since he will be delivered from the play of obedience and rewards, which Avicenna refers to as a childish dynamic. He will deepen the contemplation of the intelligible to the point of reflecting, in a specular vision, the attributes of the real.

Sadrā locates himself between the Avicennian perspective of spiritual salvation and the perspective of Ibn al-'Arabī, who valorizes divine service in a completely different way (according to Chodkiewicz). For Sadrā, ascesis and divine service will indeed be stages on the contemplative path. But at its final term we will again find the *'ibādah*, imagined as a revelation of the condition of the servant ("servitude"). This condition is conceived of in the double dimension of extinction in God and eternal existence through God. Here is a formulation of this conception, which in fact follows two quotations from Ibn al-'Arabī:

> They do not belong to the population of the heavens and the earth, for their ipseities leave the world of the body, the world of their forms and of their souls. No more renewal or temporal alteration comes to them, for they are immersed in the ocean of the superessential divine unity (*bahr al-ahadīyah*) and in the power of the divine light, as are the angels impassioned with love, whose ipseities are enveloped in the rays of divine subsistent incomprehensibility and in the blinding divine light, they who give no more attention to their own selves.... Their vivification after death and their continued existence after extinction are superior to the first vivification, for they are a real permanence without posterior extinction.[33]

Unity of the Intelligence and the Intelligible

This ultimate station brings the union of the intelligence and the intelligible to full completion.[34] Sadrā reproduces the Peripatetic doctrine of theoretical intelligence and practical intelligence. He takes over its divisions, making them stages in the substantial motion of the human soul. The soul is transformed, crosses the threshold of its first two "births," and arrives at the point where it is shaped entirely by its intellective perfection. This threshold is characterized by the freedom of the soul with respect to movements and thoughts.[35] The two faculties of theoretical intelligence and practical intelligence become one. Knowledge becomes action and action becomes knowledge, in the image of what happens in God, where science and power are a single fundamental reality. Aristotle maintained that contemplation was the highest activity. Sadrā interprets this by reconciling the act of knowing and practical guidance at the highest degree of the soul's activity. Moral activity cannot be separated from the unitive perception of the intelligible.

The degrees of theoretical intelligence, material intellect, *habitus* intellect, actual intellect, and acquired intellect, are the continuous moments of a single realization. It occurs in a passage from potency to act in which the original nature of man, potential in the first birth, is externalized and becomes fully effective.[36] From a mere empty aptitude for forms, the intelligence becomes the actualization of intelligible forms and is one with them. In itself, the soul is a "subject of knowledge by its very essence."[37] But its first birth makes it a purely corporeal form, in which it has only the potential for knowledge. The *cogito* is obscured by bodily preoccupations. Purification and perfection must gradually liberate the soul from these functions useful to the body, in order to dematerialize it in the grasping of more and more pure forms — the forms of sensible, imaginative, and finally intelligible perception.[38]

The final term of human destiny differs from that of the animal, not only because man possesses an essential difference (reason) but also because this difference reflects an act of being fundamentally distinct from that of animals. The intelligence is this act of existing; it determines the evolution of man insofar as he is fully man. The quiddity "man" is the shadow of the act of existing of the intelligence, which is intensified and is manifest finally in its total actuality. The becoming of self-consciousness thus passes through the sensible and imaginative stages and leads beyond animality, because it is, potentially, intelligible self-consciousness. The conjunction with the agent intelligence completes a return to the self that henceforth envelops all separate realities.[39] The human soul is in a process of becoming: it passes from a first birth, in which it is the final term of corporeal realities, to a third birth, in which it is the beginning of spiritual realities. The soul, says Sadrā, is the "threshold of God," and God commands his servants to go from this threshold to the "house of God." That is why the soul is, successively, the form of every faculty in this world and the matter of every form in the other world.[40]

How are we to understand this claim that human intelligence is united with the agent intelligence to the point of itself becoming agent intelligence? Sadrā does not conceive of the illumination of the potential intelligence by the agent intelligence as a simple contact or as a conjunction that leaves these two realities in a state of separation. Within the scheme of substantial motion, such a hesitation would have no meaning. The becoming-intelligence must be complete and perfect, and the fundamental unity of the thinking soul must be realized in the transfiguration leading it back to the "house of God," to the angelic world of the intelligibles, which expresses the divine reality of the divine names. The divinization of man, announced by Aristotle within the more general framework of ancient wisdom, is here taken literally.[41]

In order to overcome any objections, Sadrā distinguishes two statuses for the agent intelligence. It has an act of being in itself and an act of being in our souls. The act of being in itself is the existence of intelligence in God, or divine science. The act of being in us is the perfection of the human soul: "The completeness of its act of existing, of its form and its end, is the act of being of its own agent intelligence, its conjunction (*ittisāl*) and unification (*ittihād*) with it."[42] In the famous debate between those who argued for conjunction (the Avicennians) and those who argued for unification, Sadrā adopts an original position: he situates these two states in a movement that leads to the latter.

In its being in itself, the agent intelligence is Being in expansion (*al-wujūd al-munbasit*), corresponding to the expansion of the breath of the Merciful in Sadrā's ontology. It is the unfolding of being from out of the first silence of the divine unknowable essence; it is the integral manifestation of God, keeping in reserve, however, beyond itself, the secret of the divine essence. It is therefore no longer identified with the tenth intelligence of the Avicennian pleroma.[43] The haecceity of the monads of existence proceeds from its superabundance, from the free flow of the intelligence, which is the root of the tree of existence. The agent intelligence is the origin of existents, just as it is their end. The agent intelligence *in itself* differs from the agent intelligence *in us* only according to the familiar model of the mirror. The existences of the multiple agent intelligences are multiplied not according to a numerical law but according to the procession of monads that they constituted from the originary monad of the agent intelligence in itself. From the one proceeds only the one, by virtue of the monadizing activity of the first monad. The intelligences are thus the shadows of the act of existing pouring out the icons (*muthul*) of its unity (*wahdah*).[44]

The distinction between the intelligence in itself and the intelligence in us is a question of point of view. Do we take the perspective of the generative source or that of the image that proceeds from it? The intelligible world, this writing of the divine *qalam*, is indeed a generalized aesthetics, and it grounds the aesthetics of Islamic art, which will give form to this expansion of spiritual shadows in abstract forms or in sensible figures. The art of miniatures and sensual scenes will be the art of the intelligible – not a realist, representational art but the secondary imagination of the first ideal images that proceed from the overabundance of being. The schemes of the imagination are structures of interior space and modulations of time, not iconoclasm; they present a sensible configuration to intelligences. The icon is thus essential to the ontology of Islam. The arts bear witness to the great theological fractures within Islam, because their practice or condemnation implies an interpetation of the meaning of revelation. Sadrā's ontology, contemporary with the great artistic flourishing of the Safavid period, does not go against the prohibition on graven images but turns it toward an aesthetics of the sensible manifestation of the Idea.[45]

The agent intelligence is the necessary mediation between God, as the absolute principle of effusion (*al-fayyād*), the real Provident (*al-jawād al-haqq*), and the entirety of created species. That is why it deserves to be homologized, as we have seen, with the intimate angels, the cherubim, the lords of the species, the Platonic Ideas. The divine forms that constitute it are the "analytic sciences of God," while the synthetic and unifying science is the unity of the intelligible whole in the unity (*wahdanīyah*) immediately reflecting the essence that is ineffably one (*ahadīyah*).

This "intimate angel" assists us in becoming perfect, in the essential movement of our psychic becoming. "At the beginning of the process, the souls are obscure in their act of existing, weak in their being, dwelling in an opaque substrate like forms reflected in mirrors." This is the initial stage of the sensible and imaginative forms.

> When the soul's disposition is perfected, when its purity is made greater by means of the purification that frees it from impurities, when the perceptions and movements of thought are repeated, then the light of the agent intelligence produces its illumination upon it, upon its estimative perceptions and its imaginative forms. The soul then becomes actual intelligence. Its perceptions and its imaginative representations become actual intelligibles. The agent intelligence acts in the soul and in the imaginative forms that sojourn in it, as does the sun in the healthy eye.[46]

Sadrā is thus able to reconcile two movements with different orientations, the ascent of the forms of perception from the sensible to the intelligible, and their emanation from the "soul-giver" (*ravān-bakhsh*) to our intelligence. The forms are already latent in the soul, but they are actualized only through a purification of the mirror of the soul, a purification that is both moral and cognitive. One cannot separate the work of moral purification from the work of purification in knowledge. Eliminating the stains that arise from the functions of the body, from the passions and the desires, means at the same time eliminating the opacities that prevent the soul from reaching the threshold of intelligence. Inversely, the soul attains unity by going beyond the stage of the imagination and the estimative faculty, and by restoring the perceived form to its dimension as a universal form, no longer particularized by any material or spatial dimension.

The universal intelligible form is never an abstract universal; it is a concrete universal, the very face of the form-giver, the intimate angel. Thus the Platonic scheme of recollection can be reconciled with the Peripatetic scheme of the abstraction of the intelligible from the sensible. It remains understood that the "stripping away" of the form is not the abstraction assumed by the Peripatetics. The form is not the emergence of a general concept from a particular existent but the unveiling of the effective intelligible reality on the dim mirror of the imaginative and sensible forms.[47]

Man becomes intellective man; he is transformed and leaves

behind his previous manifestations. He is born again, and the final term of his new birth is the maximal intensification of his intelligible form, the unification with "the universal human spirit," the spirit of holiness. In him, all the sensible forms of this world are transfigured and move on to their intelligible birth, returning into God. "Ultimately, when the soul becomes intelligence, its sensible objects become actual intelligibles, and also actual intelligences."[48]

The unity of the subject of intellection, the act of intellection, and the intelligible is not merely a truth of an epistemological order. This unity expresses the meaning of intelligence (*'aql*, or *nous*), which is not, primarily, a higher human faculty but is more originarily an infinite total *reality*. The intelligence, placed within a Neoplatonic model and interpreted as the storehouse of the integral divine science, is the manifestation of the unknowable divine *real* within the integral reality of known being. It is, therefore, the fundamental unity of the subject and the object, since it is the reality of divine manifestation, the manifestation of divine unity in reality, and the reality of the act of reflection through which the real, withdrawn at first from all reflection, is rendered specular and enters the course of speculative emanation.

Man, because he is fundamentally a thinking soul, recapitulates all universes within himself. When thought is fully actualized, it envelops all its forms, which are the forms of natural existents, located in the world of angelic intelligences. Thought, and the worlds that it thinks, are therefore reality itself, in the full actuality of the divine act of being. Creation is the thought of the world, which undertakes a return to its origin. The intelligence is the world in which all reality surges forth in the element of its immaterial act of existing, rooted in eternity. It is the eternal dream of God, who contemplates himself in the vision he projects upon the angelic intelligences, as upon the mirror capable of receiving them. It is the reflection of the real in the act in which it is thought, as if the totality of worlds (sensible, imaginal, intelligible) – moments in the development of man – had no other consistency than the revelation of God by God. Man is the mirror of God giving himself to thought. Man is God revealed.[49]

This unity of the subject of intellection and the intelligible is confirmed from the point of view of the theory of knowledge. In terms of the object of intellection, it will be remarked – in order to overcome Avicennian doubts – that the intelligized form is real and is immaterial in its reality, that its act of being has no substrate. This thesis derives from the simplicity of the form of perception.

One must reject the notion that what is intelligized in actuality has one act of existing, while the subject has another. Otherwise, it would be necessary to say that the link between the two occurs through inhesion in a subject, as is the case with blackness and the body that is the substrate of blackness.[50] This is an unacceptable model. From the point of view of the subject, it is no less open to criticism: "If the subject who intelligizes were different from the thing intelligized, then the latter, by definition, without considering the subject who intelligizes, would not be *intelligized*, and its act of being would not be this intelligible act of being that is the act of being of the intelligible form."[51] The unity of the subject and the object is primary; it proceeds from the objectivity of the intelligible world, which is an emanation from the divine reality.

This fundamental unity of the knowing and the known applies to all acts of perception; it is the unity of the sensing and the sensed, of the imagining and the imagined. That is why the theory of abstraction is "vulgar":

> What is sensed actually is united in its act of being with the actually sensing substance. The senses are not as the vulgar philosophers imagine: they think that the sense separates the form of the sensed, through itself, from matter, and coincides with it by chance, with its accidents included in it, and that the imagination abstracts the form through a more powerful abstraction. It is not so, since we know that it is impossible for there to be a transferal of realities from matter to what is other than matter.[52]

Not surprising, Sadrā's originality is quite relative, by his own admission, since he discovers the source of his own doctrine in Plotinus, that is, in the *Theology of Aristotle*: "When the intellective man casts his gaze on the intelligible realities, he does not apprehend them until he and they become one thing."[53]

This Plotinian intuition of the unity of the subject, the act, and the object of knowledge enables Sadrā to counter Avicenna's critique of any doctrine unifying the subject who intelligizes with the intelligized object. But notice that Avicenna's critique is situated within a debate concerning a theme dear to Sadrā, that of the permanence of human souls after the separation from the body. The theoretical framework for this debate was in fact laid out by Nasīr al-Dīn al-Tūsī, who comments on the project of the "seventh group" of indications and remarks that the goal of Avicenna's *Ishārāt* is to explain the survival of souls after death (a survival of their intellective faculty "with" the intelligibles), and the status of divine science (the cause of the order of the universe).[54]

Here is Avicenna's critique of the complete unification of the intelligizing subject and the intelligized object: "Let us suppose that a substance intelligizes 'A,' and that it is, as they say, through itself the intelligible of 'A.' Will it then be as it was when it was not intelligizing 'A,' or did this prior state disappear from it?"[55] Avicenna demonstrates at length that there is no satisfying response to this question. Moreover, to round off his objection, Avicenna rejects all substantial motion: "When it is said that the essence of the soul itself becomes the intelligibles, this is, in my view, totally false. For my part, I do not understand what they are saying when they say that a thing becomes another thing; I cannot conceive of how this could happen."[56]

Sadrā responds in several stages. First, he recalls that the foundation of beingness and the origin of the singularity of all things are its act of existing. From this he deduces the theory of the successive births of man: "Do you not see that man's condition begins in the fetus, or even in the drop of semen, and reaches its final term as an intelligizing subject and as an intelligized object, and that the different degrees of the gradation thus occur to him, and the births are transformed for him, but that at the same time he also possesses a permanence with regard to his act of being and his singularity of being?"[57] As we see, it is not a matter of refuting

Avicenna but of posing the problem in a radically different way. Avicenna's rejection of substantial motion and the primacy of the act of being over quiddity necessarily entails the rejection of the unification of the subject and the object of perceptions. However, their assumption entails an acceptance of this unification.

What could the substrate common to the intelligized form and the perceiving subject be? That is Avicenna's question. Sadrā responds: It is not a substrate in the material sense of the term, but existence itself, the root of existentiality. The problem disappears if one conceives of the act of being as free to intensify itself. In the passage from the drop of semen to intellection and the intelligizing subject, the substance of singular man is radically transformed, and the unity of his act of being is something like the substrate of this metamorphosis.

Now we come to the most delicate concept: unification (*ittiḥād*). If it has any foundation whatever, then the unification of the subject of intellection with the intelligible and, thereby, that of the human soul with the "heaven of the intimate" can be imagined. It is not a matter of saying that one existent is unified with another or that two acts of existing belonging to two different things become a single act of being. Avicenna is right on this point. Nor is it a matter of claiming that a concept or a quiddity would become another, different concept, since transferal from one quiddity to another is absurd. The unification of the subject and the object is not the unification of two quiddities. The true concept of unification is that of gradual perfection (*istikmāl*). It is "the becoming of an existent, to the extent that a mental concept and a universal quiddity are verified for it, after not having been verified for it at an earlier time."[58] We observe this in man, who is not *intellective man* at birth but who becomes one at the term of his growth. The plasticity of his substance, which varies according to his act of existing, is sufficient for understanding the increasing unification with the intelligible.

This is not absurd, says Sadrā, but quite real, "for all the intelligible significations that one encounters as distinct in the mineral, vegetable, and animal kingdoms are found gathered together in a single man." These notions of gathering and of man understood as the microcosm that assembles the universe of forms are extremely important, for they provide a way out of the terrain chosen by Avicenna. In a single movement, existence passes from the mineral to the vegetable stage, and from there to the animal stage, then to the intellective *and* the intelligible stage, in the intensification of a single human (*al-insān al-wāhid*). It is not a matter of multiplying this man or of dispersing him along a multiplicity of separate faculties. Conversely, it must be maintained that unity is primary and that man possesses an "essential form" that "encompasses his faculties." As we know, these faculties are simply the rays effusing from the sun of the soul: they are derivatives of the soul, which is "the operator of the operations," the "sense of the senses."

Unification is the expression of the operator in its hierarchized operations. That is why the intelligence is the root of the intelligibles; "the agent intelligence, *in our souls*, is the totality of existents."[59] It recapitulates all the forms of existents, in that it recapitulates all our successive forms, envelops them, and intensifies them. The agent intelligence is the sum of reality, effusing from the divine act of being. Our soul envelops the world. The unification of the intelligence and the intelligible is this: the enveloping of worlds in the soul, the fact that all existent forms are the derivatives of a single root, the soul. "The ipseity of the agent intelligence is the touchstone for the predicative attribution of all universal significations existing in the forms of existents subject to generation and corruption in the universe."

Sadrā can thus easily dispense with Avicenna's objection, quoted above. He returns to the question of becoming. This transformation of the soul, from the stage in which it does not intelligize to the stage when it intelligizes actually — is this transformation real, and does the intellective substance remain the same? True, the unknowing intelligence "disappears," but it disappears insofar as it was deficient, "like the child when it becomes a man." What disappears from it is a mere "reality of nothingness" (*amr 'adamī*), a privation. But Avicenna says precisely this in his metaphysics:

the child is a child because he is on the path that leads him to the state of being a man. When he becomes a man, he is not corrupted but perfected; no substantial reality disappears from him, nor does any accidental reality, except that which is connected with deficiency.[60]

It is quite striking to see the Aristotelian doctrine of potency and act enlisted in the cause of substantial motion, which is what overturned Avicennian biology. In order to do this, Sadrā must overcome an objection that any Peripatetic could justifiably make: How can one maintain that the soul, at the beginning of its growth, at the origin of its *fitrah*, is a single form, while also being characterized by a potentiality, the proof of which is this soul's initial lowly materiality? How can one reconcile immaterial form, fundamental intelligible activity, and potentiality? Does Sadrā not say that in the potentiality of the soul there is already the path or pilgrimage (*sulūk*) toward the Malakūt, which assumes a long and gradual progression?[61]

Sadrā responds that "the soul is, at first, the form of some thing that belongs to corporeal existents, and in its potentiality there is a receptivity (*qabūl*) to intelligible forms, without there being any mutual incompatibility between this activity and this perfective receptivity."[62] Indeed, the fundamental plasticity of the act of being has this consequence: form and matter, activity and potentiality, are not fixed, absolute terms, as if form could not in a certain sense be matter, and vice versa. On the contrary, the psychic form, the soul in its first birth – the soul understood as the animating force of the body – is both matter for the imaginative form and a form that corresponds to its second birth, the form of resurrection. And this imaginative form is in turn matter for the intelligible form. And the first and second intelligibles emanate upon this intelligible form, according to the activity of the agent intelligence.

What, then, does the "receptivity" of the soul signify, on the first level? It is not an absolutely privative potentiality; on the contrary, it is "the fact of being the subject of an operation of renewal," the fact of being subject to metamorphosis and open to the reception of successive forms. In this sense, the soul undergoes in itself the eduction of formations opposed to those it receives first, as a block is divided, or as water becomes air when it is boiled. But in another sense, receptivity is the potentiality to be perfected, such that formal reality, too, can be qualified in terms of "receptivity," in reference to its intensification in perfection. There are thus two types of receptivity; the first corresponds to the receiving matter, the second to the form that is united to it.[63]

It is possible, then, to understand how the human soul must successively actualize its form in this world and make itself matter for an intelligible form, in which the fundamental unity of the intelligible and the intelligizing subject is produced. Sadrā writes:

> The human soul is the perfection of this world, its beauty, its completeness, its finality. It possesses two faces, with respect to which it possesses two faculties. One of them is the face the soul turns toward this world. Through it, the soul governs the body, moves it, and accomplishes the animal activities that are proper to this world. We say that this is the "practical faculty," or the "practical intelligence." The second is the face that the soul turns toward the higher world. Through it, the soul is affected by principles, it intelligizes the sciences and cognitions, and it rises up to the perfections of the otherworld, thanks to divine love and the ardent desire to encounter God, the desire for his satisfaction (*mardā*).[64]

The soul is a reality that is actual in relation to its practical faculty, for it is the completed form of the elemental body, the finality of the elemental revolutions and the natural mutations. We know what these "revolutions" (*inqilābāt*) are: the transitions from pure material potency to dust (*turāb*), to briny water, to the blood clot, to the embryo, to the fetus endowed with flesh and bones, to the living being that hears and sees, on to the final term of perfection, where the soul is capable of receiving knowledge from God and knowing that it must obey him. This is the state in which man decides whether he will be faithful or unfaithful, in which he glimpses the moral choices that will determine the future thresholds of his development.

From the perspective of the faculty of contemplation, this same soul is simple matter, innocent, naive, ingenuous, and primitive (*sādhajah*). It is a *tabula rasa*, "a tablet with nothing printed on it," a mirror in which no intelligible form has yet been reflected. How can one represent such matter, devoid of all form? How to reconcile this perspective with the Peripatetic dogma, which claims that there is no form without matter and no matter without form? This can be done by saying that this separation, in effect, has no meaning, but is necessary to hierarchize the levels where the soul is form and where the soul is matter. "In relation to the first birth, the soul is pure form, and in relation to the otherworldly birth, it is pure matter."[65]

We will therefore make a clear distinction between corporeal matter (*māddah jismānīyah*) and spiritual matter (*māddah rūhānīyah*). Corporeal matter subsists only through sensible forms, which are its first perfection, and through that which is derived from these sensible forms, the second perfections. It is a question of elementary forms, on the one hand, and the animal soul, on the other. Appetite, wrath, hope, fear, pleasure, and pain are modalities of the animal form, through which the corporeal matter of the soul subsists.

Spiritual matter subsists only through spiritual forms. We saw earlier that these forms are diversified in imaginal and intelligible forms. It follows that, with regard to its link with spiritual existence (*wujūd rūhānī*), the soul is *pure potentiality*. It is pure indigence, says Sadrā, by virtue of its rank – the lowest – in the world of the *mysterium*. Material intelligence has no act of being at all in the otherworld, which is the world of the intelligence, as long as a dimension of spiritual activity has not been actualized for it. It exists no more than a fruit does when all that exists of it, as yet, is its seed – or the living being when there is only the drop of semen.

This is how Sadrā describes the movement of growth of the intelligence, in relation to this state of nonbeing and spiritual potentiality:

> Know that the faculty, on the threshold of the state of the intelligizing subject and the intelligized object—like the rest of the things that are in potency—is sometimes distant and sometimes near. The distant potency, in the state of the intelligizing subject, is similar to what is in material intelligence, which is a substance still attached to sensible matter, and in the state of the intelligized object, is similar to what is in the specific material forms that must become intelligibles for man. As for the proximate potency, it depends on what is realized on the basis of sensible figures preserved in the imaginative faculty, the first intelligibles, held in common by all men, because some of these intelligibles are actualized without effort and without previous reasoning, or through an exercise that is easy to perform, as when we say that all earth is heavy. The actualization of these perceived objects at first makes material intelligence a habitual intelligence (*'aql bi-l-malaka*), which implies a proximate preparation in order to become actual intelligence, so that the material forms become actually intelligized for them. The actualization of the first intelligibles leads to a second perfection, which is a light from among the lights of God, projected into the heart of the faithful man who struggles on the path of God against the enemies of God, enemies who belong to the corporeal powers and the shadowy suggestions, particularly the deceptive imagination (*wahmīyah*), which paralyzes man in his accomplishment of the duties of faith.[66] Man must defend these duties through a demonstrative power, so that the soul will become healthy and purify itself through its intellective activity, with the help of the Merciful. This light is the true good, the true beatitude, through which man becomes a living being in actuality, living with an essential life, which no longer needs matter to subsist, because of its becoming among all the realities that break with matters and potentialities, subsisting eternally.[67]

This becoming of the intelligence is not conceived of without a set of ascetic practices, derived from the lives of spiritual men: examination of conscience, recollection, repeated enunciation of the divine names (*dhikr*), humility, spiritual concentration, renunciation, abstention from food, silence, and voluntary solitude.

These exercises facilitate the reception of intelligible perceptions. Thus we find, once again, many aspects of spiritual life and wisdom that we have already encountered.[68]

Sadrā is obviously not refuting Avicenna. He is completely changing the conditions of a problem that he finds unsuitable. He begins with a doctrine of being and becoming that is fundamentally different from Avicenna's, even though he inscribes himself within the Avicennian moment of philosophy. At stake in this modification is the doctrine of intelligible salvation. Avicenna conceives of this doctrine in terms of a rare and non-unitive arrival at the intelligibles. The mystical impetus of the *Ishārāt* is somewhat thwarted by this final reservation concerning the unification of the divine world. But Avicenna's visionary narratives have another significance, another kind of audacity, and we know their importance for Mullā Sadrā. For Sadrā, Avicenna stops mid-course, although he begins on good footing. Avicenna cannot understand that the differences between the stages in man's transformation do not call into question the primary unity of his soul, or that these differences "lie in the inessential accidents connected to the act of existing." The human essence is not a fixed substance; rather, it *substantializes itself* throughout its long becoming, and it passes through the degrees of intensity or weakness without ruining its unity. At the summit are the agent intelligence and a union rendered effective and living. At the bottom is a not-yet-realized unity, as with an embryo in its mother's womb, a child, or a melancholic.

Chapter Ten

The God of Epiphanies

My aim here is not to present a detailed study of Sadrā's theory but to ask how Sadrā conceives of God such that the contemplative man strives to return to him. In other words, I would like to ask how his perspective, guided by the intuition of the essential motion of the act of existing, leads to a certain representation of the real, the origin and end of this motion. Sadrā himself invites us to do this by saying that "the way to the goal is itself the goal."[1]

God is the necessary being, "free in his ipseity from what is not him," such that his essence is one with the pure act of existing, free from all quiddity.[2] Sadrā follows Avicenna by identifying the essence of God with the existent that is necessary through itself.[3] As pure existence, the maximum of the act of being, God continues to be thought in the element of being, and the conversion that leads back to him cannot guide us toward a grasp of the principle *beyond being*. The unity of the necessary being is identical to the necessity of its act of being, and the One is thought in this fundamental identity with being. This decision affects Sadrā's reading of Plotinus – that is, the *Theology of Aristotle* – since pure existence is superimposed on the principal One intuited at the summit of the *via negativa*. Let us recall here the consequences of the Sadrian doctrine of being. It clearly distinguishes existence from abstract being, from the concept of being. To say that God, in his essence, is what is necessary to being (*wājib al-wujūd*) is not to confuse him with an abstraction, the universal concept of being, for example, or some conceptual reality of absolute being that we might form. God is absolute existence, and through this simple affirmation he is delivered from all quidditative limitations, including that of quiddity, which could be thought of as pertaining to the necessary existent.[4]

The Divine Names

Rather than follow the maze of dialectical demonstrations, let us concentrate on the exegetical truth of this necessary act of being. Indeed, the divine essence is reflected in its names, which are revealed in the holy book. The knowledge of essence, origin, and return is a knowledge of this epiphany within the horizon of nomination.[5] Sadrā devotes to it a magnificent exercise of *ta'wīl*, drawing on a long tradition attributed to the sixth imam, Ja'far al-Sādiq.[6] This imam maintains that God instantiated a name "with nonsonorous letters," with "nonpronounced expressions," with "the noncorporealized individual," the "unattributed resemblance," and the "unpainted color." The primary name is a coincidence of expression and withdrawal. "It is hidden and not hidden," as if the primordial divine manifestation occurred in the infinite alternation between revelation and veiling. This name is a "complete word," divisible into four assembled parts, none of which is prior to the others. Three of these parts constitute the three names that God made manifest, in consideration of the needs of his creatures. He veils the fourth, the hidden name, which is kept secret (*al-ism al-maknūn al-makhjūn*). The initial silence of God coils into itself and contracts within this hidden name, which constitutes the secret of essence in its very revelation.

Sadrā explains that although God has names and attributes, the whole they form (despite the multiplicity of names and their mutual distinctions) cannot be added to the divine essence. There is much more in this assertion than the resolution of a scholastic question; it leads to the foundations of Sadrā's ontology, to the possibility of a revelation of divine unity in the multiplicity of existents. To that end, Sadrā carries out an astonishing synthesis of Avicenna's legacy and Ibn al-'Arabī's theosophy. In the exegesis of the imam's statement, the being that is necessary through itself will be thought as absolute Being, in the sense that this absolute Being is the divine essence.

The necessity of existence is existence itself, in the absoluteness of its act.[7] The necessary is therefore "simple in its essential reality, it is one in all of its aspects, it is therefore the totality of being."[8] Divine being, in its simple unity, is the totality of existence that unfolds from it. The essential motion of the existent thus realizes the unification of the One and the multiplicities, whose principles are the divine names, without in any way corrupting the identity of the divine essence, which is the act of existing itself. But this identity of simple being and the totality of being cannot be separated from the differences I have already pointed out: absolute Being designates that which is not defined by a particular definition, whereas interlinked being has exactly the opposite status, since man, the celestial sphere, the soul, and the intelligence are existents whose act of being is determined. There is a contradiction between indeterminateness and determinateness. The totality of things in a simple mode is the indeterminate unity of the absolute Being. Their multiplicity is a unity revealing itself in a plurality of determinations. The contradiction is resolved by the cosmological function of God, the agent of every interlinked act of being: the primary agent is not a cause distinct from its effects but the maximal perfection of the act of being of the caused, the limit of the movement of perfection. The cause's immanence in relation to its effects and the transcendence of absolute being are one, since interlinked being and absolute being are the moments of a single reality, the reality of the divine real.

The contradiction between absolute being and determinate being, and the negation that it implies, disappears in the expansive flow of extensive being. The maximal extension of being, the integral deployment of the multiple degrees of its flow, integrates all the "measures" inferior to it, all the finite degrees of intensity of the act of existing. Just as intense black integrates all the potentially infinite degrees of black and realizes blackness in a simple mode, extended being integrates all the degrees of the act of being and leads them back to its source to the simplicity of absolute Being.[9] Like absolute Being, expansive being and determinate being are one, and the identity of the identical and the different is grounded not in the labor of contradiction but in the fading away of this split in the simplicity of the divine essence.

Does this speculative boldness ruin the transcendence of God? Will we be obliged to conclude, with Hegel, that there is a pantheism of Islam?[10] This seems to be the fear of one of the great philosophers of the Savafid period, Qāzī Saʿīd Qummī, a student of Mullā Sadrā's son-in-law Muhammad Muhsin al-Fayd al-Kāshānī. In his treatise on ontology, *The Key to Paradise* (written in Persian), he maintains that the necessary Being is not multiple and is not one in the sense in which the possible existent can be. The word "being" is fundamentally homonymic, and every form of analogy between its meanings must be rejected. The necessary thus no longer remains within the concept of being, or in the science of divine things. God transcends all theological representation, which is proved by the prophets' inability to designate the giver of being. Prophetic science bears only on the manifestations of God in his attributes. God is free from all the qualifications and symbols with which one attempts to show his manifestations, since he is their absolutely ineffable cause. Theology deals with the concept of being, and the Necessary Being is external to this concept.[12]

If the divine attributes are not distinct from the divine essence, as Sadrā argues, such a transcendence of the necessary essence and the homonymy of being cannot be maintained; rather, it will be necessary to escape from pantheism in another way. Absolute transcendence must be one with radical immanence – but subject to a hierarchy of "planes" or degrees to which one must appeal in referring to the unique act of being.

Sadrā demonstrates the identity of the attributes of perfection and the divine essence by making three points: if these attributes were added to the act of existing of essence, the latter, at the rank where it is divine essence, would not be qualified by the attributes of perfection. It would therefore be deficient; it would no longer be knowing in itself, powerful in itself, living in itself, and so on. Something other than essence would have the power to effectuate in essence the perfection that it lacked. This would entail a numerical multiplication of the dimensions of activity and passivity in God, whereas these two dimensions — the gift or effusion, and reception — are simple abstract realities falling within the order of quiddity. But the simple essence of God has no quiddity.

If these attributes were added to the essence, their effusion from the essence and onto the essence would occur through a more noble dimension than the one in which the necessary Being is what it is. The essence would be more noble than the essence.

Finally, the divine essence is the principle of gradation of the monads of existence, the giver of all goods and perfections. The giver is greater than the given. If perfection and beauty were not part of the transcendental reality itself but came as a consequence of this essence, the whole formed by the essence and its attributes would be superior to the essence.[13]

We can avoid these absurdities by bringing the entire discussion out of the dialectical framework of rational theology[14] and submitting it to the theological model provided by Ibn al-ʿArabī — the theophanic model. In order to do this, Sadrā draws all the consequences from one divine attribute: knowledge.[15]

Divine science, as God's knowledge of things and of himself, is the divine act of being. It is also the reflection of God into God. God affirms his necessary act of existing and, thereby, knows his own essence, bears witness to his unicity and pure singularity. The witness of God is God, and his science, a divine attribute, is the testimony of God for God, without any differentiating relation. What we call "theophany" is this twin act of being and cognition — the conjoined revelation and testimony of he who is revealed for himself as he is in himself.

This testimony is the intelligence, or the word of God. The "bond" between the theology of essence and the theology of the word is the effusion of essence in the first order of created realities.[16] The science that God has of God, united with the essence of God, is thus united also to power, will, and the other divine attributes. Because God knows himself, and because he knows in himself all of his own expressions, in the simplicity of his essence, he wills these expressions and has the power to unfold them in the orders of the imperative and of creation. The testimony God gives to himself of himself is reflected in the angelic testimony, which is the divine act of being emanating on the plane of the intelligence.

The testimony of the angels is the unfolding of God's testimony, since it is God who testifies that there is no divinity except in God. This testimony is the angelic, intelligible act of existing, since this act of being is constituted through the divine existence. The cognition of every monad of existence is thus the expression of his being, proceeding in extended being to its singular determination. This expression emerges from out of the divine essence and from its own testimony. Revelation is existence; existence is revelation: "You know that the reality of the real testifies to its unicity and thus constitutes the act of being of something other than itself. That is what is signified by the fact that the angels possess science."[17] The simple act of being, according to its gradations, is revealed in the concomitants of science, power, and will. The attributes of existence are reflected in the created, down to the threshold of shadows, at the lowest level of material deficiency. The entire universe is a theophany.

The divine essence is the only existence. It makes God's attributes and qualifications exist, just as the essential properties of our quiddity exist only according to our individual act of existing. The multiple names are to the essence what quiddity is to the act of existing: a derivative shadow. The comparison ends at the point where God, the necessary Being, differs from us, as possible existents, since he has no quiddity. It is nonetheless true that the divine names are the multiple significations unified in the act of being and the ispseity of the real. If the universe of the theophanies is effusion and expression, the lordly world (*al-ʿālam al-rabbanī*) is the multiple unity of significations.[18] The names are "uninstantiated," but they are realized through the very effectivity of the uninstantiated necessary essence.

The names that signify the essential attributes of God—"the living," "he who provides subsistence in existing," "the knowing," "the powerful," "the one who wills"—thus designate the essence itself, which comes to be known and emerges from non-knowledge and unconsciousness. That is why divine science must unfold the internal tensions of the divine unity.

Sadrā concludes his examination of this divine science with a remarkable summary of "the doctrine of the Sūfīs."[19] When the divine ipseity ("he") knows himself, he is presented from three points of view: "he" is knowing, known, and knowledge.[20] These three points of view deploy the following three modes of knowledge: the causality of manifestation for himself (luminescence); the activity of the knowing subject and the state of the known object; and the activity of the contemplative witness and the object of testimony. The unity of the divine essence is the unity of an intradivine testimony. There is no way for us to conceive of this unity of the reflection of self in self except as love. God is love, lover, and beloved. That is why, in man, the way of lovers is the royal road to God. "A lover says: 'Love is the way, and the sight of the beloved is heaven, separation is hell. God burns the wood that grows upon the heart.'"[21]

Everything that possesses existence thereby possesses life, science, and cognition of its lord, and expresses in it the originary science and love that manifest the divine unity for itself. But for us this knowledge begins in ignorance, in the corporeal state of the soul. The body is division and separation, for each of its parts knows nothing of the others, and they are hidden from one another. The corporeal soul hasn't a shadow of cognition except insofar as it preserves the corporeal unity; it is the constitutive spiritual principle of the body. Its immaterial act of existing intensifies this original knowledge up to the intelligible.[22] In God, this is not the case at all. There is no use for intensification, since God is pure intensity of existing.

The unity of the divine essence is reflected in the three unified aspects of his science. From this reflection comes the universe of the divine names, the multiplicity of significations. These significations will in turn have sites of manifestation (*mazāhir*) in the quiddities of things and their ipseities, which require no instantiation or effectuation, for they are accompanied by the act of being. The names and their reflections in the quiddities are therefore not separated from all being, as the Muʿtazilī believe. Between pure essence and its significations, there is no need to think the space of an instantiation, an activity, and a receptivity: the nominal significations apply only to the existing essence, but they describe it as clothed by its *semblances* and "point-of-view realities."

Logic of Theophany

This scheme comes to Sadrā from Ibn al-ʿArabī. It is implicated in the ontology of the mirror that we have often encountered. Ibn al-ʿArabī summarizes it thus: "He is your mirror in your vision of yourself, and you are his mirror in his vision of his names and the manifestation of his statuses, which are nothing other than himself."[23] God sees his own names in the mirror constituted by the essential reality of the faithful – of the creature – and this manifestation in man reflects the reflection of the essence in the names. Hence "the essence from the totality within the totality is unique,"[24] but in this totality the names of God are infinite, "for they are known by what proceeds from them, and what proceeds from them is infinite, even if they are converted into finite roots, which are the mothers of the divine names, or the presences of these names.... There is only one effective reality that receives all of these relations and bonds called the divine names."[25]

This logic of light and shadow enables one to understand the status of the apparent multiple within the real unity. The eternal essences of possible existents are not luminous, says Ibn al-ʿArabī, for they are not existent through themselves. Sadrā says the same thing about the quiddities. They are nevertheless not pure nothingness, since they receive the attribute of stability (*thobūt*). But they do so without receiving being (*wujūd*), since existence is light and the quiddities are the shadow of the divine names, which are contained within the divine shadow called the world.[26]

We know that the imagination has the function of reconciling light and shadow, because it is the originary act of perception that merges with the initial unfolding of the eternal essences in effective existence:

> Know that you are imagination and all that you perceive as not being you, as you say, is imagination. All existence is imagination in imagination, and the existence of the real alone is God, particularly from the point of his essence and of his essential identity (*'ayn*), not from the point of his names. Indeed, the names have two meanings. The first meaning is the identity of the essence itself, identical to the named. The second meaning is that through which the name is separated from the other names and is distinguished from them.... You know clearly in what way each name is identical to the other names, and in what way it differs from them. That through which it is identical is the real; that through which it differs is the imagined real.[27]

The name is identical to the named from the point of view of the real. The name becomes separated from the named and its meaning is derived through its distinction from the meaning of the other names. The meaning comes to designate the imagined real, deployed in the creative imagination that creates all of reality. There is not a split between the real in itself and the imagined real but a knotting together of one with the other in the divine name itself, in the symbolic order of names. This knot is expressed in theophany.

The word for theophany, *al-tajallī*, is a verbal noun based on the fifth form of the verb *j-l-a*, meaning "to appear out in the open, in broad daylight." It is the action of "making oneself manifest," of making oneself seen with striking brilliance. Theophany is the brilliant revelation of the divine Self; it begins on the plane of the divine names, which envelops the real and expresses it. This is what justifies the human knowledge possessed by the heart, and the use that Ibn al-'Arabī and Mullā Sadrā make of Bistāmī's paradox. The heart of the gnostic proceeds from the mercy of God; it exemplifies the divine name, the Merciful. It thus envelops the divine lordship, because it perceives all the effects of this lordship in the act of perfect obedience that corresponds to it. But the divine lordship is not the real taken in its pure essence, free of every bond. It is situated in the movement of the breath of the Merciful, through which the flows of the eternal essences pour forth.[28]

Ibn al-ʿArabī distinguishes two theophanies: the manifestation of the divine *mysterium* and the appearance of the nominal manifestation of essence in the order of the sensible.[29] The divine existentiating breath is known in the mirror of the world; "the world appears in the breath (*nafas*) of the Merciful through which God has freed (*naffasa*) the divine names from the absence of manifestation of their effects."[30]

That is the scheme adopted by Sadrā in his commentary on the tradition of the imam Jaʿfar. He maintains that the names are, in this sense, identical to the unique essence (*al-dhāt al-ahadīyah*). To solve the problem of the existential status of the names, he engages in a dialectic: the names are not existents and are not nonexistents; they are not instantiated and are not noninstantiated. "More precisely, their instantiation follows the the instantiation of the act of being, and their noninstantiation follows the noninstantiation of the divine being. That is why they are eternal with the eternal, temporal with the temporal."[31] The divine identity is saved from all multiplication by a primary negation of the being of names. Their secondary affirmation, their expression in the temporal order, seems to be the negation of this negation. But that is not the case.

In the logical scheme in which Western ontology comes to completion, namely the Hegelian scheme, negation sets in motion the immediacy of universal abstract signification. The real is the becoming of this negation as it redoubles itself in the negation of itself, such that the effectivity of a concrete signification, in which the real is named, resides in this labor of the negative. The result — the absolute — is negativity returned to the immediate. The identity between the absolute and the multiplicity of its significations or names is effectuated in the long suffering, the labor, and the patience of the negative.

Sadrā's scheme is quite different. The signification of essence in the totality of its names and the reflection of essence in the mirror of names are a process without labor, suffering, or patience. Essence emerges from its immediacy, since its nomination produces no other effectivity than that of essence. The name is stricken with negation; it is, first of all, nonexistent. In order not to be a pure nothingness, it must be affirmed, and it must bring out into the open the theophany of essence, of the *mysterium*, on the plane of the totality of divine names. But this affirmation is only a second negation. In order to resemble the Hegelian scheme, the name would have had to negate the abstract universality of the essence, only to see its particularity negated in turn. Here, the name's being is barred, negated without the negation reaching as far as its essence. It is, rather, the victorial essence that negates it, only to immediately negate the negation, and to be revealed in the striking brilliance of what is identical to it. The difference in question is one between the shadow and the luminous real, not between the real and its effective moments.

The speculative power of this logic of the divine names is no less remarkable. It engenders a grammar of identity in which the name does not *effectively* differ from the named. The divine names are the "keys to the mystery," because their significations are intelligized only in the mystery of essence, without themselves being existent concrete realities (*mawjūdāt ʿaynīyāt*). One can only negate every *relation* of the name to the essence (they are not "for him," "of him," or "in him").[32] The act of being that effuses from the plane of divine names is expansive being,

> whose unity is not numerical, since it is in all things by reason of itself, and is contained within no determinate limit, nor in a particular definition, such as the eternal or the temporal, the prior or the posterior, the immaterial or the embodied, perfection or imperfection, eminence or baseness. It is eternal with the eternal, immaterial with the immaterial, corporeal with the corporeal; it is substance with substance, accident with the accident.[33]

The divine names thus comprehend all existents, their being is that of the essence, and their manifestations do not differ from the existents themselves. God is thus entirely immanent to reality, but in the element of his nominations.

The divine names are hierarchical. The supreme name is God, Allāh. It is expressed in three major names, designating the attributes of knowledge, will, and power. The four pillars of the world — intelligence, soul, nature, and body — are enveloped in the supreme name. Knowledge unfolds along four degrees: intellection, estimative faculty, imagination, and sense. A corresponding four-part division applies to the will, which expresses itself in love, inclination, desire, and passion, and to power, which is developed in instantiation, configuration, activity, and motion. The four pillars of the world enter into correspondence with the elements and with the twelve celestial constellations. Corresponding to intelligence is fire, whose "signs" are Aries, Leo, and Sagittarius; corresponding to the soul is air, whose signs are Gemini, Libra, and Aquarius; corresponding to nature is water, whose signs are Cancer, Pisces, and Scorpio; corresponding to the body is earth, whose signs are Taurus, Virgo, and Capricorn.[34]

Three fundamental names are therefore the "major imams," expressing the "imam of imams." The multiplication of their number by those of their expressions and of the celestial constellations gives thirty-six names, which are multiplied by ten, based on the ten categories of the existent (Aristotle's ten categories). Thus we obtain three hundred sixty names, the number of degrees in the celestial orb: "The entire world is created according to the form of the divine names, even if among these names there is a hierarchical diversity, as there is among the created realities. Some hold the sultanate, the government, and the imamate over others, who are considered the guards or servants."[35] This combination of mystic numerology, astrology, and the theory of the categories produces a divine politics meant to safeguard the order of the world.

Indeed, the spirit of this combinatoire, largely inspired by the theosophy of Ibn al-ʿArabī, aims at founding an aesthetic and political world order in which all contingency and monstrosity are proscribed, the only aberration being the moral evil of rebellion against the divine decree, contained entirely in the three names of knowledge, power, and will. Prophetic philosophy is a theodicy. The three hundred sixty names include the unlimited names. The three hundred sixty definite names form three concentric circles, twelve in the three, and three hundred sixty in twelve, by groups of thirty. The totalizing One is the name "Allāh," equivalent to the name "the Merciful," according to the verse "Say: 'Call upon God, or call upon the Merciful: whatever name you call him by, the most beautiful names are his.'"[36]

In conformity with the doctrine of Ibn al-'Arabī, Sadrā posits divine mercy as the element for the act of existing of all things.

> Existence is the mercy that envelops all quiddity and haecceity. From its totality arises the quiddity of the wrathful and of what is ordained by it—sufferings, maladies, tribulations, afflictions.... Mercy encompasses wrath as it encompasses all the rest.... And you, when you turn your gaze to everything that can be counted as evils, sufferings, sorrows, and maladies, you discover that they are, in themselves, existential goods and perfections.[37]

The exegesis of the supreme name, Allāh, confirms the ontology of identity. It is based on a tradition reported by the eighth imam, 'Ālī al-Ridā (d. 203/818). According to this imam, God first gave himself the name "the all high, the supereminent" (*al-'Ālī al-'Azīm*).[38] Sadrā explains that the name "the all high" designates the divine essence, for God is elevated *by himself*, whereas the other names imply the eminent *relationship* of God to what proceeds from him.[39] The signification of "Allāh" is so perfectly incomprehensible, so transcendent, that it is necessary for it to remain under the symbol of this supereminence. The names "the all high, the supereminent" allow one to approach the unfathomable meaning of the supreme name, which is the *semblance* of essence.[40] And yet "the all high" is none other than the perfect man; the name refers, all at once, to divine transcendence and the anthropomorphosis of God in the perfect man. All of the divine names are thus involuted in man.

The Perfect Man

The perfect man is the microcosm, the site of appearance of the name Allāh, signified by "the all high, the supereminent." He is the caliph of God on earth and the semblance of the divine light in its sky. The *combinatoire* of the world order is recapitulated and expressed in him: "Just as in the parts of this world there are genera and species, individuals and substances, as well as other categories, so are there, in the divine names, names for genus, species, substance, accident [for each Aristotelian category], and so does there exist in the perfect man, in the totalizing site of appearance, the entirety of what exists in the world of the names and the sites of appearance."[41]

Allāh *is* the perfect man, the totalization of the microcosm and the macrocosm. The divine names correspond to the various dimensions of the existent: al-Qayyūm (the Provident, he who gives subsistence) corresponds to substance; al-Quddūs (the Perfect) corresponds to the distinct species; al-Musawwir (he who gives form) corresponds to the substantial forms; al-Awwal al-Akhīr (the First, the Last) corresponds to the category of time; and so on. All the divine names together, in the person of the perfect man, function as an infinite number of roots—roots of substantial individualities, act-of-being singularities, monads, and their derivative expressions.

> Just as the individualities of the substances are infinite and the derivatives of the names are infinite, and just as the whole is gathered into a single existing nature—for the act of being of the possible is both a single effective reality called the pneumatic soul (*al-nafs al-rūhānī*) and the universal intelligible matter that bears the forms of the intelligible and sensible substances and their effective realities—likewise are the universal names enveloped in the single divine essence that gathers together the totality of the names according to the differentiation of their meanings.[42]

The perfect man is thus the totalizing word, the archetype of what is in the divine revealed books, the lights written in the hand of the Merciful.[43] He corresponds, in the microcosm, to the supreme spirit, gathering together the totality of the macrocosm, the principle, form, and finality of all things, the origin of intelligences and of souls. The intellective spirit characterizes the perfect man, who intelligizes the entirety of the possibles. In him, God gives birth to the "birth" that gathers together the totality of worlds and the three "births." He is instantiated by God in order to be the *semblance* of him, and that is why he is Allāh, since the name Allāh designates the meaning of the revealed divine essence, emerging from hiding. The perfect man is the mirror of the essence.[44]

The perfect man is the realization of the prophetic essence of man.[45] The essential reality of prophetic being, "with the light of his guidance, perfects the souls of believers and illuminates human intelligences, making them pass from potency to act." The prophet existentiates human intelligences, just as God existentiates the macrocosm. In this way, the prophet manifests the name Allāh. He brings forth upon men, says Sadrā, the effusion of the knowledge of the lights of being, by effectuating knowledge and faith in them. He provides them with the existence proper to the otherworld; he is the mediation between precarious and permanent existence (*al-wujūd al-baqā'ī*). He is the agent of permanent existence, of eternal establishment in being (*al-thubūt al-sarmadī*).[46] That is why the prophet and the imam, united in the same prophetic essence, are the two constitutive principles (*muqawwim*) of the essence of the believer as believer.

The total man (*al-insān al-kullī*) is therefore no longer to be regarded as owing his act of being to anything other than his own foundation in the order of the divine names. In him, existence returns to its fundamental essence. The total man is "the ground of his essence, through which he exists, or, rather, he is an act of being subsisting through himself (*wujūd qā'im bi-nafsih*)." He is existence raising itself into being through itself.

> He is light from the spiritual lights of God, a secret from the divine intelligible secrets, a face from the faces of his power, a sign from the signs of his wisdom, a source from the sources of his divinity, a word from the words of his knowledge and his will. These essential attributes all belong to him, from among the essential attributes of God and the characteristics of nobility and majesty. They are made manifest in a servant among servants.[47]

The perfect man is the perfect servant. He realizes the perfection of the real man (*al-insān al-haqīqī*), which is not man in the sense designated by his merely specific form (*al-insān al-sūrī*). He is the site of manifestation of the divine name Allāh, in that he assumes the task of spiritual guidance. This guidance does not consist only in counsel and teaching; rather, it brings to completion the totality of the essential motion of the act of existing. The perfect man is the final term of all the stations (*maqāmāt*) of existence, passing through all of them in order to bring them to the site of the supreme sojourn: the intelligible *qalam*, the tablet of the soul, nature, the divine throne delimited by space and time (the epiphany of the name "the Merciful"), the *kursī* (equivalent to the name "he who gives mercy"), the seven heavens, and the births. Such is the effect of the divine guidance given to the perfect man, who assumes its burden and realizes it as a practice.

The return of all corporeal natures into God is thus realized in the perfect man. The desire from which each act of being is woven – the movement toward the higher degree of existence – finds its destination in him. By virtue of this desire, each existent is driven to return to its origin, from which it was separated by its fixed condition: "Thus the return of the elements is similar to the rainwater that first is separated from the sea, then is united with the sea and becomes seawater, after which it becomes vapor, condenses into a cloud, falls in raindrops, flows away from springs and rivers, joins with the ocean, and becomes the ocean."[48]

The Divine Throne Is the Heart of the Faithful

The name Allāh, the supreme name unfolding itself in the hierarchy of names, is involuted into the perfect man. The God of epiphanies is the divine essence or the more-than-perfect act of being, giving itself to be known in the sum total of substantial movements, which is integrated into the becoming of man. In the topography of revelation, God is presented as sitting upright on his throne, his feet resting on a *kursī* (a "seat"). Far from giving a material meaning to this revelation, Sadrā uses it to illustrate the involution of God in man, the unity of God and man in the pure manifestation of the act of being.

Among Sadrā's numerous exegeses of the throne and the *kursī*, I would like to follow the one he gives in his commentary on the traditions of the imams.[49] Sadrā presents this text as a long conversation between the first imam and a Christian dignitary called "the Catholicos."[50]

The Catholicos asks 'Ālī if God bears the throne, or if the throne bears God. 'Ālī answers: "Allāh is the one who bears the throne, the heavens and the earth, what is in them and what is between them."[51] Sadrā comments that Allāh is "the one who raises things into being" (*qā'im*) and to say that God does not bear the throne would be to repudiate the *qiyyām*, the rising into being of all things.[52] Then 'Ālī offers an astonishing mystical exegesis: Allāh created the throne from four lights – red, green, yellow, and white. Through his majesty and his light (particularly the white light of knowledge), he sees the hearts of the believers and he sees his enemies, the people of ignorance. He discerns all existents' desire to accede to him, and their moral conduct. All that exists is thus borne by divine light, majesty, and power; Allāh is the life of all things, and he receives their praise in turn.

The Catholicos asks 'Ālī where God is. The imam answers: "He is here and he is there, above and below, he envelops us and he is with us."[53] It is the *kursī*, he says, that envelops the skies, the earth and all they contain. As for those who bear the throne, they are the *'ulamā'*, all those who practice the divine gnosis, contemplating a science identified with the Malakūt, which God showed to Abraham.[54]

This Shīʿite tradition presents a scene loaded with symbols. It can be seen as a peaceful conversation between a Christian and the imam ʿĀlī, united in a disciple-master relationship – a relationship between a demanding student who makes objections to the imam, based on common sense and referring to the Qur'ān, and a master inspired by divine gnosis, who interprets the letter of the Qur'ān by unveiling in it the very thing that inspires it. The esoteric knowledge the imam manifests in his person of light is the secret of the Throne Verse. The letter seems to be overturned, since Allāh in truth bears the throne that was supposed to bear him. But it is righted if one recalls that the bearers of the throne are in fact the subjects of inner knowledge, the exemplifications of the perfect man, who bears precisely the name Allāh. We have seen that this perfect man is the Prophet. But the Prophet, in the Shīʿite sense, is the couple formed by the prophetic person, Muhammad, who reveals the letter of the Qur'ān, and the imam, who maintains the book's meaning by unveiling the hidden knowledge rolled up within it; in this case it is the imam ʿĀlī , the "prince of believers" and founder of the lineage of the twelve imams.

Sadrā's exegesis of this conversation addresses the objections put forward by the Catholicos, who emphasizes that, according to the Qur'ān, it will be revealed on the last day that "eight, above them, will bear the throne of their Lord." According to a prophetic *hadīth*, there will be four angels holding up four others. Some will take a human form, others the form of a lion, ox, or eagle.[55] According to Sadrā, the angels bearing the throne are the "lords of the species," eight thousand in eight rows, each bearing a human or an animal form, the form of its icon. They have the status of imaginal forms and intelligible forms, so they typify the hierarchy of the imaginal world and the intelligible world.[56]

But the deeper meaning of the *hadīth* is the metamorphosis of man. He is a microcosm, possessing four powers that bear the throne in his heart. Through the motion of his substance, which carries him from his first birth to his intelligible birth, man becomes the macrocosm, greater than the universe, according to a couplet attributed to the imam ʻĀlī: "You say that you are a small body, and in you the greatest world will be enfolded." The four powers of man will be conjoined to the four angels on the Day of Resurrection, which explains why the four angels bearing the throne will become eight. The angelic becoming of man is the secret of the support of the throne.

The hidden meaning of the throne is the heart of man,

> which is the site of the gnosis of God and the support of his science and which, through the progress of perfection, becomes identical to gnosis. Science, as the sages saw, consists in man's soul – called the heart in the practice of *sharīʻah* – becoming a pure intelligence and a pure light. The Qur'ānic verse says: "And eight will, that day, bear the throne of your Lord above them" [69:17]. This means that eight angels will bear it on two sides: four of them at the highest extremity, which as a whole will be the sacred dominating lights and the separate divine forms, Lords of the elementary icons; four others, on the opposite side, will belong to the formal *semblances*, whose shadows are the forms of the four elements, in both dimensions, the high and the low, when the resurrection takes place. For the lower things, too, through the resurrection and the stripping away of matter, will become higher realities.[57]

In Suhrawardī's language, which Sadrā's exegesis borrows here, the formal *semblances* are the lights of the latitudinal gradation constituting the world of angelic forms, whereas the Lords of the icons are the archangelic lights proceeding from the longitudinal order. This hierarchy of lights brings into existence the four elements constitutive of material bodies, here identified with the eight angels, divided up according to their respective positions around the throne, the heart of man. On the Day of Resurrection, all created beings, beginning with elementary matter, are purified of their materiality and raised to their formal and intelligible archetypes, such that the transfiguration of the perfect man, in his angelic intelligible becoming, also signifies the transfiguration of the totality of the existent, which is gathered into the chorus of divine unity. This is the end of substantial motion.

The angels of the higher degree are the four angels of cognition; those of the lower degree are the four angels of practice, corresponding to the moral status of the imaginal world. Victorial lights and ruling lights — intelligences and souls — thus form the chorus of God's glorification.

The four lights spoken of by the imam are homologized by Sadrā with the four worlds: that of bodies and of natures, that of animal souls, that of universal ruling souls, and that of intelligences.[58] This provides the occasion to synthesize a number of different strands: the *ta'wīl* of the imam, the illuminative philosophy of Suhrawardī, the ontological scheme borrowed (as we have seen) from Ibn al-'Arabī, and the still-active metaphysical source, Plotinus.[59] Mullā Sadrā's Shī'ite exegesis thus strives to integrate all the elements of Greek wisdom and Islamic spirituality, in an effort to give the hidden meaning of a hermeneutics already placed under the authority of Islam.

The four colors, too, are explained by an aesthetic reference to the doctrine of the Ishrāqīyah, who think that "the marvelous colors of birds' feathers are shadows of attributes and spiritual relations that are in the luminous principles and the intelligible Lords."

Divine science, according to the imam 'Ālī, is the science of God's friends and his enemy. Here again we find the dualist insistence on the world's state of perpetual war until its end on Judgment Day. Sadrā interprets it in terms of substantial motion. The ignorant, the enemies of God and the imam, are those who, through the practice of base actions driven by appetite and wrath, have firmly rooted within themselves the ignorance that is inevitable for man at the beginning of his first growth. They become animals, as we have seen, and their resurrectional body is the body of a pig or a dog, or another of the animal bodies that amply stock the Sadrian bestiary. This is when Sadrā affirms the criterion of divine selection: whoever is the enemy of the imam is the enemy of God.[60]

The four worlds mentioned above were counted as four only according to the subdivision of the world of souls into two distinct levels. Therefore, they do not contradict the cosmological synthesis Sadrā proposes to explain the involution of all things in the heart of the perfect man, and the return of all things into God; they are the four degrees of the divine science of existents.

The first degree is divine providence (*al-'ināyah al-ilāhīyah*), a simple and totalizing science that is one with the essence of God. The second degree is the universal intelligence, or the agent intelligence, homologized with the divine decree (*al-qaḍā' al-ilāhī*). The third degree is the world of souls, or the universal soul, homologized with lordly predestination (*al-qadar al-rabbanī*). The fourth degree is "the book of effacement and establishment," the world of particular forms. The divine throne is the form of universal intelligence and the supreme spirit, which is the site of the decree. We have seen that it is the destination and the prophetic essence of man.

The *kursī* is the form of the universal soul, the tablet of predestination, on which the *qalam* of intelligence writes the forms of the world. For each emanation of the intelligence and the soul there are four supports, corresponding to the four supports of the throne. They are a nature, a sense, an imagination, and an intelligence. Here again are the various degrees of growths, from nature to intelligible birth. That is why all existents, beginning with the earth itself—the most dense of all creations—return to God according to the essential movement of growth, and undergo their resurrection.[61]

In his explication of the divine name "the all high," Sadrā distinguishes two types of elevation, that of God—who is so in his very essence—and that of man. The perfect man is elevated through the elevation of the divine real because he participates in the divine imperative and because, in truth, he is the one referred to in the verse "Glorify the name of your Lord, the most high."[62] The perfect man is the bearer of the name of the divine lordship; he glorifies it, and he is glorified by this name and under this name. Eminent dignity of man! But this dignity differs from satanic pride in that it consists of complete obedience:

> The most high servant – he who is the intimate angel – needs a place where he can wait for his participation in elevation; he needs to be educated by cultivating the state of the servant [obedience, *al-'ubūdīyah*]. . . . He does not become intoxicated, he does not leave behind gratitude, he does not enter into unbelief, which leads far away from fine actions, he does not wonder at himself, and he does not exalt himself. For then he would meet with banishment and would fall, just as it happened to Iblīs, as the verse says: "Are you too proud, or are you one of the high and mighty?" And God says: "You will have no reason to be arrogant. Get out! You are one of the wretched."[63]

"No Compulsion in Religion"

What is the meaning of this obedience? I would like to conclude this book with a reading of a text that has a very important place in the history of this question concerning human freedom in Islam. It is a commentary by Sadrā on the famous verse of the Qur'ān that states, "No compulsion in religion."[64]

What does the word "religion," *al-dīn*, refer to here? For Sadrā religion is the obedience and assent to God that are actualized in man by the knowledge that God effuses upon the satisfied heart. As knowledge, religion is conceived from the beginning as something completely different from the external acceptance of prescriptions. It is an internal movement that leads the soul to the stage where it becomes a "satisfied heart." This stage is the perfection of the third birth of man. The inner knowledge here gained is innate to the prophet, and is acquired by the faithful who are initiated into gnosis, into spiritual unveiling and certainty. But knowledge is existence; it translates a certain degree in the intensification of the act of being. Just as being is spontaneity – the freedom of its own flow out of its source in the divine act of being – so must the knowledge that comes from God be pure spontaneity in the hearts of the faithful.

The necessary cognitions "are actualized in the heart by effusion (*al-ifādah*) alone, without compulsion and without coercion." If that is the case with the knowledge that is useful for life, will it not also be thus with the speculative cognitions and the divine gnosis? Teaching prepares the mind by communicating the premises of these cognitions. It must then perfect and complete itself "solely through the dictates in the heart, through the projection of the truths of the heart, *without compulsion in the apparent, external world*." The great division between the esoteric and the exoteric thus carefully delimits what falls under juridical practice – the apparent, inessential, inferior world – from what belongs to divine freedom – the spontaneous impetus of the effusion of knowledge upon the heart, the world of the soul, and the world of the intelligence.

Sadrā formulates this important maxim: "Religion is an internal matter" (*al-dīn amr bātinī*), a maxim that does not make him a *bātinī*, an "esoterist" in the technical sense the term has when it refers to Ismā'īlī Shī'ism. But it does make him a Shī'ite who is fully aware of the danger of confounding the apparent order of the polity and the order of religion. Not that he proposes any separation between the state and revelation, which would indeed be quite surprising. Rather, he distinguishes the juridical discipline, born from history and inextricably linked to the order of the external sensible world, to which the man of the polity belongs, from the set of truths that, strictly speaking, fall within "religion."

He quotes an important tradition, which says that "when God is epiphanized for a thing, when he effects in some thing his striking and brilliant revelation, he submits what is apparent in the thing, and its esoteric dimension, to himself." Religion is the submission of the esoteric dimension of man, whereas the juridical statutes interest only his external sensibility. True obedience therefore does not consist in observing prohibitions, which are a pure negation of sins and trespasses. It is, rather, fully affirmative and a concomitant of gnosis and of certitude, "the complete spiritual view penetrating into the reality of religion." It culminates in a mystical extinction in God (*husūl al-fanā'*). Religion is the essential motion of the act of being, its growth and its progressive perfection, and can no more be confused with the law than freedom can be confused with compulsion.

The common man, who is content with an external observance of the divine commandments, is not truly obedient. He is dominated by fear and hope: fear of hell and punishment, hope for a sensual paradise located somewhere in this world. He is gripped by two passions that cause him to return to himself, not to God. The man who confuses religion and external obedience "attests to the fact that his god and the object of his adoration is himself." This degree of obedience is not without utility, but only if it rises above this station to the point where "there remains no more compulsion in religion, no more obstacles on the path of the obedient." But this degree is still foreign to the *true* Islam: "The first degree of the *true* Islam is the station of obedience to the decree *without compulsion*, because one contemplates all of creation through the eyes of obedience, and because one finds by oneself, in all that the term 'religious submission' refers to, the state of obedience." This is an inner religion, a religion of internalization, for which the individual alone is responsible.

This is still only the first degree. A separation remains between the subject of obedience and the object to which internal adherence is directed. There is still some danger of ruining the pure attestation of the divine unity in the abandon practiced through the free act of will. The station of pure extinction and self-effacement is reached only at the moment when abandon, and the freedom that animates it, are transcended in the pure emergence of divine spontaneity, without any distinction between subject and object, between effusion and its receptacle. "It is the dwelling of the people of absolute unity, I do not say of the *tawḥīd* — of the attestation of the divine unity — for the *tawḥīd* is the search for a compulsory unity, and I do not say unification, for although this latter is accomplished by nature and not by compulsion, it has the fragrance of multiplicity about it." This is no longer the stage of the assent to God, nor even of obedience; rather, it is the stage in which one attains the state of the effective servant, pure devotion (*al-'ubūdīyah wa-l-ikhlās*).

At this stage, man reaches the world of the imperative; he loses his subjected, creaturely condition, and undergoes a transfiguration that places him henceforth at the heart of the world of the imperative. He lives in the imperative, having been more than extinguished in God. But the couple freedom/constraint refers to a field of discussions that all depend on the opposition of free will and necessity. Free will belongs to the same order of illusion as the belief that religion and man's destiny are a matter of divine compulsion and the acceptance of it. Sadrā's critique of free will is integral to his critique of compulsion in religion, because he saw perfectly well that the two concepts were in solidarity.

Sadrā opposes the four predicates of the world of the imperative to the regime of compulsion and free will: will, dilection (*al-mahabbah*), love (*al-'ishq*), and ardent desire (*al-shawq*). Will is the imperative spontaneity of God. Love is the secret of the divine essence. Desire is the very essence of existents emanated from God. According to Sadrā, the Mu'tazilī err when they oppose their arguments for free will to the arguments of those for whom God is the sole agent of men's acts. The question is poorly formulated. Confusing creaturely freedom and imperative freedom, it leads to a dead end, to be exploited by adherents of a juridical order that pretends to have the final say on religion. With prudence and irony, Mullā Sadrā grants that juridical statutes based on the letter of the Qur'ānic commandments must be applied. But they do not concern religion, which does not question their validity in the name of some free choice, inseparable from compulsion, but is of another, far superior order. Authentic freedom presupposes a division between the esoteric and the exoteric. It is divine spontaneity lived in the heart of the faithful. The narrow domain of compulsion belongs to the polity. Outside the polity, where there is a question of being and of the act of being, freedom restores the rights of essential desire and of complete and integral love.

Notes

Preface

1. Christian Jambet, *La logique des Orientaux: Henry Corbin et la science des formes* (Paris: Seuil, 1983), published in the series L'Ordre Philosophique, edited by François Wahl.

2. Raymond Schwab, *The Oriental Renaissance: Europe's Rediscovery of India and the East, 1680–1880*, trans. Gene Patterson-Black and Victor Reinking (New York: Columbia University Press, 1984). First published in French in 1950, this book deals primarily with the discovery of India, but it also illuminates the appropriation of Persian culture by the philosophers of German Idealism and, more generally, the intellectual opening of Europe to "Oriental" systems of thought.

3. On contemporary Shīʿite Islam as the result of a long history in which an essentially mystical religion succumbed to a political interpretation of the question of authority, allow me to refer to a work I recently co-authored: Mohammad-Ali Amir-Moezzi and Christian Jambet, *Qu'est-ce que le shî'isme?* (Paris: Fayard, 2004).

4. Ernest Renan, *Averroès et l'averroïsme*, 3rd rev. ed. (Paris: Michel Lévy Frères, 1866).

Introduction

1. G.W.F. Hegel, *Philosophy of Mind: Being Part Three of the Encyclopaedia of the Philosophical Sciences (1830)*, trans. William Wallace and A.V. Miller (Oxford: Clarendon, 1971), sec. 564, p. 297 (Hegel's emphasis; translation emended).

2. Qur'ān 112:1. A note on quotes from the Qur'ān: While I have referred to

the translations by 'Abdullah Yūsuf 'Alī, *The Meaning of the Holy Qur'ān* (Beltsville, MD: Amana Publications, 2001), and Ahmed Ali, *al-Qur'ān: A Contemporary Translation* (Princeton, NJ: Princeton University Press, 1993), and have often borrowed their language, my priority has been to give accurate renderings of Jambet's French quotations for the sake of consistency — Trans.

3. Louis Massignon has shown that Arabic is the language of the Qur'ān not because of a mere contingency but because there occurred a "literal calcination" in "the burning winds of judgment" of the Semitic languages, according to a process that locates the revelation in Hebrew, a blossoming in Aramaic — the language of Christ — and an apocalyptic power in Arabic. Whatever we think of this periodization, which carries within it an entire philosophy of monotheistic religion, Massignon clearly situates within language — within language understood as a "literal desiccation" — what one could call the revelation of the speaker par excellence, as if, in monotheism, man were a "speaker" (*nātiq* in Arabic) because he was summoned to speech by the subject of all speech, the absolute Speaker, the *subject supposed to speak*. See Massignon, "L'arabe langue liturgique de l'Islam" (1935), *Opera Minora* (Paris: Presses Universitaires de France, 1969), vol. 2, pp. 543–46.

4. Muhammad ibn Ibrāhīm Sadr al-Dīn Shīrāzī, *al-Hikmah al-muta'ālīyah fī al-asfār al-'aqlīyah al-arba'ah*, 9 vols. (al-Najaf, Iraq: Dār al-Ma'ārif al-Islāmīyah, 1958).

5. See the *Bibliography of Mullâ Sadrâ*, ed. Nāhīd Bāqirī Khurramdashtī (Tehran: National Library of the Islamic Republic of Iran, 1999).

6. Another such conference took place in May 2004 — Trans.

7. I have translated *l'étant* as "the being" or "beings" (as here) and will use "being" for *l'être*. In cases where this distinction becomes unclear, I have provided the French. Note also that the French word *effectivité* and its cognates, which occur frequently in the present work, have been translated literally as "effectivity" (and so on); it is worth keeping in mind that Jambet's use of this term invokes, in part, the German word *Wirklichkeit*, which in philosophy is often rendered into French as *effectivité* (it is based on *Wirkung*, "effect," and *wirken*, "to effectuate or to actualize"), whereas in English *Wirklichkeit* is usually translated as "reality," or sometimes as "actuality" — Trans.

8. I have most often translated the French *instauration* and its cognates (*instaurer* and so on) as "instantiation" ("instantiate" and so on). Jambet notes that it corresponds to the Arabic *ibda'*, which can also be rendered as "innova-

tion" or "origination"; in general, it designates "the act of immediate, sudden, instantaneous production of being" – TRANS.

9. Roger Savory, *Iran Under the Safavids* (Cambridge: Cambridge University Press, 1980), p. 218.

10. *Ibid.*, p. 23.

11. See the recent overview of the question in Mohammad-Ali Amir-Moezzi, "Contribution à la typologie des rencontres avec l'imâm caché (Aspects de l'imâmologie duodécimaine II)," *Journal Asiatique* 284, no. 1 (1996), pp. 109–35.

12. Andrew J. Newman, "Towards a Reconsideration of the 'Isfāhan School of Philosophy': Shaykh Bahā'ī and the role of the Safawid 'Ulamā," *Studia Iranica* 15, fasc. 2 (1986), pp. 165–99.

13. Muhammad Bāqir al-Astarābādī, died in 1040/1631–32, grandson of al-Karakī, was known as Mīr Dāmād.

14. Said Amir Arjomand, *The Shadow of God and the Hidden Imam: Religion, Political Order, and Societal Change in Shi'ite Iran from the Beginning to 1890* (Chicago: University of Chicago Press, 1984), pp. 133–45.

15. Muhammad ibn Ibrāhīm Sadr al-Dīn Shīrāzī, *Risālah-'i sih asl*, ed. Seyyed Hossein Nasr (Tehran: Dānishkadah-'i 'Ulūm-i Ma'qūl va Manqūl, 1961).

16. Sadr al-Dīn Shīrāzī, *al-Asfār*, vol. 1, p. 2.

17. *Ibid.* Jambet frequently uses the word *science*, which I often translate literally; not to be confused with the modern concept of experimental science, it is more akin to the Latin *scientia* or the German *Wissenschaft*, both of which could be translated very literally as "knowingness." This is especially relevant when it is a question of "divine science" – TRANS.

18. Muhammad ibn Ibrāhīm Sadr al-Dīn Shīrāzī, *Risālat al-hashr*; a French translation of this work is included in Christian Jambet, *Se rendre immortel: Suivi du Traité de la résurrection, Mollâ Sadrâ Shîrâzî* (Saint-Clément-de-Rivière, France: Fata Morgana, 2000), p. 165.

19. This poignant testimony reads, in part, as follows: "When I saw the hostility one brings on oneself in our time for attempting to reform the ignorant and the uncultivated, after seeing the infernal fire of stupidity and aberration burning in all its brightness . . . and after colliding with the incomprehension of people who are blind to the lights and the secrets of wisdom, . . . people whose eyes have never looked beyond the limits of what is materially evident, whose reflection has never risen above their shadowy dwelling places and their dust,

people to whom, because of their hostility to knowledge and to gnosis (*'irfān*), and because they totally reject the path of philosophy (*hikmah*) and of the certitude that has been personally lived (*īqān*), high theosophical knowledge and the inner secrets of gnosis remain inaccessible, the knowledge that the prophets and the Friends of God (*Awlīyā'*) have shown in symbols, and that the philosophers and the gnostics have indicated in turn,... then this suffocation of intelligence and this freezing of nature that have arisen from the hostility of our age compelled me to withdraw to an isolated country, hiding myself in darkness and distress, severed from my hopes, and with a broken heart." Quoted in Henry Corbin's introduction to Muhammad ibn Ibrāhīm Sadr al-Dīn Shīrāzī, *Le livre des pénétrations métaphysiques: Kitâb al-mashâ'ir*, trans. and ed. Henry Corbin, 2nd ed. (Lagrasse, France: Verdier, 1988), p. 14.

20. Sadr al-Dīn Shīrāzī, *al-Asfār*, vol. 1, p. 7ff.

21. Muhammad ibn Ibrāhīm Sadr al-Dīn Shīrāzī, *Tafsīr al-Qur'ān al-karīm*, ed. Muhammad Khvājavī (Qum, Iran: Bīdār, 1987), vol. 3, p. 61.

22. Sadr al-Dīn Shīrāzī, *al-Asfār*, vol. 9, p. 201ff.

23. Muhammad ibn Ibrāhīm Sadr al-Dīn Shīrāzī, *al-Hikmah al-'arshīyah*, 2nd *mashreq* (place of illumination), 1st *ishrāq* (illumination), thesis 11, in James Winston Morris, *The Wisdom of the Throne: An Introduction to the Philosophy of Mulla Sadra* (Princeton, NJ: Princeton University Press, 1981), p. 150.

24. This is the subject of Sadrā's eschatology, which will be addressed in the present work only briefly and in a relatively marginal way. It is laid out in the detailed exegesis of the phases of "lesser" and "greater" resurrection, presented primarily in *al-Asfār* (vol. 9, pp. 185–380), in Muhammad ibn Ibrāhīm Sadr al-Dīn Shīrāzī, *Mafātīh al-ghayb*, ed. Muhammad Khvājavī (Tehran: Mu'assasah-'i Mutāla'āt va Tahqīqāt-i Farhangī, 1984), pp. 619–81, and in *al-Hikmah al-'arshīyah*, where it makes up the entirety of the third *ishrāq* (illumination) in the second *mashreq* (place of illumination). See also Henry Corbin's classic, *Spiritual Body and Celestial Earth: From Mazdean Iran to Shī'ite Iran*, trans. Nancy Pearson (Princeton, NJ: Princeton University Press, 1989) and Morris, *Wisdom of the Throne*, an annotated translation of *al-Hikmah al-'arshīyah*.

25. The fundamental legal prescriptions (prayer, fasting, alms, and pilgrimage) are always mentioned in a moral context and within the larger framework of virtuous actions, the enumeration of which draws on Aristotelianism, the collections of counsels, and so on. The word *sharī'ah* is very rarely used, and professions of faith in the law must be placed in the context of a writing that took

place "in a time of persecution," according to a mode of reading proposed by Leo Strauss, *Persecution and the Art of Writing* (1952; Chicago: University of Chicago Press, 1988).

26. On these authors, see Henry Corbin, *La philosophie iranienne islamique aux XVIIe et XVIIIe siècles* (Paris: Buchet/Chastel, 1981).

27. The author notes that "eduction" (which I translate literally from *éduction*) corresponds to the Arabic *hudūth*, which designates "the mode of existence of temporal beings, in contrast to what is eternal or everlasting." It also designates the emergence of beings into temporal existence — TRANS.

28. At the time of writing, the following works by Sadrā are available to Western readers who do not know Arabic: Muhammad ibn Ibrāhīm Sadr al-Dīn Shīrāzī, *Kitāb al-mashā'ir*, available in English as *The Metaphysics of Mulla Sadra: Kitab al-Masha'ir, The Book of Metaphysical Prehensions*, trans. Parviz Morewedge (New York: Society for the Study of Islamic Philosophy and Science, 1992), based on the Corbin edition cited in n.19; *al-Hikmah al-'arshīyah*, in Morris, *Wisdom of the Throne*; *Traité de la résurrection*, in Jambet, *Se rendre immortel*; *The Elixir of the Gnostics*, trans. William C. Chittick (Provo, UT: Brigham Young University Press, 2003), a translation of *Iksīr al-'ārifīn*.

29. Jambet's French translations have in turn been given English renderings, which he has reviewed and verified against the original texts. In addition, he was kind enough to review the entire manuscript after it was completed, providing comments and contributions for which the editors and I are extremely grateful — TRANS.

CHAPTER ONE: THE WITNESS OF THE REAL

1. Qur'ān 41:53, quoted in *Kitāb al-mashā'ir*, Arabic text edited and translated by Henry Corbin: Muhammad ibn Ibrāhīm Sadr al-Dīn Shīrāzī, *Le livre des pénétrations métaphysiques: Kitâb al-mashâ'ir*, trans. and ed. Henry Corbin, 2nd ed. (Lagrasse, France: Verdier, 1988), p. 88; English translation: Sadr al-Dīn Shīrāzī, *The Metaphysics of Mulla Sadra: Kitab al-Masha'ir, The Book of Metaphysical Prehensions*, trans. Parviz Morewedge (New York: Society for the Study of Islamic Philosophy and Science, 1992), p. 2. Jambet's citations of this work often refer to Corbin's introduction and notes, which are not included in the English translation; for that reason, the French citations will be retained in all cases. When Jambet cites Mullā Sadrā's text itself, references to the English translation are provided — TRANS.

2. *Ahl bayt al-walāyah.* The "people of the house" are the members of the family of the Prophet, the fourteen immaculate ones (Muhammad, Fātimah, and the twelve imams), characterized here by *walāya*, the friendship of God, the source of esoteric knowledge and exoteric prophecy. On this important notion, see Henry Corbin, *En Islam iranien: Aspects spirituels et philosophiques*, vol. 4, *L'Ecole d'Ispahan, l'Ecole shaykhie, le Douzième Imâm* (Paris: Gallimard, 1971); see the index under *walāyat.*

3. Muhammad ibn Ibrāhīm Sadr al-Dīn Shīrāzī, "Mutashābihāt al-Qur'ān," *Sih risālah*, ed. Jalāl al-Dīn Āshtiyānī (Meshed, Iran: Chāp'khānah-'i Dānishgāh-i Mashhad, 1973), p. 86.

4. See Corbin's introduction to *Kitāb al-mashā'ir*, pp. 13–15, *Le livre des pénétrations métaphysiques*, pp. 20–21.

5. Exegesis has its model in the science of the heart, granted to the imams and experienced by Muhammad, particularly during the night of the ascension; see Paul Nwyia, *Exégèse coranique et langage mystique: Nouvel essai sur le lexique technique des mystiques musulmans* (Beirut: Dar el-Machreq, 1970), p. 184ff. To appreciate the difference between this type of exegesis and the method of the *tafsīr*, or the traditional Qur'ānic commentary, see Guy Monnot, "La démarche classique de l'exégèse musulmane," in Michel Tardieu (ed.), *Les règles de l'interprétation* (Paris: Cerf, 1986), pp. 147–61. On Shī'ite exegesis, see Michel Tardieu, "Introduction à l'exégèse duodécimaine," *Annuaire de l'Ecole Pratique des Hautes Etudes* 91 (1982–83), pp. 309–17.

6. Is it still a question of "philosophy"? I would say that it is a question of not only philosophy but the highest philosophy there is in the Muslim world. The exegetic intention is in no way absent from philosophies that, like that of Avicenna, are considered "rational," in contrast with works that, like those of Suhrawardī or Mullā Sadrā, verge on unabashed mysticism. The academic separation between the former (referred to as "Hellenizing") and the latter is an abstraction. Mullā Sadrā is no less "Hellenizing" than al-Fārābī or Avicenna, and Avicenna himself is no less comfortable than Sadrā in practicing Qur'ānic exegesis or in concluding his psychology with a visionary angelology. In the long history of Islamic philosophy, it would be necessary to study the more or less pronounced inflections and emphases of a particular form or scheme, and not meaningless divisions such as that between rationalism and mysticism. It remains true, however, that these inflections have major consequences. On the question of the possible divide between *falsafah* and *hikmah*, see an important

article by Rémi Brague (whose conclusions are different from mine): "Sens et valeur de la philosophie dans les trois cultures médiévales," *Miscellanea Medievalia* 26 (1998), pp. 229–44.

7. Muhammad ibn Ibrāhīm Sadr al-Dīn Shīrāzī, "al-Masā'il al-qudsīyah," *Sih risālah*, p. 6.

8. "The reality (*haqīqah*) of a thing is the singularity of its act of being, through which it is established, for the thing's 'beingness' [*l'étantité de la chose*] and the fact that it possesses a reality have one and the same signification" (*ibid.*, p. 11). (*L'étantité* designates a thing's being a [particular] being, an *étant*; it could be translated as "being-a-being" or as "is-ness." In most cases, I render it with the literal but no less awkward "beingness" – Trans.)

9. Muhammad ibn Ibrāhīm Sadr al-Dīn Shīrāzī, *al-Shawāhid al-rubūbīyah*, ed. Jalāl al-Dīn Āshtiyānī (Meshed, Iran: University Press, 1967), p. 14.

10. Muhammad ibn Ibrāhīm Sadr al-Dīn Shīrāzī, "Kitāb 'aql va-jahl," *Sharh usūl al-kāfī*, ed. Muhammad Khvājavī (Tehran: Mu'assasah-'i Mutala'at va Tahqīqāt-i Farhangī, 1987), p. 218.

11. Muhammad ibn Ibrāhīm Sadr al-Dīn Shīrāzī, *Tafsīr al-Qur'ān al-karīm*, ed. Muhammad Khvājavī (Qum, Iran: Bīdār, 1987), vol. 4, p. 294.

12. I have borrowed this translation of the divine name *al-Qayyūm* from Guy Monnot. See *Annuaire of the Ecole Pratique des Hautes Etudes*, religious studies section, vol. 92 (1988–89), p. 249ff.

13. Sadr al-Dīn Shīrāzī, "Kitāb 'aql va-jahl," p. 228.

14. On the term "imaginal," see Chapter Seven – Trans.

15. An unveiling intuition (*kashf*) is the ultimate point of contemplation by the intelligence. To be sure, it is above intellection, but it is distinct from it not in essence but in its superior degree of perfection. Intelligence that is fully itself is "presential knowledge" and love, but it is not possible truly to transcend it in a union with the unfathomable divine essence. Still, the intelligence is an *apotheosis* "corresponding to the state in which the divine Being is himself the Subject of the acts by which he is known," since this position of the divine subject corresponds to the Intelligence, the receptacle of the influx of divine names. I would thus suggest, in relation to Sadrā, that we give some nuance to Henry Corbin's remarkable analysis concerning metaphysics as *theosophia*, in Henry Corbin, *La philosophie iranienne islamique aux XVIIe et XVIIIe siècles* (Paris: Buchet/Chastel, 1981), p. 351.

16. "Transfiguration of the subject," according to Michel Foucault's expression

in *The Hermeneutics of the Subject: Lectures at the Collège de France, 1981–1982*, trans. Graham Burchell (New York: Palgrave-Macmillan, 2005).

17. Muhammad ibn Ibrāhīm Sadr al-Dīn Shīrāzī, *Mabdā' wa-al-ma'ad*, ed. Jalāl al-Dīn Āshtiyānī and Seyyed Hossein Nasr (Tehran: Anjuman-i Shāhanshāhī-i Falsafah-'i Īrān, 1976), p. 5.

18. *Ibid.*

19. See Henry Corbin, *Temple and Contemplation*, trans. Philip Sherrard and Liadain Sherrard (London: KPI, in association with Islamic Publications, 1986); see the index under *Ka'bah*.

20. See Souâd Ayada, "Le modèle avicennien de la subjectivité," *Revue des sciences philosophiques et théologiques* 83, no. 3 (1999), pp. 491–526.

21. Sadr al-Dīn Shīrāzī, *Mabdā' wa-al-ma'ād*, p. 6.

22. Muhammad ibn Ibrāhīm Sadr al-Dīn Shīrāzī, *al-Hikmah al-muta'ālīyah fī al-asfār al-'aqlīyah al-arba'ah* (al-Najaf, Iraq: Dār al-Ma'arif al-Islāmīyah, 1958), vol. 1, p. 20.

23. This explains the difference in structure between Mullā Sadrā's *Four Spiritual Journeys* and Avicenna's *Book of Healing* or the great *Encyclopedia of the Brethren of Purity*. Self-perfection is already very clearly at the heart of Avicenna's definition of philosophy, since the soul must make itself perfect, through actualized intellection, after perfecting the activity of the body of which it is the form. In this case, however, the perfection of the self, this central theme of ancient philosophy – so opposed to the practices of defiance of the self, critique of the self, and even the radical annihilation of the self, which is valorized by many Sūfī authors – takes on an infinitely more vigorous tone.

24. See the prologue to Yahyá ibn Habash Suhrawardī, *Kitāb hikmat al-ishrāq*: "If in a given period a sage is found who has profoundly penetrated into both mystical experience and philosophical knowledge, earthly authority falls to him, and he is the caliph of God." Yahyá ibn Habash Suhrawardī, *Oeuvres philosophiques et mystiques (Opera metaphysica et mystica, vol. 2): Prolégomènes en français et édition critique*, ed. Henry Corbin (Tehran: Institut franco-iranien, 1952), p. 12, and *Le livre de la sagesse orientale (Kitâb Hikmat al-Ishrâq)*, trans. Henry Corbin, ed. Christian Jambet (Lagrasse, France: Verdier, 1986), p. 90.

25. The word *al-'aql*, translated as "intellect" or "intelligence," has a long history since al-Kindī and al-Fārābī. Its original meaning refers to the power to impede, to constrain, or to shackle [as expressed in the French verb *entraver* – Trans.]. In French, it would be necessary to refer to colloquial expressions in

which *entraver* means to understand something. [The closest English equivalent is perhaps "to get" something, as when one says, "I got it" — Trans.] It is the power of binding, and therefore of judging. In Shīʿite traditions, it is a "supra-rational" power (as Amir-Moezzi puts it) possessed above all by the imams. It is the very name of authentic reason, superior to the understanding. See the remarkable analyses in Mohammad-Ali Amir-Moezzi, *The Divine Guide in Early Shiʿism: The Sources of Esotericism in Islam* (Albany: State University of New York Press, 1994), p. 6ff. The word *ʿaql* is translated there as "hiero-intelligence."

26. Sadr al-Dīn Shīrāzī, *al-Asfār*, vol. 3, p. 108ff.

27. Allow me to refer to Christian Jambet, "Idéal du politique et politique idéale selon Nâsir al-Dîn Tûsî," in Nasr Allah Pourjavady and Ziva Vesel (eds.), *Nasir al-Din Tusi: Philosophe et savant du XIIIe siècle* (Tehran: Institut français de recherche en Iran, 2000), pp. 31–57.

28. This is why metaphysics, in Islam, opens the way to messianic waiting. This is demonstrated in Ismāʿīlism and in readings of the imams' sayings by Twelver Shīʿite philosophers. The question of the messiah thus appears to be the central question of historicity and temporality in Shīʿite Islam, but also, in a silent way, in Islam as a whole. Platonism reaches its fulfillment in messianism.

29. Avicenna's *Metaphysics* ends with a reflection on the city and on the enlightened guide it needs. It thus has an authentically political finality. The *Four Spiritual Journeys* ends with a personal eschatology. This simple fact calls for reflection.

30. See Muhsin Mahdi, *Alfarabi and the Foundation of Islamic Political Philosophy* (Chicago: University of Chicago Press, 2001), pp. 125–46.

31. See al-Kindī, *Al-Kindi's Metaphysics: A Translation of al-Kindi's Treatise "On First Philosophy,"* ed. Alfred L. Ivry (Albany: State University of New York Press, 1974), p. 55 (translation of al-Kindī emended). Ivry compares al-Kindī's statement to one in Plato's *Theaetetus* (176b): "becoming like God insofar as is possible for man" (*ibid.*, p. 117).

32. Even today, the word *maʿjūn* refers to a very popular drug that is chewed to produce effects similar to those of opium or hashish.

33. That is why it is difficult to define wisdom without speaking of practical exercises. Mullā Sadrā confirms what Pierre Hadot wrote of Plotinus: "Contemplation is not abstract knowledge but self-transformation." Pierre Hadot, *What Is Ancient Philosophy?*, trans. Michael Chase (Cambridge, MA: Harvard University Press, 2002), p. 158.

34. Sadr al-Dīn Shīrāzī, "Kitāb 'aql va-jahl," p. 373ff.

35. Yahyá ibn Habash Suhrawardī, "Kitāb al-talwīhāt," *Oeuvres philosophiques et mystiques*, ed. Seyyed Hossein Nasr and Henry Corbin, 2nd ed. (Tehran: Académie Impériale Iranienne de Philosophie, 1976–77), p. 2 of the Arabic text.

36. *Ibid.*, p. 3.

37. See Henry Corbin's prolegomena in Suhrawardī, *Oeuvres philosophiques et mystiques*, pp. xx–xxi.

38. Henry Corbin, *Itinéraire d'un enseignement: Résumé des conférences à l'Ecole Pratique des Hautes Etudes (Section des sciences religieuses), 1955–1979* (Tehran: Institut français de recherche en Iran, 1993), p. 33. The author shows that, via Mullā Sadrā, Islamic metaphysics—indissolubly bound to a divine science—did not undergo "the evolution that eventually led in the West (with Christian Wolff in the eighteenth century) to the secularization of ontology."

39. Muhammad ibn Ibrāhīm Sadr al-Dīn Shīrāzī, "Kitāb al-tawhīd," *Sharh usūl al-kāfī*, p. 67.

40. Among the abundant literature on the *Theology of Aristotle*, I will refer only to the overview of recent research presented in Jill Kraye, Charles B. Schmitt, and W.F. Ryan (eds.), *Pseudo-Aristotle in the Middle Ages: The Theology and Other Texts* (London: Warburg Institute, University of London, 1986).

41. Avicenna, *al-Shifa: al-Ilahiyyat (La métaphysique)*, ed. Georges C. Anawati and Sa'id Zayid (Cairo: Organisation générale des imprimeries gouvernementales, 1960), p. 2.

42. *Ibid.*, pp. 2–3.

43. The importance and the stakes of this question are admirably clarified by Etienne Gilson, "Avicenne et le point de départ de Duns Scot," *Pourquoi Saint Thomas a critiqué Saint Augustin; suivi de Avicenne et le point de départ de Duns Scot* (1926; Paris: Vrin, 1981), p. 133ff. See also Gilson, *Jean Duns Scot: Introduction à ses positions fondamentales* (Paris: Vrin, 1952), p. 73ff.

44. Avicenna, *al-Ilahiyyat*, p. 4.

45. On the inherent difficulties of Aristotle's text, see the very substantive remarks of W.D. Ross, *Aristotle*, 5th ed. (London: Methuen, 1977), pp. 156–59, and see especially the ingenious and profound discussion in Pierre Aubenque, *Le problème de l'être chez Aristote*, 2nd ed. (Paris: Presses Universtaires de France, 1966), pp. 368–411.

46. Avicenna, *al-Ilahiyyat*, p. 6.

47. *Ibid.*, p. 7.

48. *Ibid.*, p. 12.

49. *Ibid.*

50. Mīr Findariskī was one of Mullā Sadrā's most important contemporaries in philosophy: he died the same year as Sadrā, in 1050/1640–41. I am referring here to his *Treatise on the Arts and Human Activities* (*Risaleh-yi sana'iyeh*), written in Persian, published in Jalāl al-Dīn Āshtīyānī and Henry Corbin (eds.), *Anthologie des philosophes iraniens depuis le XVIIe siècle jusqu'à nos jours*, vol. 1 (Tehran: Département d'iranologie de l'Institut franco-iranien de recherche, 1972). He writes that "philosophers take the path of science through practice and discursive thought, whereas the prophets possess inspiration and revelation. They do not know things through discursive thought" (p. 71 of the Persian text).

51. Plotinus, *Theology of Aristotle*, in *Aflūtīn 'inda al-'Arab*, ed. 'Abd al-Rahmān Badawī (Cairo: Maktabat al-Nahdah al-Misrīyah, 1955).

CHAPTER TWO: THE LIGHT OF BEING

1. Muhammad ibn Ibrāhīm Sadr al-Dīn Shīrāzī, *al-Shawāhid al-rubūbīyah*, ed. Jalāl al-Dīn Āshtiyānī (Meshed, Iran: University Press, 1967), p. 6.

2. I will not address at any length here the problem posed by this vocabulary of being, the essential aspects of which are presented by Etienne Gilson, in *L'être et l'essence* (Paris: Vrin, 1948), and, in relation to Mullā Sadrā, by Henry Corbin, in his introduction to Muhammad ibn Ibrāhīm Sadr al-Dīn Shīrāzī, *Le livre des pénétrations métaphysiques: Kitâb al-mashâ'ir*, trans. and ed. Henry Corbin, 2nd ed. (Lagrasse, France: Verdier, 1988), pp. 58–64.

3. "The act of being is existent by itself, whereas other things, which are not the act of being, are existent not by themselves but rather through the acts of being that come to them." Muhammad ibn Ibrāhīm Sadr al-Dīn Shīrāzī, *al-Hikmah al-muta'ālīyah fī al-asfār al-'aqlīyah al-arba'ah* (al-Najaf, Iraq: Dār al-Ma'arif al-Islāmīyāh, 1958), vol. 1, p. 39. See Sadr al-Dīn Shīrāzī, *Le livre des pénétrations métaphysiques*, p. 91 (*The Metaphysics of Mulla Sadra: Kitab al-Masha'ir, The Book of Metaphysical Prehensions*, trans. Parviz Morewedge [New York: Society for the Study of Islamic Philosophy and Science, 1992], pp. 3–4), and *Mafātīh al-ghayb*, ed. Muhammad Khvājavī (Tehran: Mu'assasah-'i Mutāla'at va Tahqīqāt-i Farhangī, 1984), p. 321.

4. Sadrian ontology has nothing in common with the philosophies of "existence." Great confusion on this point has reigned among several modern

thinkers in the Muslim world, who have attempted to compare Mullā Sadrā with Sartre or even Heidegger. See, for example, Alparslan Açikgenç, *Being and Existence in Sadra and Heidegger: A Comparative Ontology* (Kuala Lumpur: International Institute of Islamic Thought and Civilization, 1993).

5. See Sadr al-Dīn Shīrāzī, *Le livre des pénétrations métaphysiques*, pp. 93 and 102ff. (*Metaphysics of Mulla Sadra*, p. 6ff.): existence is not an existent possessing existence, but "its act of being existent is precisely its very act of being existence."

6. The "Glosses" on *The Philosophy of Illumination* (*Kitāb hikmat al-ishrāq*) are included in the margins of the lithographed edition of this work (Tehran, 1315h.), and many of them were translated by Henry Corbin. This translation was published in Yahyá ibn Habash Suhrawardī, *Le livre de la sagesse orientale (Kitâb Hikmat al-Ishrâq)*, trans. Henry Corbin, ed. Christian Jambet (Lagrasse, France: Verdier, 1986), pp. 439–669. On Sadrā's critique of Suhrawardī, see Fazlur Rahman, *The Philosophy of Mulla Sadra* (*Sadr al-Din al-Shirazi*) (Albany: State University of New York Press, 1975), p. 31ff.

7. See the very detailed study by Paul Ballanfat: "Considérations sur la conception du coeur chez Mullâ Sadrâ," *Kâr-Nâmeh, Cahier de l'Association pour la Recherche Interdisciplinaire en Littérature Persane* 5 (1999), pp. 33–46, and 6 (2000), pp. 67–84.

8. Aristotle, *Metaphysics* 7.1.1028a. It should certainly be granted that "the doctrine consistently found in Aristotle is that existence precedes essence . . . that for what is, only what 'is' (*esti*) can have a 'what it is' (*ti esti*)"; Barbara Cassin and Michel Narcy (eds.), *La décision du sens: Le livre Gamma de la Métaphysique d'Aristote* (Paris: Vrin, 1989). In this sense, Sadrā is profoundly Aristotelian. But for Aristotle, being in its fundamental sense is what language grasps of substance in its quiddity, "its individual and determinate essence"; "there is a quiddity only of those things whose formula is a definition" (*Metaphysics* 7.4.1029b).

9. Sadr al-Dīn Shīrāzī, *Le livre des pénétrations métaphysiques*, p. 94; *Metaphysics of Mulla Sadra*, p. 13.

10. Sadr al-Dīn Shīrāzī, *al-Asfār*, vol. 1, p. 37: "Everything from concrete realities that is impressed, in its essence, in thoughts — this can only be their quiddity, which takes the place of their act of existing. As for being, since its effective reality resides in concrete individuals, it is impossible for it to reside in thoughts."

11. *Ibid.*, p. 263ff.; Sadr al-Dīn Shīrāzī, *al-Shawāhid al-rubūbīyah*, pp. 24–29.

12. The images of the titles ("Illumination," "Dawn rises to dissolve a shadow," and so on) are meant to say that the evidence of being is unveiled according to illuminations of the heart and the intelligence. But the metaphysical investigation that leads to a recognition of this evidence necessarily takes the form of demonstrations, or dialectical argument.

13. Sadr al-Dīn Shīrāzī, *al-Shawāhid al-rubūbīyah*, pp. 6–7.

14. Sadr al-Dīn Shīrāzī *al-Asfār*, vol. 1, p. 49. The essences referred to here are the archetypes of existents, which Ibn al-'Arabī called *al-a'yān al-thābitah*. The word *al-'ayn*, plural *al-a'yān*, means concrete essence, effective reality. It is distinguished from the word *al-dhāt*, which is translated as "essence." Sadrā interprets the discourse of the disciples of Ibn al-'Arabī as saying that the eternal essences are quiddities.

15. *Connaissance*: this word can be translated as both "knowledge" and "cognition" (I have most often chosen the former). In this context, it is worth stressing the implications of *connaissance*, both as effective knowledge of what is directly apprehended and as "cognition" in the sense of the mental or intellectual process of knowing, leaning in both cases toward the sense of "consciousness" — Trans.

16. Material forms are thus continually "fading and passing away," doomed to nothingness, and yet they are nonetheless the image and the icon of psychic and spiritual forms. Sadrā borrows his vocabulary of the icon (*sanam*) from Suhrawardī.

17. Sadrā's conception of mental existence differs fundamentally from the notion of the *objective* reality of the idea as it is found in Descartes, for example. For Sadrā, the reality of the soul is defined in Neoplatonic terms.

18. There are three types of singularization (*takhassus*) for each act of being: through its effective reality, through its relative degrees of priority and posteriority — intensity or weakness — and, finally, through its substrate. The first two types refer to the very reality of the existent; they designate a singularity intrinsic to this existent. The third type of singularization refers to the fact that the existent receives a particular quiddity; it is therefore a purely intellectual procedure, even if the act of being and quiddity are fundamentally united in the concrete. Sadr al-Dīn Shīrāzī, *al-Asfār*, vol. 1, p. 44ff.

19. See *ibid.*, p. 50ff.

20. Henry Corbin poses the question of the *absolvens*, that which absolves

being and must have a higher rank than the absolute (*absolutum*); see *La philosophie iranienne islamique aux XVIIe et XVIIIe siècles* (Paris: Buchet/Chastel, 1981), p. 65ff.

21. Sadr al-Dīn Shīrāzī, *al-Asfār*, vol. 2, p. 82ff.

22. Avicenna, *Kitāb al-najāt fī al-hikmah al-mantiqīyah wa-al-tabī'īyah wa-al-ilāhīyah* (Beirut: Dār al-Āfāq al-Jadīdah, 1985). Necessary being has neither an opposite nor a likeness: that is what Mullā Sadrā says of the act of being as such, by which it appears that the act of being as such is obviously God. Being, the real, and God, taken in absolute terms, are identical.

23. *Ibid.*, p. 343.

24. The verb used by Sadrā is *idmahallah* (in French, *évanouissement*) — TRANS.

25. The term "fading" (in English in the original) recalls Jacques Lacan's use of this word in English; see, for example, "The Subversion of the Subject and the Dialectic of Desire in the Freudian Unconscious," *Ecrits: A Selection*, trans. Alan Sheridan (New York: Norton, 1977), p. 314 — TRANS.

26. Sadr al-Dīn Shīrāzī, *al-Asfār*, vol. 1, p. 348.

27. *Ibid.*, p. 350.

28. *Ibid.*, p. 341. This conclusion is in agreement with Proclus, *On the Existence of Evils*, trans. Jan Opsomer and Carlos Steel (Ithaca, NY: Cornell University Press, 2003).

29. Sadr al-Dīn al-Qūnawī was the son-in-law of Ibn al-'Arabī, whose doctrine he systematized. He died in 671/1272 or 673/1273–74. His ontology is of great importance for Mullā Sadrā, but this will have to be examined elsewhere.

30. Sadr al-Dīn Shīrāzī, *al-Shawāhid al-rubūbīyah*, pp. 6–7.

31. It should be stressed here that this has no relationship whatsoever to the analyses of Emmanuel Lévinas.

32. Proclus, *The Elements of Theology*, ed. E.R. Dodds, 2nd ed. (Oxford: Clarendon, 1963), p. 79 (translation emended).

33. *Ibid.*, p. 93 (translation emended).

34. Sadr al-Dīn Shīrāzī, *al-Shawāhid al-rubūbīyah*, p. 10.

35. This word is usually translated in the Qur'ān as "the self-subsisting" — TRANS.

36. Muhammad ibn Ibrāhīm Sadr al-Dīn Shīrāzī, *Tafsīr al-Qur'ān al-karīm*, ed. Muhammad Khvājavī (Qum, Iran: Bīdār, 1987), vol. 4, pp. 88–95 (on Qur'ān 2:255).

37. I used this concept to designate the status of the One in Shīʿite ontology in a work on the Ismāʿīlī Shīʿism of the Alamūt period. See Christian Jambet, *La grande résurrection d'Alamût: Les formes de la liberté dans le shi'isme ismaélien* (Lagrasse, France: Verdier, 1990), pp. 139–76.

38. Sadr al-Dīn Shīrāzī, *al-Shawāhid al-rubūbīyah*, p. 7.

39. *Ibid.*, p. 8.

40. *Ibid.*, pp. 7–8.

41. Abū al-Hasan Bahmanyār ibn al-Marzubān, died in 458/1066.

42. Sadr al-Dīn Shīrāzī, *al-Shawāhid al-rubūbīyah*, p. 9.

43. *Ibid.*, p. 10.

44. *Ibid.*, p. 11.

45. At the risk of adding yet another language to the many already in play here, it is worth noting that the terms Jambet uses cannot fail to evoke the Heideggerian notions of *Befindlichkeit* (loosely, the fact of "finding" oneself, and what is, within a certain determinate situation) and *Da-sein* (being-there) —TRANS.

46. Sadr al-Dīn Shīrāzī, *al-Shawāhid al-rubūbīyah*, p. 12.

47. Attributed by Sadrā to Avicenna's *Kitāb al-Tāʿlīqāt*, quoted in *ibid.*, p. 12.

48. *Ibid.*, p. 13.

49. Nasīr al-Dīn al-Tūsī, *Kitāb Sharh al-Ishārāt*, in *Ibn Sīnā, al-Ishārāt wa-l-tanbīhāt* (n.p.: Daftar Nashr al-Kitāb, 1403 h.), vol. 3, p. 245. Tūsī writes: "When a thing proceeds from the First Originator, this thing possesses an ipseity that is different from the First, and necessarily so. The concept of its being-emanated from the First [Principle] is something other than the fact, for it, of possessing a particular ipseity. There are thus two intelligized realities here: first, the reality that proceeds from the First [Principle], which we call *existence*; second, the ipseity that is concomitant to this act of existing, which we call *quiddity*. This latter, from the point of view of the concrete existent, follows this existence. Indeed, if the First Originator did not make this thing, there would be no quiddity at all. But, from the point of view of the intelligence, it is existence that follows quiddity, for existence is then an attribute of quiddity."

50. See the analysis of the union of the intelligence and the intelligible in Part Three.

51. Sadr al-Dīn Shīrāzī, *al-Shawāhid al-rubūbīyah*, p. 14.

Chapter Three: The Avicennian Moment

1. Muhammad ibn Ibrāhīm Sadr al-Dīn Shīrāzī, *Le livre des pénétrations métaphysiques: Kitâb al-mashā'ir*, trans. and ed. Henry Corbin, 2nd ed. (Lagrasse, France: Verdier, 1988), p. 57.

2. Avicenna, *al-Mantiq: Book One, Isagoge, of the Part of al-Shifa' of Ibn Sina Dealing with Logic*, ed. Ibrāhīm Madkūr (Cairo: al-Matba'ah al-Āmīrīyah, 1952), p. 14.

3. I will not address here the question of whether Avicenna is himself a radical beginning. This question has received various responses that indicate Avicenna's multiple dependencies and underscore the lack of absolute beginnings in philosophy. This is a historical question with a perfectly legitimate place, but it is not the question I am attempting to ask here. Nor is it my goal to situate Sadrā historically. My aim is to examine how Sadrā modifies what he receives as an absolute beginning, namely Avicenna's metaphysics. In short, how is Iranian Avicennism, for Sadrā, something like a pedestal that can be modified but is nonetheless constitutive, and what are its characteristics? The exposition that follows is offered in this sense and does not claim to provide an "objective truth" concerning Avicenna, a truth I doubt one can know outside its effective development in its real element, the Muslim East. The fact is that there is no real becoming in philosophy without the affirmation of an absolute beginning, and without granting a future generated by this beginning.

4. The expression "that which is above perfection" (*fawq al-tammām*) is used by Avicenna to mean "that with which existence is superabundant outside itself." But it is used to describe what "the philosophers" think and not what he himself thinks, although he shows no antipathy for this conception. Mullā Sadrā will adopt it to designate the principle. See Avicenna, *al-Shifa: al-Ilahiyyat (La Métaphysique)*, ed. Georges C. Anawati and Sa'id Zayid (Cairo: Organisation générale des imprimeries gouvernementales, 1960), p. 188.

5. *Ma'nah al-wujūd, ma'nah al-shay'*; *ibid.*, bk. 1, ch. 5, p. 31.

6. Guy Monnot, *Penseurs musulmans et religions iraniennes: 'Abd al-Jabbar et ses devanciers* (Paris: Vrin, 1974), p. 40.

7. On the notion of "thing" in Avicenna, see Robert Wisnovsky, "Notes on Avicenna's Concept of Thingness (Shay'iyya)," *Arabic Sciences and Philosophy* 10, no. 2 (2000), pp. 181–221, and Jean Jolivet, "Aux origines de l'ontologie d'Ibn Sînâ," in Jean Jolivet and Rushdi Rashid (eds.), *Etudes sur Avicennne* (Paris: Belles Lettres, 1984). On "entities," see Avicenna, in Muhammad ibn 'Abd al-Karīm

Shahrastanī, *Livre des religions et des sectes*, vol. 2 (Paris: UNESCO, 1993), p. 408. (I have given the cognate of the French word from Jolivet's translation that Jambet refers to here: *entités* — TRANS.)

8. Indeed, these two "significations" will be universal significations, and "no individuality will ever result from adding something universal to the universal" (Sadr al-Dīn Shīrāzī, *Le livre des pénétrations métaphysiques*, p. 97).

9. See A.M. Goichon, *Lexique de la langue philosophique d'Ibn Sînâ (Avicenne)* (Paris: Desclée de Brouwer, 1938), p. 78. On Aristotle's reference to the distinction between the fact of being and essence (in *Posterior Analytics* 2.7.92b10), see Goichon, *La distinction de l'essence et de l'existence d'après Ibn Sînâ (Avicenne)* (Paris: Desclée de Brouwer, 1937), p. 132.

10. This is the ultimate and founding decision, which Sadrā will also adopt: the fact that the existent *is* is not in itself determined by a radical contingency. The ontology of our contemporaries (it is quite evident in Heidegger) stands in sharp contrast to this decision.

11. Toshihiko Izutsu, "The Fundamental Structure of Sabzawari's Metaphysics," in Hādī ibn Mahdī Sabzavārī, *Sharh-i ghurar al-farā'id*, pt. 1, *Metaphysics*, ed. Mahdī Muhaqqiq and Toshihiko Izutsu (Tehran: Institute of Islamic Studies, McGill University, Tehran Branch, 1969), p. 66.

12. The division (*al-qismah*) between the sensible and the intelligible is not, for Avicenna, the division between "two things" in each thing, "like two men within the contents of the entity of humanity," a sensible man and an intelligible man. There is no "archetypal existence" (*wujūd al-mithālī*). This has enormous consequences: on the one hand, Avicenna does not think of quiddity as an "archetype" (*mithāl*) or as the reflection of an archetype. Moreover, this major term, *al-mithāl*, is explicitly located within a Platonic conception and is rejected as such. Its subsequent fate in Islamic ontology is well known; one will speak, for example, of an *'ālam al-mithāl*, a *mundus imaginalis*, a world of image-archetypes, or of an intelligible world, *'ālam 'aqlī,* also thought within an archetypal schema. Avicenna, for his part, does not conceive of a "separate intelligible reality" (*al-ma'nah al-ma'qūl al-mufāriq*), which becomes an issue only through a kind of "lapse," a sliding or slippage that occurs in Socrates and Plato. See Avicenna, *al-Ilahiyyat*, bk. 7, ch. 2, p. 310ff.

13. *Ibid.*, bk. 1, ch. 5, p. 32.

14. *Ibid.*, p. 31.

15. What I mean by contradiction here is not that Avicenna's definitions are

fraught with logical absurdity, which would be quite surprising, but that they testify to a movement immanent to the existent and passing between quiddity and existence, a movement that characterizes the Avicennian moment as such. The term of this movement will be stated by Hegel: essence *is* existence. This is precisely what is aimed at by the ontology of Islam in Sadrā. In Hegelian terms, the movement will never reach the threshold of the effective Concept, but it will reach that of the essence whose being consists in existing, or pure essence.

16. Avicenna, *al-Ilahiyyat*, bk. 5, ch. 1, p. 200.

17. *Ibid.*, ch. 6, p. 231.

18. *Ibid.*, p. 232.

19. Avicenna, *al-Mantiq*, vol. 1, p. 28.

20. *Ibid.*

21. *Ibid.*, p. 37.

22. Avicenna, *al-Ilahiyyat*, bk. 5, ch. 8, p. 244ff.

23. *Ibid.*, p. 245 (my emphasis).

24. This expression has an important place in the discourse of Jacques Lacan, where it is usually translated as "lack to being." See "Problèmes cruciaux pour la psychanalyse," *Autres écrits* (Paris: Seuil, 2001), pp. 199–202 – Trans.

25. Avicenna, *al-Mantiq*, vol. 1, ch. 6, p. 34.

26. *Ibid.*

27. *Ibid.*, vol. 1, p. 15.

28. *Ibid.*, p. 22.

29. Avicenna, *al-Ilahiyyat*, bk. 5, ch. 1, p. 198.

30. *Ibid.*, p. 199.

31. *Ibid.*, p. 201.

32. *Ibid.*

33. *Ibid.*, pp. 201–202.

34. *Ibid.*, p. 203.

35. *Ibid.*, p. 204.

36. Goichon quotes Avicenna in relation to nature in itself: *mutaqaddimah fī-l-wujūd* (nature in itself "precedes in being"). And she asks: "What then is the existence proper to nature in itself? In what sense does Avicenna say that essence preexists not only concrete nature, which goes without saying, but even intelligible nature? Since it cannot be a question of a return to the Platonic Ideas, nature in itself is the nature whose being is the divine being itself, it is thought by God inseparably from God's own essence, and God thinks and acts necessar-

ily, such that nature in itself will receive the concomitant of concrete or mental existence" (*Distinction*, pp. 80–84).

37. Avicenna, *al-Ilahiyyat*, bk. 8, ch. 4, p. 343.

38. *Ibid.*, p. 344.

39. Unless it is thought that existence cannot be deduced *a priori*, but can *only* be experienced in empirical cognition, which radically modifies the status of existence. This is what Kant does, such that the result of his critique is present in the very foundation this critique is given in the existential status of the phenomenon. But we know that this gives rise to a question: What about the being of the thing in itself? Does Avicenna deduce *a priori* the existence of God? He maintains that existence is observed empirically. But it is observed among possible existents, and the possibility of existing assumes, logically and *in reality*, the priority of the necessity of existing. The existent that is necessary through itself therefore necessarily exists. Avicenna would not grant Kant's notion that the concept of the necessary existence of God falls within the domain of reason, in the Kantian sense of the term, or that it is a question of the Idea of the "maximum" of existence, formed from the representation of *possible* existence. Indeed, existence, in God, is not a predicate, and to say that God necessarily exists is not to think in God the maximum of existence, imagined as a predicate.

40. Avicenna, *al-Ilahiyyat*, bk. 8, ch. 4, p. 346.

41. *Ibid.*, p. 353.

42. *Ibid.*, ch. 6, p. 355.

43. *Ibid.*, p. 356.

44. *Ibid.*, ch. 7, p. 362ff.

45. *Ibid.*, p. 363.

46. *Ibid.*, p. 366.

47. 'Abd al-Rahmān Badawī, *Aflūtīn 'inda al-'Arab* (Cairo: Dār al-Nahdah al-Arabīyah, 1966), p. 22. The thinkers of Islam interpret this passage as if it described the experience of union with the One. According to Dominic J. O'Meara, it is rather a question of a union with the intelligible: see *Plotinus: An Introduction to the Enneads* (Oxford: Clarendon, 1993), ch. 10.

48. Avicenna, *al-Ilahiyyat*, bk. 8, ch. 7, p. 368.

49. *Ibid.*, p. 369.

50. Avicenna, *al-Ishārāt wa-al-tanbīhāt*, ed. Sulaymān Dunyā, pt. 1 (Cairo: Dār al-Ma'ārif, 1947), p. 154.

51. *Ibid.*, pp. 158–62. Goichon usefully recalls these definitions: the

constitutive is the thing intrinsic to quiddity; the concomitant (*lāzim*) is that which will necessarily qualify the thing after the verification of its essence, insofar as that follows its essence, but not insofar as it is intrinsic to the truth of its essence. The accidental character is the one by which the thing is sometimes described, provided that it is not necessary that the thing always be described by it (*Distinction*, pp. 111–12). Goichon's book is very useful, although the solution she adopts is problematic. As stated above, we must be wary of saying that quiddities exist in the divine science, absolutely speaking; rather, it must be said that they are established in it—in the pure potency of existing—without confusing this in the least with the conception of a "divine understanding" distinct from the divine unity.

52. Louis Gardet, *La pensée religieuse d'Avicenne (Ibn Sînâ)* (Paris: Vrin, 1951), p. 61.

53. That this contingency of existence is a literary phenomenon and not at all a concept is made clear in *Nausea* by the metaphorical exuberance of its ontological descriptions. *Existence* becomes the weapon of choice in this novel's war against philosophy. And, no doubt, it is a war well waged. Jean-Paul Sartre, *Nausea*, trans. Lloyd Alexander (New York: New Directions, 1964).

54. Avicenna, *al-Ilahiyyat*, bk. 1, ch. 5, p. 35. See Avicenna, *al-Mantiq: Book Four, al-Qiyas, On the Syllogism, of the Part of al-Shifa' of Ibn Sina Dealing with Logic*, ed. Ibrāhīm Madkūr (Cairo: al-Hay'ah al-'Āmmah li-Shu'ūn al-Matābi' al-Amīrīyah, 1964), pt. 3, ch. 4, p. 162ff.

55. Hence, "there is no universal that cannot be reduced to the possible. Even death, since this is indeed the only point upon which death can be articulated. However universal we posit it to be, it always remains only possible." Jacques Lacan, "L'étourdit," *Autres écrits*, p. 451.

56. It is in this sense that we must understand the following: "Since there is no whole, nothing is everything." See Jacques Lacan, "Radiophonie," *Autres écrits*, p. 441.

57. Avicenna, *al-Ilahiyyat*, bk. 1, ch. 5, p. 36.

58. *Tychē* and *automaton*; see Aristotle, *Physics* 2.4.196a.

59. Muhammad ibn Ibrāhīm Sadr al-Dīn Shīrāzī, *Tafsīr al-Qur'ān al-karīm*, ed. Muhammad Khvājavī (Qum, Iran: Bīdār, 1987), vol. 4, p. 212.

60. Such a history has yet to be undertaken. It is rendered all the more difficult by the fact that "Avicennism" in the Muslim world is a term with multiple and often contradictory meanings.

61. In Avicenna, God has no need to be in some way "absolved," nor is he, rigorously speaking, "absolute," since he could never be compared with relative realities.

62. Nasīr al-Dīn al-Tūsī (597/1201–672/1274) is a particularly colorful figure in Islamic politics, science, and philosophy. Carried away by the Ismā'īlī Shī'ite adventure to the point of going to live with the imam of Alamūt, whom he eventually betrayed – no doubt out of pragmatism – to the Mongol invaders, he converted late in life to Twelver Shī'ism (or he returned to this doctrine after spending years in the service of radical Ismā'īlism). He was a mathematical genius, an astronomer, and a philosopher of the first order, and he wrote a commentary on Avicenna's *Ishārāt* that would long serve as the basis for future readings. He is one of Mullā Sadrā's major points of reference. For a minimal bibliography, see Nasr Allah Pourjavady and Ziva Vesel (eds.), *Nasir al-Din Tusi: Philosophe et savant du XIIIe siècle* (Tehran: Institut français de recherche en Iran, 2000). The philosopher's autobiography is now available in an excellent edition and translation by S.J. Badakhchani, *Contemplation and Action: The Spiritual Autobiography of a Muslim Scholar* (London: Tauris, 1998).

63. Avicenna, *Livre des directives et remarques*, trans. A.M. Goichon (Paris: Vrin, 1951), p. 362. Tūsī's text and commentary, as well as Rāzī's commentary, can be found in Sulaymān Dunyā's edition of Avicenna, *al-Ishārāt wa-al-tanbīhāt*, pt. 3 (Cairo: Dār al-Ma'ārif, 1966), p. 30ff.

64. Fakhr al-Dīn Rāzī was born in Rayy, a city close to present-day Tehran, in 543/1149 and died in Herat in 606/1209; he left behind an immense amount of work as a philosopher, theologian, and commentator on the Qur'ān. Sadrā places him within the lineage of those who claim that God, in his instantiation of beings, gives priority to quiddities. To this Sadrā opposes the priority of the act of being and thus rescues the meaning of spiritual practices (cf. Sadr al-Dīn Shīrāzī, *Tafsīr al-Qur'ān*, vol. 1, pp. 48–50).

65. The question of the meaning of the word *al-tashkīk*, rendered here for the sake of convenience as "analogy," is quite thorny. We will return to it later, in a more direct discussion of Sadrā's analogy, in which this term plays an important role. I will refer for now to the remarkably clear and well-informed study of the problem by Cécile Bonmariage, "Le réel et les réalités: La structure de la réalité de l'être chez Mullâ Sadrâ Shîrâzî," Ph.D. diss., Université catholique de Louvain, Institut supérieur de philosophie, 1998, vol. 1, p. 67ff. Bonmariage's translation of *tashkīk* as "modulation" works very well.

66. See Christian Jambet, *Se rendre immortel: Saivi du Traité de la resurrection, Mollâ Sadrâ Shîrâzî* (Saint-Clément-de-Rivière, France: Fata Morgana, 2000), pp. 7–11. The concept of intensity is indispensable to philosophers influenced by some form of Neoplatonism, such as Gilles Deleuze, whose use of the term, however, is very different from Sadrā's. Deleuze says "becoming-animal"; Sadrā says "becoming-angel": the final ends are antagonistic, but they have comparable grounds. Here is Bergson's definition most suited to an understanding of this common ground: "Things have happened just as though an immense current of consciousness, interpenetrated with potenialities of every kind, had traversed matter to draw it towards organization and make it, notwithstanding that it is necessity itself, an instrument of freedom." Henri Bergson, *Mind-Energy: Lectures and Essays*, trans. H. Wildon Carr (New York: Henry Holt and Co., 1920), p. 25.

Chapter Four: Freedom and Intensity

1. Muhammad ibn Ibrāhīm Sadr al-Dīn Shīrāzī, *al-Hikmah al-muta ʻālīyah fi al-asfār al-aqlīyah al-arbaʻah*, (al-Najaf, Iraq: Dār al-Maʻārif al-Islāmīyah, 1958), vol. 1, p. 48.

2. "Being, or existing, is therefore the reality of everything that possesses a reality, but it does not itself need some other reality in order to possess a reality." See Muhammad ibn Ibrāhīm Sadr al-Dīn Shīrāzī, *Kitāb al-Mashāʻir*, sec. 16: *Le livre des pénétrations métaphysiques: Kitâb al-Mashâʻir*, trans. and ed. Henry Corbin, 2nd ed. (Lagrasse, France: Verdier, 1988), p. 91, and *The Metaphysics of Mulla Sadra: Kitab al-Mashaʻir, The Book of Metaphysical Prehensions*, trans. Parviz Morewedge (New York: Society for the Study of Islamic Philosophy and Science, 1992), p. 10.

3. Sadr al-Dīn Shīrāzī, *al-Asfār*, vol. 1, p. 340ff.

4. We have seen that Avicenna distinguished quiddity in the *lā bi-shart* state (the state without condition), in the *bi sharti-lā* state (the condition negating all determination, the universal concept), and in *bi-shart-shay'*, a state determined by the condition of something else (concrete individuality). Sadrā demonstrates that none of these states possesses reality through itself. See Sadr al-Dīn Shīrāzī, *Le livre des pénétrations métaphysiques*, p. 186.

5. Sadr al-Dīn Shīrāzī, *al-Asfār*, vol. 1, p. 49.

6. Sadr al-Dīn Shīrāzī, *Kitāb al-Mashāʻir*, sec. 54 (*ittisāf al-māhīyah bi-l-wujūd amrʻaqlī*); *Le livre des pénétrations métaphysiques*, p. 107; *Metaphysics of Mulla Sadra*, p. 28.

7. Mīr Dāmād, *Kitāb al-qabasāt*, ed. Mahdī Muhaqqiq (Tehran: Institute of Islamic Studies, 1977), p. 39.

8. *Ibid.*, p. 73.

9. Ahmad al-'Alawī died between 1054/1644 and 1060/1650. Not only was he a great philosopher and theologian; he was also well known for his exceptional knowledge of the Jewish and Christian scriptures. See Henry Corbin, "Théologoumena iranica," *Studia Iranica* 5 (1976), pp. 232–35.

10. Ahmad al-'Alawī, *Sharh Kitāb al-Qabasāt* (Tehran: Institute of Islamic Studies, 1997), p. 258, and Mīr Dāmād, *Taqwīm al-īmān* (Tehran: Institute of Islamic Studies, 1998), p. 235ff. Ahmad al-'Alawī maintains, classically, that existence comes to the possible existent from the outside (*min khārij*). On this point, there is no divergence from Sadrā, except that this caused existence is added to quiddity. The entire debate rests on the pertinence of the concept of addition.

11. Sadr al-Dīn Shīrāzī, *Kitāb al-Mashā'ir*, sec. 57; *Le livre des pénétrations métaphysiques*, p. 109; *Metaphysics of Mulla Sadra*, p. 30.

12. "Mais rendre la lumière / Suppose d'ombre une morne moitié." Paul Valéry, "The Graveyard by the Sea," *The Collected Works of Paul Valéry*, ed. Jackson Matthews, vol. 1, *Poems*, trans. David Paul (Princeton, NJ: Princeton University Press, 1971), pp. 214–15.

13. "This figure is the pure, all-embracing and all-pervading *luminous essence* [*Lichtwesen*] of sunrise, which preserves itself in its formless substantiality." G.W.F. Hegel, *Phenomenology of Spirit*, trans. Arnold V. Miller (Oxford: Oxford University Press, 1977), p. 419 (Hegel's emphasis; translation emended).

14. Sadr al-Dīn Shīrāzī, *al-Asfār*, vol. 1, p. 69.

15. The possible is the "impenetrable threshold of absolute nonbeing," and the reality of light confronts the Ahrimanian shadow of nonbeing, according to an impressive dualist scheme referring to the Zoroastrian duality of Ahura Mazda and Ahriman, in the reflections of the abovementioned Ahmad al-'Alawī, son-in-law of Mīr Dāmād. The latter's conception of quiddity as shadow, evil, and ontological baseness is an echo of these remarkable elaborations. See Henry Corbin's remarks on Ahmad al-'Alawī, "Key to the Shifā'," MS 5, Department of Iranology, Institut franco-iranien, Tehran (n.d.), in *Avicenna and the Visionary Recital*, trans. Willard R. Trask (New York: Pantheon, 1960), p. 58ff.

16. That is why the concepts of unveiling (*kashf*) and the veil (*hijāb*) do not correspond to what we read in the discourse of modern Western phenomenology.

Unveiling means proceeding to the act by which the veritable existent, the intelligible divine light, is uncovered, not grasping the "thing itself" in its reality as a being given "in the world." Indeed, for Sadrā, the reality of the thing is fully "in the world" only if this world is situated in the hierarchy of worlds, at its summit, only if it is the world of pure light. *A fortiori*, there is a great deal of confusion in the comparison often made between the experience of being in the Eastern thought of Islam and Heidegger's statements in *Being and Time*. If one keeps this in mind, it becomes possible to elaborate some fruitful correlations.

17. Sadr al-Dīn Shīrāzī, *al-Asfār*, vol. 1, p. 70.

18. *Ibid.*, p. 70ff.

19. *Lum'āt al-nūr al-haqīqī al-wājibī*. See *The Book of Radiance* (*Partaw 'nāmah*) by Yahyá ibn Habash Suhrawardī, Persian text appearing in *Oeuvres philosophiques et mystiques*, ed. Henry Corbin, vol. 2 (Tehran: Académie Impériale Iranienne de Philosophie, 1976), selections translated by Henry Corbin in Yahyá ibn Habash Suhrawardī, *L'archange empourpré: Quinze traités et récits mystiques,* ed. Henry Corbin (Paris: Fayard, 1976), p. 133ff. See also the admirable meditation on epiphany in *Lawa'ih*, by the great Persian poet and mystic Jāmī (d. 898/1492): *Les jaillissements de lumière* (*Lavayeh*), trans. Richard Yann (Paris: Deux Océans, 1982).

20. Muhammad ibn Ibrāhīm Sadr al-Dīn Shīrāzī, *Mafātīh al-ghayb*, ed. Muhammad Khvājavī (Tehran: Mu'assasah-'i Mutāla'āt va Tahqīqāt-i Farhangī, 1984), p. 335ff.

21. Muhammad ibn Ibrāhīm Sadr al-Dīn Shīrāzī, "Mutashābihāt al-Qur'ān," *Sih risālah*, ed. Jalāl al-Dīn Āshtiyānī (Meshed, Iran: Chāp'khānah-'i Dānishgāh-i Mashhad, 1973), p. 95.

22. *Ibid.*

23. As one can read in the al-Rahmaān sura (Qur'ān 55: 26–27). Speaking of "the ships sailing smoothly through the seas, lofty as mountains," the Qur'ān states: "Whomever they carry will perish, but will abide the Face of your Lord, full of majesty, worthy of reverence" (I have adopted here the reading of Jacques Berque).

24. Yahyá ibn Habash Suhrawardī, *Kitāb hikmat al-ishrāq*, sec. 256; *Oeuvres philosophiques et mystiques*, vol. 2, p. 240; *Le livre de la sagesse orientale* (*Kitâb Hikmat al-Ishrâq*), trans. Henry Corbin, ed. Christian Jambet (Lagrasse, France: Verdier, 1986), p. 220.

25. Honoré de Balzac, *A Passion in the Desert* (Gloucester: Sutton, 1985).

Elsewhere I have written at greater length on this story by Balzac and what it reveals regarding the theophanic space in the Muslim world; see Christian Jambet, "L'appel du désert," in Daniel Rondeau (ed.), *L'appel du Maroc* (Paris: Institut du monde arabe, 1999), p. 246ff. (A *grognard* is a soldier of the old guard of Napoleon I — TRANS.)

26. Are existents mirages or dreams, or are they manifestations of authentic existence? They are indissolubly one and the other. According to 'Azīz Nasafī, these two positions characterize, respectively, the "fire people" and the "light people," and the latter know that the distinction between being and appearing must disappear in its turn. See the remarkable analysis of Hermann Landolt, "Le paradoxe de 'la Face de Dieu': 'Azīz-e Nasafī (VIIe/XIIIe siècle) et le 'monisme ésotérique' de l'islam," *Studia Iranica* 25 (1996), pp. 177–79. Nasafī homologizes the *nūn* (from the word *nūr*, light) with the prophet, the *waw* with the *wali*, the friend of God, and the *rā* with illuminative intelligence; see *Kitāb al-insān al-kāmil*, ed. Marijan Molé (Tehran: Département d'iranologie de l'Institut franco-iranien, 1962), p. 221. A systematic comparison between Nasafī and Mullā Sadrā would be extremely fruitful. For a recent bibliography, see Sima Orsini-Sadjed, "Note bibliographique sur 'Azīz-e Nasafi," *Studia Iranica* 26 (1997), pp. 269–80.

27. Sadr al-Dīn Shīrāzī, *al-Asfār*, vol. 1, p. 54.

28. *Ibid.*

29. *Ibid.*, p. 63.

30. *Ibid.*

31. Yahyá ibn Habash Suhrawardī, *Kitāb hikmat al-ishrāq*, sec. 107; *Oeuvres philosophiques et mystiques*, vol. 2, p. 106; *Le livre de la sagesse orientale*, p. 97.

32. Cécile Bonmariage, "Le réel et les réalités: La structure de la réalité de l'être chez Mullâ Sadrâ Shîrâzî," Ph.D. diss., Université catholique de Louvain, Institut supérieur de philosophie, 1998, vol. 1, p. 70. The author recalls the translations proposed by several specialists, including "systematic ambiguity" (Fazlur Rahman), "analogical gradation" (Toshihiko Izutsu), and "restlessness of being" (Henry Corbin).

33. Sadrā thus realizes the "skepticism that is integral to philosophy," which affirms "pure negativity" and ruins "the dogmatism of common consciousness," "this indifference of the mind that makes all that is procured by the phenomenon or the understanding vacillate, in a vacillation of all that is finite" (Hegel, commenting on the tropes used by Sextus Empiricus in the article written

against the undercurrent of dogmatism in the Kantian critique "The Relation of Skepticism to Philosophy" (1802), *Jenaer Schriften 1801–1807* (Frankfurt: Suhrkamp, 1970). It remains true, however, that Sadrian negation is not Hegelian negation; it is closer to the truth of Pyrrhonian phenomenalism, in that the phenomenon translates not a negativity that is the concept, but the existence that is identical to essence, the essential and infinite movement of being.

34. Sadr al-Dīn Shīrāzī, *al-Asfār*, vol. 1, p. 36.

35. Which corresponds to the Latin *primaritas*. See A.M. Goichon, *Lexique de la langue philosophique d'Ibn Sînâ (Avicenne)* (Paris: Desclée de Brouwer, 1938), p. 34.

36. Sadr al-Dīn Shīrāzī, *al-Asfār*, vol. 1, p. 37.

37. The father is prior to the son, not through his identification as a *man*, but through his *act of being*. See Muhammad ibn Ibrāhīm Sadr al-Dīn Shīrāzī, *Tafsīr al-Qur'ān al-karīm*, ed. Muhammad Khvājavī (Qum, Iran: Bīdār, 1987), vol. 1, p. 53.

38. Sadr al-Dīn Shīrāzī, *al-Asfār*, vol. 1, p. 65.

39. "Know that accidents are of two kinds: accidents of existence and accidents of quiddity. Accidents of existence are, for example, the accidents, *in concreto*, of whiteness for a body or of 'being above' for the sky, or the universality and the reality of species for man, or the reality of genera for animals. An accident of quiddity is, for example, specific difference or individuation in species." See Muhammad ibn Ibrāhīm Sadr al-Dīn Shīrāzī, *Kitāb al-Mashā'ir*, sec. 31; *Le livre des pénétrations métaphysiques*, p. 98; *Metaphysics of Mulla Sadra*, p. 18.

40. Sadr al-Dīn Shīrāzī, *al-Asfār*, vol. 1, pp. 65–66. It will be noticed that there is a contradiction between this passage and the allusion, cited above, to eternal essence as conceived of by Ibn al-'Arabī

41. *Ibid.*, p. 63.

42. *al-Mawjūd huwa al-wujud bi-l-haqīqa*, *ibid.*, p. 67.

43. *Amran 'aqlīyyan*, *ibid.*, p. 68.

44. *Mahd al-tahaqquq al-'aynī.*

45. The solution to the question posed above – "What is the being of quiddities?" – would be, for Ibn al-'Arabī, the distinction between the *establishment* (*thubūt*) of eternal essences (*al-a'yān al-thābitah*) by God and their effective *existentiation*. Would this distinction have any meaning for Sadrā? This seems unlikely. And yet Sadrā seems to adopt it when he distinguishes the status of essences, understood as models of the quiddities on the plane of divine names, from their status as the shadow of the act of existing on the plane of the world of

creation. See Ibn al-'Arabī, *Les illuminations de La Mecque*, ed. Michel Chodkiewicz (Paris: Sindbad, 1988), p. 494, n.69.

46. *Ibid.*, p.69.

47. *Izhār li-nafsih.*

48. Sadr al-Dīn Shīrāzī, *al-Asfār*, vol. 1, p. 40.

49. Muhammad ibn Ibrāhīm Sadr al-Dīn Shīrāzī, "al-Masâ'il al-qudsîyah," *Sih risālah*, ed. Jalāl al-Dīn Āshtiyānī (Meshed, Iran: Chāp'khānah-'i Dānishgāh-i Mashhad, 1973), p. 13.

50. Sadr al-Dīn Shīrāzī, *al-Asfār*, vol. 2, p. 327ff.

51. *Wah huwah bi-hasb dhātih al-muqaddasah laysa mahdûdan muqayadan bi-ta'ayun lā mutlaqan.*

52. *Umūr i'tibārīyah 'aqlīyah.*

53. *al-Mawjūd al-muta'alliq bi-ghayrih.*

54. *al-Wujūd al-munbasit al-mutlaq.*

55. The analysis of this existential revolution, centered on the becoming of man, is the central theme of Part Two.

56. Henry Corbin, *Creative Imagination in the Sufism of Ibn 'Arabi*, trans. Ralph Manheim (Princeton, NJ: Princeton University Press, 1969), pp. 184ff. and 222ff. It is nonetheless true that this act of imaginal creation assumes the entire structure of the divine names and the intelligibles. As Michel Chodkiewicz writes, "It is in a second stage, and only then, that it 'takes a body' in the *'alam al-khayāl*, and it is then that it takes on words and images that will allow its transmission to those who do not have access to this universe of pure light": *An Ocean without Shore: Ibn 'Arabī, the Book, and the Law*, trans. David Streight (Albany: State University of New York Press, 1993), p. 83.

57. According to al-Qūnawī, as quoted by Sadrā in *al-Asfār*, vol. 2, p. 330.

58. *Ibid.*, vol. 1, p. 70.

Chapter Five: Essential Motion

1. Muhammad ibn Ibrāhīm Sadr al-Dīn Shīrāzī, *Kitāb al-'arshīyah*, 1st *mashreq*, p. 13. I am translating from the edition of the Arabic text with a commentary by Shaykh Ahmad al-Ahsā'i (Kermān, Iran: Tchāpkhaneh-e Sa'ādat, 1361 h.). The passage quoted is from vol. 1, p. 265. See James Winston Morris, *The Wisdom of the Throne: An Introduction to the Philosophy of Mulla Sadra* (Princeton, NJ: Princeton University Press, 1981), pt. 1, sec. 13, pp. 119–20; references will be given to this translation, which has in each case been modified to reflect the

author's French. Jambet's references to Shaykh Ahmad al-Ahsā'i's commentary will cite the Arabic edition given above — TRANS.

2. Sadr al-Dīn Shīrāzī, *Kitāb al-'arshīyah,* p. 202ff. Shaykh Ahmad al-Ahsā'i was born in 1166 /1753 and died in 1241/1826; since he was the founder of the Shaykhi sect, I refer to him by his most commonly used name, Shaykh Ahmad. This sect, which still exists today, was persecuted in the first stages of the Islamic revolution in Iran; it professes a spiritual Shī'ism far removed from the now dominant "political" Shī'ism. Shaykh Sarkār Āqā, who died in 1969, maintained regular contact with Henry Corbin. On the Shaykhis, see Henry Corbin, *En Islam iranien: Aspects spirituels et philosophiques*, vol. 4, *L'Ecole d'Ispahan, l'Ecole shaykhie, le Douzième Imâm* (Paris: Gallimard, 1971), pp. 205–300; *Spiritual Body and Celestial Earth: From Mazdean Iran to Shi'ite Iran*, trans. Nancy Pearson (Princeton, NJ: Princeton University Press, 1977), pp. 180–221, and *Itinéraire d'un enseignement: Résumé des conférences à l'Ecole Pratique des Hautes Etudes (Section des sciences religieuses), 1955–1979* (Tehran: Institut français de recherche en Iran, 1993), p. 174ff; see also Mohammad-Ali Amir-Moezzi, "Contributions à la typologie des rencontres avec l'imâm caché (Aspects de l'imâmologie duodécimaine II)," *Journal Asiatique* 284, no. 1 (1996), pp. 109–35, and "Une absence remplie de présences: Herméneutiques de l'Occultation chez les Shaykhiyya (Aspects de l'imâmologie duodécimaine VII)," *Bulletin of the School of Oriental and African Studies* 64, no. 1 (2001), pp. 1–18. Henry Corbin bequeathed to the Department of Religious Studies of the Ecole Pratique des Hautes Etudes a very significant archive of Shaykhi texts, which are catalogued and analyzed in an article by Amir-Moezzi and Sabine Schmidtke, "Twelver-Shī'ite Resources in Europe," *Journal Asiatique* 285, no. 1 (1997), pp. 73–122.

3. In his commentary on this passage from Sadrā, Shaykh Ahmad presents a veritable summation of Sadrā's metaphysics: for him, the act of being is matter, and quiddity is form composed of definitions through which the existent is particularized, whereas existents are distinguished by the differences between these definitions (quantity, quality, relation, position, location, time, dimension). These seven categories correspond to the seven days of the creation of the temporal universe, the seven stages of the creation of man (sperm, clot, embryo, bone, flesh, birth, inbreathing of spirit), and the seven days of the heavens and the earth (Intelligence, soul, nature, cloud, image, matter, form). According to him, and in conformity with the *Theology of Aristotle*, souls are not temporal. They have nonelemental bodies, which have no location. It is a question here of

the great distinction between the elemental body and the *barzakh* body, an imaginal body to which we will return. It is this imaginal body that constitutes Jābalqā and Jābarsā in its lower world and Hūrqalyā in its higher world. See Sadr al-Dīn Shīrāzī, *Kitāb al-ʻarshīyah*, vol. 1, pp. 266–70.

4. Muhammad ibn Ibrāhīm Sadr al-Dīn Shīrāzī, *al-Hikmah al-mutaʻālīyah fī al-asfār al-ʻaqlīyah al-arbaʻah* (al-Najaf: Dār al-Maʻārif al-Islāmīyah, 1958), vol. 3, p. 37.

5. Avicenna, *al-Shifa: al-Tabiiyyat* (*La physique*), ed. Saʻid Zayid and Ibrahim Madkur (Cairo: Organisation egyptienne générale du livre, 1983), vol. 1, p. 81.

6. Sadr al-Dīn Shīrāzī, *al-Asfār*, vol. 3, p. 40.

7. *Ibid.*, p. 61.

8. Aristotle, *Categories* 5.3b.

9. Qur'ān 28:88.

10. Sadr al-Dīn Shīrāzī, *al-Asfār*, vol. 3, p. 62.

11. Fazlur Rahman has pointed out a certain oscillation on this point in Mullā Sadrā, who sometimes says that form remains stable while existence is in motion and sometimes says the contrary. In my view, it is a matter of two easily reconcilable points of view, since the quiddity of an existent composed of matter and form varies according to its degree of existence, and, conversely, this movement of the act of existing intensifies a formal reality that remains delimited between a point of origin and a final term, and which is therefore one. See Rahman, *The Philosophy of Mulla Sadra* (*Sadr al-Din al-Shirazi*) (Albany: State University of New York Press, 1975), p. 105.

12. Sadr al-Dīn Shīrāzī, *al-Asfār*, vol. 3, p. 65.

13. Avicenna, *al-Tabiiyyat*, vol. 1, p. 98.

14. Vegetative powers can, however, metamorphose into animal powers. Sadrā inherits the extensive tradition according to which there are "thresholds" between the natural kingdoms, points of passage (coral, the palm tree, the black Ethiopian, and — why not — the philosopher, the point of passage from man to angel). For example: "One of the species of the vegetative power is poured out in drops of semen and ends up rising to completion at the rank of animal." See Christian Jambet, *Se rendre immortel: Suivi du Traité de la resurrection, Mollâ Sadrâ Shîrâzî* (Saint-Clément-de-Rivière, France: Fata Morgana, 2000), p. 139.

15. Sadr al-Dīn Shīrāzī, *al-Asfār*, vol. 3, p. 67. "The agent and the direct cause of motion is therefore not a pure intelligence without mediation, since the Intelligence is not subject to any change. Nor is it a soul, insofar as the essence

of the soul is intelligible. No! Rather, if the soul is moved, then it is insofar as it resides in the body, or insofar as it is attached to it. Either it becomes a nature, or it becomes within the status of a nature." See Muhammad ibn Ibrāhīm Sadr al-Dīn Shīrāzī, *Risālah fī al-hudūth*, in *Rasā'il*, lithographed edition (Tehran, 1884), p. 18.

16. See Jean Trouillard, "Le Parménide de Platon et son interpretation néoplatonicienne," *Etudes néoplatoniciennes* (Neuchâtel: Baconnière, 1973), pp. 9–26. The "fourth rank" granted to nature is expressly mentioned by Mullā Sadrā, *Traité de la resurrection*, p. 120. The scheme varies slightly in the corresponding text of *al-Asfār*, vol. 9, p. 243, where natures are located at the fifth degree, because souls are distributed along the third degree (imaginal souls) and the fourth degree (vegetal souls).

17. Plotinus, *Enneads* 3.8.3.

18. *Ibid.*, 2.1.4.

19. *Ibid.*, 2.1.1.

20. *Ibid.*, 3.8.4. Jean Trouillard comments on this passage with a very beautiful and enigmatic description: "Nature is a diffuse and somnolent thought. It produces without reflection or choice, it pours forth a translation of its dream." *La procession plotinienne* (Paris: Presses Universitaires de France, 1955), p. 28.

21. Plotinus, *Enneads* 3.7.11.

22. *Ibid.*, 3.8.10.

23. *Theology of Aristotle*, bk. 8.

24. *Ibid.*, bk. 7.

25. *Ibid.*

26. Ikhwān al-Safā', *Rasā'il Ikhwān al-Safā wa-Khullān al-Wafā'* (Qum, Iran: al-Maktab al-islāmī, 1985), vol. 2, p. 63. According to this encyclopedia, only the soul possesses an activity and carries out its operations through the potency of nature in bodies. All bodies are the organs and instruments of nature, as thought and cognition are the instruments of the soul in the perception of cognized and intelligized realities (p. 64). See Yves Marquet, *La philosophie des Ihwan al-Safa'* (Algiers: Société Nationale d'Editions et de Diffusion, 1973), p. 160ff.

27. Nāsir-i Khusraw, *Kitāb-i zād al-musāfirīn* (Tehran: Kitabfurushi-i Mahmudi, 1923), p. 390ff; see also *Le livre réunissant les deux sagesses*, trans. Isabelle de Gastines (Paris: Fayard, 1990), pp. 143–54.

28. Ishāq ibn Ahmad Abū Ya'qūb al-Sijistānī, *Kashf al-mahjûb*, ed. Henry Corbin (Tehran: Institut franco-iranien, 1949), vol. 1, p. 42; *Le dévoilement des*

choses cachées (Lagrasse, France: Verdier, 1988), p. 77; see also, by the same author, *Kitāb al-yanābī'*, in Paul E. Walker, *The Wellsprings of Wisdom: A Study of Abu Ya'qub al-Sijistani's "Kitab al-Yanabi'"; Including a Complete English Translation with Commentary and Notes on the Arabic Text* (Salt Lake City: University of Utah Press, 1994), pp. 76 and 164, and Hamīd al-Dīn Ahmad ibn 'Abd Allāh Kirmānī, *Rāhat al-'aql* (Cairo: Dār al-Fikr al-'Arabī, 1953), p. 149ff.

29. Sadr al-Dīn Shīrāzī, *al-Asfār*, vol. 5, p. 249ff.

30. *Ibid.*, p. 260ff.

31. *Ibid.*, p. 261.

32. On the Plotinian conception of substantial motion as an "act internal to substance," see Pierre Hadot, *Porphyre et Victorinus* (Paris: Etudes augustiniennes, 1968), vol. 1, p. 232ff.

33. Sadr al-Dīn Shīrāzī, *Risālah fi al-hudūth*, p. 25. See *al-Asfār*, vol. 3, p. 104.

34. See the detailed exposition in Jambet, *Se rendre immortel*, pp. 63–65.

35. "The substrate of substantial motion in material natures is such that its singular unity is preserved by virtue of an active intelligible unity, through the intelligible agent's quality as preserver – which quality falls to the natural individual in the hierarchized degrees of essential operations and existential modalities – and through an obscure, receptive unity of matter, itself preserved in its unity in the hierarchized degrees of passivities and metamorphoses." Sadr al-Dīn Shīrāzī, *al-Asfār*, vol. 4, p. 273.

36. Sadr al-Dīn Shīrāzī, *Kitāb al-'arshīyah*, vol. 1, p. 299; *Wisdom of the Throne*, p. 124. Sadrā opposes "philosophers" who profess the eternal existence not only of the Intelligences but also of the celestial souls, the heavens, and the elements in their universal state. He vigorously challenges Suhrawardī on this point. See the gloss cited below on the *Kitāb hikmat al-ishrāq*: Yahyá ibn Habash Suhrawardī, *Le livre de la sagesse orientale (Kitâb Hikmat al-Ishrâq)*, trans. Henry Corbin, ed. Christian Jambet (Lagrasse, France: Verdier, 1986).

37. *Theology of Aristotle*, bk. 9.

38. *Ibid.*, cited by Sadrā in numerous variants. The two citations correspond to Plotinus, *Enneads* 4.7.3. The first citation glosses the following passage from Plotinus: "For there would not even be any body, if the power of the soul did not exist; for it flows away, and its nature is transitory."

39. Sadr al-Dīn Shīrāzī, *Risālah fi al-hudūth*, p. 25. See *al-Asfār*, vol. 3, p. 111ff.

40. This practice is legitimated by a belief in the existence of a prophetic community to which Aristotle belongs.

41. *Mécomptes*: also "disappointments" — Trans.

42. Sadr al-Dīn Shīrāzī, *al-Asfār*, vol. 3, p. 95.

43. *Ibid.*, p. 96.

44. *Ibid.*, p. 97.

45. *Ibid.*

46. "This notion of Time embodied, of years past but not separated from us, it was now my intention to emphasize as strongly as possible..." Marcel Proust, *In Search of Lost Time*, vol. 6, *Time Regained*, trans. Andreas Mayer and Jerence Kilmartin, revised by D.J. Enright (New York: Modern Library, 1993), p. 529.

47. Sadr al-Dīn Shīrāzī, *al-Asfār*, vol. 3, p. 104.

48. Sadr al-Dīn Shīrāzī, *Risālah fi al-hudūth*, p. 24.

49. Sadr al-Dīn Shīrāzī, *al-Asfār*, vol. 3, p. 115ff. On time as fundamentally dependent on the body and its substantial motion, see Rahman, *Philosophy of Mulla Sadra*, p. 109ff.

50. Sadr al-Dīn Shīrāzī, *al-Asfār*, vol. 3, p. 124ff.

51. *Ibid.*, p. 121.

52. It will be noticed that there is a departure here from Plotinus's view. Shaykh Ahmad al-Ahsā'ī contends, against Mullā Sadrā, that the being of souls is not temporal. Souls are above time, above souls there is the Intelligence, and above the Intelligence there is the Water from which God created all living things, the first Effusant. See al-Ahsā'ī, *Sharh al-'arshīyah*, p. 270.

53. Sadr al-Dīn Shīrāzī, *al-Asfār*, vol. 3, p. 127.

54. *Ibid.*, pp. 179–81. Rest has no reality; it is a "thing of nothingness" (*amr 'adamī*, p. 182). What is at rest from a certain point of view is in motion from another point of view. There is nothing stable in the world of creation: "all things are passing away."

55. Sadr al-Dīn Shīrāzī, *Kitāb al-'arshīyah*, vol. 1, p. 285; *Wisdom of the Throne*, pp. 121–23.

56. For this commentary, see al-Ahsā'ī, *Sharh al-'arshīyah*, vol. 1, pp. 286–89.

57. More generally, it is a question of the lesson found in all the religions of the Book: "For all the true religions agree in affirming that the world is innovated, in the sense that God was [first] and that nothing was with him." Suhrawardī, *Le livre de la sagesse orientale*, p. 586ff.

58. Sadr al-Dīn Shīrāzī, *Traité de la résurrection*, p. 169.

59. Qur'ān 29:64.

60. Qur'ān 29:19–20.

61. Sadr al-Dīn Shīrāzī, *Kitāb al-'arshīyah*, vol. 1, p. 274; *Wisdom of the Throne*, part 1, sec. 13, p. 120.

62. Sadr al-Dīn Shīrāzī, *Kitāb al-'arshīyah*, vol. 1, p. 274; *Wisdom of the Throne*, p. 121. It will be noticed that here Sadrā takes up the Aristotelian definition of nature as a principle of movement and *rest*. The notion of rest is modified, since it is affected by the concept of essential motion. There is no true rest except in the intelligible.

63. See Sadr al-Dīn Shīrāzī, *Kitāb al-'arshīyah*, vol. 1, p. 291; *Wisdom of the Throne*, p. 123–24.

64. al-Ahsā'ī, *Sharh al-'arshīyah*, p. 291ff.

65. Muhammad ibn Ibrāhīm Sadr al-Dīn Shīrāzī, "Kitāb al-tawhīd," *Sharh usūl al-kāfī*, ed. Muhammad Khvājavī (Tehran: Mu'assasah-'i Mutāla'āt va Tahqīqāt-i Farhangī, 1987), p. 39.

66. Sadr al-Dīn Shīrāzī, *Kitāb al-'arshīyah*, vol. 1, pp. 304–307; *Wisdom of the Throne*, pp. 125–26.

Chapter Six: Births of the Soul

1. This chapter expands on some of the analyses presented in Christian Jambet, "L'âme humaine d'Aristote à Mollâ Sadrâ Shîrâzî," *Studia Iranica* 26 (1997), pp. 211–36.

2. Muhammad ibn Ibrāhīm Sadr al-Dīn Shīrāzī, *al-Shawāhid al-rubūbīyah*, ed. Jalāl al-Dīn Āshtiyānī (Meshed, Iran: University Press, 1967), p. 199.

3. Aristotle, *On the Soul* 2.1.412a.

4. As the title of the fourth journey of *al-Asfār* indicates, Muhammad ibn Ibrāhīm Sadr al-Dīn Shīrāzī, *al-Hikmah al-muta'ālīyah fi al-asfār al-'aqlīyah al-arba'ah* (al-Najaf, Iraq: Dār al-Ma'ārif al-Islāmīyah, 1958), vol. 8, p. 2.

5. Sadr al-Dīn Shīrāzī, *al-Asfār*, vol. 8, p. 4.

6. *Ibid.*, pp. 5–7.

7. Avicenna, *Livre des définitions* (*Kitab al-hudud*), ed. and trans. A.M. Goichon (Cairo: Institut français d'archéologie orientale du Caire, 1963), pp. 14 and 20. See Avicenna, *Avicenna's De Anima (Arabic Text): Being the Psychological Part of Kitab al-Shifa'*, ed. Fazlur Rahman (London: Oxford University Press, 1959), p. 12.

8. Avicenna, *Avicenna's De Anima*, p. 4.

9. *Ibid.*, p. 7.

10. *Ibid.*, p. 8.

11. *Ibid.*, p. 6.

12. *Ibid.*, p. 8.

13. *Ibid.*, p. 9ff.

14. *Ibid.*, p. 10ff. Aristotle writes: "Hence the soul must be a substance in the sense of the form of a natural body having life potentially within it. But substance is actuality, and thus soul is the actuality of a body as above characterized." *On the Soul* 2.1.412a. (See also *Metaphysics* 5.8.1017b, 7.10.1035b, 7.11.1037a.)

15. Avicenna, *Avicenna's De Anima*, p. 29.

16. Sadr al-Dīn Shīrāzī, *al-Asfār*, vol. 8, p. 11ff.

17. *Ibid.*, p. 12ff.

18. *Ibid.*, p. 13.

19. *Ibid.*, p. 15ff.

20. "To be sure, you know that the act of being of the soul and its psychicity are one and the same. The soul, because of this act of being, is a form relative to the body, and it exercises its government over it. This does not mean that its relation to the body and its government over it belong for it among the consequent accidents posterior to its act of being, to the point of disappearing, like the relation between the magnet and the iron, as Qutb al-Dīn [al-Shīrāzī] thinks. The soul's act of being requires the body, and this implies a corporeal connection." *Ibid.*, p. 375.

21. Avicenna, *Avicenna's De Anima*, p. 16. See the translation of Avicenna's text, and a commentary on it, in Souâd Ayada, *Avicenne*: *980–1037* (Paris: Ellipses, 2002).

22. Sadr al-Dīn Shīrāzī, *al-Asfār*, vol. 8, pp. 42–44. Sadrā speaks of the living animal in general; I have taken the liberty of choosing the familiar example of the cat to illustrate his argument.

23. Sadr al-Dīn Shīrāzī, *al-Shawāhid al-rubūbīyah*, p. 198, quoting Qur'ān 104:6–7.

24. Sadrā quotes Avicenna (*Avicenna's De Anima*, p. 39ff.) almost literally: *al-Asfār*, vol. 8, pp. 53–57.

25. *al-Quwwá al-shahwānīyah*, the "appetitive faculty," *al-quwwá al-ghadabiyah*, the "irascible faculty."

26. If it were not likely to cause confusion, *idrāk* could be correctly translated as *Begriff*, concept. *Daraka*, to grasp, is precisely *begreifen*.

27. Quoted in Sadr al-Dīn Shīrāzī, *al-Asfār*, vol. 8, p. 56.

28. For example, *ibid.*, p. 205, which echoes Avicenna. The classical doctrine of the common sense as that which effectuates the synthesis of the universal man and the particular individual in a single perception is presented on p. 206ff. A faculty is necessary that initiates the work by which I judge that this particular man whom I perceive through my external senses is indeed "a man," in conformity with the universal quiddity of man. Not only does the common sense unify the sensations, but the reflection of the particular in the universal also begins with it. Kant is not far removed from such considerations.

29. *Ibid.*, p. 211.

30. *Ibid.*, p. 65.

31. *Ibid.*, p. 66.

32. *Ibid.*, p. 67.

33. Everything concerning the first "birth" of the soul should be of interest to readers of Maurice Merleau-Ponty, from whom Sadrā is not so distant, despite the obvious heterogeneity of their theoretical frameworks.

34. Sadr al-Dīn Shīrāzī, *al-Asfār*, vol. 8, pp. 133–37.

35. Sadrā is quoting Abū Hāmid al-Ghazzālī's chapter devoted to "the property of the heart," in *ibid.*, p. 137ff., and in his commentary on the al-Baqara sura of the Qur'ān: Muhammad ibn Ibrāhīm Sadr al-Dīn Shīrāzī, *Tafsīr al-Qur'ān al-karīm*, ed. Muhammad Khvājavī (Qum, Iran: Bīdār, 1987), vol. 4, p. 287ff. al-Ghazzālī's text, which Sadrā quotes at great length, is found in al-Ghazzālī, *Ihyā' 'ulūm al-dīn* (*The Revitalization of the Sciences of Religion*), ed. 'Abd al-Rahīm ibn al-Husayn 'Irāqī (Cairo: Mu'assasat al-Halabī, 1967–68), vol. 3, p. 6ff.

36. Qur'ān 74:31.

37. See the remarkable study by Paul Ballanfat cited above, "Considérations sur la conception du coeur chez Mullâ Sadrâ," *Karnameh* 5 (1999), pp. 33–46, and 6 (2000), pp. 67–84. The texts I am discussing here could also provide support for this study, alongside the many other references found there.

38. The perfect man, the caliph of God, is created after the form of the Merciful. He is the manifestation of the form of the revelation of the divine name. Sadrā cites a passage from ch. 361 of Ibn al-'Arabī, *Futūhāt al-Makkīyya; Les illuminations de La Mecque*, ed. Michel Chodkiewicz (Paris: Sindbad, 1988), vol. 3, p. 295, in this chapter of *al-Asfār*, as a complement to the long al-Ghazzālī quote, and in a gloss of Yahyá ibn Habash Suhrawardī, *Le livre de la sagesse orientale* (*Kitâb Hikmat al-Ishrâq*), trans. Henry Corbin, ed. Christian Jambet (Lagrasse, France: Verdier, 1986), p. 664.

39. Qur'ān 51:56.

40. It goes without saying that the title of Mullā Sadrā's summa, *Four Spiritual Journeys*, is explained by this notion. The entirety of metaphysics, physics, and eschatology describes the journey of the existent both away from and back to God. The *journey* designates this dynamics of being, whose moral meaning is spiritual struggle, and whose final term is the return to God.

41. After the passage from al-Ghazzālī, Sadrā quotes a passage from the Brethren of Purity that ends with these words: "Every time the thinking soul is preoccupied with something sensible, the sentient faculty is configured by that which preoccupies it. This it perceives and carries to the thinking soul, instantaneously and without delay. Just so is the angels' obedience to the Lord of worlds." The instantaneity of our perception is likened to an image of the instantaneity of angelic service.

42. Qur'ān 12:31. This verse from the Joseph sura concerns Joseph's beauty, which is considered the archetype of prophetic beauty and inspires, among other things, the mystical meditation of the great poet and mystic Jāmī.

43. Qur'ān 17:85.

44. "At times the soul governs the body and dominates it with the assistance of God and his Malakūt, and at times the soul submits to the body and undergoes the victorious domination of its powers, through the seduction of Satan and through the intermediary of the clothing donned by the deceptive imagination (*wahm*). It then adorns itself with the objects of bestial desire. When its submission to the body is repeated, the soul suffers from great passivity in relation to it, and it becomes submissive (*inqiyād*) and takes on self-destructive habits, such that something that was not previously difficult – namely, diminishing the strength of its own corruption – becomes difficult for it now. However, when its dominance over its chains is repeated, it acquires a dimension of superiority that was not easily acquired previously." Sadr al-Dīn Shīrāzī, *al-Asfār*, vol. 9, p. 127. Mullā Sadrā goes on to a discussion based on Aristotle's definition of the "golden mean" between excess and deficiency.

45. *Ibid.*, p. 219.

46. "We know that the soul is not a complete singular essence, essentially separated, to which the connection with the body would then occur, as a merchant in the market is connected to his stall." *Ibid.*, vol. 8, p. 377.

47. *Ibid.*, p. 328ff.

48. *Ibid.*, p. 329; Qur'ān 76:1.

49. Sadr al-Dīn Shīrāzī, *al-Asfār*, vol. 8, p. 329ff.

50. For Sadrā, the ancients are the Greeks, from the earliest sages ("the most ancient") to Socrates, Plato, and Aristotle. The moderns are Avicenna and his successors. He situates himself outside these two categories, at the end of the lineage of "inspired men of knowledge" (*'urufā'*, "men of learning in spiritual science"), enlightened by all the prophetic, imamic, and philosophical traditions as a whole. He sees himself, if I may say so, as "postmodern."

51. Avicenna's position is clear: souls have a temporal eduction, which corresponds to their connection to the body. "Before the body, the soul is only quiddity, purely and simply." Avicenna, *Kitāb al-najāt fī al-hikmah al-mantiqīyah wa-al-tabī'īyah wa-al-ilāhīyah* (Beirut: Dār al-Āfāq al-Jadīdah, 1985), p. 376. Sadrā reverses this problematic by affirming that before the body the soul is an intelligible act of being, not pure and simple quiddity without existence.

52. Sadr al-Dīn Shīrāzī, *al-Asfār*, vol. 8, p. 330ff.

53. *Ibid.*, p. 333.

54. On Mullā Sadrā's attempt to rescue the Platonic doctrine of the forms or Ideas, see Christian Jambet, *Se rendre immortel: Suivi du Traité de la résurrection, Mollâ Sadrâ Shîrâzî* (Saint-Clément-de-Rivière, France: Fata Morgana, 2000), pp. 58–71.

55. Sadr al-Dīn Shīrāzī, *al-Asfār*, vol. 8, p. 332.

56. *Ibid.*, p. 334.

57. Sadrā quotes Suhrawardī's *Philosophy of Illumination*, secs. 213 and 214; see Yahyá ibn Habash Suhrawardī, *Le livre de la sagesse orientale (Kitâb Hikmat al-Ishrâq)*, trans. Henry Corbin, ed. Christian Jambet (Lagrasse, France: Verdier, 1986), p. 191ff., as well as the glosses of Qutb al-Dīn Shīrāzī referring to these pages (*ibid.*, pp. 378–82).

58. See Guy Monnot, "La transmigration et l'immortalité," *Mélanges de l'Institut Dominicain d'Etudes Orientales* 14 (1980), pp. 149–66; Sabine Schmidtke, "The Doctrine of the Transmigration of Soul According to Shihab al-Din al-Suhrawardi (killed 587/1191) and His Followers," *Studia Iranica* 28, no. 2 (1999), pp. 237–54; Hermann Landolt, "La transmigration de l'âme dans le chîisme et le soufisme," *Annuaire de l'Ecole Pratique des Hautes Etudes* 108 (1999), pp. 242–44.

59. Sadr al-Dīn Shīrāzī, *al-Asfār*, vol. 8, pp. 340–42.

60. Avicenna, *al-Tā'līqāt*, lithograph edition (Tehran, 1315 h.), p. 476; *Le livre de la sagesse orientale*, pp. 603–604.

61. Sadrā conceives of palingenesis as a regeneration, a new birth, not without affinities with the Hermeticist doctrine. See the commentary on treatise 13 of the *Corpus hermeticum* by A.J. Festugière, *La révélation d'Hermès Trismégiste*, vol. 4, *Le dieu inconnu et la gnose* (Paris: Gabalda, 1954), p. 200ff.

62. Sadr al-Dīn Shīrāzī, *al-Asfār*, vol. 8, p. 344.

63. *Ibid.*, pp. 345–47.

64. The degrees of the corporeal birth of the soul are the following: elemental birth, natural birth, mineral birth, vegetable birth, and sentient (animal) birth. Intelligible birth includes the following degrees: passive intelligence, actual intelligence, and agent intelligence (*ibid.*, vol. 8, p. 378).

65. *Ibid.*, vol. 9, p. 238.

66. *Ibid.*, p. 239.

67. *Ibid.*, p. 241.

68. This expression is used a number of times by Jacques Lacan, especially in his seventh seminar, *The Ethics of Psychoanalysis, 1959–1960*, trans. Dennis Porter (New York: Norton, 1997) — Trans.

69. Sadr al-Dīn Shīrāzī, *Tafsīr al-Qur'ān al-karīm*, vol. 4, p. 291.

70. Qur'ān 4:56.

71. Yahyá ibn Habash Suhrawardī, "Qissat al-ghurbat al-ghurbatīyah" (Tale of Occidental Exile), *Oeuvres philosophiques et mystiques*, ed. Henry Corbin (Tehran: Institut franco-iranien, 1952), p. 274ff. Translated from Arabic by Corbin as "Le récit de l'exil occidental" in *L'archange empourpré: Quinze traités et récits mystiques* (Paris: Fayard, 1976), p. 265ff. More recently, Abdelwahah Meddeb has completed a new translation and commentary of this narrative (Montpellier: Fata Morgana, 1993). (For an English translation, see "A Tale of Occidental Exile" in Suhrawardī, *The Philosophical Allegories and Mystical Treatises*, ed. Wheeler M. Thackston [Costa Mesa, CA: Mazda Publishers, 1999] — Trans.) Suhrawardī wanted to supplement Avicenna's teaching on one major point: the gnostic revelation of the lived experience of the eschatological promises. His text is intended as the continuation of Avicenna's recitals of *Salāmān and Absāl* and *Hayy ibn Yaqzān*. See the texts and translations discussed by Henry Corbin in *Avicenna and the Visionary Recital*, trans. Willard R. Trask (New York: Pantheon, 1960).

72. Suhrawardī, *Kitāb hikmat al-Ishrāq*, bk. 4, secs. 211–12; *Le livre de la sagesse orientale*, pp. 190–91.

73. The Arabic text of the gloss can be read in the margins of the lithograph

edition of Suhrawardī, *Kitāb hikmat al-Ishrāq* (Tehran, 1315 h.), p. 445ff. See Sadr al-Dīn Shīrāzī, *al-Asfār*, vol. 8, p. 353.

74. Sadr al-Dīn Shīrāzī, *al-Asfār*, vol. 8, p. 349.

75. *Ibid.*, pp. 349–50. Only this monadology can justify the prophetic traditions: "We are those who precede, the *lāhiqūn*..." and "I was a prophet when Adam was between the water and the clay." Sadrā accuses Suhrawardī of being unfaithful to himself and not respecting his own intuition of the singularity of the reigning lights.

76. *Ibid.*, vol. 8, p. 352.

77. *Ibid.*

78. *Ibid.*, p. 353.

79. The body is not the cause of the soul, neither an agent cause nor a receptive cause, neither a formal cause nor a final cause. (See *ibid.*, p. 381.) But it is nevertheless false that the soul is the cause of the body. The "binding together" of the soul and the body is not a simple "being with" that joins a cause with what it has caused: "The soul needs the body, not because of its essential absolute intelligible reality, but in relation to the existence of its individual determination and of the eduction of its ipseity into temporal psychic existence" (*ibid.*, p. 382).

80. "And thus what certain Persian Orientals are said to have put forth, namely that the shadow imprisoned the light and imprisoned it for a time, then that the angels brought it aid and assistance, such that it gained victory over Ahriman, who is the shadow, and such that it was victorious over the shadow: this does not mean that a time limit was passed, or that the shadow would come from the light because of a rebellious thought. This event too comes from the soul, for the soul is a luminous substance in its aspect as actual intelligence, as we have shown. And the shadow is the natural animal power, which encircles and dominates the powers and attracts them to the lower world. As for the assistance of the angels, it is the opportune moment for the (divine) decree of the soul's guidance by an intelligible illumination, and thus its passage to the act, up to the time fixed for the persistence of the powers until the moment of death, or the rupture of the bodily attachment. As for the rebellious thought, it is the soul's affection for material things" (*ibid.*, p. 366). This is a striking example of a moral exegesis — in Aristotelianizing terms — of an ancient Persian symbol.

81. *Ibid.*, p. 355.

82. See Henri-Charles Puech, *En quête de la gnose* (Paris: Gallimard, 1978), vol. 1, pp. 55–82.

83. See Henry Corbin, *En islam iranien: Aspects spirituels et philosphiques* (Paris: Gallimard, 1971), vol. 2, *Sohrawardî et les platoniciens de Perse*, p. 117.

84. Sadrā brings together verses 2:38, 2:36, 101:1–11 (the entire "calamity" or "strife" sura), 19:71–72, and 7:29–30.

85. Sadr al-Dīn Shīrāzī, *al-Asfār*, vol. 8, pp. 355–57.

86. John 3:3.

87. Sadr al-Dīn Shīrāzī, *al-Asfār*, vol. 8, p. 356.

88. Sadrā first quotes this long passage: "Its descent to this world does not hurt her at all; indeed it benefits by it, for it derives from this world the knowledge of evil, and learns what its nature is, after expending its powers on it and manifesting its noble deeds and acts, the quiescent, that were within it when it was in the intelligible world. Had it not manifested its activities and expended its powers and had it not made them come into view, those powers and activities would have been idle in her and the soul would have forgotten the perfections and the perfect deeds, because they would have remained hidden and not apparent. Were this so, one would not know the power of the soul and would not know its nobility, for action is but the indication and manifestation of the hidden power, and if the power of the soul lay hidden and did not appear, it would decay and become as though it had never been." *Theology of Aristotle* 7; Plotinus, *Enneads* 4.8.5. With Lewis, I read *sharr*, evil, instead of *shay'*, thing.

89. Georges Vajda, "Les notes d'Avicenne sur la Théologie d'Aristote," *Revue thomiste* 51 (1951), p. 394.

90. Sadr al-Dīn Shīrāzī, *al-Asfār*, vol. 8, p. 358.

91. A passage from the *Phaedrus* (and not from the *Phaedo*, as the edition of *al-Asfār* states) and two passages attributed to the *Timaeus*; none of the three occurs literally in the dialogues, but they are very significant. This is how Sadrā quotes the *Phaedrus*: "The soul's fall into this world is caused by the falling off of its wings, and when it finds these wings again, it rises toward its originary world"; this corresponds roughly to *Phaedrus* 246d, 248b–c, 251b–c. Sadrā takes from Plato the well-known doctrine according to which the soul returns into this corporeal world in the cycle of palingenesis and, according to its sins, receives its punishment and retribution.

92. Sadr al-Dīn Shīrāzī, *al-Asfār*, vol. 8, p. 360.

93. *Theology of Aristotle* 2.33, 2.35, 7.87ff., in Plotinus, *Aflūtīn 'inda al-'Arab*, ed. 'Abd al-Rahmān Badawī (Cairo: Maktabat al-Nahdah al-Misrīyah, 1955).

94. Sadr al-Dīn Shīrāzī, *al-Asfār*, vol. 8, pp. 364–65.

95. See the explanation of the "secret of the fall of Adam" in the commentary on Qur'ān 2:36: "The most eminent bodily events are the spirits connected to human receptacles. It is not possible that all thinking souls pass from potency to act at a single moment, according to the *sunnah* of instantiation, without being connected to bodies.... At each moment, human souls proceed from the divine holy world. Whatever in them is perfected through knowledge and moral strengthening returns to the original homeland and to the divine place. And whatever is not perfected remains in a lower *barzakh*, for a greater or lesser time" (Sadr al-Dīn Shīrāzī, *Tafsīr al-Qur'ān al-karīm*, vol. 3, pp. 110–11). On the becoming decreed by God: "Man has three births, according to the order of the descent. And the same is true along the order of the reascent through the process of perfection. He thus has two falls and two ascensions. The birth from the world below is the end of the descent and of the fall, and the first degree of the reascent. It is the land of opposition and deficiency" (*ibid.*, p. 126). See also the quotation of the verses of Avicenna, in a *ta'wīl* of the fall of Adam: *ibid.*, pp. 160–61. Avicenna says that Adam fell from "the highest place," which Sadrā interprets thus: "The highest place is the supreme luminous world, entirely separated from the impurities of the body. It is the highest degree and belongs to the world of paradise. For paradise is corporeal and the world of pure light is immaterial and intelligible."

96. Sadr al-Dīn Shīrāzī, *al-Asfār*, vol. 8, pp. 366–77.

97. *Ibid.*, p. 366.

98. *Ibid.*, pp. 367–68.

99. *Ibid.*, pp. 368–69.

100. *Ibid.*, pp. 369–70.

101. *Ibid.*, p. 370.

102. *Ibid.* The dialogue quoted here is attributed to Pythagoras. This tradition of a "perfect nature" is a hermeticist notion that Henry Corbin identified with the personal angel. For an overview of its field of application, see Corbin, *En islam iranien*, vol. 4, p. 525, and the index under *nature parfaite*, and *The Man of Light in Iranian Sufism*, trans. Nancy Pearson (Boulder, CO: Shambhala, 1978).

103. Sadr al-Dīn Shīrāzī, *al-Asfār*, vol. 8, p. 371.

Chapter Seven: The Imagination

1. Sadiq Hidayat, *The Blind Owl*, trans. D.P. Costello (London: Calder, 1957), p. 44.

2. He thus revives the Mazdean hell, which was the first of all. See *Le livre*

d'Arda Viraz, transliteration, transcription, and translation of the Pahlavi text by Philippe Gignoux (Paris: Recherche sur les civilisations, 1984).

3. It suffices to refer to the "prelude" that, toward the end of his life, Henry Corbin wrote for the second edition of *Terre céleste et corps de resurrection de l'Iran mazdéen à l'Iran Shî'ite*, which became *Corps spirituel et terre céleste de l'Iran mazdéen à l'Iran Shî'ite* (Paris: Buchet/Chastel, 1979), titled "Pour une charte de l'imaginal." (This text does not appear in the translation, *Spiritual Body and Celestial Earth*, trans. Nancy Pearson [Princeton, NJ: Princeton University Press, 1977], which is not based on the second edition – Trans.) After a masterful discussion of the term's definition, Corbin writes: "I have noticed with pleasure, but not without some disquiet, that the word 'imaginal,' used in reference to my research, is becoming more widespread. I would like to make the following point: If one uses this term in order to apply it to something other than the *mundus imaginalis* and the imaginal Forms, as they are situated within the schema of the worlds that necessitate and legitimate them, there is a great danger that the term will be degraded and that its meaning will be lost" (p. 18).

4. The separation of the imagination, its distinction "from either perceiving or discursive thinking," is a thesis of Aristotle's (*On the Soul* 3.3.427b). Its definition as an intermediate formative faculty between the common sense and intellection is maintained up to Sadrā's time.

5. Muhammad ibn Ibrāhīm Sadr al-Dīn Shīrāzī, *al-Hikmah al-muta'ālīyah fī al-asfār al-'aqlīyah al-arba'ah* (al-Najaf, Iraq: Dār al-Ma'ārif al-Islāmīyah, 1958), vol. 3, p. 278.

6. *Hāla wijdānīyah nafsānīyah*: the existential, passionate feeling of an intensity of psychic existence. Knowledge is the soul's self-consciousness; *ibid.* See Chapter One.

7. As Edmund Husserl shows, an expression such as "golden mountain" (a classic example also used by Sadrā) can have a meaning even though it has no object. See *Logical Investigations*, trans. J.N. Findlay (London: Routledge and Kegan Paul, 1970), vol. 1, p. 193. Avicenna or Sadrā would maintain that judgment alone is responsible for the error that gives this meaning an objective value.

8. Sadr al-Dīn Shīrāzī, *al-Asfār*, vol. 3, p. 281.

9. *Ibid.*, p. 282.

10. Qur'ān 30:27, my emphasis. Like Jacques Berque, I am translating *al-mathal* as semblance. One could also translate it as similitude, image, or icon, since *al-mathal* is the equivalent of *al-mithāl*.

11. Bahman is the name of the first archangel proceeding from Ohrmazd. Suhrawardī homologizes him with the first Intelligence, as part of an attempt to establish a correspondence between the Mazdean angelology and the cosmology inherited from Avicenna. See Yahyá ibn Habash Suhrawardī, *L'archange empourpré: Quinze traités et récits mystiques*, ed. Henry Corbin (Paris: Fayard, 1976), p. 487 and the index under *Bahman*.

12. Muhammad ibn Ibrāhīm Sadr al-Dīn Shīrāzī, *Mafātīh al-ghayb*, ed. Muhammad Khvājavī (Tehran: Mu'assasah-'i Mutāla'āt va Tahqīqāt-i Farhangī, 1984), pp. 450–51.

13. *Laysah fī-l-wujūd ilā-Allāh*, a classic formulation in the Sūfism inherited from Ibn al-'Arabī, who states the complete and spiritual *tawhīd*, in opposition to an attestation of God that keeps him at a distance from the being of the creature, in a duality that is a form of idolatry and agnosticism.

14. Qur'ān 28:88 and 43:4; Sadrā also mentions Qur'ān 13:29 in connection with this.

15. Sadr al-Dīn Shīrāzī, *Mafātīh al-ghayb*, p. 447; allow me to refer once again to Christian Jambet, *Se rendre immortel: Suivi du Traité de la résurrection, Mollâ Sadrâ Shîrâzi* (Saint-Clément-de-Rivière, France: Fata Morgana, 2000), p. 54ff., where I discuss this passage, in which Sadrā is referring explicitly to *al-Shawāhid al-rubūbīyah*, ed. Jalāl al-Dīn Āshtiyānī (Meshed, Iran: University Press, 1967).

16. The use of the expression "lord of the icon" implies a precise conception of the relationship between the intelligible archetype and sensible, corporeal individuals. In Suhrawardī's language, it is a matter of the Intelligences proceeding from the primordial archangelic lights, each one the source of a different species. From each of these lords of the species, bodies emanate according to the dimension of indigence, and the souls ruling over bodies proceed according to the victorial dimension. The vocabulary used here is that of theurgy: the species is the result of an emanation that is an act of theurgy to which corresponds the icon's resemblance to its intelligible model, and nature is thus the iconostasis of the immaterial lights. See Yahyá ibn Habash Suhrawardī, *Le livre de la sagesse orientale (Kitâb Hikmat al-Ishrâq)*, trans. Henry Corbin, ed. Christian Jambet (Lagrasse, France: Verdier, 1986), pp. 140–41, and Sadrā's glosses, *ibid.*, p. 542.

17. This dialectical deduction stands in for a presential grasp or an immediate "unveiling" of the Idea.

18. Sadr al-Dīn Shīrāzī, *Mafātīh al-ghayb*, pp. 443–46.

19. Qur'ān 2:257.

20. Sadr al-Dīn Shīrāzī, *Mafātīh al-ghayb*, p. 445.

21. Sadr al-Dīn Shīrāzī, *al-Asfār*, vol. 3, p. 297.

22. Sadr al-Dīn Shīrāzī, *Mafātīh al-ghayb*, pp. 445–46. The important notion of *ghanā'* signifies wealth, self-sufficiency. It thus implies the freedom that is necessitated through itself. It corresponds exactly to the Aristotelian concept of autarchy.

23. *Ibid.*

24. *Ibid.*, p. 456; Qur'ān 96:3–5. On the homologation of the pen and the intelligence according to Ibn al-'Arabī, implicitly present here, see Ibn al-'Arabī, *Les illuminations de La Mecque*, ed. Michel Chodkiewicz (Paris: Sindbad, 1988), p. 60.

25. According to Qur'ān 4:1: "He created you from a single soul."

26. Sadr al-Dīn Shīrāzī, *Mafātīh al-ghayb*, pp. 453–54. Mullā Sadrā cites Ibn al-'Abbās's interpretation (the water is the water of knowledge), and others as well (the water is the grace of effusion, the water is the Qur'ān). These interpretations refer to Qur'ān 13:17. For Sadrā, they are equivalent.

27. Pierre Duhem carried out the first modern study of this notion: Pierre Duhem, *Medieval Cosmology: Theories of Infinity, Place, Time, Void, and the Plurality of Worlds*, trans. Roger Ariew (Chicago: University of Chicago Press, 1985), p. 173ff. On the work of Ibn al-Haytham (430/1038), who, following Simplicius, proposed the ninth sphere, or the sphere of spheres, see Seyyed Hossein Nasr, *An Annotated Bibliography of Islamic Science* (Lahore: Suhail Academy, 1975), vol. 1, p. 247ff.

28. See Mullā Sadrā's analysis in his exegesis of Qur'ān 62:2: "It is he who has sent amongst the unlettered a messenger from among themselves, to recite to them his signs, to purify them, and to instruct them in scripture and wisdom – although they had been, before, in manifest error." Muhammad ibn Ibrāhīm Sadr al-Dīn Shīrāzī, *Tafsīr al-Qur'ān al-karīm*, ed. Muhammad Khvājavī (Qum, Iran: Bīdār, 1987), vol. 7, pp. 152–54.

29. The structure of the "births" and the worlds is therefore the following: the sensible birth (*nash'at al-hiss*) corresponds to the lower world (*'ālam al-dunyā'*); the birth of the soul (*nash'at al-nafs*) corresponds to the otherworld (*'ālam al-akhira*); the birth of the intelligence corresponds to the intelligence in the world of lordliness (*'ālam al-rubūbīyah*).

30. This conception of the prophet can be compared to that of Maimonides and to the entire doctrine of hermeneutics in the work of Joseph ben Abraham Ibn Waqār, the fourteenth-century cabbalist of Toledo. See Georges Vajda, *Recherches sur la philosophie et la kabbale dans la pensée juive du Moyen Age* (Paris: Mouton, 1962), pp. 148–70.

31. According to Qur'ān 18:88.

32. Sadr al-Dīn Shīrāzī, *Tafsīr al-Qur'ān al-karīm*, vol. 7, p. 122 (commenting on Qur'ān 56:83–87).

33. Sadrā refers to the statement attributed to the Prophet according to which the Islamic community includes within itself, and overcomes, all the great communities that came before: the Qadarīyah are the magi of Islam, the Zāhirīyah or the Mushabbiha are the Jews of Islam, and the Ismā'īlī Shī'ites (the Bātinīyah) are the Christians. Pure obedience to the external letter (identified here with Judaism) and integral esoterism, which abandons the level of external meaning (identified with Christianity), are equally blameworthy. See Sadr al-Dīn Shīrāzī, *Tafsīr al-Qur'ān al-karīm*, vol. 7, p. 187.

34. *al-'Alam al-mutawassit bayn al-'ālamīn.*

35. Here the *himma* signifies a precise complex of powers, including enlightened resolution, force of soul, and well-informed prudence. It also has a mystical meaning in the language of Sūfism. It is through the *himma* that the imagination unfolds the inner space of its spiritual revelations. The spatialization produced by the imagination is an effect of its *himma*, its power. We will see this later in Sadrā. On the articulation of the theme of space with that of the *himma*, see Hermann Landolt, "Sakralraum und mystischer Raum im Islam," *Eranos* 44 (1975), pp. 231–65.

36. On the complex notion of *walāyah* in Twelver Shī'ism, see Mohammad-Ali Amir-Moezzi, "Notes à propos de la *walâya* imamite (Aspects de l'imâmologie duodécimaine X)," in Geneviève Gobillot (ed.), *Mystique musulmane: Parcours en compagnie d'un chercheur: Roger Deladrière* (Paris: Cariscript, 2002), and Hermann Landolt, "Walayah," in Mircea Eliade (ed.), *The Encyclopedia of Religion* (New York: Macmillan, 1987), pp. 316–23.

37. This harmony or correspondence is described by Mullā Sadrā in his commentary on Qur'ān 56:78, or, more precisely, on the expression "a hidden book" (*kitāb maknun*). Sadr al-Dīn Shīrāzī, *Tafsīr al-Qur'ān al-karīm*, vol. 7, pp. 107–108.

38. Qur'ān 6:75.

39. Sadr al-Dīn Shīrāzī, *Mafātīh al-ghayb*, pp. 149–50.

40. Sadr al-Dīn Shīrāzī, *Tafsīr al-Qur'ān al-karīm*, vol. 7, p. 108.

41. See Michel Chodkiewicz, *Seal of the Saints: Prophethood and Sainthood in the Doctrine of Ibn 'Arabi*, trans. Liadain Sherrard (Cambridge: Islamic Texts Society, 1993).

42. Qur'ān 89:27–30.

43. Sadr al-Dīn Shīrāzī, *Tafsīr al-Qur'ān al-karīm*, vol. 4, p. 239.

44. al-Ghazzālī vigorously reproached "the philosophers" – especially Avicenna – with denying bodily retribution. Mullā Sadrā takes up this accusation, which is not groundless, although it is somewhat unjust, as Jean R. Michot shows in *La destinée de l'homme selon Avicenne: Le retour à Dieu (ma'ad) et l'imagination* (Louvain, Belgium: Peeters, 1986), pp. 192–218. In many respects, Sadrā's conception of the eschatological function of the imagination in the "return" (*ma'ād*) is similar to Avicenna's, as will be clear to readers of Michot's analysis. But I do not agree that Avicenna, much less Sadrā, commits an excess of intellectualism in locating imaginal paradise and hell at a degree inferior to the supreme destination, which is and remains the encounter with the agent intellect – and which, for Sadrā, is a becoming-agent intellect. On the contrary, such a structure is essential to these thinkers, who want to save the letter of revelation without falling into literalism and without appearing to give their assent to the triumph of literalism. If the supreme destiny of man is intelligence, then the way is barred to juristic dogmatism, and thus to its consequences, the most serious of which is the attempt to center Islam on positive law and the prescriptions of *sharī'a*.

45. Sadr al-Dīn Shīrāzī, *al-Shawāhid al-rubūbīyah*, p. 231ff., and *al-Asfār*, vol. 9, pp. 1–55.

46. Alexander, cited by Sadrā, following Shahrastānī: *al-Shawāhid al-rubūbīyah*, p. 226. See Muhammad ibn 'Abd al-Karīm Shahrastānī, *Livre des religions et des sectes*, vol. 2 (Paris: UNESCO, 1993), p. 354ff.

47. Mullā Sadrā distinguishes between different terms that are translated here simply as "body": *al-badan*, which designates the natural elemental body; *al-jism*, which means the body in general and can mean the imaginal body; and *al-jirm*, which means more particularly the celestial body. The separation of the imagination is a separation from the body in the sense of *al-badan*, not from every body. At times, however, his use of the terms varies.

48. Qur'ān 29:64. Berque translates *al-Hayawān* as the fullness of living.

This is a *hapax* in the Qur'ān, and the term does indeed designate life in its maximum of vital intensity. Sadrā homologizes it with the plenitude of the animal life of the soul, in the first sense of the term, not in the sense in which the soul is the principle ruling over this material body. We have seen above that this animal life has the experience of the immateriality of its "self" (Sadr al-Dīn Shīrāzī, *al-Shawāhid al-rubūbīyah*, p. 227).

49. The imagination "can imagine the sphere of spheres as well as the mustard seed, it can imagine the ray of sunlight and the heat from the fire, while it can also imagine the flash of lightning and the moderate warmth of the air, and it can imagine the noise of thunder or the sound of a whisper" (Sadr al-Dīn Shīrāzī, *al-Asfār*, vol. 8, p. 299). Freedom, plasticity, variable particularity, the union of opposites – all these prove the immateriality of the imagination.

50. *Ibid.*, vol. 3, p. 476ff.

51. *Ibid.*, p. 478ff.

52. *Ibid.*, pp. 478–84.

53. *Ibid.*, vol. 8, p. 211ff.

54. This analysis can be compared with Hume's. Whereas Hume speaks of the human mind, Sadrā speaks of the immaterial imagination, in its function as remembrance, as a power of habit. Sadrā is a Platonist Hume (*ibid.*, vol. 8, p. 213).

55. *Ibid.*, p. 214.

56. *Ibid.*

57. On the process of stripping away (*tajrīd*) form, see Avicenna, *al-Mabda' wa-al-ma'ād*, ed. 'Abd Allāh Nūrānī (Tehran: Dānishgāh-i Tihrān, 1984), pp. 102–103.

58. "For indeed when painters themselves wish to represent sirens and satyrs by means of especially bizarre forms, they surely cannot assign to them utterly new natures. Rather, they simply fuse together the members of various animals." René Descartes, *Meditations on First Philosophy: In Which the Existence of God and the Distinction of the Soul from the Body Are Demonstrated,* trans. Donald A. Cress, 3rd ed. (Indianapolis, IN: Hackett, 1993), meditation 1, p. 15.

59. Avicenna, *Avicenna's De Anima (Arabic Text): Being the Psychological Part of Kitab al-Shifa'*, ed. Fazlur Rahman (London: Oxford University Press, 1959), ch. 4, sec. 2, p. 169ff.

60. This is exactly what will be said in the phenomenology of the imaginary, particularly in Jean-Paul Sartre's well-known work *The Imaginary: A*

Phenomenological Psychology of the Imagination, trans. Jonathan Webber (1940; London: Routledge, 2004).

61. Avicenna, *Avicenna's De Anima*, p. 173.

62. Avicenna, *al-Ishārāt wa-al-tanbīhāt*, ed. Sulaymān Dunyā, pt. 3 (Cairo: Dār al-Ma'ārif, 1966), p. 407.

63. See Avicenna's commentary on Tūsī, *ibid.*, p. 407.

64. Ahmad Ghazzālī, brother of the great theologian. *Sawānih* is the title of his "treatise on love." See Ahmad ibn Muhammad Ghazzālī, *Sawanih: Inspirations from the World of Pure Spirits, the Oldest Sufi Treatise on Love*, trans. Nasr Allah Pourjavady (London: KPI in association with Iran University Press, 1986). See also Ahmad ibn Muhammad Ghazzālī, *Gedanken über die Liebe*, trans. (into German) Richard Gramlich (Mainz, Germany: Akademie der Wissenschaften und der Literatur, 1976).

65. Michel Foucault, *The History of Sexuality*, vol. 3, *The Care of the Self*, trans. Robert Hurley (New York: Pantheon, 1986), p. 5.

66. "Nevertheless the ancient belief that dreams foretell the future is not wholly devoid of truth. By picturing our wishes as fulfilled, dreams are after all leading us into the future. But this future, which the dreamer pictures as the present, has been molded by his indestructible wish into a perfect likeness of the past." These are the final sentences of Sigmund Freud's *Interpretation of Dreams*; see *The Standard Edition of the Complete Psychological Works of Sigmund Freud*, ed. James Strachey (London: Hogarth Press, 1995), vol. 5, p. 621.

67. Avicenna, *Avicenna's De Anima*, p. 178.

68. Nasīr al-Dīn al-Tūsī, in Avicenna, *al-Ishārāt wa-al-tanbihāt*, vol. 3, p. 408.

69. Sadrā draws from this the following argument: "Certain shaykhs or friends of God are such that their imagination (*takhayyul*) and their configurative power (*tasawwur*) take place because of the state of immaterial intelligence. If their imaginative faculty subsisted through this natural body, would there be a deficiency in their imagination or in their estimative faculty every time they became sick? Not at all, since they have no defect in their operations" (*al-Asfār*, vol. 8, p. 294). The imagination's independence from lower matter is thus demonstrated, as if Sadrā had the sense that he was completing an analysis that Avicenna had not taken to its logical conclusion.

70. Nasīr al-Dīn al-Tūsī, in Avicenna, *al-Ishārāt wa-al-tanbihāt*, vol. 3, p. 408ff. Tūsī presupposes the existence of the imaginal world, according to the versions of it that he had read in the disciples of Suhrawardī.

71. Yahyá ibn Habash Suhrawardī, *Kitāb Hikmat al-ishrāq*, bk. 4, ch. 8, *Oeuvres philosophiques et mystiques (Opera metaphysica et mystica, vol. 2): Prolégomènes en français et édition critique*, ed. Henry Corbin (Teheran: Institut franco-iranien, 1952), p. 211; *Le livre de la sagesse oriental (Kitâb Hikmat al-Ishrâq)*, trans. Henry Corbin, ed. Christian Jambet (Lagrasse, France: Verdier, 1986), p. 199.

72. See the glosses translated in *Le livre de la sagesse orientale*, p. 387. Qutb al-Dīn Shīrāzī (634/1236–710/1311) developed the concept of the imaginal world from his readings of Ibn al-ʿArabī and Suhrawardī. Its distinction from the world of the Ideas, the specular model, the discernment of the traces of the imaginal world in dreams, visions, and post mortem experiences—these and a number of other themes from his work can be found in Sadrā. See John Walbridge, *The Science of Mystic Lights: Qutb al-Din Shirazi and the Illuminationist Tradition in Islamic Philosophy* (Cambridge, MA: Harvard University Press, 1992), pp. 155–59. On Shahrazuri, see Sabine Schmidtke, "The Influence of Shams al-Din Shahrazuri (7th/13th century) on Ibn Abi Jumhur al-Ahsaʿi (d. after 904/1499): A Preliminary Note," in Lutz Edzard and Christian Szyska (eds.), *Encounters of Words and Texts* (Hildesheim, Germany: Olms, 1997), pp. 23–32, and especially *Theologie, Philosophie und Mystik im zwölferschiitischen Islam des 9./15. Jahrhunderts* (Leiden: Brill, 2000), pp. 212–33.

73. Shams al-Dīn Muhammad ibn Mahmūd Shahrazūrī, *Sharh Hikmat al-Ishrāq*, ed. Husayn Ziyāʾī Turbatī (Tehran: Mu'assasah-'i Mutālaʿāt va Tahqīqāt-i Farhangī [Pizhūhishgāh], 1993), p. 509.

74. *Ibid.*

75. Jorge Luis Borges, "Al espejo" (To the Mirror), *Obras completas* (Buenos Aires: Emecé, 1974), p. 1133.

76. Suhrawardī, *Le livre de la sagesse orientale*, bk. 5, sec. 259, p. 222.

77. We see this liberating pedagogy of love and imagination enacted in the novel by Nizami Ganjavi, *Les sept portraits*, trans. Isabelle de Gastines (Paris: Fayard, 2000). The structure of the imagination in Islam seems to be a transhistorical, transcultural phenomenon. The traits characterizing the women in Ganjavi's novel can be found today in the experience of women, and in an experience of desire, in which events of an imaginal type take place. See Aline Tauzin's beautiful book, *Figures du féminin dans la société maure, Mauritanie: Désir nomade* (Paris: Karthala, 2001).

78. Mullā Sadrā writes: "For if man had a strong enough active imagination, if the power of his heart (*himmah*) were intense enough, if his soul were not

submerged in matter, if his attention were not dispersed in the multitude of preoccupations, he would not need any bodily movement to attain the object of his desire, once he turns toward it in his soul. Or rather, all that he desires would be present to him, in a perfect presence"; in Suhrawardī, *Le livre de la sagesse orientale*, p. 621.

79. The perfect man has an entirely spiritual enjoyment. For Sadrā, this pleasure owes nothing more to the imagination, but it is the unification of the intelligence with the archangelic world, the perpetual praise of God. He interprets illuminative ecstasy in terms of the extinction of the self (*fanā'*) and permanent abiding in God.

80. Suhrawardī, *Kitāb Hikmat al-ishrāq*, bk. 5, sec. 240; *Oeuvres philosophiques et mystiques*, p. 226; *Le livre de la sagesse orientale*, p. 211.

81. Suhrawardī's text gives rise to a certain perplexity in his commentator Qutb al-Dīn al-Shīrāzī (*Kitāb Hikmat al-ishrāq*, pp. 229–30; *Le livre de sagesse orientale*, p. 213 and p. 403). I interpret the expression "the blessed among the moderately advanced and the ascetics among those who have acquired moral purity" to mean – given the use of the conjunction – that Suhrawardī defines this rank of election through the practice of moral ascesis. A gloss suggests this, but the point remains doubtful.

82. Suhrawardī, *Kitāb Hikmat al-Ishrāq*, p. 230; *Le livre de la sagesse orientale*, pp. 213–14.

83. See Shahrazūrī, *Sharh Hikmat al-Ishrāq*, pp. 549–50.

84. Much could be gained by comparing this conception of the soul's imaginal destiny with the doctrine that Georges Vajda presents, with numerous references to the Sabians and to Muslim authors, in *Juda ben Nissim Ibn Malka: Philosophe juif marocain* (Paris: Larose, 1954) and "La doctrine astrologique de Juda ben Nissim Ibn Malka," in *Homenaje a Millás-Vallicrosa*, vol. 2 (Barcelona: Consejo Superior de Investigaciones Científicas, 1956), pp. 483–500. In his discussion of the doctrine of the Sabians, Shahrastānī lays out their doctrine of celestial "abodes" and the representations or idols made of them by the faithful. There is no trace here of a doctrine of the imaginal, but it is not difficult to see the importance of this Sabian "idolatry," interpreted as an iconostasis. On the Sabians, see the rich and erudite synthesis of Guy Monnot, in Shahrastānī, *Livre des religions et des sectes*, vol. 2, pp. 3–13, and his translation of Shahrastānī, *ibid.*, pp. 159–62.

85. The imagination thus becomes the vehicle of the soul. Henry Corbin

compared this conception with that of Proclus and his view of "perpetual bodies" and the "middle vehicle" of the soul. On closer examination, however, it appears that the concept of the "middle vehicle" is based entirely on the Platonic notion of the soul, and Suhrawardī's philosophy of the imagination, as we are examining it here, has no place in its definition there. The text referred to by Jean Trouillard designates an intermediate status between the sensibles and the intelligibles, but nothing that resembles the imaginal world. We must say, rather, that the *ishrāqī* doctrine imposed something on the Proclusian scheme that is in no way valorized in it, and that following Suhrawardī, Mullā Sadrā interpreted the median degree of the soul in terms of the imagination and the configuration of the psychic body. See Trouillard, *L'un et l'âme selon Proclos* (Paris: Belles Lettres, 1972), p. 187, and Proclus, *Commentaire sur le "Timée,"* trans. A.J. Festugière (Paris: Vrin, 1967), vol. 3, p. 340ff. This also applies to the vehicle of the soul in the tradition of the Chaldaean oracles; see Yochanan Lewy, *Chaldaean Oracles and Theurgy: Mysticism, Magic and Platonism in the Later Roman Empire* (Cairo: Institut français d'archéologie orientale, 1956), p. 178ff. The imaginal world, in the sense meant by the Ishrāqīyah, takes on the function of the ether, the sun, the moon, and the air, fragments of which form the "vehicle of the soul."

86. See Suhrawardī, *Kitāb Hikmat al-ishrāq*, bk. 5, sec. 247; *Oeuvres philosophiques et mystiques*, p. 252; *Le livre de la sagesse orientale*, p. 215.

87. See the references to the Mazdean lexicon provided by Henry Corbin, *En Islam iranien: Aspects spirituels et philosophiques*, vol. 2, *Sohrawardî et les platoniciens de Perse* (Paris: Gallimard, 1971), pp. 105–106.

88. Shahrazūrī, *Sharh Hikmat al-Ishrāq*, p. 553.

89. *Ibid.*, pp. 553–54.

90. *Ibid.*, p. 554.

91. Suhrawardī, *Le livre de la sagesse orientale*, p. 544.

92. *Ibid.*, p. 213.

93. *Ibid.*, pp. 647–49.

94. Yves Marquet, "Sabéens et Ikhwân al-Safâ'," *Studia Islamica* 24 (1966), pp. 35–81.

95. Here we would have to recognize the full value of Shahrastānī's testimony, both in his *Livre des religions et des sectes (Milal wa-al-nihal)* and in his commentary on the Qur'ān. Unfortunately, I cannot expand on this reference within the framework of the present study. Shahrastani pointed out the connection made by the Sabians between, on the one hand, the dogma of the angel's

appearance in human form and the demon's appearance in animal form and, on the other, the dogma of transmigration; this connection confirms the interpenetration of these speculations (on astral religion, transmigration, and the destination of the soul and its retribution) within a structure of thought found again, albeit implicitly, in the reflections of the Ishrāqīyah. See *Livre des religions et des sectes*, vol. 1, p. 512; on transmigration in Ismāʿīlī circles, see Wilfred Madelung, "Abu Yaʿqub al-Sijistani and Metempsychosis," *Iranica Varia: Papers in Honor of Professor Ehsan Yarshater* (Leiden: Brill, 1990), pp. 131–43.

96. Avicenna opened the way for such an interpretation of reward and punishment, adopting the conclusions of astral theology and an "imaginal beyond," but without theorizing an imaginal world, strictly speaking and in the full sense of the term. See Michot, *La destinée de l'homme selon Avicenne*, pp. 190–98.

97. Shahrazuri, *Sharh Hikmat al-Ishrāq*, p. 554ff.

98. Guy Monnot, *Islam et religions* (Paris: Maisonneuve et Larose, 1986), p. 122.

99. See Guy Monnot, *Penseurs musulmans et religions iraniennes: ʿAbd al-Jabbar et ses devanciers* (Paris: Vrin, 1974).

100. Shahrastani, *Livre des religions et des sectes*, vol. 1, p. 659.

101. Michel Tardieu, *Le Manichéisme* (Paris: Presses Universitaires de France, 1981), p. 109.

102. See Henri-Charles Puech, *Sur le manichéisme et autres essais* (Paris: Flammarion, 2001), pp. 43–44. Here is a quote from the hymn to the four great days: "The path is the perfect man: whoever walks it has a confident heart. The vessels are the sun and the moon: no price is demanded from he who steps on board. The treasure house is the god of truth." André Villey, *Psaumes des errants: Ecrits manichéens du Fayyum* (Paris: Cerf, 1994), p. 60. On the detail of the mechanism involving the moon and the sun, see Villey's commentary in his translation of Alexander of Lycopolis, *Contre la doctrine de Mani* (Paris: Cerf, 1985), pp. 156–58.

103. Qur'ān 56:19; Shahrazūrī, *Sharh Hikmat al-Ishrāq*, p. 552.

104. Shahrazūrī, *Sharh Hikmat al-Ishrāq*, p. 552.

105. As Robert Klein puts it: "There is no point in imagining one's judges after death: on its own, by the weight of what it has thought, the soul is carried to the place of its punishment or its reward. The reincarnation spoken of by the Platonists is only the mythic expression of the fact that the soul chooses its destiny." *La forme et l'intelligible* (Paris: Gallimard, 1970), p. 78. (This essay is not

included in the English translation of the book.) Klein's studies of the Renaissance imagination and the authors of the period, particularly Marsilio Ficino and Giordano Bruno, illuminate Sadrā's formulations remarkably well.

106. Shahrazūrī, *Sharh Hikmat al-Ishrāq*.

107. *Lā fī 'ālam al-mithāl*: "not in the imaginal world," since Sadrā distinguishes the authentic world of the active imagination, which is the world of the soul, from the imaginal world as conceived of by the Ishrāqīyah. See Sadr al-Dīn Shīrāzī, *Tafsīr al-Qur'ān al-karīm*, vol. 5 (on the Yāsīn sura), p. 378.

108. *Ibid.*

109. This phenomenology of knowledge is presented in its entirety in Sadr al-Dīn Shīrāzī, *al-Asfār*, vol. 3, pp. 300–305.

110. Sadr al-Dīn Shīrāzī, *Tafsīr al-Qur'ān al-karīm*, vol. 5, pp. 378–79.

111. Sadr al-Dīn Shīrāzī, *al-Shawāhid al-rubūbīyah*, pp. 227–78.

112. Sadr al-Dīn Shīrāzī, *Tafsīr al-Qur'ān al-karīm* , vol. 1, p. 299.

113. Qur'ān 19:17. These quotes are from next section of the Qur'ānic commentary, Sadr al-Dīn Shīrāzī, *Tafsīr al-Qur'ān al-karīm*, vol. 1, pp. 299–301.

114. Sadr al-Dīn Shīrāzī, *Tafsīr al-Qur'ān al-karīm*, vol. 1, pp. 299–301.

115. Muhammad ibn Ibrāhīm Sadr al-Dīn Shīrāzī, *Mabda'wa-al-ma'ād*, ed. Jalāl al-Dīn Āshtiyānī and Seyyed Hossein Nasr (Tehran: Anjuman-i Shāhanshāhī-i Falsafah-'i Īrān, 1976), pp. 423–30.

116. Sadrā quotes the last lines of the *Ilāhīyāt*: Avicenna, *al-Shifa: al-Ilahiyyat (La métaphysique)*, ed. Georges C. Anawati and Sa'id Zayid (Cairo: Organisation générale des imprimeries gouvernementales, 1960), p. 432. It is remarkable that the entire edifice of Avicenna's metaphysics ends this way, with internal enjoyment or suffering, with the dream of heaven or the heaven of dreams.

117. For al-Ghazzālī, dreams have the function of bringing premonitions and revealing the states of the otherworld. In dreams, important witnesses – the companions of the Prophets, for example – come to tell the dreamer the retribution they have received from God. There is even a dream in which 'Ālī and Mu'āwiyah both come to tell of their salvation: the first was rewarded, the second forgiven – a touching and improbable reconciliation. But then heaven does not seem to be an imaginal heaven, even though it is a heaven revealed in a dream. See al-Ghazzālī, *Ihyā' 'ulūm al-dīn (The Revitalization of the Sciences of Religion)*, ed. 'Abd al-Rahīm ibn al-Husayn 'Irāqī (Cairo: Mu'assasat al-Halabī, 1967–68), vol. 4, p. 536ff. al-Ghazzālī, however, warns against identifying the

heavenly land and the material land. It is no doubt the land of the otherworld, admirably described by al-Ghazzālī, that Sadrā is thinking of when he develops his doctrine of the imaginal land. See *ibid.*, vol. 4, p. 546ff.

118. Sadr al-Dīn Shīrāzī, *Mabdā ʻwa-al-ma ʻād*, p. 424.

119. In sleep, as in death, our soul is awakened to itself, to the world it makes from itself, and it unfolds the special duration of its internal senses, condensed in the imagination alone.

120. Sadr al-Dīn Shīrāzī, *al-Asfār*, vol. 9, p. 332.

121. Sadr al-Dīn Shīrāzī, *Mabdā ʻwa-al-ma ʻād*, p. 428. In a handwritten note that remains unpublished, Henry Corbin wrote these remarkable sentences: "In general, the soul is itself that which imagines. It no longer needs a faculty called the imagination." In view of the text I am discussing, I would say, rather: In general, the soul is itself something that *senses*, something that produces *sensible truth*. It no longer needs a faculty called the imagination. Still, these productive senses of the soul are internal, configurative, and memorial, much like the imagination. The imagination will be the power that survives the ruin of the body and will provide the matter of the visions of the tomb.

122. Sadr al-Dīn Shīrāzī, *al-Asfār*, vol. 9, p. 378.

123. *Ibid.*, p. 428ff.

124. Marcel Proust, *In Search of Lost Time*, vol. 2, *Within a Budding Grove*, trans. C.K. Scott-Moncrieff and Terence Kilmartin, revised by D.J. Enright (London: Chatto and Windus, 1992), pp. 461–62.

Chapter Eight: A Philosophy of Spirit

1. I am translating expressions using the term *psychique* literally (as here: *l'homme psychique*), but the strong connotation of "soul" in these expressions should be kept in mind, such that this subtitle, for example, could also be rendered as "The Man of Soul" — Trans.

2. Muhammad ibn Ibrahim Sadr al-Dīn Shīrāzī, *Kitāb al-ʻarshīyah*, pt. 2, 1st illumination, 9th thesis; *The Wisdom of the Throne*, trans. James Winston Morris (Princeton, NJ: Princeton University Press, 1981), p. 142 (translation emended, here and in all other quotes, to reflect Jambet's French — Trans.). Shaykh Ahmad Ahsāʼī comments: "This psychic man, a median substance between intelligible man and natural man, signifies in general that he is not in intelligible simplicity, but neither is he in material density. Indeed, the intelligible is entirely separate from elementary natural matter and from substantial or imaginal form,

as well as from the temporal and natural duration proper to the temporal matter/form composite. The psychic, however, is neither elementary nor natural, but remains formal (like what is natural), and substantial and perpetual (like what is intelligible)" (*Kitāb al-'arshīyah*, p. 94).

3. "This was precisely the approach of his teachers, Plato and Socrates, concerning the forms (*suwar*, Ideas). But the author of the *Shifā'* (Healing) did not find it easy to comprehend this subject or to follow this path, so that he began to criticize this talk of the existence of the Ideas and to attack Plato and Socrates on this subject quite vehemently. It is as though he had never looked at the *Theology*, or as though he had attributed it not to Aristotle but rather to Plato" (Sadr al-Dīn Shīrāzī, *Kitāb al-'arshīyah*, p. 96; *Wisdom of the Throne*, pp. 143–44). To attribute to Plato a book consisting of Plotinian texts would have demonstrated great perspicacity. Sadrā contends that the book comes from Aristotle, and this allows him to believe in the unity of the Greek sages and to reproach Avicenna with an inconsistency of which he himself becomes guilty. But his confusion is fruitful. It authorizes this debate on the Ideas and the reality of the intelligible world, which in turn conditions the philosophical interpretation of the return to God.

4. Sadr al-Dīn Shīrāzī, *Kitāb al-'arshīyah*, vol. 2, p. 98; *Wisdom of the Throne*, pp. 144–45 (translation emended).

5. See Shaykh Ahmad Ahsā'ī's commentary in Sadr al-Dīn Shīrāzī, *Kitāb al-'arshīyah*, pp. 98–99.

6. *Ibid.*, p. 100.

7. The Neoplatonic scheme had another destiny in Ismā'īlī Shī'ism, where it was the basis of an authentic philosophy of history, including the seven cycles or periods corresponding to the six prophets announcing a *sharī'ah*, followed by the seventh period, that of the resurrector. This could be called an *Ismā'īlī Shī'ite theology* of history.

8. *Ibid.*, p. 98; *Wisdom of the Throne*, p. 145.

9. Sadr al-Dīn Shīrāzī, *Kitāb al-'arshīyah*, pp. 98, 109, 110; *Wisdom of the Throne*, pp. 145–46 (translation emended).

10. See the tradition that speaks of "the armies of intelligence and of ignorance," related by Kulaynī, among others, and commented on by Mullā Sadrā, in Mohammad-Ali Amir-Moezzi, "Fin du temps et retour à l'origine (Aspects de l'imâmologie duodécimaine VI)," *Revue des mondes musulmans et de la Méditérranée* 91-94 (2001), pp. 59–61.

11. For example, the Satanic estimative faculty. The *wahmīyah* or *wahm*, is, in the strict sense, the estimative faculty, the inferior degree of the faculty of cognitive or practical judgment. But it is also a power of imaginary configuration that fashions deceptive forms. Here, the *wahmīyah* thus extends to the sense of a deceptive imagination that causes one to judge badly, during earthly life, and to choose to orient oneself toward false goods and deceptive appearances. The *wahm* is the faculty of deceptive appearances. Therefore, the intelligible form that is united with the spiritual matter of the soul, nourished by this false appearance, can only take a deceptive form, as Satan does. Satan does indeed have a real existence, in the hell of the imagination and of the imaginal birth of the soul, but this existence has no more consistency than the evil it incarnates; it is the existence of a deceptive appearance, as is taught throughout the Qur'ān. On the *wahm*, I refer the reader to an old but still suggestive article by Harry Austryn Wolfson, "The Internal Senses in Latin, Arabic, and Hebrew Philosophic Texts," *Harvard Theological Review* 28, no. 2 (1935), pp. 69–133.

12. This refers to a famous tradition on which the authority of the imams is based; it says that 'Ālī is the threshold (*bāb*) of the city of knowledge whose prophet is Muhammad. See Chapter Seven, pp. 343ff.

13. Sadr al-Dīn Shīrāzī, *Kitāb al-'arshīyah*, vol. 3, p. 227ff; *Wisdom of the Throne* ("Principle, on the inner meaning of *Tūbā*"), p. 231ff. An analysis of Shaykh Ahmad's admirable commentary on this text, which ends with a significant quotation from Ibn al-'Arabī, is still to be undertaken.

14. Muhammad ibn Ibrāhīm Sadr al-Dīn Shīrāzī, "Kitāb al-tawhīd," in *Sharh usūl al-kāfī*, ed. Muhammad Khvājavī (Tehran: Mu'assasah-'i Mutāla'āt va Tahqīqāt-i Farhangī, 1987), p. 380ff.

15. Qur'ān 15:29, 17:85, 32:9, 38:72, 78:38, 97:4, among others.

16. Or the "possessors of hearts," those who are eminently endowed with the spiritual organ of the heart.

17. This gradual scheme is classic. See Fakhr al-Dīn Muhammad ibn 'Umar Rāzī, *Kitāb al-nafs wa-al-rūh wa-sharh quwāhumā*, ed. Muhammad Saghīr Hasan al-Ma'sūmī (Tehran: n.p., 1985), p. 78. One finds it, for example, in Rūzbihān Baqlī of Shiraz, in a different form. Not the hierarchy of imaginal soul, intelligence, heart, and spirit, but rather one of principle vital soul, intelligence, heart, spirit. On the doctrine of spirit in Rūzbihān, see Paul Ballanfat, *Quatre traités inédits de Rûzbehân Baqlî Shîrâzî* (Tehran: Institut français de recherche en Iran, 1998), pp. 91–180.

18. In the sense given to the subtle organ of the heart and the *himma* in Ibn al-ʿArabī, whom Mullā Sadrā rather tamely follows here. See Henry Corbin, *Creative Imagination in the Sufism of Ibn ʿArabi*, trans. Ralph Manheim (Princeton, NJ: Princeton University Press, 1969), pp. 222–30.

19. Sadr al-Dīn Shīrāzī, "Kitāb al-tawhīd," p. 381. Sadrā quotes Qur'ān 7:54: "It is his to create and to command."

20. See Paul Nwyia, *Exégèse coranique et langage mystique: Nouvel essai sur le lexique technique des mystiques musulmans* (Beirut: Dar el-Machreq, 1970), pp. 56–57. Sadrā begins with the breathing of spirit into Adam and Jesus in order to examine whether the spirit is the Creator, created, or a "part of God," as the Christians think. A tradition going back to the sixth imam concerning the spirit breathed into Jesus says that "this spirit is created" (Sadr al-Dīn Shīrāzī, "Kitāb al-tawhīd," p. 375).

21. Qur'ān 15:29.

22. Qur'ān 17:85.

23. Qur'ān 32:9.

24. Qur'ān 17: 85; Sadr al-Dīn Shīrāzī, "Kitāb al-tawhīd," pp. 383–84.

25. Sadr al-Dīn Shīrāzī, "Kitāb al-tawhīd," p. 382.

26. *Ibid.*, p. 383.

27. This exegesis is based on a tradition of the sixth imam, Jaʿfar al-Sādiq: "The spirit is moved like the wind, and one calls it spirit (*rūh*) because its name is the root of the wind (*rīh*), and certainly it comes forth according to what is expressed in the wind, because spirits are of the same kind. It is only in relation to itself, because he elected it from among the rest of the spirits, just as he called the house of houses 'my house' and called the messenger of messengers 'my friend.' All that is fashioned and produced and all that is created is subject to its lord and ruler."

28. Qur'ān 15:29.

29. Sadr al-Dīn Shīrāzī, "Kitāb al-tawhīd," p. 383.

30. *Ibid.*, p. 385.

31. On the notion of the subtle luminous *pneuma*, see Yahyá ibn Habash Suhrawardī, *Kitāb Hikmat al-Ishrāq*, bk. 8, secs. 218 and 272; *Le livre de la sagesse orientale (Kitâb Hikmat al-Ishrâq)*, trans. Henry Corbin, ed. Christian Jambet (Lagrasse, France: Verdier, 1986), p. 194ff. and sec. 272; and *The Shape of Light (Hayākil al-nūr)*, Persian version in *Oeuvres philosophiques et mystiques*, vol. 3, p. 85ff.; French version in *L'archange empourpré: Quinze traités et récits mystiques*,

ed. Henry Corbin (Paris: Fayard, 1976), p. 45. See also Yahyá ibn Habash Suhrawardī, *Risalah-'i Hayākil al-nūr: Matn-i 'Arabi, tarjumah-'i kuhan-i Fārsī, sharh-i Fārsī az 'ahd-i Āl-i Muzaffar*, ed. Muhammad Karīmī Zanjānī Āsl (Tehran: Nashr-i Nuqtah, 2000).

32. Shams al-Dīn Muhammad ibn Mahmūd Shahrazūrī, *Sharh Hikmat al-Ishrāq*, ed. Husayn Ziyā'ī Turbatī (Tehran: Mu'assasah-'i Mutāla'āt va Tahqīqāt-i Farhangī [Pizhūhishgah], 1993), pp. 396–97.

33. In Arabic: *aqrāb al-qawālib*, the most proximate of the "envelopes," in terms of their proximity to the divine world. It is interesting to compare the mystical status of the *qālib*, plural *qawālib*, with that of the *qelippot* in Jewish mysticism. Sadrā develops an original theory of the receptacle in relation to his theory of essential motion. See Muhammad ibn Ibrāhīm Sadr al-Dīn Shīrāzī, *al-Hikmah al-muta'ālīyah fī al-asfār al-'aqlīyah al-arba'āh* (al-Najaf, Iraq: Dār al-Ma'ārif al-Islāmīyah, 1958), vol. 3, pp. 330–31.

34. Qur'ān 39:69.

35. Sadr al-Dīn Shīrāzī, "Kitāb al-tawhīd," pp. 385–86.

36. Sadrā justifies this angelic monadology with the Qur'ān: "And truly we are ranged in ranks; and truly we are those who sing praises to God" (37:165–66), and a prophetic tradition: "Those who bow their bodies do not prostrate themselves, and those who prostrate himself themselves not bow, and there is none who has not a well-defined station."

37. Sadr al-Dīn Shīrāzī, "Kitāb al-tawhīd," p. 389.

Chapter Nine: The Return into God

1. Qur'ān 55:26–27.

2. Qur'ān 40:16.

3. Qur'ān 97:1; Muhammad ibn Ibrāhīm Sadr al-Dīn Shīrāzī, *al-Mabdā' wa-al-ma'ād*, ed. Jalāl al-Dīn Āshtiyānī and Seyyed Hossein Nasr (Tehran: Anjuman-i Shāhanshāhī-i Falsafah-'i Īrān, 1976), pp. 433–35.

4. Muhammad ibn Ibrāhīm Sadr al-Dīn Shīrāzī, *Risālat al-Hashr*, ed. Muhammad Khvājavī (Tehran: Mawlá, 1984), quoted in Christian Jambet, *Se rendre immortel: Suivi du Traité de la resurrection, Mollâ Sadrâ Shîrâzî* (Saint-Clément-de-Rivière, France: Fata Morgana, 2000), p. 169ff.

5. Jambet, *Se rendre immortel*, p. 126. There is a parallel text in Muhammad ibn Ibrāhīm Sadr al-Dīn Shīrāzī, *al-Hikmah al-muta'ālīyah fī al-asfār al-'aqlīyah al-arba'āh* (al-Najaf, Iraq: Dār al-Ma'ārif al-Islāmīyah, 1958), vol. 9, p. 246.

6. Sadr al-Dīn Shīrāzī, *al-Asfār*, vol. 9, p. 224ff.

7. "Everything is unspeakably lacking to us. We die from the nostalgia of Being.... For as long as the suffering race of Adam's children continues, there will be men starved for Beauty and for Infinity, as one is starved for bread." Léon Bloy, "Belluaires et porchers," *Oeuvres*, ed. Joseph Bollery and Jacques Petit (Paris: Mercure de France, 1964), vol. 2, p. 177. Bloy writes the following, which fits with the feeling Sadrā has for this world: "We are becoming brutal, I dare say. We are becoming brutal – utterly, superabundantly, and quite thoroughly. We are sick and tired of political or literary clichés. We are sick at heart over everything that went to make up moral life in the world of the past, and the immutable nature of man fiercely insists, nonetheless, on appealing to the ideal. This tiger will have its victim, on pain of devouring its pitiful keeper" (*ibid.*, p. 79).

8. Qur'ān 2:255; Muhammad ibn Ibrāhīm Sadr al-Dīn Shīrāzī, *Tafsīr al-Qur'ān al-karīm*, ed. Muhammad Khvājavī (Qum, Iran: Bīdār, 1987), vol. 4, pp. 294–300.

9. As Spinoza will say, "As soon as he ceases to be passive, he at once ceases to be at all." See *The Ethics and Selected Letters*, trans. Samuel Shirley (Indianapolis, IN: Hackett, 1982), pt. 5, prop. 42, scholium, p. 225.

10. Note the homologizing of the agent intelligence with the spirit of holiness and with the "giver of souls" (*ravān-bakhsh*), according to a Suhrawardian scheme here attributed to the "imams of Persia," that is, to the "sages of ancient Persia."

11. Sadr al-Dīn Shīrāzī, *Tafsīr al-Qur'ān al-karīm*, vol. 4, p. 297.

12. Sadrā makes his own use of this *ishrāqī* formulation: "All existence is light and all light is existence, since existence and light are a single reality and a unique effective reality, although they are differentiated by intensity and weakness, priority and posteriority." Muhammad ibn Ibrāhīm Sadr al-Dīn Shīrāzī, *Mafātīh al-ghayb*, ed. Muhammad Khvājavī (Tehran: Mu'assasah-'i Mutāla'āt va Tahqīqāt-i Farhangī, 1984), p. 264.

13. Sadr al-Dīn Shīrāzī, *al-Asfār*, vol. 9, p. 122.

14. Pleasure is not to be condemned, since it occurs "because of something that has the nature of light" (Yahyá ibn Habash Suhrawardī, *Kitāb hikmat al-ishrāq*, bk. 5, sec. 241). Enjoyment, says Sadrā, is all the more intense when "the influx of spiritual substances" increases. In a Platonic style, he explains why "the freshness of years in beautiful animals is loved and desired, whereas that is not

the case for those advanced in age." The movement of our existence makes us grow old, and we pass from the plane of sensibility to the plane of intelligence, which makes us better but renders us less desirable to the senses. Sexual pleasure corresponds, therefore, to that paradoxical age when we have not yet left our sensible condition and are still quite imperfect but can seduce with our youthfulness. And yet there is nothing bad about sexual pleasure, and Sadrian love is both more Platonic and less Platonic than Socratic love: the same man integrates all these "increases," so "he enjoys the company of adolescents or women, musicians, dancers, and wealth, all this by means of the physic part of his being, at the level of the senses; he enjoys the company of men of spirit and is a lover of men of knowledge by means of the psychic part of his being and his imagination; he enjoys the company of the perfect sages and of spiritual men and men of piety, by means of the intellective and spiritual part of his being." *Ta'liqā (Glosses on the Book of Oriental Wisdom)*, lithograph edition (Tehran, 1315 h.), p. 504; Yahyá ibn Habash Suhrawardī, *Le livre de la sagesse orientale (Kitâb Hikmat al-Ishrâq)*, trans. Henry Corbin, ed. Christian Jambet (Lagrasse, France: Verdier, 1986), pp. 634–35.

15. Aristotle, *Nicomachean Ethics* 10.4.1174b.

16. Sadr al-Dīn Shīrāzī, *Tafsīr al-Qur'ān al-karīm*, vol. 4, p. 297.

17. Sadr al-Dīn Shīrāzī, *al-Asfār*, vol. 9, p. 123.

18. *Ibid.*, p. 125. On God as the "real beloved," see vol. 7, p. 160ff.

19. Gloss, in Suhrawardī, *Le livre de la sagesse orientale*, p. 636.

20. Sadr al-Dīn Shīrāzī, *Tafsīr al-Qur'ān al-karīm*, vol. 4, p. 298.

21. *Ibid.*

22. See Richard Walzer, *Al-Farabi on the Perfect State: Abu Nasr al-Farabi's Mabadi' ara' ahl al-madina al-fadila* (Oxford: Clarendon, 1985), pp. 241–47; Abū Nasr al-Fārābī, *Risālah fī'l-'aql*, ed. Maurice Bouyges, 2nd ed. (Beirut: Dar el-Machreq, 1983), p. 12ff.; *Kitāb al-siyāsah al-madanīyah: al-Mulaqqab bi-Mabādi' al-mawjūdāt*, ed. Fawzī Mitrī Najjār (Beirut: al-Matba'ah al-Kāthūlīkīyah, 1993), pp. 79–80; *Kitāb tahsīl al-sa'ādah*, ed. Ja'far Āl Yāsīn (Beirut: Dar al-Manāhil, 1992), p. 92; *Kitāb al-millah wa-nusūs ukhrá*, ed. Muhsin Mahdī (Beirut: Dar el-Machreq, 1986), p. 58; and *Deux traités philosophiques: L'harmonie entre les opinions des deux sages, le divin Platon et Aristote et De la religion*, ed. and trans. Dominique Mallet (Damascus: Institut français de Damas, 1989), p. 135.

23. One can admire all the more the astonishing effort of distortion that was necessary for Khomeini, as a reader of Mullā Sadrā, to accomodate this phi-

losophy to the political theology that, according to him, gives authority to the expert jurist, the *velāyat-e fāqih*.

24. See Georges C. Anawati, "Un cas typique de l'ésoterisme avicennien: Sa doctrine de la résurrection des corps," *Etudes de philosophie musulmane* (Paris: Vrin, 1974), p. 274.

25. al-Ghazzālī, whom Sadrā places in the chorus of inspired thinkers, worked against the notion of complete mystical union in order to valorize the theme of conjunction. See Farid Jabre, *La notion de la ma'rifa chez Ghazali* (Beirut: Lettres Orientales, 1958), pp. 72–76. Nevertheless, the same Plotinian scheme plays a decisive role for both Sadrā and al-Ghazzālī, who is one of the important sources of Sadrā's thought.

26. Avicenna, *al-Ishārāt wa-al-tanbīhāt*, ed. Sulaymān Dunyā, pt. 3 (Cairo: Dār al-Ma'ārīf, 1966), p. 375. The ninth "group" of indications, to which this text belongs, can be clarified, I think, when read in the light of the conversations between Avicenna and the Shaykh Abū Sa'īd (967/1049), who was the first great mystic in the Persian language. The substance of these conversations is reported by Muhammad ibn Munavvar, a great-grandson of the shaykh, who says that the *Ishārāt* and other works by Avicenna were written "to explain the spiritual degrees" of the "friends of God" and to describe "the means of progressing in the mystical path and the path of Truth," that is, the concern for the real. Avicenna reportedly said of Abū Sa'īd, "All that I know, he sees," and Abū Sa'īd supposedly said of Avicenna, "All that I see, he knows." See Muhammad ibn al-Munavvar, *Les étapes mystiques du shaykh Abu Sa'id: Mystères de la connaissance de l'Unique*, trans. Mohammad Achena (Paris: Desclée de Brouwer, 1974), pp. 199–200, and *The Secrets of God's Mystical Oneness; or, The Spiritual Stations of Shaikh Abu Sa'id (Asrar al-towhid fi maqamat al-Seyk Abi Sa'id)*, trans. John O'Kane (Costa Mesa, CA: Mazda Publishers in association with Bibliotheca Persica, 1992), pp. 300–302. Why refuse to consider such testimony, whose value for the history of Iranian Avicennism is considerable?

27. Avicenna, *Ishārāt*, vol. 3, p. 369; *al-Ishārāt wa-al-tanbīhāt*, ed. Sulaymān Dunyā, pt. 4 (Cairo: Dār al-Ma'ārīf, 1968), p. 57. See Abu al-Qasim Junayd ibn Muhammad, *Enseignement spirituel: Traités, lettres, oraisons et sentences*, trans. Roger Deladrière (Paris: Sindbad, 1983), p. 119.

28. Michel Chodkiewicz, *An Ocean without Shore: Ibn 'Arabî, the Book, and the Law*, trans. David Streight (Albany: State University of New York Press, 1993).

29. This statement is attributed to the imam Ja'far al-Sādiq, quoted by Hujvīrī: 'Ālī ibn 'Usmān al-Hujviri, *The Kashf al-Mahjúb: The Oldest Persian Treatise on Súfiism*, trans. Reynold Alleyne Nicholson (Leiden: Brill, 1911), p. 79.

30. Avicenna, *Ishārāt*, vol. 3, p. 369; vol. 4, p. 58.

31. *Ibid.*, vol. 3, p. 383.

32. *Ibid.*, p. 380.

33. Sadr al-Dīn Shīrāzī, *al-Asfār*, vol. 9, p. 277.

34. Sadrā claims that the doctrine of the unity of the subject of intellection and the intelligible originates with him: "The question of the mode of being of the soul that intelligizes the intelligized forms of things is the most obscure philosophical question, and it has not been correctly examined by any of the philosophers of Islam up to our day. When we see the difficulty of this question, and when we meditate on the problems arising from the fact that the knowledge of substance is both substance and accident, we do not see in the books of the common philosophers — such as the books of the leading figure of this tradition, Abū 'Alī [Avicenna], the *Shifā'* [*Healing*], the *Najāt*, the *Ishārāt*, the *'Uyūn al-hikmat* [*Sources of Wisdom*], and so on — anything that might cure sickness and quench a burning thirst. No, but I have found it." Sadr al-Dīn Shīrāzī, *al-Asfār*, vol. 3, p. 312.

35. *Istighnā' 'an al-harakā wa-l-afār*; Muhammad ibn Ibrāhīm Sadr al-Dīn Shīrāzī, *al-Shawāhid al-rubūbīyah*, ed. Jalāl al-Dīn Āshtiyānī (Meshed, Iran: University Press, 1967), p. 200.

36. Sadr al-Dīn Shīrāzī, *al-Shawāhid al-rubūbīyah*, pp. 204–206, *Mafātīh al-ghayb*, pp. 520–22, *al-Mabdā' wa-al-ma'ād*, pp. 261–63.

37. Sadr al-Dīn Shīrāzī, *al-Shawāhid al-rubūbīyah*, p. 202.

38. On this stripping away (*tajrīd*) and the dematerialization of forms (*tajarrud*), see Sadr al-Dīn Shīrāzī, *al-Asfār*, vol. 3, p. 360ff. The axiom is "All perception must have within it some separation [some stripping away], and the perceptions are hierarchized according to this separation."

39. Sadr al-Dīn Shīrāzī, *al-Shawāhid al-rubūbīyah*, p. 203.

40. *Ibid.*, p. 204. Sadrā quotes Qur'ān 57:13.

41. Aristotle, *Nicomachean Ethics* 10.7.1177b.

42. Sadr al-Dīn Shīrāzī, *al-Asfār*, vol. 9, p. 140.

43. Here Ibn al-'Arabī's scheme has been substituted for Avicenna's.

44. Sadr al-Dīn Shīrāzī, *al-Asfār*, vol. 9, p. 141.

45. On why the use of Kantian concepts is legitimate, see Christian Jambet,

La logique des Orientaux: Henry Corbin et la science des formes (Paris: Seuil, 1983), pp. 52–71.

46. Sadr al-Dīn Shīrāzī, *al-Asfār*, vol. 9, p. 143.

47. Sadrā rejects the Avicennian problematic of the representation of the concrete form in the intelligized form. Avicenna argues that there must be a congruence between the two forms, but he stresses that the intelligized form of substance is not a substance. How is it possible to save this congruence? By maintaining that in the act of intellection one does not abstract a form but makes the thing itself—the substance, for example—pass from the fluctuating perishable act of being in the material world to its immaterial act of being. See *ibid.*, vol. 3, p. 305, which quotes Avicenna, *al-Shifa: al-Ilahiyyat (La métaphysique)*, ed. Georges C. Anawati and Sa'id Zayid (Cairo: Organisation générale des imprimeries gouvernementales, 1960), pp. 140–41.

48. Sadr al-Dīn Shīrāzī, *al-Asfār*, vol. 9, p. 143.

49. Not only is the face of man the face of God, but man's name is also the divine name in which all his other names are recapitulated. The original Shī'ism, of which Ismā'īlī Shī'ism gives a fairly clear idea, maintains that Allāh is the name of the perfect man. God does not become man, but the revelation of God is man. Between these two formulations lies the difference between the ontology of Christianity and that of Islam. Most surprising, once the distinction is made between the unknowable, unnamable divine essence and its revelation, spiritual Islam bases its authority on formulations that Christianity does not put forth, for the simple fact that it does not recognize the distinction in question. These formulations are as radical as the "paradoxes" of the Sūfīs (Bistāmī: "Glory to me"; Hallāj: "I am the real") or as vigorous as the Shī'ite professions of faith ("Who has seen the imam has seen God").

50. Sadr al-Dīn Shīrāzī, *al-Asfār*, vol. 3, pp. 312–15.

51. *Ibid.*, p. 315.

52. *Ibid.* There follow critiques of the supposed movement of the sensing faculty toward the sensed form and of the Suhrawardian theory of vision.

53. *Theology of Aristotle* 8.162–64, corresponding to Plotinus, *Enneads* 5.8, quoted in Sadr al-Dīn Shīrāzī, *al-Asfār*, vol. 3, p. 315.

54. Avicenna, *al-Ishārāt wa-al-tanbīhāt*, pt. 3, p. 263ff.

55. *Ibid.*, p. 292.

56. Avicenna, *Avicenna's De Anima (Arabic Text): Being the Psychological Part of Kitab al-Shifa'*, ed. Fazlur Rahman (London: Oxford University Press, 1959), p. 239.

57. Sadr al-Dīn Shīrāzī, *al-Asfār*, vol. 3, p. 324.

58. *Ibid.*, p. 325.

59. *Ibid.*, p. 326.

60. *Ibid.*, p. 327.

61. *Ibid.*, p. 330ff.

62. *Ibid.*, p. 331.

63. *Ibid.*, pp. 331–32.

64. Sadr al-Dīn Shīrāzī, *Tafsīr al-Qur'ān al-karīm*, vol. 4, p. 293. This interpretation of practical intelligence and theoretical intelligence is indebted to an amalgamation combining Aristotle with Plato's *Timaeus*, by way of Plotinus's reading.

65. *Ibid.*, p. 234. See Chapter Six.

66. This is the true meaning of *jihād*; it is an inner *jihād*, a moral struggle.

67. Sadr al-Dīn Shīrāzī, *Tafsīr al-Qur'ān al-karīm*, vol. 4, p. 296ff.

68. *Ibid.*, p. 297. Does the sage have a nature different from that of other men? No doubt, since he brings about a "divinization" that metamorphoses his nature. But in doing this, he accomplishes everything that other men would accomplish if they were faithful to their nature. On a doctrinal point that is comparable in Spinoza, see Pierre Macherey's reflections in *Introduction à l'Ethique de Spinoza: La cinquième partie; Les voies de la libération* (Paris: Presses Universitaires de France, 1994), pp. 196–204.

Chapter Ten: The God of Epiphanies

1. Muhammad ibn Ibrāhīm Sadr al-Dīn Shīrāzī, *al-Hikmah al-muta'ālīyah fī al-asfār al-'aqlīyah al-arba'ah*, 9 vols. (al-Najaf, Iraq: Dār al-Ma'ārif al-Islāmīyah, 1958), vol. 6, p. 13.

2. *Ibid.*, p. 16.

3. Avicenna, *al-Shifa': al-Tabiiyyat*, ed. Sa'id Zayid and Ibrahim Madkour (Cairo: Organisation egyptienne générale du livre, 1983), bk. 8, pp. 344–46. God is "above perfection" (p. 355) and has no peer (p. 354).

4. On the deduction of the Necessary Being, see Muhammad ibn Ibrāhīm Sadr al-Dīn Shīrāzī, *al-Shawāhid al-Rubūbīyah*, ed. Jalāl al-Dīn Āshtiyānī (Meshed, Iran: University Press, 1967), pp. 35–46, and *al-Asfār*, vol. 6, pp. 12–91. God is thought as what is in excess of actuality; nothing in being suffices to him; he is without genus, difference, or definition, such that the name Allāh does not define him but designates what the existence of existents as a whole proves concerning God; it expresses the manifestation of God in and for them.

5. The exegesis of the divine names "the Living, the Provident" (Qur'ān 2:255) enables Sadrā to present a systematic exposition of dogmatic theology. Muhammad ibn Ibrāhīm Sadr al-Dīn Shīrāzī, *Tafsīr al-Qur'ān al-karīm*, ed. Muhammad Khvājavī (Qum, Iran: Bīdār, 1987), vol. 4, pp. 88–95.

6. Included in the work by Kolaynī, this *hadīth* is commented on by Sadrā in Muhammad ibn Ibrāhīm Sadr al-Dīn Shīrāzī, "Kitāb al-tawhīd," in *Sharh usūl al-kāfī*, ed. Muhammad Khvājavī (Tehran: Mu'assasah-'i Mutāla'āt va Tahqīqāt-i Farhangī, 1987), pp. 235–50.

7. The necessary is the very reality of being (*al-wajīb nafs haqīqat al-wujūd*). The difference between the necessary essence and the possibles is the same as that between pure light and what is obscured by what is not the reality of being (Sadr al-Dīn Shīrāzī, *al-Asfār*, vol. 6, p. 138).

8. *Ibid.*, p. 110.

9. *Ibid.*, p. 116.

10. See G.W.F. Hegel, *Philosophy of Mind: Being Part Three of the 'Encyclopaedia of the Philosophical Sciences' (1830)*, trans. William Wallace (Oxford: Clarendon, 1971), sec. 573, pp. 302–13. The question of pantheism has great philosophical dignity, being the very question of the "system" and of the ground of reality in the absolute real. See Martin Heidegger, *Schelling's Treatise on the Essence of Human Freedom*, trans. Joan Stambaugh (Athens: Ohio University Press, 1985), pp. 62–83. Nevertheless, it seems to me that Heidegger gives too much importance to this thematic and that beyond the debate on pantheism, which has an equivalent in Islam in the attacks on the disciples of Ibn al-'Arabī, the question is, rather, one of understanding the infinite in the finite, or of an apprehension of the existent that combines apophatic rigor with the identity of the absolute principle and its irradiations. We can only invite the reader to compare Sadrā's investigation of this fundamental point with that of Schelling, in his second philosophy of nature, and refer to the pages and references in Xavier Tilliette, *Schelling: Une philosophie en devenir* (Paris: Vrin, 1970), vol. 1, pp. 381–407, and to Jean-Louis Vieillard-Baron, "L'interprétation hégélienne du *Timée*; ou, La philosophie de la nature," *Revue de métaphysique et de morale* 3 (1976), pp. 376–95. On the relationship between Hegel and the texts of the Islamic tradition, see Souâd Ayada, "Hegel et l'islam," Ph.d. diss., University of Lille, 1994.

11. Qāzī Sa'īd al-Qummī was born in 1043/1639 and died in 1103/1691. See Henry Corbin, *En islam iranien: Aspects spirituels et philosophiques*, vol. 4,

L'Ecole d'Ispahan, l'Ecole shaykhie, le Douzième Imâm (Paris: Gallimard, 1971), pp. 123–201.

12. Muhammad Sa'īd ibn Muhammad Mufīd al-Qummī, *Kilīd-i bihisht*, ed. Muhammad Mishkāt (Tehran: Majlis, 1937), pt. 2, ch. 2.

13. Sadr al-Dīn Shīrāzī, *al-Asfār*, vol. 6, pp. 133–35.

14. That is, the theology of the Kalām. Sadrā is close to Ash'ārism in his conception of the act, but he is equally dismissive of the Ash'ārī and the Mu'tazilī in his discussion of the divine attributes.

15. On the modes of divine knowledge, see Sadr al-Dīn Shīrāzī, *al-Asfār*, vol. 6, pp. 174–87. Divine science is not a relationship between a subject and a separate object. It is a concomitant of essence but is not added to essence. God knows all things principially and supereminently. Sadrā writes: "Certain ancient philosophers denied that God's knowledge of a thing among existents other than his essence and his attributes is identical to his essence. Those philosophers who deny that God has knowledge of the principle of something support their claim by saying that, according to them, knowledge is a relationship between the knowing subject and the object that is known." There can be no such relationship in God, since it would render God multiple. God's knowledge of himself and of things would then not be through himself. Sadrā responds to this agnosticism thus: "They commit an extraordinary error and do us obvious harm. It is unspeakably repugnant to proclaim that a created being can understand, through himself, the subtle realities of the Mulk, the subtleties of the Malakūt, and thus give himself the name of metaphysical philosopher, then deny that the knowledge of anything whatever comes from his creator, the sage, the knowing one, who caused the effusion of the ipseities of those who know, and illuminated their hearts with a direct cognition of things!" (*ibid.*, p. 179ff.).

16. In the absence of any Christology, the theology of the word will be angelology and prophetology. Prophetology will culminate in the theology of the imam.

17. Sadr al-Dīn Shīrāzī, *al-Asfār*, vol. 6, p. 139. The revelation of God in himself and in the angelic testimony does not assume any coming out of himself. In Sadrā, there is no equivalent to the very beautiful exegesis proposed by Schelling of the person of the Son, "far from God and from the Father," of the return of the extradivine to the final *homoousia*, after the moment of *heteroousia*. The inevitable absence of all Trinitarian theology will lead to an internal tension in the divine essence, since we cannot in any way break the absolute unity of identity. However, we will see a trinitary movement appear in divine science.

See Friedrich Wilhelm Joseph von Schelling, *Philosophie der Offenbarung: 1841–42* (Frankfurt: Suhrkamp, 1977), pp. 271–77.

18. Sadr al-Dīn Shīrāzī, *al-Asfār*, pp. 142–43.

19. Sadr al-Dīn Shīrāzī, *Mafātīh al-ghayb*, pp. 267–68.

20. Note that in Arabic these three terms, "he knows" (*'alima*), "he is known" (*'ulima*), and "knowledge" (*'ilm*) are all identical when written in the unvocalized form (*'-l-m*).

21. Quoted and commented on in Sadr al-Dīn Shīrāzī, *Tafsīr al-Qur'ān al-karīm*, vol. 4, p. 414 (in the commentary on the Light Verse, Qur'ān 24:35).

22. Sadr al-Dīn Shīrāzī, *Mafātīh al-ghayb*, p. 262.

23. Ibn al-'Arabī, *Fusūs al-Hikām*, ed. Abū 'Alā Afīfī (Beirut: Dār al-Kitāb al-'Arabī, 1946), p. 62.

24. *Ibid.*, p. 76 (*al-'ayn wāhidah min al-majmū' fī-l-majmū'*). Unity in totality is *wāhdīyah*, coming after the plane of pure essential unity, *al-ahadīyah*, without any distinction in being between the two.

25. *Ibid.*, p. 65.

26. *Ibid.*, p. 102. I have already noted this distinction between establishment and existence. At bottom, Sadrā is obliged to adopt it. But it presents a number of difficulties, which reveal the essential problem of ontology: what is the ontological stability of a shadow — whose reality depends on that of the individual or essence of which it is a shadow — if it does not have something like an act of being? How is it possible to free oneself completely from a logic of essences? Leibniz, for example, would maintain that the possible, as such, is real, that it has an act of existing by virtue of its essence as a possible. But his logic, which is a logic of essences, is not that of Ibn al-'Arabī or Sadrā. Moreover, the distinction between the act of being and quiddity, fully elaborated by Sadrā in the Avicennian moment of metaphysics, is not given an adequate philosophical elucidation by Ibn al-'Arabī.

27. *Ibid.*, p. 104.

28. *Ibid.*, pp. 119–20.

29. *Ibid.*, pp. 120–21. The heart is disposed to receive the revelation of the *mysterium*, a brilliant essential revelation. It is the divine ipseity itself, designated by God under the indexical "he." But this theophany of essence is manifest only in the form that becomes manifest for the heart of the faithful, in his witnessing, according to the form of his faith. On the "God created in the faiths," see Henry Corbin, *Creative Imagination in the Sufism of Ibn 'Arabi*, trans. Ralph Manheim (Princeton, NJ: Princeton University Press, 1969), pp. 195–200.

30. Corbin, *Creative Imagination*, p. 145.

31. Muhammad ibn Ibrāhīm Sadr al-Dīn Shīrāzī, *Sharh usūl al-kāfī*, ed. Muhammad Khvājavī (Tehran: Mu'assasah-'i Mutāla'āt va Tahqīqāt-i Farhangī, 1987), p. 237.

32. *Ibid.* Sadrā quotes Ibn al-'Arabī, *Fusūs al-Hikām*, pp. 51–52.

33. *Ibid.*, p. 239. Sadrā quotes (on p. 242) a long passage from Ibn al-'Arabī, *Les illuminations de La Mecque*, ed. Michel Chodkiewicz (Paris: Sindbad, 1988), on Qur'ān 19:109 and 4:171. al-'Arabī sees in the existents the words of God, such that the earth would run dry if it held the ink to write them with (*ibid.*, ch. 198). He also quotes a passage from the *Fusūs al-Hikām*, p. 153, and a commentary by Qūnawī on the co-expression of the names and the essence (pp. 246–47.)

34. Sadr al-Dīn Shīrāzī, *Sharh usūl al-kāfī*, pp. 247–48.

35. *Ibid.*, p. 248. On two occasions Sadrā writes "three hundred" instead of "three hundred sixty."

36. Qur'ān 17:110.

37. Sadr al-Dīn Shīrāzī, *Sharh usūl al-kāfī*, p. 250, commenting on Ibn al-'Arabī, *Fusūs al-Hikām*, p. 177.

38. According to Qur'ān 2:255. See Daniel Gimaret, *Les noms divins en islam: Exégèse lexicographique et théologique* (Paris: Cerf, 1988), pp. 208–209.

39. Sadr al-Dīn Shīrāzī, *Sharh usūl al-kāfī*, p. 252.

40. Here, too, Sadrā follows Ibn al-'Arabī, *Fusūs al-Hikām*, p. 79.

41. Sadr al-Dīn Shīrāzī, *Tafsīr al-Qur'ān al-karīm*, vol. 4, p. 390.

42. *Ibid.*, p. 395.

43. The perfect man is thus the perfect Qur'ān, in the sense that the Jewish Cabala was thought of as the "perfect Torah." See Moshe Idel, *Kabbalah: New Perspectives* (New Haven: Yale University Press, 1988), pp. 210–18, see also pp. 42–44 for an analysis of Ezra ben Solomon of Gerona's work on the union with the intelligible.

44. Sadr al-Dīn Shīrāzī, *Tafsīr al-Qur'ān al-karīm*, vol. 4, pp. 398–400.

45. Sadrā refers to Qur'ān 33:6.

46. Sadr al-Dīn Shīrāzī, *Tafsīr al-Qur'ān al-karīm*, vol. 4, p. 401.

47. *Ibid.*, p. 402.

48. *Ibid.*, vol. 1, pp. 101–102 (on the *fātiha*, "*uhdinā-l-sirāt al-mustaqīm*," "guide us on the straight path"). Sadrā gives a detailed presentation of the return of existents into God in *Risālat al-hashr* (Treatise on Resurrection).

49. Here is the Throne Verse: "Say: There is no god but he, the Living, the

Provident. Neither does somnolence affect him nor sleep. To him belongs all that is in the heavens and on the earth. And who can intercede with him except by his leave, he who knows what is present before men and what is hidden (in time past and time future), and not even a little of his knowledge can they grasp except what he will? His seat (*kursī*) extends over the heavens and the earth, and he tires not in protecting them. He is the All High, the Supereminent" (Qur'ān 2:255). Sadrā devotes more than three hundred pages to this verse and those that follow it (*Tafsīr al-Qur'ān al-karīm*, vol. 4, pp. 8–337). There he develops, among other things, his doctrines of the *walāyah* (p. 227ff.) and of the Garden and the Fire (pp. 264–304), in a brief treatise on ethics.

50. Sadr al-Dīn Shīrāzī, "Kitāb al-tawhīd," pp. 330ff.

51. The imam quotes Qur'ān 35:41. The Catholicos raises an objection by quoting verse 69:17.

52. Allah is the agent of the *taqwīm*, the act of making beings arise into being, to which corresponds the *taqawwum*, the fact of being raised into being. Sadr al-Dīn Shīrāzī, *Sharh usūl al-kāfī*, pp. 332–33.

53. He quotes Qur'ān 58:7.

54. Qur'ān 6:75.

55. This is the revelation given to Ezekiel in his vision of glory (Ezekiel 1:5–11), which has given rise to a considerable amount of commentary, both in Jewish mysticism and in Christian exegesis. Without entering into a detailed comparison, which would require several books, it can be pointed out that, like the Jewish mystics, Sadrā conceives of "the interpretation of the throne-world as the true center of all mystical contemplation." Gershom Scholem, *Major Trends in Jewish Mysticism*, 3rd rev. ed. (New York: Schocken, 1954), p. 44. On the Jewish exegesis of the throne within the framework of theurgy, see Charles Mopsik, *Les grands textes de la Cabale: Les rites qui font Dieu; Pratiques religieuses et efficacité théurgique dans la Cabale, des origines au milieu du XV–IIe siècle* (Lagrasse, France: Verdier, 1993).

56. Sadr al-Dīn Shīrāzī, *Sharh usūl al-kāfī*, p. 334.

57. *Ibid.*, p. 335.

58. *Ibid.*, p. 336.

59. "This is shown by demonstrations, and it is what the master of philosophers [Aristotle, alias Plotinus] indicated in his book *Theology*, in the language of the Greeks, which is translated as 'the gnosis of lordliness' (*ma'rifat al-rūbūbīyah*). Whatever is a derivative in the world of manifestation is not without

a root among the roots and a hidden mystery among the mysteries in the lordly world. Otherwise it would be like a shadow without an individual, like a fleeting mirage and an imagination fallen into ruin. In the world of the higher Malakūt, there is no intelligible light and no imperative spirit that does not possess a shadow in this world. Otherwise, it would be a root without derivative, like someone who was liberal without liberality, or as if what was proved remained without proof" (*ibid.*).

60. *Ibid.*, p. 338.

61. *Ibid.*, p. 335. For the details concerning the gathering together of all things in God, Sadrā refers here to his *Risalāt al-hashr* in Christian Jambet, *Se rendre immortel: Suivi du Traité de la résurrection, Mollâ Sadrâ Shîrâzî* (Saint-Clément-de-Rivière, France: Fata Morgana, 2000), pp. 119–60.

62. Qur'ān 87:1.

63. Sadr al-Dīn Shīrāzī, *Sharh usūl al-kāfī*, p. 349; Qur'ān 38:75 and 7:13.

64. Qur'ān 2:256: "*Lā ikrāha fī-l-dīn*"; Sadr al-Dīn Shīrāzī, *Tafsīr al-Qur'ān al-karīm*, vol. 4, pp. 191–95. I have presented a more detailed analysis of Sadrā's commentary in a separate work: *Pas de contrainte en religion: Une approche de la question de la liberté en Islam*, Seminar on the History of Liberalism in Europe, brochure 15 (Paris: Center for Research in Applied Epistemology [Ecole Polytechnique]/Center for Research in Economic Philosophy [ESCP-EAP], 2004).

Index of Names

Zone Books series design by Bruce Mau
Typesetting by Archetype
Printed and bound by Maple-Vail on Sebago acid-free paper